THE  BEST

AMERICAN

MAGAZINE

WRITING

2010

THE BEST
AMERICAN
MAGAZINE
WRITING
2010

**Compiled by
the American
Society of
Magazine
Editors**

Columbia University Press   New York

Columbia University Press
Publishers Since 1893
New York   Chichester, West Sussex
Copyright © 2011 Columbia University Press
All rights reserved

Library of Congress Cataloging-in-Publication Data
ISSN 1541-0978
ISBN 978-0-231-15753-7 (pbk.)

Columbia University Press books are printed on permanent and durable
acid-free paper.
This book is printed on paper with recycled content.
Printed in the United States of America
p 10 9 8 7 6 5 4 3 2 1

Contents

xi   *Introduction*
      Jon Meacham

xv   *Acknowledgments*
      Sid Holt, chief executive, American Society of
      Magazine Editors

3   The Deadly Choices at Memorial
                 Sheri Fink
                     The New York Times Magazine
                     WINNER—Reporting

45   Still Life
                 Skip Hollandsworth
                 Texas Monthly
                 WINNER—Feature Writing

69 Marc Dreier's Crime of Destiny

Bryan Burrough

Vanity Fair

FINALIST—Profile Writing

99 The Last Abortion Doctor

John H. Richardson

Esquire

FINALIST—Feature Writing

129 The Cost Conundrum

Atul Gawande

The New Yorker

WINNER—Public Interest

155 A Death in Texas

Tom Barry

Boston Review

FINALIST—Public Interest

185 Vanish

Evan Ratliff

Wired

FINALIST—Feature Writing

215 Out West

Joe Wilkins

Orion

FINALIST—Essays

231 Theocracy and Its Discontents

Fareed Zakaria

Newsweek

WINNER—Columns and
Commentary

239 Lead Us Not Into Debt

Megan McArdle

The Atlantic

FINALIST—Columns and
Commentary

247 Bacon: The Other White Heat

Theodore Gray

Popular Science

FINALIST—Columns and
Commentary

251 In Defense of Tourism

Peter Jon Lindberg

Travel & Leisure

FINALIST—Columns and
Commentary

257   *Excerpts from* For and Against Foreskin
                    Michael Idov, Christopher
                    Bonanos, and Hanna Rosin
                    New York
                    Winner—Personal Service

277   There's a Sucker Born Every Minute
                    Tom Carson
                    GQ
                    Finalist—Reviews and
                    Criticism

285   War Games
                    Steve Erickson
                    Los Angeles
                    Finalist—Reviews and
                    Criticism

291   Suburban Ghetto
                    Jonathan Dee
                    Harper's Magazine
                    Finalist—Reviews and
                    Criticism

309 Obituary Columns: Danny La Rue, Benson,
William Safire

Ann Wroe

The Economist

Finalist—Columns and
Commentary

319 Top Ten State Fair Joys

Garrison Keillor

National Geographic

Winner—Essays

327 The Man Who Never Was

Mike Sager

Esquire

Winner—Profile Writing

359 Trial by Fire

David Grann

The New Yorker

Finalist—Reporting

409 Raw Water

Wells Tower

McSweeney's Quarterly

Winner—Fiction

445 And Yet . . .

Mitch Albom

Sports Illustrated

Finalist—Essays

459 *National Magazine Awards 2010 Finalists and Winners*

469 *National Magazine Awards for Digital Media 2010 Finalists and Winners*

475 *National Magazine Awards 2010 Judges*

483 *ASME Board of Directors, 2010–2011*

485 *Permissions*

489 *List of Contributors*

Jon Meacham

Introduction

I t is, to say the least, not a cheerful hour for magazines as they have been written, edited, published, and read for nearly 300 years. It is true that every generation tends to think of itself as challenged and under siege; the questions of the present, whether of a political, economic, or cultural nature, assume outsize and urgent importance for they are, after all, the questions that shape and suffuse the lives of those living in the moment. Humankind seems to be forever coping with crisis. Even the most placid of historical eras seems placid only from the perspective of the future. Those living in, say, the Gilded Age or the Roaring Twenties or the allegedly idyllic 1950s by and large did not see themselves as the blessed citizens of peaceful and enviable times.

Still, not every historical juncture is equal, and some eras are manifestly more consequential than others. An example from the world of warfare comes to mind. Always bloody and tragic and disorienting, from the first time one caveman struck another with a stone, war nevertheless changed forever in the summer of 1945, when the United States built and deployed atomic weapons. The Nuclear Age was like all preceding ages in that weapons were being developed and used to subdue one's enemies and impose one's will, but it was (and is) unlike all that came before in that previously unimaginable destruction was suddenly quite imaginable. The existential became the commonplace: any hour could be the last for whole ways of life.

Connecting the fate of the magazine business of the early twenty-first century to the dawn of the Nuclear Age is admittedly and purposely hyperbolic, but the intellectual point remains: in war, the world was one way before August 1945 and another way afterward. In magazine publishing, the world was one way before the rise of digital technology and the decline of the traditional advertising model and another way afterward.

We are at the end of one great era and on the threshold of another. That much is certain. What is uncertain is the precise shape of the new age—how stories are to be told, how they will be read, who will pay what for them, and what resources will be at our disposal to create and sustain great creative endeavors.

The answers to these questions have significance for people far beyond the industry of magazine editing, writing, and designing. The answers matter to those who care about the world, and about literature, and about photography and art and reporting. Magazines are not the only sources of insight, entertainment, and original information—but they are important such sources, and we need them.

In this bleak economic season there is a special joy in reading the pieces collected in the following pages for they bear witness to the enduring role of magazine narrative and reporting far better than any polemic, or any introduction, can. Young writers are always told to show, not tell, and these National Magazine Award winners and nominees brilliantly and memorably show why the genre matters now more than ever.

From John H. Richardson's *Esquire* profile of "The Last Abortion Doctor" to Fareed Zakaria's *Newsweek* essay on Iran to Wells Tower's *McSweeney's Quarterly* short story "Raw Water," the pieces offer writing and analysis and observation that is substantively different from much of what is now produced digitally. Though digital technology is evolving with characteristically epic speed, the online medium remains, for the time being, better suited to the immediate and the visceral than to the considered and the reflective. It is true that the ASME digital award finalists and winners testify to the exceptional journalistic and creative talent being brought to the digital world, which is rapidly becoming the world. And yet print—and all of the work here appeared in print—remains a gratifying and fulfilling experience—an ancient technology made new every week or every month or every quarter, brought to fresh life by the hearts and minds of those so passionate about their craft to devote themselves to the painstaking work of magazine making.

But here is the oft-overlooked good news: depending on the business model, the digital possibilities for the creation and consumption of magazine journalism are boundless and thrilling. Yes, there are differences, big, real ones. The simple transfer of one's print magazine to the Web—long what passed for "digital strategy" at many places—has already proved a failure. Will the iPad or some similar tablet device totally displace the printed magazine? Probably, and that hour will likely come sooner than many of us once thought.

I love print because I grew up with it, but I am a member of the last generation who came of age in a totally analog world. To state the obvious, our task is not to mourn but to build. At this point, grief over the slow but inexorable decline of mass print publications is self-indulgent. The values and visions that informed the printed page for so long are perennial, and lovers of magazines would do well, I think, to focus on platform-agnostic virtues: accuracy, wit, eloquence, beauty, memorability. To give up the fight to find ways for old-fashioned storytelling to adapt and live on is not an option for such a capitulation would probably mark the end of the kind of journalism celebrated in this collection.

I slipped in a crucial phrase a moment ago: depending on the business model. On those five words hang everything. Will enough readers engage, pay for, and become attractive to advertisers to underwrite the great work you are about to read? I do not know. But I do know this: from Homer to Addison and Steele to Hayes and Shawn, the love of story is what endures through the storms and crises of the ages. Read the pieces in this book and you will believe, with me, that the love of story will not only endure but triumph, and that three centuries from now people will still be savoring the work of storytellers like our colleagues here.

Or so one hopes. Fervently.

Sid Holt

Acknowledgments

W hen the American Society of Magazine Editors was founded nearly half a century ago, the organizers included the editors of magazines that are still well known today: *Glamour, Reader's Digest, Family Circle, Businessweek, Good Housekeeping, The Atlantic, Popular Science.* But there were also editors at that meeting in September 1963 whose magazines are now largely—in some cases, entirely—forgotten: *U.S. Lady, Mother's Manual, Hairdo, Modern Romances, Silver Screen, Ingenue,* even *Holiday,* whose editor, Ted Patrick, was the first president of ASME.

And then there were the editors of magazines that would, within a few years, change out of all recognition. *Cosmopolitan,* the general-interest magazine edited by Robert C. Atherton (a cover story written the following year by a thirty-year-old Gloria Steinem was titled "John Lennon: Beatle With a Future"), would soon give way to *New Cosmopolitan,* edited for a quite different audience by the quite different Helen Gurley Brown. Arnold Gingrich was among those present, but Harold T. P. Hayes was already transforming *Esquire,* the magazine Gingrich had founded in the 1930s, into a bastion of the New Journalism. And *Look*—whose editor, Daniel D. Mich, reported that he had invited President Kennedy to attend ASME's next conference, in 1964—would soon falter and collapse under the weight of its 6-million-plus circulation.

Look would survive long enough to win the first National Magazine Award in 1966. The creation of the National Magazine Awards was in fact one of the reasons ASME had been founded. "The society," read the first bylaws, "will undertake . . . the development of specifications for a program of National Magazine Awards." At first, there was only one award, and ASME members were skeptical of the need for more. So *Look* was followed by *Life*, then *Newsweek*, and finally *American Machinist* (which, after more than 125 years of publication, only recently shuttered its print edition). But beginning in 1970, the awards began to expand. That year five awards were presented—for Public Service (*Life* again), Reporting (*The New Yorker*), Fiction and Belles Lettres (*Redbook*), Specialized Journalism (*Philadelphia*), and Visual Excellence (*Look*, in its last hurrah). New categories were slowly added—Essays and Criticism in 1978, General Excellence in 1981 (after a cameo presentation to *Businessweek* in 1973), Photography in 1985, Feature Writing in 1988—but by 1999, there were still only fifteen categories, including General Excellence in something called New Media.

Just ten years later there are thirty-five award categories. What happened? In a word (or two), the Internet. In response to the growth of the Web, the National Magazine Awards began to grow in 2000, adding more categories for print magazines (such as Profile Writing and Photo Portfolio) as well as for online content (Interactive Feature and Personal Service Online). But as magazines expanded online, it became clear that the very definition of a magazine had changed since ASME first convened fifty years ago. The result: in 2010, ASME and our partners at the Columbia University Graduate School of Journalism introduced the National Magazine Awards for Digital Media—twelve categories, ranging from General Excellence and News Reporting to Blogging and Podcasting—and a new category for Magazine of the Year, which "honors publications that successfully use both print and digital media in fulfilling the editorial mission of the magazine."

What does all this have to do with this book? Besides providing the material for this compilation, the National Magazine Awards have always been a chance for magazine editors to get together and talk about what they like best about magazines, which is the same thing readers like best about magazines— stories and pictures. Every year nearly 300 magazine journalists get together for three days in New York to judge the National Magazine Awards. Those who participate in the judging come away impressed by the work being published across the country—not just by the magazines that are nominated but by all the work being done by literary magazines, by political journals, by independent magazines whose editors and readers share the same special interests, and by the big publishing companies.

A couple of months after the judging many of the same people get together again in New York at the presentation of the awards. Each winner receives a statuette, a reproduction of a stabile called "Elephant" (hence the nickname of the awards, the Ellies) by the great American artist Alexander Calder. As someone who has both won and lost on these occasions, I can tell you that winning is better, but even the losers know that the awards celebrate the best magazine journalism there is.

This book is made possible first and foremost by the writers and editors whose work is included here as well as by the hundreds of editors, art directors, photography editors, and educators who sacrifice work days and weekends to judge the awards. Thanks are also due to the Board of Directors of ASME, who oversaw both the awards judging and the awards shows. The names of both the judges and the board members are printed at the back of the book.

Since 1966, ASME has presented the National Magazine Awards in association with the Columbia University Graduate School of Journalism. On behalf of ASME, I want to thank our colleagues at Columbia, chiefly the dean and Henry R. Luce Professor, Nicholas

Lemann, and the associate dean of prizes and programs, Arlene Notoro Morgan.

Thanks to Jon Meacham, who agreed to write the introduction to this book during an especially eventful time at his magazine, *Newsweek*. It is a testament to Jon's skill and dedication that his magazine continues to achieve the highest standards of excellence, as reflected this year by *Newsweek*'s winning of the National Magazine Award for Columns and Commentary.

The members of ASME are grateful to our agent, David McCormick of McCormick & Williams, for his skillful representation of our interests, and I am especially thankful for the patience and enthusiasm of our editors at Columbia University Press, Philip Leventhal and Michael Haskell.

On behalf of ASME, I also want to thank our colleagues at Magazine Publishers of America, both the board, chaired by John Q. Griffin of *National Geographic*, and the many staff members whose support makes the awards possible. I especially want to thank Nina B. Link, Howard Polskin, and Ja-Shin Tsang. Finally, I want to thank my colleagues at ASME: Marlene Kahan, who recently stepped down from her position as executive director of ASME after twenty years of outstanding service, and Nina Fortuna, without whose hard work, keen enthusiasm, and "MMMBop"-ing good cheer, nothing around here would get done.

THE BEST
AMERICAN
MAGAZINE
WRITING

2010

The New York Times Magazine

WINNER—REPORTING

Of all the tragedies associated with Hurricane Katrina, perhaps the most disturbing is the story told here. "Deadly Choices at Memorial" has the unique distinction of having won both the Pulitzer Prize for Investigative Reporting and the National Magazine Award for Reporting (because the piece was published in the New York Times Magazine, *it was eligible for both awards—the Pulitzer for newspapers, the Ellie for magazines). This is not only an outstanding piece of journalism but also an indication of changes in the newspaper and magazine businesses that have only just begun—the reporting and writing of the story was supported by the independent, nonprofit news organization ProPublica.*

Sheri Fink

The Deadly Choices at Memorial

The smell of death was overpowering the moment a relief worker cracked open one of the hospital chapel's wooden doors. Inside, more than a dozen bodies lay motionless on low cots and on the ground, shrouded in white sheets. Here, a wisp of gray hair peeked out. There, a knee was flung akimbo. A pallid hand reached across a blue gown.

Within days, the grisly tableau became the focus of an investigation into what happened when the floodwaters of Hurricane Katrina marooned Memorial Medical Center in Uptown New Orleans. The hurricane knocked out power and running water and sent the temperatures inside above one hundred degrees. Still, investigators were surprised at the number of bodies in the makeshift morgue and were stunned when health care workers charged that a well-regarded doctor and two respected nurses had hastened the deaths of some patients by injecting them with lethal doses of drugs. Mortuary workers eventually carried forty-five corpses from Memorial, more than from any comparable-size hospital in the drowned city.

Investigators pored over the evidence, and in July 2006, nearly a year after Katrina, Louisiana Department of Justice agents arrested the doctor and the nurses in connection with the deaths of four patients. The physician, Anna Pou, defended herself on national television, saying her role was to "help" patients "through their pain," a position she maintains today. After a New Orleans grand jury declined to indict her on second-degree murder charges, the case faded from view.

In the four years since Katrina, Pou has helped write and pass three laws in Louisiana that offer immunity to health care professionals from most civil lawsuits—though not in cases of willful misconduct—for their work in future disasters, from hurricanes to terrorist attacks to pandemic influenza. The laws also encourage prosecutors to await the findings of a medical panel before deciding whether to prosecute medical professionals. Pou has also been advising state and national medical organizations on disaster preparedness and legal reform; she has lectured on medicine and ethics at national conferences and addressed military medical trainees. In her advocacy, she argues for changing the standards of medical care in emergencies. She has said that informed consent is impossible during disasters and that doctors need to be able to evacuate the sickest or most severely injured patients last—along with those who have Do Not Resuscitate orders—an approach that she and her colleagues used as conditions worsened after Katrina.

Pou and others cite what happened at Memorial and Pou's subsequent arrest—which she has referred to as a "personal tragedy"— to justify changing the standards of care during crises. But the story of what happened in the frantic days when Memorial was cut off from the world has not been fully told. Over the past two and a half years, I have obtained previously unavailable records and interviewed dozens of people who were involved in the events at Memorial and the investigation that followed.

The interviews and documents cast the story of Pou and her colleagues in a new light. It is now evident that more medical professionals were involved in the decision to inject patients— and far more patients were injected—than was previously understood. When the names on toxicology reports and autopsies are matched with recollections and documentation from the days after Katrina, it appears that at least seventeen patients were injected with morphine or the sedative midazolam, or both, after a long-awaited rescue effort was at last emptying the hospital. A number of these patients were extremely ill and might not have survived the evacuation. Several were almost certainly not near death when they were injected, according to medical professionals who treated them at Memorial and an internist's review of their charts and autopsies that was commissioned by investigators but never made public.

In the course of my reporting, I went to several events involving Pou, including two fund raisers on her behalf, a conference and several of her appearances before the Louisiana Legislature. Pou also sat down with me for a long interview last year, but she has repeatedly declined to discuss any details related to patient deaths, citing three ongoing wrongful-death suits and the need for sensitivity in the cases of those who have not sued. She has prevented journalists from attending her lectures about Katrina and filed a brief with the Louisiana Supreme Court opposing the release of a 50,000-page file assembled by investigators on deaths at Memorial.

The full details of what Pou did, and why, may never be known. But the arguments she is making about disaster preparedness— that medical workers should be virtually immune from prosecution for good-faith work during devastating events and that lifesaving interventions, including evacuation, shouldn't necessarily go to the sickest first—deserve closer attention. This is particularly important as health officials are now weighing, with little public discussion and insufficient scientific evidence, protocols for making the kind of agonizing decisions that will, no doubt, arise again.

At a recent national conference for hospital disaster planners, Pou asked a question: "How long should health care workers have to be with patients who may not survive?" The story of Memorial Medical Center raises other questions: Which patients should get a share of limited resources, and who decides? What does it mean to do the greatest good for the greatest number, and does that end justify all means? Where is the line between appropriate comfort care and mercy killing? How, if at all, should doctors and nurses be held accountable for their actions in the most desperate of circumstances, especially when their government fails them?

A Shelter from the Storm

Memorial Medical Center was situated on one of the low points in the bowl that is New Orleans, three miles southwest of the city's French Quarter and three feet below sea level. The esteemed community hospital sprawled across a neighborhood of double-shotgun houses. Several blocks from a housing project but a short walk to the genteel mansions of Uptown, it served a diverse clientele. Built in 1926 and known for decades as Southern Baptist, the hospital was renamed after being purchased in 1995 by Tenet Healthcare, a Dallas-based commercial chain. For generations, the hospital's sturdy walls served as a shelter when hurricanes threatened: employees would bring their families and pets, as well as coolers packed with muffulettas.

By the time Katrina began lashing New Orleans in the early hours of Monday, August 29, some 2,000 people were bunking in the hospital, including more than 200 patients and 600 workers. When the storm hit, patients screamed as windows shattered under a hail of rocks from nearby rooftops. The hospital groaned and shook violently.

At 4:55 A.M., the supply of city power to the hospital failed. Televisions in patient rooms flicked off. But Memorial's auxiliary generators had already thumped to life and were humming reassuringly. The system was designed to power only emergency lights, certain critical equipment, and a handful of outlets on each floor; the air-conditioning system shut down. By that night, the flooding receded from the surrounding streets. Memorial had sustained damage but remained functional. The hospital seemed to have weathered one more storm.

The Evacuation Begins

Anna Pou was a forty-nine-year-old head- and neck-cancer surgeon whose strong work ethic earned respect from doctors and nurses alike. Tiny and passionate, with coiffed cinnamon hair and a penchant for pearls, Pou was funny and sociable, and she had put her patients at the center of her life.

The morning after Katrina hit, Tuesday, August 30, a nurse called to Pou: "Look outside!" What Pou saw from the window was hard to believe: water gushing from the sewer grates. Other staff members gaped at the dark pool of water rimmed with garbage crawling up South Claiborne Avenue in the direction of the hospital.

Senior administrators quickly grasped the danger posed by the advancing waters and counseled L. René Goux, the chief executive of Memorial, to close the hospital. As at many American hospitals in flood zones, Memorial's main emergency-power transfer switches were located only a few feet above ground level, leaving the electrical system vulnerable. "It won't take much water in height to disable the majority of the medical center," facilities personnel had warned after Hurricane Ivan in 2004. Fixing the problem would be costly; a few less-expensive improvements were made.

Susan Mulderick, a tall, no-nonsense fifty-four-year-old nursing director, was the rotating "emergency-incident commander" designated for Katrina and was in charge—in consultation with the hospital's top executives—of directing hospital operations during the crisis. The longtime chairwoman of the hospital's emergency-preparedness committee, Mulderick had helped draft Memorial's emergency plan. But the 246-page document offered no guidance for dealing with a complete power failure or for how to evacuate the hospital if the streets were flooded. Because Memorial's chief of medical staff was away, Richard Deichmann, the hospital's soft-spoken medical-department chairman, organized the physicians.

At 12:28 P.M., a Memorial administrator typed "HELP!!!!" and e-mailed colleagues at other Tenet hospitals outside New Orleans, warning that Memorial would have to evacuate more than 180 patients. Around the same time, Deichmann met with many of the roughly two dozen doctors at Memorial and several nurse managers in a stifling nurse-training room on the fourth floor, which became the hospital's command center. The conversation turned to how the hospital should be emptied. The doctors quickly agreed that babies in the neonatal intensive-care unit, pregnant mothers, and critically ill adult I.C.U. patients would be at great risk from the heat and should get first priority. Then Deichmann broached an idea that was nowhere in the hospital's disaster plans. He suggested that all patients with Do Not Resuscitate orders should go last.

A D.N.R. order is signed by a doctor, almost always with the informed consent of a patient or health care proxy, and means one thing: A patient whose heartbeat or breathing has stopped should not be revived. A D.N.R. order is different from a living will, which under Louisiana law allows patients with a "terminal and irreversible condition" to request in advance that "life-sustaining procedures" be withheld or withdrawn.

But Deichmann had a different understanding, he told me not long ago. He said that patients with D.N.R. orders had terminal or irreversible conditions, and at Memorial he believed they should go last because they would have had the "least to lose" compared with other patients if calamity struck. Other doctors at the meeting agreed with Deichmann's plan. Bill Armington, a neuroradiologist, told me he thought that patients who did not wish their lives to be prolonged by extraordinary measures wouldn't want to be saved at the expense of others—though there was nothing in the orders that stated this. At the time, those attending the meeting didn't see it as a momentous decision, since rescuers were expected to evacuate everyone in the hospital within a few hours.

There was an important party missing from the conversation. For years, a health care company known as LifeCare Hospitals of New Orleans had been leasing the seventh floor at Memorial. LifeCare operated a "hospital within a hospital" for critically ill or injured patients in need of twenty-four-hour care and intensive therapy over a long period. LifeCare was known for helping to rehabilitate patients on ventilators until they could breathe on their own. LifeCare's goal was to assist patients until they improved enough to return home or to nursing facilities; it was not a hospice.

The eighty-two-bed unit credentialed its own doctors, most of whom also worked at Memorial. It had its own administrators, nurses, pharmacists, and supply chain. It also had its own philosophy: LifeCare deployed the full array of modern technology to keep alive its often elderly and debilitated patients. Horace Baltz, one of the longest-serving doctors at Memorial, told me of spirited debates among doctors over coffee about what some of his colleagues considered to be excessive resources being poured into hopeless cases. "We spend too much on these turkeys," he said some would say. "We ought to let them go."

Many of the fifty-two patients at LifeCare were bedbound or required electric ventilators to breathe, and clearly, they would be at significant risk if the hospital lost power in its elevators. The doctors I spoke to who attended the meeting with Deichmann did not recall discussing evacuating LifeCare patients specifically, despite the fact that some of the doctors at the meeting worked with both Memorial and LifeCare patients.

In the afternoon, helicopters from the Coast Guard and private ambulance companies began landing on a long-unused helipad atop an eight-story parking garage adjacent to the hospital. The pilots were impatient—thousands of people needed help across the city. The intensive-care unit on the eighth floor rang out with shouts for patients: "We need some more! Helicopters are waiting!" A crew of doctors, nurses, and family members carried Memorial patients down flights of stairs and wheeled them to the hospital wing where the last working elevator brought them to the second floor. Each patient was then maneuvered onto a stretcher and passed through a roughly three-by-three-foot opening in the machine-room wall that offered a shortcut to the parking garage. Many patients were placed in the back of a pickup truck, which drove to the top of the garage. Two flights of metal steps led to the helipad.

At LifeCare that afternoon, confusion reigned. The company had its own "incident commander," Diane Robichaux, an assistant administrator who was seven months pregnant. At first everything seemed fine; Robichaux established computer communications with LifeCare's corporate offices in Texas and was assured that LifeCare patients would be included in any FEMA evacuation of Memorial. But as the day wore on, the texts between Life-Care staff members and headquarters grew frantic as it became clear that the government's rescue efforts and communications were in chaos.

According to the messages, Robichaux asked Memorial administrators to add her fifty-two patients to transport plans being organized with the Coast Guard. An executive at the hospital told Robichaux that permission would be requested from Memorial's corporate owner, Tenet Healthcare. "I hope and pray this is not a long process for getting their approval," Robichaux said in an e-mail message to her colleagues at headquarters. (A Tenet spokesman, David Matthews, wrote me in an e-mail message that LifeCare staff members turned down several offers of evacuation assistance from Memorial staff members on Tuesday afternoon.)

The doctors had now spent days on duty, under stress and sleeping little. Ewing Cook, one of the hospital's most senior physicians, told me that he decided that in order to lessen the burden on nurses, all but the most critical treatments and care should be discontinued. When Bryant King, a thirty-five-year-old internist who was new to Memorial, came to check on one of his patients on the fourth floor, he canceled the senior doctor's order to turn off his patient's heart monitor. When Cook found out, he was furious and thought that the junior doctor did not understand the circumstances. He directed the nurse to reinstate his instructions.

It was dark when the last of the Memorial patients who had been chosen for immediate evacuation were finally gone. Later that night, the Coast Guard offered to evacuate more patients, but those in charge at Memorial declined. The helipad had minimal lighting and no guard rail, and the staff needed rest.

Memorial had shaved its patient census from 187 to about 130. On the seventh floor, all fifty-two LifeCare patients remained, including seven on ventilators. "Been on the phone with Tenet," a LifeCare representative outside the hospital wrote to Robichaux. "Will eventually be to our patients. Maybe in the morning."

Fateful Triage Decisions

At about 2 A.M. on Wednesday, August 31—nearly forty-eight hours after Katrina made landfall near New Orleans—Memorial's backup generators sputtered and stopped. Ewing Cook later described the sudden silence as the "sickest sound" of his life. In LifeCare on the seventh floor, critically ill patients began suffering the consequences. Alarm bells clanged as life-support monitors and ventilators switched to brief battery reserves while continuing to force air into the lungs of seven patients. In about a half-hour, the batteries failed and the regular hiss of mechanical breaths ceased. A Memorial nurse appeared and announced that the Coast Guard could evacuate some critical patients if they were brought to the helipad immediately. Volunteers began carrying the LifeCare patients who relied on ventilators down five flights of stairs in the dark.

A LifeCare nurse navigated the staircase alongside an eighty-year-old man on a stretcher, manually squeezing air into his lungs with an Ambu bag. As he waited for evacuation on the second floor, she bagged him for nearly an hour. Finally a physician stopped by the stretcher and told her that there was no oxygen for the patient and that he was already too far gone. She hugged the man and stroked his hair as he died.

Anna Pou began bagging another patient on the second floor to relieve a nurse whose hands were growing tired. That patient, along with two other LifeCare patients who relied on ventilators, also died early that morning, but the others were evacuated by helicopter. The hospital chaplain opened a double door with stained-glass windows down the hallway, and the staff began wheeling bodies into the chapel. Distraught nurses cried, and the chaplain held them and prayed with them.

The sun rose and with it the sultry New Orleans temperature, which was on its way to the mid-nineties. The hospital was stifling, its walls sweating. Water had stopped flowing from taps, toilets were backed up, and the stench of sewage mixed with the odor of hundreds of unwashed bodies.

Visitors who had come to the hospital for safety felt so desperate that they cheered when two airboats driven by volunteers from the Louisiana swamplands roared up to the flooded emergency-room ramp. The flotilla's organizers, Mark and Sandra Le-Blanc, had a special reason to come to Memorial: Vera LeBlanc, Mark's eighty-two-year-old mother, was at LifeCare, recovering from colon-cancer surgery. Sandra, an E.M.T., knew that her mother-in-law couldn't swallow, so she was surprised when she saw that Vera and other patients who needed IVs to keep hydrated were no longer getting them. When her husband asked a Memorial administrator why, the administrator told him that the hospital was in survival mode, not treating mode. Furious, Mark LeBlanc asked, "Do you just flip a switch and you're not a hospital anymore?"

．　　　．　　　．

That morning, doctors and nurses decided that the more than one hundred remaining Memorial and LifeCare patients should be brought downstairs and divided into three groups to help speed the evacuation. Those who were in fairly good health and could sit up or walk would be categorized "1's" and prioritized first for evacuation. Those who were sicker and would need more assistance were "2's." A final group of patients were assigned "3's" and were slated to be evacuated last. That group included those whom doctors judged to be very ill and also, as doctors agreed the day before, those with D.N.R. orders.

Though there was no single doctor officially in charge of categorizing the patients, Pou was energetic and jumped into the center of the action, according to two nurses who worked with her. Throughout the morning, makeshift teams of medical staff and family members carried many of the remaining patients to the second-floor lobby where Pou, the sleeves of her scrubs rolled up, stood ready to receive them.

In the dim light, nurses opened each chart and read the diagnoses; Pou and the nurses assigned a category to each patient. A nurse wrote "1," "2," or "3" on a sheet of paper with a Marks-A-Lot pen and taped it to the clothing over a patient's chest. (Other patients had numbers written on their hospital gowns.) Many of the 1's were taken to the emergency-room ramp, where boats were arriving. The 2's were generally placed along the corridor leading to the hole in the machine-room wall that was a shortcut to the helipad. The 3's were moved to a corner of the second-floor lobby near an A.T.M. and a planter filled with greenery. Patients awaiting evacuation would continue to be cared for—their diapers would be changed, they would be fanned and given sips of water if they could drink—but most medical interventions like IVs or oxygen were limited.

Pou and her coworkers were performing triage, a word once used by the French in reference to the sorting of coffee beans and applied to the battlefield by Napoleon's chief surgeon, Baron Dominique-Jean Larrey. Today triage is used in accidents and disasters when the number of injured exceeds available resources. Surprisingly, perhaps, there is no consensus on how best to do this. Typically, medical workers try to divvy up care to achieve the greatest good for the greatest number of people. There is an ongoing debate about how to do this and what the "greatest good" means. Is it the number of lives saved? Years of life saved? Best "quality" years of life saved? Or something else?

At least nine well-recognized triage systems exist. Most call for people with relatively minor injuries to wait while patients in the worst shape are evacuated or treated. Several call for medical workers to sort the injured into another category: patients who are seen as having little chance of survival given the resources on hand. That category is most commonly created during a devastating event like a war-zone truck bombing in which there are far more severely injured victims than ambulances or medics.

Pou and her colleagues had little if any training in triage systems and were not guided by any particular triage protocol. Pou would later say she was trying to do the most good with a limited pool of resources. The decision that certain sicker patients should go last has its risks. Predicting how a patient will fare is inexact and subject to biases. In one study of triage, experienced rescuers were asked to categorize the same patients and came up with widely different answers. And patients' conditions change; more resources can become available to help those whose situations at first appear hopeless. The importance of reassessing each person is easy to forget once a ranking is assigned.

After several helicopters arrived and rescued some of the Life-Care patients, Air Force One flew over New Orleans while President Bush surveyed the devastation. Few helicopters arrived after that. Pou told me she heard that the Coast Guard was focusing on saving people stranded on rooftops around the city. Meanwhile dozens of patients sweltered on the lower two floors of Memorial and in the parking garage as they waited to leave.

Many of the doctors and nurses had shifted from caring for patients to carrying them and were loading people onto helicopters and watercraft. Vera LeBlanc, the LifeCare patient whose son arranged the airboat flotilla that had arrived hours earlier, was among the patients massed on the second floor. Her chart read "Do Not Resuscitate," as it had during several hospital admissions for more than a decade, so that her heart would not be restarted if it were to stop. Mark LeBlanc decided he was going to put his mother on one of the airboats he and his wife had directed to the hospital. When the LeBlancs tried to enter the patient area on the second floor, a staff member blocked them, and several doctors told them they couldn't leave with Vera. "The hell we can't," Sandra said. The couple ignored the doctors, and Vera smiled and chatted as Mark and several others picked her up and carried her onto an airboat.

On a seventh-floor hallway at LifeCare, Angela McManus, a daughter of a patient, panicked when she overheard workers discussing the decision to defer evacuation for D.N.R. patients. She had expected her frail seventy-year-old mother, Wilda, would soon be rescued, but her mother had a D.N.R. order. "I've got to rescind that order," Angela begged the LifeCare staff. She says they told her that there were no doctors available to do it.

By Wednesday afternoon, Dr. Ewing Cook was physically and mentally exhausted, filthy and forlorn. A sixty-one-year-old pulmonary specialist, he'd had his semiautomatic Beretta strapped to him since he heard on Monday that a nurse was raped while walking her dog near the hospital (a hospital official denies that this happened). Cook had had two heart attacks and could not help transport patients in the heat.

That afternoon, Cook stood on the emergency-room ramp and caught sight of a mattress floating up Napoleon Avenue. On it lay an emaciated black woman, with several young men propelling her through the fetid water. "The hospital is closed," someone shouted. "We're not accepting anybody."

René Goux, the hospital's chief executive, told me he had decided, for reasons of safety, that people floating up to Memorial should generally be directed to dry ground about nine blocks south. Medical workers finally insisted that the woman and her husband be allowed to enter, but the men who swam in the toxic soup to rescue her were told to leave. When a couple with small children rowed up and were told to "go away," Bryant King, who was one of Memorial's few African American physicians, lost his temper.

"You can't do this!" King shouted at Goux. "You gotta help people!" But the family was turned away.

King was out of touch with reality, Cook told me he thought at the time. Memorial wasn't so much a hospital anymore but a shelter that was running out of supplies and needed to be emptied. Cook also worried that intruders from the neighborhood might ransack the hospital for drugs and people's valuables.

Recently retired from clinical practice, Cook became a Memorial administrator a week before Katrina hit, but he had spent many years working on the eighth floor in the I.C.U. That afternoon, he climbed slowly upstairs to check what was happening there. Most of the patients had been evacuated on Tuesday, but a few with D.N.R. orders had not.

"What's going on here?" he asked the four nurses in the unit. "Whaddya have left?" The nurses said they were down to one patient: Jannie Burgess, a seventy-nine-year-old woman with advanced uterine cancer and kidney failure. She was being treated for comfort only and had been sedated to the point of unconsciousness with morphine. She was so weighted down by fluid from her diseases that Cook sized her up at 350 pounds.

Cook later told me he believed several things: 1. Given how difficult it had been for him to climb the steps in the heat, there was no way he could make it back to the I.C.U. again. 2. Given how exhausted everyone was and how much this woman weighed, it would be "impossible to drag her down six flights of stairs." 3. Even in the best of circumstances, the patient probably had a day or so to live. And frankly, the four nurses taking care of her were needed elsewhere.

To Cook, a drug that had been dripping into Burgess's IV for days provided an answer. Morphine, a powerful narcotic, is frequently used to control severe pain or discomfort. But the drug can also slow breathing, and suddenly introducing much higher doses can lead to death.

Doctors, nurses, and clinical researchers who specialize in treating patients near the ends of their lives say that this "double effect" poses little danger when drugs are administered properly. Cook says it's not so simple. "If you don't think that by giving a person a lot of morphine you're not prematurely sending them to their grave, then you're a very naïve doctor," Cook told me when we spoke for the first time, in December 2007. "We kill 'em."

In fact, the distinction between murder and medical care often comes down to the intent of the person administering the drug. Cook walked this line often as a pulmonologist, he told me, and he prided himself as the go-to man for difficult end-of-life situations. When a very sick patient or the patient's family made the decision to disconnect a ventilator, for example, Cook would prescribe morphine to make sure the patient wasn't gasping for breath as the machine was withdrawn.

Often Cook found that achieving this level of comfort required enough morphine that the drug markedly suppressed the patient's breathing. The intent was to provide comfort, but the result was to hasten death, and Cook knew it. To Cook, the difference between something ethical and something illegal "is so fine as to be imperceivable."

Burgess's situation was "a little different," as Cook described it. Being comatose and on painkillers, she wasn't uncomfortable. But the worst thing Cook could imagine would be for the drugs to wear off and for Burgess to wake up and find herself in her ravaged condition as she was being moved. "Do you mind just increasing the morphine and giving her enough until she goes?" Cook told me he asked Burgess's nurse.

Cook scribbled "pronounced dead at" in Burgess's chart, left the time blank and signed the note with a large squiggle. Then he walked back downstairs, believing that he had done the right thing for Burgess. "To me, it was a no-brainer, and to this day I don't feel bad about what I did," he told me. "I gave her medicine so I could get rid of her faster, get the nurses off the floor." He added, "There's no question I hastened her demise."

The question of what to do with the hospital's sickest patients was also being raised by others. By the afternoon, with few helicopters landing, these patients were languishing. Susan Mulderick, the "incident commander" who had worked with Cook for decades, shared her own concerns with him. According to Cook, Mulderick told him, "We gotta do something about this." Mulderick, who declined to be formally interviewed about the days after Katrina, did tell me: "We were well prepared. We managed that situation well."

Cook sat on the emergency-room ramp smoking cigars with another doctor. Help was coming too slowly. There were too many people who needed to leave and weren't going to make it, Cook said, describing for me his thinking at the time. It was a desperate situation and he saw only two choices: quicken their deaths or abandon them. "It was actually to the point where you were considering that you couldn't just leave them; the humane thing would be to put 'em out."

Cook went to the staging area on the second floor where Anna Pou and two other doctors were directing care. Cots and stretchers seemed to cover every inch of floor space. Rodney Scott, an obese I.C.U. patient who was recovering from heart problems and several operations, lay motionless on a stretcher, covered in sweat and almost nothing else. A doctor had decided that he should be the last patient to leave the hospital because he weighed more than 300 pounds and might get stuck in the machine-room hole, backing up the evacuation line. Cook thought Scott was dead, and he touched him to make sure. But Scott turned over and looked at him.

"I'm O.K., Doc," Scott said. "Go take care of somebody else."

Despite how miserable the patients looked, Cook said, he felt there was no way, in this crowded room, to do what he had been thinking about. "We didn't do it because we had too many witnesses," he told me. "That's the honest-to-God truth."

Richard Deichmann, Memorial's medical-department chairman, also remembers being stopped by Mulderick for a quick conversation that afternoon, an episode he wrote about in *Code Blue*, a memoir he published in 2006 about the days after Katrina. He was startled, he wrote, when Mulderick asked him his thoughts about whether it would be "humane" to euthanize the hospital's D.N.R. patients. "Euthanasia's illegal," he said he told her. "There's not any need to euthanize anyone. I don't think we should be doing anything like that." He had figured the D.N.R. patients should go last, but the plan, he told Mulderick, was still to evacuate them eventually. Through her lawyer, Mulderick denied that she discussed euthanasia of patients with Deichmann or anyone else at Memorial.

As darkness fell, rumor spread that evacuations would halt for the night because people were shooting at rescuers. In the adjacent parking garage, Goux distributed guns to security and maintenance staff, who cordoned off the hospital's entrances. That night, dozens of LifeCare and Memorial patients lay on soiled and sweaty cots in the second-floor lobby. Pou, several doctors, and crews of nurses worked in the dim light of a few lamps powered by a portable generator. For the third night in a row, Pou was working with scarcely an hour's sleep, changing patients' diapers, giving out water, comforting, and praying with nurses.

Kamel Boughrara, a LifeCare nursing director, walked past the A.T.M. area on the second floor where some of the sickest patients—most of whom had been given 3's—lay. Carrie Hall, a seventy-eight-year-old LifeCare patient with long, braided hair whose vast family called her Ma-Dear, managed to grab him and indicate that she needed her tracheostomy cleared. The nurse was surprised at how fiercely Hall was battling to stay alive. He suctioned her with a portable machine and told her to fight hard.

Comfort Care or Mercy Killing?

Soon after sunrise on Thursday, September 1—more than seventy-two hours into the crisis—Memorial's chief financial officer, Curtis Dosch, delivered good news to hospital staff gathered on the emergency-room ramp. He had reached a Tenet representative in Dallas and was told that Tenet was dispatching a fleet of privately hired helicopters that day. Dosch later said that the dejected staff was skeptical. But soon the hospital's voice chain began echoing with shouts for women and children to evacuate. Boats were arriving, including fishing vessels that had been parked on trailers in the neighborhood and were now commandeered by hospital workers. Helicopters at last converged on the hospital within a couple of hours of daylight, according to a Memorial nurse from the Air Force Reserve who oversaw helipad operations. The Tenet spokesman and testimony by Mulderick in a 2008 deposition also confirm this. The hospital filled with the cacophony of military and private crafts hovering and landing.

Down on the emergency-room ramp that morning, stone-faced State Police officers wielding shotguns barked that everyone had to be out of the hospital by 5 P.M. because of civil unrest in New Orleans; they would not stay later to protect the hospital.

Meanwhile, Cook strapped on his gun again and prepared to leave the hospital by boat to rescue his son, who had been trapped at his house since Tuesday's flooding. He told me that Mulderick asked him before he left to talk to Pou.

On the second floor, Cook says, he and Pou, both weary, discussed the Category 3 patients, including nine who had never been brought down from the seventh floor. According to Cook, Pou was worried that they wouldn't be able to get them out. Cook hadn't been on the seventh floor since Katrina struck, but he told me that he thought LifeCare patients were "chronically deathbound" at the best of times and would have been horribly affected by the heat. Cook couldn't imagine how the exhausted Memorial staff would carry nine patients down five flights of stairs before the end of the day. Nobody from outside had arrived to help with that task. If there were other ways to evacuate these patients, he didn't see them.

Cook said he told Pou how to administer a combination of morphine and a benzodiazepine sedative. The effect, he told me, was that patients would "go to sleep and die." He explained that it "cuts down your respiration so you gradually stop breathing and go out." He said he believed that Pou understood that he was telling her how to achieve this. He said that he viewed it as a way to ease the patients out of a terrible situation.

In an interview with *Newsweek* in 2007, Pou acknowledged that after discussions with other doctors, she did inject some Category 3 patients. But she said her intention was only to "help the patients that were having pain and sedate the patients who were anxious" because "we knew they were going to be there another day, that they would go through at least another day of hell." Beyond that, Pou has not talked about the details of what happened on that Thursday, citing the pending legal cases and sensitivity to patients and their families. What follows is based on the recollections of others, some of which were recounted in interviews with Louisiana Justice Department investigators, as well as in interviews with me.

Therese Mendez, a LifeCare nurse executive, had worked overnight on the first floor, she later told investigators. (She declined to speak with me.) After daybreak, she heard the sound of helicopters and watched the evacuation line begin to move. According to Mendez, she returned at around 8 or 9 A.M. to the seventh floor and walked along a corridor. The patients she saw looked bad. Several were unconscious, frothing at the mouth and breathing in an irregular way that often heralds death. Still, while two patients died on the LifeCare's seventh floor on Wednesday, the others had lived through the night, with only a few given small doses of morphine or the sedative lorazepam for comfort.

Mendez heard that Pou was looking for her. They sat down in an office with an open window. Pou looked distraught and told her that the LifeCare patients probably were not going to survive. Mendez told investigators that she responded, "I think you're right."

Mendez said she watched Pou struggle with what she was saying, telling investigators that Pou told her that "the decision had been made to administer lethal doses" of morphine and other drugs. (Pou, through her lawyer, Richard Simmons Jr., denied mentioning "lethal doses.") Were the LifeCare patients being singled out? Mendez asked. She knew there were other sick patients at Memorial. Mendez recalled that Pou said "no" and that there was "no telling how far" it would go.

According to Mendez, Pou told her that she and other Memorial staff members were assuming responsibility for the patients on the seventh floor; the LifeCare nursing staff wasn't involved and should leave. (Pou, through her lawyer, disputes Mendez's account.) Mendez later said she had assumed that the hospital was under martial law, which was not the case, and that Pou was acting under military orders. Mendez left to dismiss her employees, she said, because she feared they would be forced downstairs by authorities.

Diane Robichaux, the senior leader on the LifeCare floor, later walked into the office, she recalled in interviews with investigators. (She declined to talk to me.) She and other LifeCare workers had gone downstairs at around 9:30 A.M. to ask Susan Mulderick when the LifeCare patients on the seventh floor would be evacuated. According to Robichaux, Mulderick said, "The plan is not to leave any living patients behind," and told her to see Pou.

In Robichaux's interview with investigators, she could not recall exactly what Pou told her, but she said that she understood that patients "were not going to be making it out of there." She said that Pou did not use the word "euthanize." Prompted by investigators, she said she thought Pou might have used the word "comfortable" in describing what she was trying to do for the patients.

Robichaux remembered Pou saying that the LifeCare patients were "not aware or not alert or something along those lines." Robichaux recounted to investigators that she told Pou that that wasn't true and said that one of LifeCare's patients—Emmett Everett, a 380-pound man—was "very aware" of his surroundings. He had fed himself breakfast that morning and asked Robichaux, "So are we ready to rock and roll?"

The sixty-one-year-old Honduran-born manual laborer was at LifeCare awaiting colostomy surgery to ease chronic bowel obstruction, according to his medical records. Despite a freakish spinal-cord stroke that left him a paraplegic at age fifty, his wife and nurses who worked with him say he maintained a good sense of humor and a rich family life, and he rarely complained. He, along with three of the other LifeCare patients on the floor, had no D.N.R. order.

Everett's roommates had already been taken downstairs on their way to the helicopters, whose loud propellers sent a breeze through the windows on his side of the LifeCare floor. Several times he appealed to his nurse, "Don't let them leave me behind." His only complaint that morning was dizziness, a Life-Care worker told Pou.

"Oh, my goodness," a LifeCare employee recalled Pou replying.

Two Memorial nurses—identified as Cheri Landry and Lori Budo from the I.C.U. to investigators by a LifeCare pharmacist, Steven Harris—joined the discussion along with other LifeCare workers. (Through their lawyers, Landry and Budo declined to be interviewed. Harris never returned my calls.) They talked about how Everett was paralyzed and had complex medical problems and had been designated a "3" on the triage scale. According to Robichaux, the group concluded that Everett was too heavy to be maneuvered down the stairs, through the machine-room wall, and onto a helicopter. Several medical staff members who helped lead boat and helicopter transport that day say they would certainly have found a way to evacuate Everett. They say they were never made aware of his presence.

In his interviews with investigators, Andre Gremillion, a Life-Care nurse, said that the female physician in the office (he didn't know Pou's name) asked if someone who knew Everett could explain to him that because he was so big they did not think they would be able to evacuate him. They asked Gremillion whether he could "give him something to help him relax and explain the situation." Gremillion told investigators that he didn't want to be the one who told Everett that "we would probably be leaving and he would be staying." At that point, Gremillion said, he lost his composure.

Gremillion's supervisor and friend, a LifeCare nursing director, Gina Isbell, told me she walked into the room around 11 A.M. and saw Gremillion crying and shaking his head. He brushed past her into the hallway, and Isbell followed, grabbing his arm and guiding him to an empty room. "I can't do this," he kept saying.

"Do what?" Isbell asked. When Gremillion wouldn't answer, Isbell tried to comfort him. "It's going to be O.K.," she said. "Everything's going to be all right."

Isbell searched for Robichaux, her boss. "What is going on?" she asked, frantic. "Are they going to do something to our patients?"

"Yes, they are," Isbell remembers Robichaux, in tears, saying. "Our patients aren't going to be evacuated. They aren't going to leave." As the LifeCare administrators cleared the floor of all but a few senior staff members, Robichaux sent Isbell to the back staircase to make sure nobody reentered. It was quiet there, and Isbell sat alone, drained and upset. Isbell said she thought about her patients, remembering with guilt a promise she made to the daughter of one of her favorites, Alice Hutzler, a ninety-year-old woman who came to LifeCare for treatment of bedsores and pneumonia. Isbell fondly called her Miss Alice and had told Hutzler's daughter that she would take good care of her mother. Now Isbell prayed that help would come before Hutzler and her other patients died.

· · ·

According to statements made to investigators by Steven Harris, the LifeCare pharmacist, Pou brought numerous vials of morphine to the seventh floor. According to investigators, a proffer from Harris's lawyer said that Harris gave her additional morphine and midazolam—a fast-acting drug used to induce anesthesia before surgery or to sedate patients for medical procedures. Like morphine, midazolam depresses breathing; doctors are warned to be extremely careful when combining the two drugs.

Kristy Johnson, LifeCare's director of physical medicine, said she saw what happened next. She told Justice Department investigators that she watched Pou and two nurses draw fluid from vials into syringes. Then Johnson guided them to Emmett Everett in Room 7307. Johnson said she had never seen a physician look as nervous as Pou did. As they walked, she told investigators, she heard Pou say that she was going to give him something "to help him with his dizziness." Pou disappeared into Everett's room and shut the door.

As they worked their way down the seventh-floor hallway, Johnson held some of the patients' hands and said a prayer as Pou or a Memorial nurse gave injections. Wilda McManus, whose daughter Angela had tried in vain to rescind her mother's D.N.R. order, had a serious blood infection. (Earlier, Angela was ordered to leave her mother and go downstairs to evacuate.) "I am going to give you something to make you feel better," Pou told Wilda, according to Johnson.

Johnson took one of the Memorial nurses into Room 7305. "This is Ms. Hutzler," Johnson said, touching the woman's hand and saying a "little prayer." Johnson tried not to look down at what the nurse was doing, but she saw the nurse inject Hutzler's roommate, Rose Savoie, a ninety-year-old woman with acute bronchitis and a history of kidney problems. A LifeCare nurse later told investigators that both women were alert and stable as of late that morning. "That burns," Savoie murmured.

According to Memorial workers on the second floor, about a dozen patients who were designated as "3's" remained in the lobby by the A.T.M. Other Memorial patients were being evacuated with help from volunteers and medical staff, including Bryant King. Around noon, King told me, he saw Anna Pou holding a handful of syringes and telling a patient near the A.T.M., "I'm going to give you something to make you feel better." King remembered an earlier conversation with a colleague who, after speaking with Mulderick and Pou, asked him what he thought of hastening patients' deaths. That was not a doctor's job, he replied. Patients were hot and uncomfortable, and a few might be terminally ill, but he didn't think they were in the kind of pain that calls for sedation, let alone mercy killing. When he saw Pou with the syringes, he assumed she was doing just that and said to anyone within earshot: "I'm getting out of here. This is crazy!" King grabbed his bag and stormed downstairs to get on a boat.

Bill Armington, the neuroradiologist, watched King go and was upset at him for leaving. Armington suspected that euthanasia might occur, in part, he told me, because Cook told him earlier that there had been a discussion of "things that only doctors talk about." Armington headed for the helipad, "stirred up," as he recalls, "to intensify my efforts to get people off the roof." Neither Armington nor King intervened directly, though King had earlier sent out text messages to friends and family asking them to tell the media that doctors were discussing giving medication to dying patients to help accelerate their deaths. King told me that he didn't think his opinion, which hadn't mattered when he argued against turning away the hospital's neighbors, would have mattered.

.   .   .

Only a few nurses and three doctors remained on the second floor: Pou; a young internist named Kathleen Fournier; and John Thiele, a fifty-three-year-old pulmonologist, who had never before spoken publicly about his Katrina experiences until we had two lengthy interviews in the last year. Thiele told me that on Thursday morning, he saw Susan Mulderick walking out of the emergency room. "John, everybody has to be out of here tonight," he said she told him. He said René Goux told him the same thing. Mulderick, through her lawyer, and Goux both say that they were not given a deadline to empty the hospital and that their goal was to focus their exhausted colleagues on the evacuation. "We'd experienced the helicopters' stopping flying to us," Goux told me, "and I didn't want that to occur again."

Around a corner from where the patients lay on the second floor, Thiele and Fournier struggled to euthanize two cats whose owners brought them to the hospital and were forced to leave them behind. Thiele trained a needle toward the heart of a clawing cat held by Fournier, he told me later. While they were working, Thiele recalls Fournier telling him that Mulderick had spoken with her about something to the effect of putting patients "out of their misery" and that she did not want to participate. (Fournier declined to talk with me.) Thiele told her that he understood, and that he and others would handle it. Mulderick's lawyer says that Mulderick did ask a physician about giving something to patients to "make them more comfortable," but that, however, was not "code for euthanasia."

Thiele didn't know Pou by name, but she looked to him like the physician in charge on the second floor. He told me that Pou told him that the Category 3 patients were not going to be moved. He said he thought they appeared close to death and would not have survived an evacuation. He was terrified, he said, of what would happen to them if they were left behind. He expected that the people firing guns into the chaos of New Orleans—"the animals," he called them—would storm the hospital, looking for drugs after everyone else was gone. "I figured, What would they do, these crazy black people who think they've been oppressed for all these years by white people? I mean if they're capable of shooting at somebody, why are they not capable of raping them or, or, you know, dismembering them? What's to prevent them from doing things like that?"

The laws of man had broken down, Thiele concluded, and only the laws of God applied.

"Can I help you?" he says he asked Pou several times.

"No," she said, according to Thiele. "You don't have to be here."

"I want to be here," Thiele insisted. "I want to help you."

Thiele practiced palliative-care medicine and was certified to teach it. He told me that he knew that what they were about to do, though it seemed right to him, was technically "a crime." He said that "the goal was death; our goal was to let these people die."

Thiele saw that morphine, midazolam, and syringes had been set up on a table near the A.T.M. There were about a dozen patients, and he took charge of the four closest to the windows— three elderly white women and a heavyset African American man—starting IVs on those who didn't have one. Apart from their breathing and the soft moans of one, the patients appeared "lifeless" and did not respond to him. Thiele saw Pou and several nurses working on patients lying near the hallway.

Thiele wavered for a moment. He turned to Karen Wynn, the I.C.U. nurse manager at Memorial who led the hospital's ethics committee. "Can we do this?" he remembers asking the highly respected nurse.

Wynn felt that they *needed* to medicate the patients, she said when she described her experiences publicly for the first time in interviews with me over the past year. She acknowledged having heard rumors that patients were being euthanized, but she said no one had told her that that was what was happening to these patients and that her only aim was to make patients comfortable by sedating them. Wynn said she did not fear staying in the hospital after the 5 P.M. curfew announced by the State Police—she had already decided to ignore the evacuation deadline and stay at the hospital until everyone alive had been taken out. Instead, she said, she was motivated by how bad the patients looked.

Wynn described turning to an elderly woman who was unconscious with labored breathing. She then prepared a syringe with morphine and midazolam, pushed it slowly into the woman's IV line and watched her breathing ease. The woman died a short time later, which didn't disturb Wynn because she had appeared to be close to death. Wynn told me that at that point all the staff could offer was "comfort, peace, and dignity." She said: "We did the best we could do. It was the right thing to do under the circumstances."

She added: "But even if it had been euthanasia, it's not something we don't really do every day—it just goes under a different name."

Thiele gave other patients a shot of morphine and midazolam at doses he said were higher than what he normally used in the I.C.U. He held their hands and reassured them, "It's all right to go." Most patients, Thiele told me, died within minutes of being medicated. But the heavyset African American man didn't.

His mouth was open, his breathing was labored, and everyone could hear his awful death rattle. Thiele tried more morphine. He tried prayer. He put his hand on the man's forehead; Wynn and another nurse manager took the man's hands in theirs. Together they chanted: "Hail Mary, full of grace. The Lord is with thee." They recited the Lord's Prayer. They prayed for the man to die.

The man kept breathing, and Wynn says she and her colleagues took that as a sign. "God said, 'O.K., but I'm not ready for him.' Or he wasn't ready." She remembers passing him through the hole in the machine-room wall on his way to the evacuation helicopters.

Thiele has a different memory of what happened. "We covered his face with a towel" until he stopped breathing, Thiele told me.

He says that it took less than a minute for the man to die and that he didn't suffer. "This was totally against every fiber in my body," Thiele told me, but he also said he knew what he did was right. "We were abandoned by the government, we were abandoned by Tenet, and clearly nobody was going to take care of these people in their dying moments." He added, "I did what I would have wanted done to me if the roles were reversed."

Both Thiele and Wynn recall that they, Pou, and the other nurses covered the bodies of the dead and carried them into the chapel, filling it. Thiele said the remaining bodies were wrapped in sheets and placed on the floor in the corridor and in a nearby room.

"It was very respectful," Thiele told me. "It's not like you would think."

. . .

That afternoon, Memorial's pathologist and laboratory director walked though the hospital, floor by floor, to record the locations of the dead and make sure that nobody alive was left behind. They found Pou on the seventh floor with a nurse. Pou was working on the IV of a patient who seemed barely alive. The laboratory director told investigators that Pou asked for help moving the patient; the pathologist remembered it differently and said in a deposition that he offered Pou help with evacuating the patient, but Pou did not respond, and later, when he asked her again, she said she needed to speak with an anesthesiologist first.

Dr. John Walsh, a surgeon, told me that he was sitting on a bench, too tired to move, when Pou and the pathologist came downstairs. Pou looked upset. She sat down beside him. "What's wrong?" he asked. He said she mentioned something about a patient, or patients, dying and about someone, or some people, questioning her.

Walsh had known Pou for about only a year, but he knew, he told me, that she was compassionate and dedicated to her patients. "I'm sure you did the right thing," he remembers telling her. "It'll work itself out. It'll all turn out O.K."

Throughout the day, boats and helicopters drained the hospital of nearly all of its patients and visitors. At around 9 P.M., Rodney Scott, the obese I.C.U. patient who was recovering from surgery and heart trouble, at last felt himself being hoisted up the open metal steps to the helipad. Weighing more than 300 pounds and unable to walk, Scott was the last living patient to leave the hospital grounds. He felt relief. The four men surrounding him shouted, "Push! Push!" and rolled his heavy wheelchair into a Coast Guard helicopter. Evacuating someone as large as Scott had a cost—a nurse was briefly pinned against the helicopter, bruising his ribs and spleen—but it had been done.

Scott, Thiele, and Wynn were flown separately to Louis Armstrong New Orleans International Airport, where their ordeals continued. Hundreds of hospital and nursing-home patients had been dropped there from across the disaster zone; they were met by federal disaster-management teams that were so understaffed and undersupplied that they couldn't provide even basic nursing care to many patients. Reflecting on the scene at the airport, Thiele told me that if the patients he injected with drugs had made it there, "They wouldn't have survived."

The Coroner's Dilemma

On Sunday, September 11, 2005, thirteen days after the storm hit, mortuary workers recovered forty-five decomposing bodies from Memorial Medical Center. The next day the Louisiana attorney general, Charles Foti Jr., opened investigations into hospital and nursing-home deaths during Hurricane Katrina. The Justice Department's phones were soon ringing with allegations of patient abandonment and euthanasia.

One of the people who called was a LifeCare lawyer who relayed a report that nine of the company's patients may have been given lethal doses of medicines by a Memorial doctor and nurses. State and federal investigators interviewed LifeCare witnesses and descended on the mold-ridden hospital to search for evidence. Separately, Foti's staff asked the Orleans Parish coroner, Dr. Frank Minyard, to perform autopsies and drug tests on approximately one hundred bodies that were recovered from more than a half-dozen hospitals and nursing homes in New Orleans.

The burden was unwelcome for Minyard, a seventy-six-year-old obstetrician-gynecologist who was already struggling to oversee the autopsies and identification of hundreds of hurricane victims. Minyard was inspired by a Catholic nun to devote his life to public service. For thirty-one years as the city's elected coroner, he peered into bodies in the basement office of the colonnaded criminal courthouse, emerging in cowboy boots and white suits to play jazz trumpet at city charity events. As New Orleans flooded, Minyard says, he got out of his car and swam to work. He was trapped there for four days.

After autopsies were done and specimens removed, workers at National Medical Services, a private laboratory in Pennsylvania, quickly detected morphine in nine bodies—the same nine patients LifeCare staff identified as potential victims.

The attorney general's office hired a forensic pathologist, Cyril Wecht, who worked on the John F. Kennedy assassination case and the O. J. Simpson murder trial, to review evidence in the deaths of four patients whose full toxicology reports and medical records they obtained first: Emmett Everett, Rose Savoie, and two other LifeCare patients. Wecht concluded that all four deaths were homicides, caused by human intervention.

After months of conducting interviews and collecting documents, investigators came to believe, they said, that doctors and nurses euthanized as many as two dozen patients at Memorial. But medical records were needed to substantiate the findings, and according to investigators, Tenet's lawyers said that many of those belonging to Memorial patients were unavailable. (The Tenet spokesman said via e-mail that Tenet produced all records in its possession.) Armed with the testimony of LifeCare workers and the medical records of the four patients on the seventh floor, state prosecutors decided their strongest case was against Anna Pou, Cheri Landry, and Lori Budo for those deaths.

·   ·   ·

At about 9 P.M. on July 17, 2006—nearly a year after floodwaters from Katrina swamped Memorial hospital—Pou opened the door of her home to find state and federal agents, clad in body armor and carrying weapons. They told her they had a warrant for her arrest on four counts of principal to second-degree murder.

Pou was wearing rumpled surgical scrubs from several hours of surgery she performed earlier in the day. She knew she was a target of the investigation, but her lawyer thought he had assurance that she could surrender voluntarily. "What about my patients?" she asked reflexively. An agent suggested that Pou call a colleague to take over their care. She was allowed to freshen up and then was read her rights, handcuffed, and ultimately driven to the Orleans Parish jail. On the way, she prayed silently. (Landry and Budo were arrested the same night.)

Pou was booked and released after midnight. The next day the attorney general, Foti, held a news conference carried on CNN, which had broken some of the initial reports of the investigation and the possible euthanasia at Memorial. "This is not euthanasia," Foti said emphatically. "This is plain and simple homicide."

At a news conference later that day, Pou's lawyer blamed the storm—not Pou—for the deaths. He said his client was innocent and accused Foti, who was about to run for reelection, of orchestrating a media event with the arrests. He announced his intention to bring the results of his own investigation to the Orleans Parish district attorney, whose office had jurisdiction over the case after the arrests and would bring it before a grand jury.

As the government investigation progressed, Carrie Everett, Emmett Everett's widow, spoke out on CNN. After Katrina she searched for her husband for two weeks before learning that he was dead. She filed wrongful death lawsuits against Tenet, Life-Care, Pou, Landry, and Budo.

"Who gave them the right to play God?" Mrs. Everett demanded. "Who gave them the right?"

.   .   .

A successful murder prosecution in Orleans Parish typically requires a coroner's medical determination of homicide—that a death was caused by the actions of another human being—without regard to fault or legal responsibility. It is a step toward a criminal finding of homicide, in which a Louisiana court assigns fault for a killing.

Minyard, the coroner, brought together Cyril Wecht, Michael Baden—another well-known forensic pathologist—and Robert Middleberg, the director of the toxicology laboratory where the autopsy samples were tested, to discuss the toxicology findings. Minyard's flood-ravaged offices still hadn't been repaired, so they met for three days in his temporary quarters in a vacant funeral home.

Records showed that more than half of the forty-one bodies from Memorial that were analyzed by Middleberg's lab tested positive for morphine or midazolam, or both. Middleberg had handled thousands of cases in his career, and the high drug concentrations found in many of the patients stuck out "like a sore thumb," he told me.

The group considered the ninety-year-old pneumonia patient Alice Hutzler, whom the LifeCare nurse Gina Isbell had promised to care for during the hurricane. Morphine and midazolam were found in her liver, brain, and muscle tissue, but neither drug had been prescribed, according to her chart, which contained notes until the night before her death on September 1. That chart showed that she was "resting calmly" the previous afternoon, and during the evening her nurses did not document any complaints of pain or distress that indicated she needed the drugs.

Hutzler was one of the nine LifeCare patients found on the seventh floor with one or both drugs in their systems. All were seen alive the morning of September 1, and all were listed as dead by Memorial's pathologist that afternoon.

"Homicide," Wecht wrote on a sheet of paper with Hutzler's name on top, underlining it twice. "Homicide," he wrote for seven of the eight other seventh-floor patients, including Emmett Everett, Wilda McManus, and Rose Savoie. The last patient, whose records indicated she was close to death, he marked as undetermined. Baden said he thought all nine were homicides.

The group considered one death on the eighth floor in the I.C.U.: Jannie Burgess was the comatose patient who was found by Ewing Cook when he climbed the stairs in the heat on Wednesday, August 31. Burgess's medical chart showed that she was given 15 milligrams of morphine seven times on Wednesday between 2:10 P.M. and 3:35 P.M. on spoken orders from Cook. This was more than seven times the maximum dose she was receiving for comfort care. But because she had already been receiving morphine and because of her advanced cancer, she was "not a clear, strong case," Wecht wrote in his notes. He marked her death as undetermined.

Besides the nine patients who remained on the LifeCare floor and Burgess, the group also reviewed thirteen Memorial and LifeCare patients whose deaths were recorded by Memorial's pathologist on the second-floor lobby near the A.T.M. and elsewhere. (Other deaths struck investigators as suspicious, but because not all bodies were tested for drugs after autopsy, they were not considered.) Of those thirteen, nine tested positive for midazolam and four for morphine, too. Investigators searching the hospital found prescriptions for large amounts of morphine for three of them, including Carrie Hall, the woman who fought hard to survive on Wednesday night. The prescriptions were dated Thursday, September 1, and were signed by Dr. Anna Pou.

Despite Wecht and Baden's strong opinions that the LifeCare deaths were the result of drug injections, Minyard wanted additional information to help him make his decision. He sent the patients' medical, autopsy, and toxicology records to three other experts for an independent review.

"Homicide," Dr. Frank Brescia, an oncologist and specialist in palliative care, concluded in each of the nine cases. "Homicide," wrote Dr. James Young, the former chief coroner of Ontario, Canada, who was then president of the American Academy of Forensic Sciences. "All these patients survived the adverse events of the previous days, and for every patient on a floor to have died in one three-and-a-half-hour period with drug toxicity is beyond coincidence."

A local internal-medicine specialist concluded that while medical records and autopsies for several of the patients revealed medical issues that could reasonably have led to their deaths, most of the patients' records did not. In his report to Minyard, he wrote that it was "evident" that Emmett Everett was "in stable medical status with no clear evidence that death was imminent or impending." (Pou's lawyer says that Everett almost certainly died of an enlarged heart, not an overdose of medication.)

As Minyard deliberated, he continued his own inquiry, inviting several LifeCare administrators to his office for interviews. Their stories focused on Anna Pou. Minyard had never met Pou, but two months after her arrest he watched her defend herself and her nurse colleagues with passion on *60 Minutes*. "I want everybody to know that I am not a murderer," she told Morley Safer. "I do not believe in euthanasia."

After the *60 Minutes* story, some of Minyard's longtime colleagues questioned why he was even investigating the case. The day after the CBS broadcast, the American Medical Association released a statement: "The A.M.A. is very proud of the many heroic physicians and other health care professionals who sacrificed and distinguished themselves in the aftermath of Hurricane Katrina."

Minyard told me that after Pou appeared on national television, he had an urge to meet her, to chat over a cup of coffee and try to "get a handle on her." He had done this before with people accused of crimes. "Science is great, but there is a point where you have to go beyond science; you have to go by your gut feeling, whatever you do." He invited Pou's lawyer to bring her to his office for a visit.

Pou sat across from Minyard, "a very ladylike lady, real Southern charming lady." On his desk was a Bible, on his wall a crucifix, and all around them were framed pictures of life in their native city. Soon they were discovering mutual friends and chatting about several members of Pou's large Catholic family with whom Minyard was close. They reminisced about Pou's deceased father, a family doctor who had been especially kind to Minyard and had referred patients to him when Minyard opened his ob-gyn practice.

They talked for about an hour. She told him that she had been trying to alleviate pain and suffering. Given that Pou's lawyer was there, Minyard was careful not to put her on the spot with direct questions about what she had done. The conditions she described at Memorial took him back to the days he spent trapped in the courthouse after Katrina. How precious food and water had seemed. How impossible it was to sleep at night with gunshots echoing all around.

Minyard told me that his feelings were less sympathetic than he let Pou know. He believed he would have at least tried to save Emmett Everett. There must have been a way to get the 380-pound man downstairs, he said he thought. It also bothered Minyard that documentation suggested that few of the elderly patients who died were being treated for pain.

Minyard reached out to the noted University of Pennsylvania bioethicist Arthur Caplan for more advice. Caplan reviewed the records and concluded that all nine LifeCare patients on the seventh floor were euthanized, and that the way the drugs were given was "not consistent with the ethical standards of palliative care that prevail in the United States." Those standards are clear, Caplan wrote, in that the death of a patient cannot be the goal of a doctor's treatment.

Despite all the expert determinations of homicide, Minyard was still struggling with what to tell the grand jury. He consulted one more pathologist, Dr. Steven Karch. Karch had staked his career on advancing the argument that the level of drugs found in a cadaver may have no relationship to the levels just before death.

Karch flew to New Orleans, examined the evidence and concluded that it was absurd to try to determine causes of death in bodies that had sat at one hundred degrees for ten days. In all of the cases, he advised, the medical cause of death should remain undetermined.

The coroner said he believed that if the case went to trial, the defense would bring in someone like Karch to provide reasonable doubt. "We'd lose the case," Minyard told me. "It would not be good for the city, for the recovery. It's just a bigger picture that I had to consider than just that pure basic scientific thing."

Minyard agonized. Willfully taking a life was "a very bad, bad thing," he thought. "Only God knows when you're going to die." The case occupied Minyard's life, his thoughts, and the dreams that awoke him in the middle of the night. He called his experts again and again for support and advice.

The Grand Jury's Decision

In March 2007, the grand jurors who would consider Anna Pou's fate were sworn in. That spring, they began meeting about once a week at a secret location. Normally prosecutors are advocates for indictment, calling their strongest witnesses to testify and granting immunity in exchange for critical information. But the assistant district attorney, Michael Morales, whose office received condemnatory letters every day for bringing a case against Pou, told me that he and the Orleans Parish district attorney, Eddie Jordan, "weren't gung-ho" about prosecuting the case. "We were going to give some deference to the defendant," he said, because Pou wasn't the usual career criminal accused of murder. At the same time, because a judge had signed a warrant to arrest Pou and multiple witnesses were willing to testify, "we weren't going to shirk our duties and tank it." He said that he personally "didn't care one way or the other" about the outcome.

Rather than presenting the evidence to the jurors and seeking an indictment, as he typically did, he said he invited the jurors, in conjunction with the district attorney's office, to act as investigators and decide what evidence they wanted to consider. This didn't sit well with the attorney general and his staff. Foti told me that he repeatedly asked the district attorney's office to present all the evidence and the experts.

Grand-jury hearings are conducted in secret, making it difficult to know exactly what jurors hear. Minyard told me that in the end, he decided that four of the nine deaths on the seventh floor were homicides, including Emmett Everett and Rose Savoie. Until now, he has never publicly revealed that conclusion. He also said of Pou, "I strongly do not believe she planned to kill anybody, but it looks like she did."

The jury heard from Minyard but not from any of his forensic experts; nor from two family members who were present on the LifeCare floor during most of the ordeal; nor the main Justice Department investigator, who worked the case for a year and helped collect 50,000 pages of evidence. Only two of the main LifeCare witnesses were brought before the jury late in the process. Budo and Landry, who were compelled to testify after the district attorney decided not to prosecute them, had publicly expressed their support for Pou.

The grand jurors lived among the general public, which was firmly in Pou's corner. Pou had one of New Orleans's premier public-relations agencies representing her. A poll commissioned by her lawyer's office to assess the potential jury pool found that few New Orleanians favored indictment.

Any grand jurors who might have turned on their radios or TVs, or opened the *Times-Picayune*, or surfed the Web would have heard samples of the community's drumbeat of support. Nearly every day, New Orleans's most popular talk-radio host, Garland Robinette, raised his bass voice on WWL's *Think Tank* in outrage at "what's being done to these three . . . for trying to save lives." On July 17, 2007, a support rally to mark the first anniversary of Pou's arrest garnered top billing on Robinette's show and on every local news program. Hundreds gathered in City Park. Speakers aimed their comments directly at the grand jury, warning that medical professionals, whose ranks had already been depleted by Katrina, would flee Louisiana in droves if a doctor was indicted after serving in a disaster.

The week of the rally, the grand jurors stopped hearing evidence. The district attorney's office prepared a ten-count bill of indictment against Pou for the grand jury to consider—one count of second-degree murder in Emmett Everett's case and nine counts of the lesser conspiracy to commit second-degree murder, one for each of the LifeCare patients on the seventh floor.

This meant that the grand jurors were being asked to decide whether the evidence they heard persuaded them that Pou had "a specific intent to kill"—part of Louisiana's definition of second-degree murder.

On July 24, 2007, the jurors filed into Section E of Orleans Parish Criminal District Court, the building where Minyard survived Katrina. Judge Calvin Johnson read aloud the ten counts of indictment. The grand jury did not indict Pou on any of them.

. . .

Four years after Katrina, it's summer again in New Orleans, and the myrtle trees are in bloom. Rodney Scott, the patient whom Ewing Cook once took for dead, is still alive.

Scott is grateful to be with his family. A former nurse, he says he does not know whether euthanasia occurred at Memorial; but if it had, he wonders what the doctors and nurses could have been thinking. "How can you say euthanasia is better than evacuation?" he asked me not long ago. "If they have vital signs," he said, "get 'em out. Let God make that decision."

The debate among medical professionals about how to handle disasters is intensifying, with Pou and her version of the Memorial narrative often at the center. At a conference for hospital executives and state disaster planners a few months ago in Chicago, she did not mention that she injected patients, saying that helicopters arrived in the afternoon of Thursday, September 1, and "we were able to evacuate the rest."

Pou projected the booking photo from her arrest onto the screen as she argued for laws to shield health workers from civil and criminal liability in disasters.

Before delivering the keynote address, Pou participated in a panel on the "moral and ethical issues" that could arise if standards of care were altered in disasters. At one point, one of the panelists, Father John F. Tuohey, regional director of the Providence Center for Health Care Ethics in Portland, Ore., said that there are dangers whenever rules are set that would deny or remove certain groups of patients from access to lifesaving resources. The implication was that if people outside the medical community don't know what the rules are or feel excluded from the process of making them or don't understand why some people receive essential care and some don't, their confidence in the people who care for them risks being eroded. "As bad as disasters are," he said, "even worse is survivors who don't trust each other."

Texas Monthly

WINNER—FEATURE
WRITING

Now edited by Jake Silverstein, Texas Monthly *has won eleven National Magazine Awards, including four for General Excellence—more than any other regional publication in the history of the awards, indeed more than only a handful of other monthly magazines. This piece goes a long way toward explaining why.*

Written by Skip Hollandsworth, who joined Texas Monthly *in 1989, "Still Life" tells the story of John McClamrock and his mother, Ann—of three decades of fierce devotion to a son paralyzed during a high school football game in the early 1970s.*

Skip Hollandsworth

Still Life

Compared with the glistening two-story mansions that surrounded it, the house looked like something from another time. It was only 2,180 square feet. Its red-brick exterior was crumbling, and its gutters were clogged with leaves. Faded, paint-chipped blinds sagged behind the front windows. Next to the concrete steps leading to the front door, a scraggly banana plant clung to life.

Built in 1950, it was one of the last of the original single-story homes on Northport Drive, in Dallas's Preston Hollow neighborhood. The newer residents, almost all of them affluent baby boomers, had no idea who lived there. Over the years, they'd see an ambulance pull up to the front of the house, and they'd watch as paramedics carried out someone covered in a blanket. A few days later, they'd see the paramedics return to carry that person back inside. But they'd never learned who it was or what had happened. Some of the local kids were convinced that the house was haunted. They'd ride their bikes by the lot at dusk, daring one another to ring the doorbell or run across the unwatered lawn.

None of the neighbors knew that mailmen once delivered boxes of letters to the front door and that strangers left plates of food or envelopes stuffed with money. They didn't know that high school kids, whenever they drove past the house, blew their horns, over and over. They didn't know that a church youth group had stood on that front yard one afternoon, faced the house, and sung a hymn.

In fact, it wasn't until the spring of last year that they learned that the little house used to be one of Dallas's most famous residences, known throughout the city as the McClamrock house. It was the home of Ann McClamrock and her son John, the boy who could not move.

．　　．　　．

On the morning of October 17, 1973, John McClamrock bounded out of bed; threw on bell-bottom jeans and a loud, patterned shirt with an oversized collar; jumped into his red El Camino with a vinyl roof; and raced off to Hillcrest High School, only six blocks away. He was seventeen years old, and according to one girl who had dated him, he was "the all-American boy, just heartbreakingly beautiful." He had china-blue eyes and wavy black hair that fell over his forehead, and when he smiled, dimples creased his cheeks. Sometimes, when he sacked groceries at the neighborhood Tom Thumb, Hillcrest girls would show up to buy watermelons so that he'd carry them out to their cars. On weekend nights, they'd head for Forest Lane, the cruising spot for Dallas teenagers, hoping to get a look at him in his El Camino—or better yet, catch a ride. One cute Hillcrest blonde, Sara Ohl, had been lucky enough to go out with John on her first-ever car date, to play miniature golf. After he took her home, she called all her friends and told them she had had trouble breathing the entire time they were together.

That morning, John sat restlessly through his classes. When the lunch period bell rang, he drove to the nearest Burger King to grab a Whopper. He pushed buttons on the radio until he found the Allman Brothers' "Ramblin' Man," turned up the volume, and pressed down on the gas pedal to get back to school. He walked past the auditorium, where the drama club was rehearsing Neil Simon's *Plaza Suite*; made a left turn; and then walked on toward the boys' locker room to put on his football uniform. John—or "Clam," as he was known among his friends— had a game that afternoon.

Earlier that summer, John had quit playing for the Hillcrest Panthers so he could work extra hours at Tom Thumb to pay off his El Camino. When he tried to rejoin the team at the start of his junior year, the coaches had ordered him to spend a few weeks on the JV squad. He was five feet eleven inches tall and weighed 160 pounds. He played tackle on offense, linebacker on defense, and he was the wedge buster on the kickoffs, assigned the task of breaking up the other team's front line of blockers. That afternoon, the junior varsity was playing Spruce High School, and John was determined to show the coaches what he could do. This was the week, he vowed to his buddies, that he would be promoted to varsity.

On Hillcrest's opening kickoff, he burst through the Spruce blockers and zeroed in on the ball carrier. He lowered his head, and as the two collided, John's chin caught the runner's thigh. The sound, one teammate later said, was like "a tree trunk breaking in half."

John's head snapped back, and he fell face-first to the ground. For the next several seconds, another teammate recalled, "there was nothing but a terrible silence." Because there were no cell phones in that era, a coach had one of the players run to the high school's main office to call an ambulance. When it arrived fifteen minutes later, John was still on the ground, his body strangely still. "You've got some pinched nerves," a referee told him, speaking into the ear hole of his helmet. "You'll be up in no time."

But as soon as he was wheeled into Presbyterian Hospital, doctors knew he was in trouble. They gave him a complete neurological exam, scraping a pencil across the bottoms of his feet and taking X-rays, then ordered that his head be shaved and two small holes be bored into the top of his skull. Large tongs, like the ones used to carry blocks of ice, were attached to the holes, and seventy pounds of weight was hung from the tongs in an attempt to realign his spine.

A Hillcrest administrator called John's mother at her office at a local bank. Ann McClamrock was fifty-four years old, a striking woman, green-eyed with strawberry-blond hair. She was, as her niece liked to say, "perpetually good-natured." She always had extra food in the refrigerator for the neighborhood kids who came running in and out of the house, and on weekends she loved to throw boisterous dinner parties, most of them ending with her exhorting everyone around the table to sing corny old songs like "Skinnamarink." When she arrived at the hospital, a doctor took her aside and quietly asked if she had any religious preference.

"I'm Catholic," Ann said, giving him a bewildered look.

"Maybe you should call your priest, in case you need to deliver your son his last rites," the doctor said. "We're not sure he's going to make it through the night."

The doctor told Ann that John had severely damaged his spinal cord and was paralyzed from his neck down. He was able to swivel his head from side to side, but because his circulatory system had been disrupted, causing his blood pressure to fluctuate wildly, he could not lift his head without blacking out. "It couldn't be any worse," the doctor said.

At least outwardly, Ann seemed to take the diagnosis rather calmly. Or maybe, she later told her friends, she had simply been unable to comprehend the full meaning of what the doctor was saying. She stood at her son's bedside until her husband, Mac, who had been out of town that day—he worked for a company that insured eighteen-wheelers—arrived with the McClamrocks' other child, Henry, a quiet boy who was a freshman at Hillcrest. It was right then, with the family all together, that Ann felt the tears coming.

She slowly turned to the doctor, her hands trembling. "My Johnny is not going to die," she said. "You wait and see. He is going to have a good life." And then, her voice choking, she fell into Mac's arms.

.   .   .

John made it through the night and then through the next day. His friends flocked to the hospital, many of them dropped off at the front door by their parents. One night, nearly one hundred kids were in the ICU waiting room, all of them signing their names on a makeshift guest register—a legal pad—pinned to a wall. There were so many phone calls coming into the hospital about John that extra operators were brought in to work the switchboard.

The local newspapers jumped on the story, and soon just about everyone in Dallas was following John's struggle to stay alive. Dallas Cowboys coach Tom Landry and star defensive back Charlie Waters came to see him. The owner of the local Bonanza steakhouse chain held a Johnny McClamrock Day, donating 10 percent of all the restaurants' sales to a medical fund. "Buy a Drink for Johnny" booths were set up at shopping malls all over the city, with proceeds from the $1 soft drinks going to the family. And at Hillcrest alone, there was a bake sale, a benefit basketball game, a bowl-a-thon, a fifties dance, and even a paper drive conducted by the Ecology Club.

After one of the national wire services ran a story about John, letters began pouring in from all over the country. A group of North Carolina women who attended Sunday school together mailed John a card with an encouraging Bible verse. A faith healer from Michigan sent a note to let John know that "healing sensations" were coming his way ("You will begin to feel sensation . . . KNOW you are going to be UP and around very SOON"). John received hand-drawn get-well cards from

Texas schoolchildren and sentimental notes from teenage girls who had never met him. (A girl named Patti wrote to let him know that she had played "Bad, Bad Leroy Brown" on her record player in his honor.) Then, in November, a letter arrived at the hospital from the most unlikely place of all: the White House. President Richard Nixon, who was in the midst of his spectacular downfall from the Watergate scandal—he was only ten days away from delivering his "I am not a crook" speech—had read about John and stopped what he was doing to write him a sympathetic note.

"Mrs. Nixon and I were deeply saddened to learn of the tragic accident which you suffered," he began, "but we understand that you are a very brave young man and that your courage at this difficult time inspires all who know you. You have a devoted family and many friends cheering for you, and we are proud to join them in sending warm wishes to you always."

• • •

In December doctors suggested that John be moved to the Texas Institute for Rehabilitation and Research, in Houston, which specialized in spinal injuries. Maybe someone down there could figure out a way to get him to move, they said. When he left Presbyterian, there were nearly four thousand names listed on the guest register. Students stood by the hospital's exit and held up signs that read "Good Luck, Clam!"

While Ann lived in an apartment near the rehabilitation center and Mac and Henry visited on weekends, John stayed in a ward with other paralyzed men, going through two hours of physical therapy every day. The following March, when forty of his high school friends showed up to surprise him on his eighteenth birthday—they gave him the new albums by Elton John and Chicago—he was too weak to blow out the candles on his cake.

But he assured them that the therapy was working. Speaking into a telephone receiver held by his mother, he told a *Dallas Morning News* reporter that he would walk again and "probably" would go back to playing football. "I will never give up," he said in as firm a voice as he could muster.

But late that spring, doctors met with Ann, Mac, and Henry in a conference room. Staring at their notes, they said that not a single muscle below John's neck had shown any response. He still couldn't raise his head without losing consciousness, they added, which meant there was almost no chance he would be able to sit in a wheelchair.

One of the staffers took a breath. "We've found that 95 percent of the families that try to take care of someone in this condition cannot handle it," she said. "The families break up." She handed them a sheet of paper. "These are the names of institutions and nursing homes that will take good care of him."

Ann nodded, stood up, and said, "We will be taking Johnny home, thank you." A relative arrived with a station wagon, John was loaded into the back, and the McClamrocks returned to Northport Drive, where a newspaper photographer and some friends were waiting. Mac, Henry, and a couple of others carried John, who was wearing his Hillcrest football jersey, into the house. They twisted him into a sort of L shape as they turned down the hall and turned again into the guest bedroom, where they laid him on a hospital bed with a laminate headboard.

To make everything look as normal as possible, Ann redecorated the bedroom, hanging photos on the wall of John in his uniform. On a set of shelves she displayed footballs that had been autographed by members of various NFL teams, and she also placed the football from the Spruce game, which had been signed by his teammates. Because she had heard John tell his friends that he was determined to go hunting again, she had Mac buy a Remington twelve-gauge shotgun, which she hung on another wall. Then she told her son, "Here we are. Here is where you are going to get better."

•   •   •

Every morning before sunrise, she got out of bed, did her makeup and hair, put on a nice dress or pantsuit, dabbed perfume on her neck, and walked into John's room. She shaved him, clipped his nails, brushed his teeth, gave him a sponge bath, shampooed his hair, and scratched his nose when it itched. She fed him all his meals, serving him one bite of food after another, and she taped a straw to the side of his glass so that he could drink on his own. She changed his catheter and emptied the drainage bag when it filled up with urine, and she dutifully cleaned his bottom as if he were a newborn whenever he had a bowel movement. To prevent bedsores, she turned him constantly throughout the day, rolling him onto one side and holding him in place with pillows, then rolling him onto his back, then rolling him to his other side—over and over and over.

From Monday through Saturday, she almost never left the house. On Sunday mornings, she went to Mass at Christ the King Catholic Church, lit a candle for John, and put a $10 check in the collection box. Afterward, she drove to Tom Thumb, the same one where John used to work, to buy groceries. Once a month she'd treat herself to a permanent at the hair salon at JCPenney. But that was it: Every other minute was devoted to John.

Perhaps Ann kept up such a schedule because she thought he didn't have long to live. Within weeks after their return from Houston, he developed a kidney infection so severe it caused blood poisoning. An ambulance pulled up to the house. Paramedics ran inside, picked up John from his bed, and drove him to Presbyterian Hospital. Somehow he recovered, and when the paramedics brought him home, Ann kissed him on the forehead and said, "I'm so proud of you." A few weeks later, he developed pneumonia, which forced another trip to the hospital. Once again, he made a comeback, and once again, as he was returned home, Ann went through her ritual, kissing his forehead and saying how proud she was.

For the next few months, his friends constantly dropped in to visit. Driving past the house on their way to and from school, they always honked their horns. When John's friend Jeff Brown bought a classic 1939 Chevy Coupe, he drove it onto the Mc-Clamrocks' front yard so John could see it from his window. And because the newspapers in those days printed the home addresses of people they wrote about, strangers did indeed show up with food and gifts. At least five well-wishers gave him copies of *Joni*, the autobiography of a young woman who was paralyzed at the age of seventeen but became a skillful artist, using only her mouth to guide her brush.

One Saturday night in May 1975, Ann left home for a few hours with Mac so that they could accept John's diploma at Hillcrest High School's graduation ceremony. When his name was announced and Ann began to walk across the stage, the cheers were so loud that people put their hands to their ears. The reporters wrote about his graduation; "Gridder Scores" was the *Dallas Times Herald's* headline. When one journalist came to see him, John remained upbeat, saying he might take business law courses and someday try to pass the bar exam. "I really appreciate all the help everyone has given me and my family," he said. "Tell everyone thanks." But when the reporter asked him about his dream of walking again, he simply said, "Oh, I don't know."

Later that summer, before heading off to college, John's friends came over to say their goodbyes. In September the sound of the crowds cheering at the Hillcrest football games on Friday night began drifting across the neighborhood. Although John's window was always shut—his mother didn't want pollen coming into the house because it might congest his already weak lungs—the sound slipped in anyway. John would listen to the band play the school fight song, and he knew exactly the place in the song where the cheerleaders would kick their long, beautiful legs. "Right there," he'd softly say. "Right there."

"Come on, Johnny, we can get through this," Ann would say when she saw that look of despair cross his face. She would often read to him her favorite lines from a Catholic book of devotions she owned: "You can find the good in what seems to be the most horrible thing in the world. . . . God tells us that in all misfortunes we must seek the good. . . . Acting hopeless is easy. The real challenge is to hope."

She would also show him a small, well-worn card, titled "Prayer of Thanksgiving," which she kept on her bedside table. The prayer ended with the lines "Lord Jesus, may I always trust in your generous mercy and love. I want to honor and praise you, now and forever. Amen." She told John that she read that prayer every night. "We must pray for God's mercy," she said. "That's all we can do."

But a lot of people who knew the McClamrocks could not help but wonder if God had abandoned them. In 1977, during Henry's senior year at Hillcrest, doctors found cancerous lymph nodes in his neck. After removing them, the doctors told Ann and Mac that there was no guarantee the cancer was gone. A few months later, after paying his own visit to the doctor, Mac came home and told Ann that his nagging cough had been diagnosed as acute emphysema. Ann couldn't believe what she was hearing. She had been married once before, right out of high school, and she had given birth to a son named Cliff, who was now grown. But her first husband had died of liver disease before she turned thirty, and now here was Mac—"the genuine love of my life," she liked to say—telling her he too was going to die.

As Mac's breathing worsened, oxygen tanks piled up in their bedroom. In January 1978 he walked down the hall to sit with John. Wheezing, he patted his son on the shoulder and said he was going to need to spend a little time in the hospital. He walked out of the house and died four days later.

The funeral was held on a frigid afternoon. Ann dressed John in a suit he hadn't worn in five years and had him driven in a van to Christ the King Catholic Church. Other than his emergency trips to the hospital, it was the only time he had been out of the house. As he was pulled from the van and placed onto a stretcher outside the church, he exhaled heavily. "I can see my breath," he said, his eyes widening. "I can see my breath." He was pushed to the front of the sanctuary, next to the family's front-row pew, and he turned his head so that he could watch a priest swing a burner of incense over his father's casket. When John started to sob, Henry wiped the tears from his eyes with a tissue.

Incredibly, just two years later, Cliff called to say he had been diagnosed with lung cancer. He died in 1981, at the age of thirty-nine. At that funeral, people looked at Ann, convinced she was at the breaking point. Two husbands and one of her sons were dead. Another son was battling cancer. And, of course, there was John. Her niece, Frances Ann Giron, who always called her "Pretty Annie," told her to take a vacation. "Go someplace you've always wanted to go, like New York City," Frances Ann said. "I'll take care of John. A long weekend. That's all."

But Ann shook her head. She drove home from the funeral, walked into John's room, and put on her best smile for her son. "We're going to keep fighting," she said. "That's all I ask—just keep fighting."

·   ·   ·

They lived on Social Security disability benefits and a little insurance money. To help make ends meet, Ann, who had never gone back to her bank job after John's injury, found part-time work with an answering service, taking after-hour phone calls for a Dallas heating and air-conditioning company that were forwarded to the McClamrock house. To save money, she ordered inexpensive clothes for herself from catalogs, and she continued to wear the same clip-on earrings she had bought when she first met Mac.

She and John developed a daily routine. In the mornings, either she read to him, mostly stories out of *Reader's Digest*, or he read alone, using a page-turning device that he could operate with a nod of his head. They watched game shows and *Guiding Light*. They watched all the news broadcasts and movies on a VCR. Henry, who by then was living in his own apartment and working as a car salesman, would come over to sit with John on Sundays so that Ann could go to church and the grocery store. When she returned, she would fix a huge meal, usually chicken or pot roast with potatoes. Finally, at the end of each night, she would kiss John on the forehead and go off to her own bed, always reading her prayer of thanksgiving before falling asleep.

At least once a year, John came close to dying. He developed a urinary tract infection that nearly caused renal failure. Bladder stones clogged his catheter. His lungs filled with fluid, nearly drowning him. During his stays at the hospital, the doctors would say to Ann, "It's touch and go." But he always recovered, and as he was brought back into the house, Ann would always kiss him on the forehead and say, "I'm so proud of you."

One afternoon, as paramedics carried him back into the home, he looked at his mom and Henry and said, "Here I am, still kicking." He grinned and added, "Well, maybe not kicking."

Ann was delighted. "That's the spirit," she said.

Although John had found it impossible to get through a college correspondence course because he couldn't write anything down, he began watching all the history documentaries on PBS, he studied encyclopedia entries in hopes that someday he would be able to answer all the questions on *Jeopardy*, and he carefully read the newspaper (his mother folding the pages and putting them in front of him) so that he could have a better chance at guessing who would be the Person of the Week on ABC's Friday-evening newscast.

Sometimes, he'd blow into a specially designed tube that allowed him to turn off the radio or television, and he'd stare at the ceiling, letting his mind wander. He kept a mental list of places he wanted to see: Alaska, the Swiss Alps, and the Colosseum, in Rome. He imagined himself taking a trip down the Nile or exploring Yellowstone National Park in the winter. And he spent hours thinking back on his life before his injury: the street baseball games he played with neighborhood kids in the fourth grade, the time he put twenty pieces of bubble gum in his mouth in junior high school, the students who passed by him in the halls, the Saturday nights cruising in his El Camino. He seemed to remember some days at Hillcrest in their entirety, right down to the food he ate in the cafeteria. "It's like everyone else has all these new memories filling up their brains," he told one of his closest friends, Mike Haines, a former lineman on the football team who had become a lawyer. "All I've got are the ones before October 1973."

In March 1986, to nearly everyone's surprise, he made it to his thirtieth birthday. Ann threw one of her old-fashioned dinner parties, inviting relatives and friends. At the end of the meal she made everyone sing "Skinnamarink." Then she sang the ballad "How Many Arms Have Held You?" The dining room got strangely quiet. Everyone stared at Ann, this woman in her sixties who refused to be broken. At the end of the song, they turned to look at the motionless John, who was smiling at his mother, cheerfully telling her she still sang off-key. "You simply could not fathom how they were able to do it, day after day," Ann's niece, Frances Ann, later said. "I'd say to Pretty Annie, 'Don't you ever feel overwhelmed? Aren't you ever bitter at what has happened to you?' And she'd say, 'Frances Ann, we can either act hopeless or we can make the best out of the life we have been given.' And she'd show me that prayer of thanksgiving card and she'd say, 'God will provide. I know he will.'"

.   .   .

Another year passed, and then another. Around the neighborhood, older residents began to sell off their little houses to a new
generation of wealthy Dallasites, who would almost immediately tear them down to build mansions with high-ceilinged
foyers and impressive "great rooms." Ambitious young real estate agents would knock on the front door of the McClamrock
home, and when Ann answered, they'd tell her that they could
get her a large amount of money if she'd sell too. But she would
quickly turn them away, their business cards still in their hands.
"I'm sorry," she'd say politely, "but this is our *home*."

It was perfectly understandable that the new residents knew
nothing about the McClamrocks. By then, John was no longer
being written up in the newspapers: Reporters, predictably, had
found other senseless tragedies to write about. In fact, by the time
the nineties rolled around, a lot of people in Dallas who had once
followed John's struggles had forgotten all about him. Many of
John's classmates—the very ones who had flocked to the intensive-
care waiting room so many years ago—had also lost touch with
him. They'd certainly meant to visit, but one thing or another had
gotten in the way, and now, after so many years, they were no longer sure how to restart the friendship they'd once had.

But in 1995, the organizers of the twentieth reunion festivities
for Hillcrest's class of '75 put out the word that John, his mother,
and Henry would be more than happy to entertain visitors.
(Henry had moved back home after a divorce and undergone two
more cancer surgeries on his already scarred neck.) During the
reunion weekend, fifty or so classmates went by the house, and
they were stunned at what they saw. Perhaps because he had not
spent a day in the sun since 1973, John hardly seemed to have
aged. His skin was perfectly smooth and his hair was still jet-
black and long over the ears, exactly the way all the guys used to
wear their hair in high school. And except for the shotgun—John

had told Henry years earlier to take it down and give it to someone who could use it—nothing in his room had changed. The
photos of John in his football uniform were still on the wall, and
his clothes from high school, including his jersey, his bell-bottom
jeans, and his loud, patterned shirts with oversized collars, were
still in the closet. Even the same shag carpet covered the floor.

A couple women who had once dated him blinked back tears
when they saw him. Another classmate, Sara Foxworth, a Dallas
housewife and mother, gasped when she walked into his room
and he called her name.

"But I thought you didn't know who I was," she exclaimed. "I
was too shy to talk to you."

"You sat three seats behind me in English," he said. "And your
locker was over by the cafeteria." He gave her a gentle smile. "I
remember," he said.

Several of his old teammates, still muscular and narrow-
waisted, had no idea what to say to him. They certainly didn't
want to make John feel worse about his plight by telling him
about all the things they had done since high school. But John
asked them about their careers, their wives and children, and
where they went on vacations. He also assured them that he was
doing just fine—that he even watched football on weekends and
didn't flinch when he saw a jarring tackle. "I'm the same person
I've always been—only I don't move," he joked. And when each
of his visitors told him goodbye, he said cheerfully, "Come on
back, anytime you want. Believe me, I'm not going anywhere."

Some of his classmates did come back around. A few of them
brought along their children to meet John so they could learn
about courage. (As soon as they got back to their homes, the kids
would go lie in their beds, trying to see how long they could stay
still.) Bill Allbright, a trainer on the junior varsity team who had
become a successful financial adviser, found himself driving over
to see the McClamrocks after he lost his wife to cancer, knowing
they would understand his loss. And when Sara Foxworth was

diagnosed with leukemia, she too showed up at the McClamrocks'. After she left, John asked his mother to come into his room with some stationery so that he could dictate a letter for Sara. He had his mom write the lines "You can find the good in what seems to be the most horrible thing in the world. Take good care of yourself. Sincerely, John McClamrock."

.   .   .

Ann was then in her late seventies, and she was still maintaining her daily schedule, changing John's catheter, cleaning his bottom, and turning him every couple hours, refusing any help. A few years earlier, after reading an article about exercise and a healthy heart, she had ordered a cheap stationary bicycle from a catalog, which she put in her bedroom and faithfully pedaled each night. Wearing ancient, cracked tennis shoes, she had also been taking quick walks around the block, pumping her arms back and forth.

But she knew that time was catching up with her. It wasn't long after the twentieth reunion that she began adding a single sentence to the end of her prayer of thanksgiving. She asked God to let her live one day longer than John—only one day, she fervently prayed—so that she could always take care of him. "I'm not going to leave him," she told Henry. "He's hung on for me. I'm going to hang on for him."

John did continue to hang on. He came down with another urinary tract infection. His intestines suddenly twisted, which forced doctors to push a tube down his throat and pump everything out of his stomach to provide him some relief. He got a bedsore so severe that plastic surgery was required to mend it. His lungs again filled up with fluid. But each time, he bounced back. As paramedics carried him inside the house, he would say, "Still kicking," and his mother, following her ritual, would kiss him on the forehead and say, "I'm so proud of you."

One afternoon, a pretty brunette named Jane Grunewald, who had been a classmate of John's, called and asked if she could visit. Jane had married soon after graduating from Hillcrest and spent twenty years trying to be what she described as "the perfect PTA mom," raising two children in the suburbs. But her marriage had fallen apart, and she was struggling. On that first visit, she and John talked for two hours. She began returning once a month, often wearing a lovely black dress, always bringing along Hershey's Kisses for John. Before she arrived, John would have his mother wash his hair, comb his mustache, dab some cologne on his neck, and then pull his bedsheet up to his chin so she wouldn't see his painfully thin body. Sometimes, Ann would fix them cocktails, carrying them into John's room on a tray (with a straw always taped to the side of John's glass). Then she'd leave them alone.

During one visit, Jane told him that he was the kind of man she longed for—someone who genuinely appreciated her. "And you're always there for me," she said.

"That's true, you never have to worry about me running around on you," John replied. He told Jane to look in the top dresser and pull out his old Saint Christopher pendant. "It's yours," he said. "I never did get the chance to give it to someone in high school." She leaned down and kissed him on the cheek, leaving a thick red lipstick print.

He later told Henry that his monthly visits from Jane were his version of a love affair. "Not that we are going to have sex," he said with a sort of resigned smile. "You know, I never had sex. I'll never make love to a woman." He gave his brother a look. "Is there any way you can tell me what it feels like?"

•　　•　　•

For Ann's eighty-second birthday, on January 12, 2001, Henry brought home a gift, along with a takeout chicken-enchilada dinner from El Fenix and a bag of red licorice, her favorite candy. "To Mom, still kicking," John said as she opened her present, a small bottle of perfume that Henry had bought at Dillard's. Five years later, on her eighty-seventh birthday, Henry again brought home takeout enchiladas and a bag of red licorice, and John again said, "To Mom, still kicking."

By then, it was obvious she was slowing down. Instead of getting dressed as soon as she got out of bed, she spent her mornings in her nightgown and her favorite green terrycloth bathrobe. She was having trouble hearing, and her eyesight was weakening. She began to wobble when she walked and once fell while cooking breakfast. A doctor told her that she had a type of vertigo and that she needed to stay off her feet. "Absolutely not," she replied.

But in the fall of 2007, she fell again, breaking a bone in her right shoulder and tearing her left rotator cuff. It was the first time she had been admitted to the hospital since Henry's birth, in 1959. Still, she left a couple days earlier than the doctors wanted so that she could get back to John. "I have to keep going," she said when Henry came to take her home, and she suddenly burst into tears. "Henry, I can't leave him."

Only then did she allow Henry to take over the task of turning John in his bed. She let him make the instant coffee in the morning for the three of them. Because of her eyesight, she also agreed to let Henry drive her to Christ the King and the grocery store on Sundays. But she still had precise rules for their excursions. She told Henry that as soon as he dropped her off at the church, he had to immediately return to the house to sit with John. He then could pick her up at the end of the service and take her to the grocery store, but he had to drive right back to the house again to sit with John, and he could return to the store only when she called.

In January 2008, Ann, John, and Henry celebrated her eighty-ninth birthday with another takeout meal from El Fenix and another bag of licorice. A few weeks later, in the middle of the night, she thought she heard the sound of bedsprings squeaking in John's room. She heard footsteps and then a hesitant cry.

"Mom . . ."

She sat up, pulled her green terrycloth bathrobe over her gown, and headed down the hall. Because she could barely see in the darkness, she kept one hand on the wall to keep herself from falling. When she reached John's bedroom doorway, she stepped forward and peered toward his bed, in the corner of the room.

"Johnny?" she asked. "Johnny?"

She was nearly out of breath. She turned on a lamp and there he was, fifty-one years old, lying on his back in his bed just as he had been for the past thirty-four years. He turned his head a few inches to the side and looked at her.

"Mom, are you okay?"

She took a breath and said, "I thought . . ." And then she paused for a moment.

"I thought you had . . ." But she paused again, unable to bring herself to say the words.

It was the first time, she later said, that she had ever dreamed that John could walk again. "What does it mean?" she asked Henry. "What do you think it means?"

Not long after the dream, two new bedsores appeared on the backs of John's knees. In late February, he was taken to Presbyterian. The doctors, realizing the tissue of his skin was wearing out and unable to withstand the constant pressure from the bed, suggested that he be admitted to a nearby rehabilitation facility, where a wound-care specialist could treat him.

Within days, he developed a fever, and because he could not cough with any strength, he was unable to expel any dust or mucus from his lungs. His weight dropped to ninety-eight pounds. "You have to admit, my body held up for a long, long time," he said when Henry dropped by to check on him.

"Come on now, you can get through this," Henry said, using one of their mother's phrases. "All you have to do is keep fighting."

"Why don't you bring Mom over?" John said. "Have her look pretty. She'd like for me to see her that way."

"John, are you giving up?"

There was a long silence. A food cart rattled down the hall and a nurse's sneakers squeaked on the hallway floors. From other rooms came the beeps of heart monitors and the deep whooshing sounds of ventilators.

"We know about her prayer," John finally said. "We know she doesn't want to go first." He looked at Henry and said, "I need to go so she can go."

·   ·   ·

On March 18, Henry drove Ann to JCPenney to get her hair done before he took her to the rehabilitation facility. Because she was so feeble, Henry put her in a wheelchair. He pushed her into John's room, where she immediately began to check his catheter and inspect the bandages on his bedsores. "Mom, it's okay," John said.

She smoothed John's hair along the temples. She touched his forehead, and she slowly ran her hand down one side of his face, past his cheekbones and the curls of his hair. She said, as if she knew what was about to happen, "Johnny, we'll be back together soon."

"I know we will," John said.

Then he told his mother something he had never said before. "I know how hard it's been for you."

"Hard?" Ann asked. "Johnny, it's been an honor."

Henry took her home, helped her into her bed and made sure she had her prayer of thanksgiving card. After she fell asleep, he drove back to the rehabilitation facility to check on John one last time. A nurse greeted him at the door. John had died about thirty minutes earlier, she said. He had closed his eyes and quietly drifted away, not making a single sound.

.   .   .

It was standing room only for the funeral. Some of John's childhood friends had flown in from around the country. Jane Grunewald, of course, arrived in one of her black dresses, and Sara Foxworth, less than a year away from death herself, was also there, gingerly taking a seat at the end of a pew. John's schoolmate Jeff Whitman, a prominent Dallas eye surgeon, came straight from a hospital, still wearing his scrubs, and Dave Carter, the former Hillcrest swimming coach, who had named his dog after John, already had tears in his eyes when he walked into the sanctuary.

The mourners looked toward the front rows to get a glimpse of Ann. But just before the service began, a priest walked up to the pulpit to announce that she and Henry would not be there. Earlier that morning, the priest said, Ann had collapsed while getting dressed for the funeral and Henry had rushed her to Presbyterian Hospital.

The organist launched into the opening hymn, and John's casket was rolled down the main aisle. He was dressed in the suit he'd worn to his father's funeral. The priest waved a burner of incense over John's casket and said, "May the Lord bless this man who is finally freed of the binds that have held him. May he run over fields of green."

Ann returned home a couple of days later. Clearly disoriented, she wandered through the house, always holding onto a wall, not sure what to do. At one point, she picked up the phone and asked Henry for the number of a Dallas department store that had been closed for decades. She asked to talk to her father, who had been dead for fifty years. She then stood in the doorway of John's bedroom, staring blankly at his bed. "Johnny?" she said. "Johnny, are you walking?"

Eight weeks after John's death, Ann died in her bed, her prayer of thanksgiving card on the bedside table. Henry was sitting beside her, holding her hand. He had her cremated and her ashes put in an urn, which he decided to bury in the ground directly over John's casket, at a cemetery near Love Field. At her service, the same priest who had presided over John's funeral said, "We send off Ann today to be with the son she loved. We send her to the mansions of the saints." The priest was about to say something else about Ann, but he saw Henry holding his hands to his face. "And may God bless Henry, who gave his life to his family," the priest said. "God bless Henry."

. . .

For days, Henry just sat in the little house on Northport Drive, not sure what to do. He finally got rid of John's hospital bed and, except for his mother's terrycloth robe, donated her clothes to charity. He then planted a For Sale sign in the front yard. Many of the neighborhood's residents were no doubt relieved: The old house was finally going to be demolished so that a new mansion could be built.

But one afternoon, when he was in the front yard watering the banana plant, two young mothers on their power walk slowed down and waved at him. They said they had read a sports column in the newspaper eulogizing the McClamrocks. "We're sorry we never got a chance to meet your mother and brother," one of the women said, grabbing Henry's hand. A few days later, a man got out of a luxury car, rang the doorbell, and told Henry he lived down the street. "If there's anything we can do for you, let us know," he said.

In March, a year after John's death, Henry still hadn't accepted any offers to sell. "I know I need to move on and get my life started again," he recently told a visitor while the two of them sat in John's room. "But I keep hearing Mom's and John's voices. In the mornings, I keep making three cups of instant coffee. When I go to the grocery store, I drive back home as fast as I can, thinking someone might need me."

The visitor noticed that Henry had started remodeling, pulling out the old shag carpet and repainting the walls. Henry shrugged. "I don't know if I can ever leave," he said. "This has been a good home. It's been a very good home."

Vanity Fair

Marc Dreier wanted—needed—a beachfront house in the Hamptons. That, anyway, is how it all started—a four-year crime spree, during which Dreier defrauded thirteen hedge funds and stole $380 million. It ended with the fifty-nine-year-old, Ivy League–educated lawyer sentenced to twenty years in federal prison. Vanity Fair described this as "Dreier's blow-by-blow account of what it's like to turn bad." The National Magazine Award judges called it "a thrilling narrative and a story for our times."

Bryan Burrough

Marc Dreier's Crime of Destiny

The sun-drenched apartment, perched high in a Midtown Manhattan building looking down on the famed restaurant Le Cirque, is as luxurious as one would expect for space that cost $10.4 million. Lined with floor-to-ceiling glass, the living room features low divans wrapped in rich golden fabric. On the vast outdoor deck, as big as many apartments, the views stretch north and east, all the way across Long Island Sound toward Connecticut.

Yet even a casual visitor would notice that something is amiss. Dozens of bare hooks line the white walls; all the paintings are gone. Boxes of paperwork litter the floors. In the kitchen, the knives are missing. Bags of trash overflow. The dining-room table is strewn with containers of half-eaten Chinese food. In an adjacent nook, an older man slumps on a sofa watching CNN on a wall-mounted flat-screen television. Unpaid bills are piling up. As nice as this apartment once was, it now feels like a $10 million dorm room.

That's because it's a jail. Sort of. On the orders of a federal judge, its owner is living here under house arrest. That man watching CNN? He's a retired F.B.I. agent, one of several who rotate through all week long. One morning I arrive after eleven. The owner, the man the security guards are watching, is just getting out of bed.

His name is Marc Dreier, he is fifty-nine years old, and his life is over. A smallish, tightly wound man with red, stubbled cheeks and a silvery pompadour, Dreier was once a hotshot New York litigator with multimillionaire clients. Then he stole $380 million from a bunch of hedge funds, got caught, and was arrested in Toronto under bizarre circumstances, having attempted to impersonate a Canadian pension-fund lawyer as part of a scheme to sell bogus securities to the big American hedge fund Fortress Investment Group. Now, as he wanders into the living room rubbing sleep from his eyes, Dreier is waiting for the judge to tell him just how many years he will spend in prison.

As he takes a seat across from me, he is wearing a loose-fitting black sweater and black jeans. And then, in the lifeless monotone of a death-row inmate, Marc Dreier begins to tell his story.

Maybe you remember the Dreier case. Or maybe you don't, given that just five days after Dreier's arrest, last December, federal authorities announced the discovery of the largest Ponzi scheme in U.S. history and the detention of its mastermind, Bernard Madoff; ironically, you can just glimpse a corner of Madoff's Fifty-third Street headquarters from Dreier's kitchen windows. Once the Madoff scandal hit, Dreier all but vanished from the headlines. If he's remembered today, it's probably for the details of his arrest, the sheer audacity of impersonating that Toronto attorney inside the man's own offices.

The Canadian incident turned out to be the tip of one very dirty iceberg. Re-arrested upon his return to La Guardia Airport, Dreier was revealed to have defrauded more than a dozen hedge funds, not counting the $45 million or so he stole from his own clients' escrow accounts. His 270-lawyer Park Avenue firm, Dreier L.L.P., imploded practically overnight. He was indicted, thrown in a jail cell, then allowed to spend several months under house arrest at his Fifty-eighth Street apartment. In June, after our interviews, he pleaded guilty to all charges. A judge sentenced him to twenty years in prison. As of this writing, he is in the Metropolitan Correctional Center Chicago. Dreier's downfall left half the New York bar scratching their heads. Here was a lawyer who seemingly had every toy a middle-aged American man could want: not one but two waterfront homes in the Hamptons, condominiums in the Caribbean, a 120-foot yacht moored in St. Martin, a $200,000 Aston Martin, an ocean-side condominium in Santa Monica, plus his own Los Angeles sushi restaurant, not to mention a collection of modern art that included works by Warhol, Hockney, Picasso, Matisse, and Lichtenstein.

There were all kinds of theories, though, most assuming that Dreier had resorted to theft to cover losses at his firm, or perhaps to support his outsize lifestyle. Some veteran trial attorneys, however, noting how addictive the adrenaline of courtroom combat can be, came up with a novel notion: Dreier, they speculated, did it out of boredom. "People caught in these situations—Madoff, whoever—they all share a similar profile," muses David Keyko, a partner at the Manhattan law firm Pillsbury Winthrop Shaw Pittman. "At some point this stops being about the money. They've got enough money. At some point this becomes about the thrill of getting away with it."

There was at least one other theory you heard, mostly from those who grappled with Dreier in court. "You know everyone's theory about Dreier is that this guy went bad because he overreached financially, that he got in over his head," says Jerome Katz, a Ropes & Gray attorney, who had clashed with Dreier in the past. "I'm sorry, but I don't buy that. I think this guy has always been bad."

They were all wrong. What no one understood is something that Dreier, the first of the Madoff-era criminals to tell his story publicly, explains here for the first time. This wasn't the case of a man who had everything going bad, Dreier makes clear. What no one understood is that everything Dreier owned—the cars, the mansions, the yacht, the sushi restaurant, even the law firm itself—was made possible by his crimes. This was a man who went bad to have everything.

I Confess

Back in April, two months before his sentencing, Dreier consented to a wide-ranging set of interviews with *Vanity Fair* and *60 Minutes*. (The only condition was that publication be held until after his sentencing.) Talking with Dreier was like talking with a dying man. During our conversations in that sunny living room above Le Cirque, he was all but a zombie, breaking a smile exactly once during five hours of discussion, a wry chuckle as he described what it was like occupying a darkened prison cell with a urine-covered floor and a triple murderer. Dreier's blue eyes, dull and lifeless, seldom made contact with mine. His speech, marred by a slight lisp, was formal and repetitive, almost stilted, as if he had rehearsed exactly what he wanted to say.

"Obviously, people who knew me are puzzled by what I did," Dreier says, "and I hope talking to you helps begin to explain it. I obviously am sincerely, deeply remorseful and sorry about what I did, and hopefully an interview can convey to people I hurt how remorseful I am. That's the truth. I am deeply sorry. And the frustrating thing is not to be able to say that." He wants the world to see he is not some comic-book villain, he says, that he was once a decent man who found himself swept up in a culture that rewards material gains. All he ever wanted, Dreier says, was to be viewed as a success, and when he wasn't, he began to steal to get the things he craved,

"Even a good person can lose their way," he goes on. "This is not just a story about someone who engaged in a significant crime, but the less dramatic point, you know, is people who are following a certain path, who go to the right schools, who do the right things. . . . You can still lose your way. In a terrible way. As I did."

Marc Stuart Dreier was born in 1950 and grew up in Lawrence, Long Island, one of the fabled, affluent "Five Towns." His father was a captain in the Polish Army who, assigned to the New York World's Fair in 1939, found himself marooned in America by the start of war. He stayed, married, and went on to found a string of movie theaters in Manhattan and on Long Island. The elder Dreier retired to Florida in the 1970s, but restless there, he started a second string of theaters that Marc's brother, Mitchel, runs today. Dreier describes the family as close and loving, which sounds right; they paid the $70,000 a month it cost for private-security men during his house arrest.

From childhood, Dreier was a golden boy. At Lawrence High he was head of the student council and voted "Most Likely to Succeed." He was very smart, a good talker, and from an early age, perhaps unsurprisingly, he wanted to become a courtroom attorney. Talk to those who have known him the longest and the one fault some cite was Dreier's mercenary streak. Marc Dreier was in it for Marc Dreier. He was charming, ambitious, hardworking, and determined to excel. Everyone who knew him, especially his parents, predicted great things.

"I [grew] up experiencing a lot of success, even in elementary school," Dreier says. "I had always been a leader. Things just came easy to me. People expected I would achieve real success in my life."

He got into Yale, earned a degree in 1972, and went on to Harvard Law School, where he graduated in the middle of his class in 1975. He was hired as a litigation associate at the white-shoe Manhattan firm of Rosenman & Colin, where he fell under the supervision of its litigation chief, Max Freund, who was also the firm's co-chairman. Dreier started out carrying Freund's briefcase, then graduated to "third chair" in Freund's trials, then moved up to second chair. His baptism by fire came during years of work alongside Freund in the so-called Betamax case, in which the plaintiffs, Disney and Universal Studios, sued Sony,

Rosenman's client, makers of the Betamax videocassette player, for copyright infringement. By the time the trial finally wrapped up, in 1979, Dreier was known within the firm as "Max's boy." As they had since he was a child, people predicted great things.

Into the 1980s, Dreier lived alone in a sadly neglected Upper East Side apartment, grinding through hundred-hour weeks working for Freund. A fervid fan of the New York Mets, he pitched on the Rosenman softball team—one of his few outside pursuits. In 1985, to no one's surprise, he made partner. At the same time, he began dating an attractive Rosenman associate named Elisa Peters. They married in 1987, honeymooned in Italy and France, and later had two children, a boy and a girl, both now in their teens.

But if Dreier's career was thriving, Rosenman wasn't. The old-line firm had lost its most important client, CBS, on the day Dreier joined, in 1975, and some said it never recovered. Older lawyers jealously guarded their clients, frustrating their younger colleagues, many of whom, especially the litigators, began to grow restless. Some attorneys began to leave. (Rosenman eventually merged with a larger firm in 2002.)

Dreier, for one, found making partner didn't bring him the money or the responsibility he felt he deserved. "Life didn't change as much as I would've wanted it to change," he says. "I was disappointed the position didn't mean everything I had hoped for. I guess you would say I didn't get either the financial success or the recognition I would've liked."

Just as Dreier's eye began to roam, he received a job offer from Fulbright & Jaworski, the massive Houston firm, which was opening a New York office. Dreier leapt at the chance to head Fulbright's New York litigation section. The move meant more money and more recognition, and Dreier hoped he would be representing Fulbright's big Texas clients in their courtroom battles. Instead, as at Rosenman, he found older lawyers not willing to let go of their clients. For the most part, Dreier and his group were obliged to find their own clients, which was difficult.

Dreier did manage to snag one large fish, a medium-size Wall Street firm named Wertheim Schroder & Company, which hired him in 1991 to sue Avon, the consumer-products giant. It was a complex securities case involving the disputed redemption price of some Avon preferred stock, and Dreier plunged into it with zeal, eventually persuading a New York judge to make it a class action, meaning Dreier was named to represent all the preferred holders. If he could win the suit, Dreier thought, the damages might run into the hundreds of millions of dollars. His own payday could easily run into the tens of millions.

But it was not to be. Dreier's frustrations with Fulbright management had been building for several years when, in 1994, Wertheim was purchased by a British investment bank, Schroders P.L.C. To Dreier's dismay, executives at Schroders had no interest in pursuing the Avon litigation. Fulbright's management committee in Houston, hoping to keep the British bank as a client, agreed and told Dreier to drop the lawsuit. Dreier, unwilling to surrender a case he felt could make him very rich, angrily refused. When Fulbright insisted, Dreier asked the case judge to replace him, thus embarrassing both Fulbright and Schroders, which quickly backed off. Instead, his bosses ordered Dreier to settle the case for a nominal sum. A settlement was reached, but Dreier opposed it in court, at which point Fulbright tried to push him aside and named another attorney to help run the case.

It was the final straw. In March 1995, Dreier pulled a Jerry Maguire, sending a long resignation memo to Houston and taking his one piece of major litigation, the Avon lawsuit, with him. He joined a tiny law firm, Duker & Barrett, to pursue the case. The three lawyers didn't get along, however, and Dreier left within a year, determined now to go it alone. "I saw a small firm wasn't that hard to run," Dreier says. "I thought I could do it myself." (Ironically, Duker's founding partner, William Duker, would later plead guilty to fraud for overbilling the U.S. government $1.4 million; he received thirty-three months in prison.)

Striking out on his own, Dreier rented a small office suite in Rockefeller Center and hired a few associates. Shortly after, in 1996, he agreed to partner with a friend of his brother-in-law's, Neil Baritz, who practiced in Boca Raton, Florida. Their new firm, Dreier & Baritz, muddled along for several years with little distinction; Dreier argued a string of cases for various small businesses, and for a time he felt content. "I was much happier," Dreier says. "I loved being my own boss. For the first time I felt like I was doing something meaningful."

Running his own firm, however, presented a host of new challenges, chiefly the pressure of luring clients. That meant entertaining, and Dreier quickly realized that prospective clients judged him in large part not on his legal talent but on the trappings of his success. He moved his family into a duplex on Seventy-sixth Street, then into a far larger apartment on Fifty-eighth Street, which he rented because he couldn't afford to buy it. He spent nearly $1 million on renovations, then thousands more buying art and furnishings. In 1998 he moved his offices to 499 Park Avenue, designed by I. M. Pei.

"I needed to give people the idea I was doing very well," he says. "That was the first step in a pattern toward living above my means."

His new surroundings, in fact, soon drove Dreier into debt. The only way to get out, he realized, was to expand his firm and its revenues. Neil Baritz had a friend in Oklahoma City named William Federman, and Dreier, impressed with Federman's practice, lured him into their partnership. The new firm, Dreier, Baritz & Federman, had twenty lawyers in New York, Boca Raton, and Oklahoma, and Dreier, as lead partner, used it to launch a series of new class-action securities lawsuits, similar to the strategy he was employing in the Avon case, which was still dragging on.

By 2000, after two full years, the expanded firm was having "modest success," Dreier says. "We were paying the bills." Dreier turned fifty that year, a point when many men assess their lives. As he took stock, Dreier began to realize he hadn't fulfilled the potential so many had seen in him. Friends from Harvard were heading giant firms and bringing in multi-million-dollar judgments. It was depressing that, after all those years as a golden boy, Dreier was still mired in a small firm, still hustling to pay his bills. It was then that 9/11 hit, bringing on the dark days when Dreier's world began to collapse.

Middle-Age Crazy

Dreier watched the towers fall from his Park Avenue office. He doesn't blame any of what happened on the events of that day, but he does trace the source of almost all his ensuing difficulties to the months after 9/11. "I had a very emotional response to that," he says. "I remember feeling an emptiness I couldn't shake in the last quarter of '01, feeling emotionally drained and looking to find myself."

Dreier won't say it, but in some inescapable way he found the fiery fall of the Twin Towers a metaphor for his career, for his entire life. Part of it was the conclusion of his ten-year fight against Avon, which finally ended in November 2001; only later would a judge rule against Dreier, sending the biggest case of his life spiraling down the drain. But it was more than that. He and Elisa had been growing apart. They began to argue more. Dreier won't explain what happened, only that he was to blame, saying, "I wasn't attentive enough to my family." Elisa filed for divorce in January 2002. This, in turn, exacerbated simmering tensions with Dreier's Florida partner, Neil Baritz; the wives were close. Dreier and Baritz agreed to split up. William Federman left as well, after objecting not only to Dreier's penchant for secrecy— he says he never received the monthly financial statements he was promised—but also to the exorbitant sums Dreier had spent on their Park Avenue offices.

All this sent Dreier into an emotional tailspin. "I was very distraught," he says. "I was very disappointed in my life. I felt my career and my marriage were over. I was fifty-two and [I felt] maybe life was passing me by. . . . I felt like I was a failure." His feelings of despair were deepened by his keen, lifelong sense of entitlement, a hard-core belief that he was destined to achieve great things.

And now, suddenly, he realized he hadn't. Worse, for the first time since early adulthood he was alone. "I didn't go into therapy," Dreier says, "though I should have. It might have helped to have someone to talk to, to make me stay grounded." He pauses for a long moment. "I thought I was too smart, I was too confident," he says finally. "You can lose your way a little bit. It was all my fault. I didn't have a therapist, a wife, or a friend. I didn't have anyone I could talk to. I don't do that. I kept everything inside."

There have been rumors that Dreier engaged in a man's typical divorce-era vices—alcohol, women, even recreational drugs—but he waves it all away. His only vice, he insists, was work, but it couldn't lift the gloom. For months he brooded over the wreckage of his life. His epiphany, Dreier remembers, came in the summer of 2003, during a long walk he took on the beach near his vacation home, in Westhampton Beach, New York. He experienced a moment of clarity, he says, in which he saw the path he needed to take; unfortunately, it was a path that would lead to his downfall.

It happened one day when he found himself staring at a palatial beachfront home. His own house was inland. He had always wanted one right on the beach. It was at that moment, Dreier says, that he came to two conclusions. He would buy himself a big house on the beach. And he would get the money by dramatically expanding his firm, now renamed Dreier L.L.P. Dreier knows how ridiculous this sounds, that his criminal behavior can be traced to his yearning for a better beach house. "I wanted to just, well, appease myself," he says. "Well, not appease myself. Gratify myself . . . I was very, very caught up in seeing the criteria of success in terms of professional and financial achievement, which I think was a big part of the problem. But I thought it would make me happy. And I wanted to be happy again."

He returned to his Park Avenue office that fall determined to lure teams of all-star lawyers to Dreier L.L.P. Each would get a guaranteed salary, plus a bonus based on performance. But unlike other major U.S. firms, Dreier L.L.P. would not be a partnership. Dreier himself would own it all.

The plan looked promising on paper, but in practice there was one major problem. "It required a lot of cash," Dreier admits. Each lawyer had to be paid up front, and as more came on board Dreier was obliged to lease an entire new floor of offices, complete with furniture and computers. Every penny had to come from his own pocket—money, needless to say, that he simply didn't have. In fact, given the support he was required to pay his wife, he was already living far beyond his means. He had tried borrowing from banks, but "the banks all turned me down," he says. "I had no assets. No credit history." To begin his expansion, he had resorted to borrowing money from factors, firms willing to lend against his receivables—but at steep interest rates. "The factors," Dreier says today, "were just killing me."

Still, within a year, Dreier managed to bring almost forty new attorneys into his firm, including an entire group or two, such as the four-lawyer wealth-advisory practice he snagged from Kaye Scholer. An essential part of the recruiting process, at least in Dreier's mind, remained draping his life in the trappings of success. He had moved into a large rental on Fifty-seventh Street after the separation and, as before, plowed nearly $1 million into a renovation. "Lawyers are very risk-averse," he says. "They want to see someone who is very successful already. That was key. The problem was, I had to succeed immediately, or at least present the appearance I was succeeding."

Easy Money

It was during this period, in the first half of 2004, that he began considering, as he puts it, "crossing the line" into illegal behavior, into fraud. "I was [still] very unhappy," he says. "I was really desperate for a solution. I wanted to have more success in my life. There was that desperate component for me that made it easier to cross the line. The second part of it was an irrational overconfidence in myself. I had always been able to will myself through problems."

Dreier says he can't remember the moment he actually began considering fraud. But he acknowledges the decision was made easier by a long track record of what he calls "cutting corners." As he acknowledges, "Yeah, I took advantage of expense accounts, statements on tax returns, that kind of thing. You know, I discovered once you cross a gray line it's much easier to cross a black line." And once he did begin thinking about fraud, he rationalized it as a onetime event that was necessary to fuel his expansion plans. "I thought I could do what I had to do, and get out of it relatively quickly," he explains. "How much did I struggle with the ethical issue? I'd like to say I have a clear recollection of going through some great ethical analysis and agonizing over it. But I don't believe I did. I should have. I just don't remember that kind of angst. I don't."

If he was to become a thief, Dreier reasoned, his target was obvious: hedge funds. It was 2004, and every dinner party he attended seemed to be thronged with young hedge-fund billionaires eager to throw around investment money. "I had to come up with some quote-unquote great idea for a hedge fund," Dreier remembers. "I couldn't sell anything tangible. It had to be a financial instrument at some level to sell to a hedge fund. So I came up with the idea of selling debt."

He would sell an IOU, a one-year note with an interest rate of 8 or 9 percent. But it would need to come from a bogus issuer. No hedge fund would invest in Dreier L.L.P. itself. The issuer needed to be an attractive firm, something to excite a hedge fund. In a perfect world, the issuer should be exceedingly private, someone it would be difficult to ask questions of, the better to conceal his scheme. The more Dreier thought it over, the more obvious it was who the putative issuer of his fake debt had to be: his best client, Sheldon Solow.

Well known for building 9 West Fifty-seventh Street, the office tower where Henry Kravis and Ross Johnson squabbled throughout *Barbarians at the Gate*, Solow is a cantankerous, eighty-one-year-old Brooklyn-born developer renowned in Manhattan real-estate circles for all manner of legal wrangling. And he has plenty of money to wrangle with: in 2008, Forbes named him the world's 605th-richest man, with a net worth estimated at $2 billion. Dreier met Solow in the mid-1990s through a family friend, and argued his first case for him several years later.

Solow became Dreier's dream client, a deep-pocketed billionaire whose appetite for corporate combat meant a string of big-money assignments. Wherever Solow went into battle, Dreier led the charge. In 1998, when Solow became embroiled in a nasty tussle with Hard Rock Café chain co-founder Peter Morton over a Hamptons mansion they both sought to buy, Dreier sued Morton in state court, lost, appealed the verdict, and lost, then filed two federal lawsuits, losing both. When Dreier filed a third federal lawsuit, a judge named Loretta Preska dismissed it, saying that Solow "had so many bites at the apple, [he] has swallowed the core." Dreier and Solow appealed, but at that point the upper court lost all patience, fining both men for filing a frivolous action.

Then there was the time in 2005 when Solow had Dreier sue the owners of 380 Madison Avenue, alleging a conspiracy to inflate the rent Solow was paying to them. During oral arguments, the defendants' attorney, Jerome Katz, then of Chadbourne & Park, marveled at Dreier's ability to make his implausible conspiracy theory sound coherent and reasonable. "This guy is a combination of great intellect and complete sleaze; he is very clever, very smooth, very agile, a high-I.Q. guy," Katz says. "He is a guy who, in my case, drafted a complaint that was extremely clever but based on a pure fantasy, where he concocted this alleged conspiracy that just didn't exist. He would speak in these sentences that were silky smooth, but his argument made absolutely no sense."

The judge agreed wholeheartedly, throwing out the case. Katz then asked the court to impose the maximum sanction against both Dreier and Solow, forcing them to pay the defendants' legal fees. "I don't believe in my entire career I had ever made a motion for legal fees, and I've been practicing law for thirty-four years," Katz says. The judge consented to the unusual order. Four years later, thanks to a blizzard of legal protests from Dreier, Katz is still trying to collect. (Sheldon Solow did not respond to requests for comment.)

A third case involving Dreier and Solow suggests behavior even more questionable. Its pivot was a long-running feud between Solow and another prominent Manhattan developer, Peter Kalikow. The incident began in February 2004, when Kalikow opened both the *New York Post* and the *New York Times* and, to his dismay, found large, bogus legal notices listing more than 400 creditors from a bankruptcy he had endured more than a decade earlier, in 1991. The ads suggested that the bankruptcy was somehow ongoing and, worse, that Kalikow had understated his assets. It concluded, "You may have additional rights of recovery based upon a failure by the debtors to make truthful disclosure."

Kalikow was incensed; the ads were utterly untrue. He was convinced that someone had placed them to humiliate him personally. Seeking to find out who, he turned to Stanley Arkin, a crafty New York attorney who specializes in ferreting out corporate espionage and all kinds of international intrigues; it was Arkin who famously built the case that American Express had hired private detectives to plant articles defaming the late international banker Edmond Safra, a story I told in a 1992 book. In the intervening years Arkin has become his own mini-conglomerate, forming an intelligence agency, Arkin Group, run by a former top official at the Central Intelligence Agency.

It took Arkin and his men barely a week to identify the secret hand behind the strange ads. At the bottom of the ads was a company name, Evergence Capital Advisors; a check of Florida records indicated Evergence was a dissolved corporation formerly headed by someone named Kosta Kovachev. A crosscheck of records revealed that Kovachev was the target of an S.E.C. lawsuit involving some kind of time-share scam; his attorney was listed as Marc Dreier. Even more telling, a telephone number on the ads was answered at Dreier's office.

Kalikow wasn't surprised; he and Solow had been squabbling for years, ever since Kalikow had repaid a loan from Solow earlier than Solow had hoped, leaving Solow irked at the lost income. Once Dreier was linked to the ads, Kalikow sued, drawing both Solow and Dreier into a series of court pleadings and depositions in which Dreier was forced to admit the entire scheme. The presiding judge, Burton R. Lifland, ruled firmly in Kalikow's favor, declaring Dreier's actions "somewhat sleazy," then reached for a thesaurus to add a few more choice adjectives, including "tacky, shabby, base, low, malicious, petty, nasty [and] unsavory." Judge Lifland ordered Solow to once again pay his opponent's court costs, then went a step further, suggesting that Kalikow explore filing some sort of action against Dreier before "professional or legal tribunals that govern professional conduct."

His work for Solow, including the sanctions and the embarrassing Kalikow case, damaged Dreier's reputation and left him deeply resentful. Though he won't go into details, it's clear the relationship with Solow was irrevocably damaged. During our talks, Dreier's face reddens as he discusses formulating his revenge on Solow.

"You rationalize your behavior," he says. "Mr. Solow is a difficult client whom I had served with enormous hours, with enormous stress and sacrifice. I felt, for good reason, underappreciated. I felt a little victimized. I had gone out on a limb for him, and I felt like he cut off the limb." For a moment it appears Dreier will lose his composure. "That's childish [to say]; it doesn't justify anything," he goes on. "But at the time, I didn't believe I was being treated fairly." He takes a deep breath. "I had a good relationship with Mr. Solow. I had a lot of affection for Mr. Solow. Obviously, I exploited that. I betrayed Mr. Solow. . . . That is a terrible thing to do."

The scam, once it began, wasn't that hard to pull off. Alone at his office computer, Dreier opened an Excel spreadsheet and began constructing a fake Solow Realty financial statement he could show to a hedge fund. "It wasn't easy," he says. "I don't have a financial background. I would find financial statements of similar firms and extrapolate from them." He knew Solow's auditor and placed the fake financial statements under its letterhead. In another file, he drafted the note he would sell. He decided it would be in the amount of $20 million. Through a friend, Dreier offered to sell the note to a big Connecticut hedge fund named Amaranth, run by a trader named Nicholas Maounis. (The fund later failed spectacularly after a bad bet on natural-gas futures in 2006.) Dreier explained that Solow Realty needed the $20 million to expand. To his mild surprise, the transaction went off without a hitch.

"I don't recall how I identified the first fund, but it was common knowledge they had a very big appetite," Dreier says with a sigh. "I mean, it was easier than you might think. I had the impression the hedge funds were under a mandate: they had money, they had to invest it. I said I was representing Mr. Solow. All the meetings [with Amaranth] were either in their office or mine."

And like that Dreier walked off with $20 million. He used it to hire more lawyers, build out more office space, and buy the beachfront home he had dreamed of, a sprawling mansion in the Hamptons town of Quogue. The problem was, once Dreier got a taste of the good life, he wanted more. The law firm's growth, in particular, he found intoxicating. For years he had supervised barely a dozen lawyers. By the end of 2004 he had close to fifty, and with their healthy new salaries, these new attorneys all but worshipped him. "Meeting him at his office, it was like seeing the Wizard of Oz," marvels one Dreier client. "Everyone was so deferential, just kowtowing to him like he was God—he could do no wrong. Because, I guess, he was making them all rich."

After that first $20 million, Dreier quickly sold a series of additional phony notes in amounts ranging from $40 million to $60 million, eventually totaling roughly $200 million. He kept track of the sales in a series of small black notebooks. "The initial misappropriation proved to be inadequate to make the firm what I wanted," Dreier notes dryly. "So I did it again. I had one leg into building this law firm, you know, and I couldn't bring myself to take that leg out. It was a little like quicksand. So I kept doing it."

Dreier pauses in his retelling, his eyes searching the skyline outside his apartment windows. "Each time I always thought it was the last one," he says. "I never thought I'd have to do it again."

The "Dreier Model"

Practically overnight, the new money created the life of Dreier's dreams. He added a second waterfront home in Quogue. He drove an Aston-Martin for fun, while a chauffeur ferried him around Manhattan in a Mercedes 500 for work. He laid out $10.4 million for the apartment overlooking Le Cirque. The *pièce de résistance* was *Seascape*, the $18 million yacht he kept docked in St. Martin; it came with a crew of ten and a Jacuzzi. But the lion's share of the illegal cash went into the law firm. By the end of 2006, Dreier L.L.P. had again doubled in size, to more than 100 lawyers. By the end of 2007 there were 175. His offices expanded in tandem, eventually taking up eleven floors at 499 Park Avenue. Dreier went on an art-buying spree, shelling out $40 million to fill the firm's walls with Hockneys, Warhols, and Picassos. Some clients were impressed; others weren't. "These were major pieces of art," recalls one client. "You had to ask yourself, 'Who would spend $10 million on a piece of art and hang it in the receptionist area?' That's always a bad sign, when they spend the money glorifying themselves."

In Southern California, beginning in 2006, Dreier hired two large groups of attorneys, more than fifty individuals in all. Mostly entertainment lawyers and litigators, they brought with them a string of celebrity clients, including Jay Leno, the Olsen twins, Rob Lowe, Andy Pettitte of the New York Yankees, singer Diana Krall, and the band Wilco. Dreier's start-up costs were enormous: a number of lawyers worked with guaranteed salaries of $1 million or more. To house them, Dreier rented and renovated office space in the Century City skyscraper featured in the movie *Die Hard*—the lease alone cost him an estimated $300,000 a month.

Dreier began spending a week every month in Los Angeles, where, as in New York, he spent heavily to impress prospective clients. He paid $180,000 to play golf as a member at the Brentwood Country Club, rented a condominium on Ocean Drive in Santa Monica, then opened a branch of a sushi restaurant called Tengu nearby. When in L.A., Dreier could be found most nights there, surrounded by attractive young women and potential clients.

Within the legal community, Dreier was viewed as a rising star. He told anyone who would listen that Dreier L.L.P. was a new kind of law firm, one where lawyers could work with freedom, unburdened by old-school bureaucracy and administration, all of which Dreier handled himself. In a 2007 article for *The National Law Journal*, Dreier argued that the "Dreier Model," as he christened it, freed attorneys from petty bickering over profits and allowed them to operate as true legal entrepreneurs. It certainly appeared to work. Dreier L.L.P.'s functions were glittering. In 2007, he and Michael Strahan, of the New York Giants, cohosted a charity golf tournament for which William Shatner served as M.C. and Diana Ross was the entertainment. Alicia Keys sang the next year. One of the firm's Christmas parties was held at the Waldorf-Astoria, where Dreier danced wildly to the song "Shout," from *Animal House*. At a firm party at his Quogue beach house a plane flew overhead trailing a banner that said, DREIER LAWYERS ROCK.

Through it all, Dreier kept quietly selling bogus notes. During the first three years of his scheme, in fact, from 2004 until the summer of 2007, he found it simple to keep going. Almost every time a note came due, the hedge fund in question would simply renew it for another year, usually with a slightly higher interest rate. No one ever asked to meet Solow or any of his executives; they simply accepted that Dreier was operating on their behalf.

The trouble began in mid-2006, when the housing market started to weaken. By the fall there were rumblings that Wall Street firms would begin taking losses. Those worries blossomed into something like panic the following June, when two massive Bear Stearns hedge funds imploded, nearly bankrupting Bear. At first, Dreier's hedge funds only began rethinking their decisions to renew his notes. With several, Dreier secured renewals by offering better interest rates, as high as 11 or 12 percent. But by early 2008, even that wasn't enough. For the first time, several funds refused to renew and demanded their money back. Dreier managed to repay a few by selling more notes to other funds, the classic Ponzi tactic. He kept still others on board by selling new notes at a steep discount; these new notes not only offered 12 percent interest but cost 30 percent less.

Wall Street's "credit crunch," however, deepened all that winter, eventually leading to the collapse of Bear Stearns, in March 2008. After that, almost every hedge fund refused to renew; all they wanted was their money back. For the first time, Dreier began to sweat. By that summer, he was facing a full-blown crisis. Almost all his outstanding notes were coming due that fall. During walks on the beach at Quogue, he confronted the unthinkable: $48 million of notes due in September, another $15 million in November, a whopping $100 million in December, plus $60 million in January 2009. All told, he would need almost $225 million to cover these redemptions.

"Obviously," Dreier observes without a hint of irony, "I had put myself in a ridiculous predicament."

For the first time, he began to think he might not, as he puts it, "pull out of this." Still, he clung to hope. After all, he had raised this much before. He had a line on some Persian Gulf investors who might inject awesome sums. And Dreier L.L.P. was expecting a good year in 2009; its profits might yet make a dent in what he owed.

Dreier began his sales push after Labor Day. It was rough going. No one wanted to buy anything, only sell. In desperation, Dreier resorted to offering notes due in less than a year, in some cases as little as eight months. He was digging himself quite a hole: a 12 percent note, sold at a steeply discounted price, to be repaid the following May. He managed to sell a small note, for $13.5 million, to a hedge fund named Verition, but the big catch was the $100 million note he sold to a fund named Elliott Associates, a $10 billion fund run by a lawyer turned money manager named Paul Singer. All told, the two sales raised half the money Dreier needed.

As it became harder to market his notes, Dreier found himself relying increasingly on the same hedge funds. By October, in fact, four held almost all his debt, roughly $100 million apiece: Fortress, one of America's largest hedge funds; the new buyer, Elliott Associates; Eton Park Capital Management, run by thirty-one-year-old wunderkind Eric Mindich, once the youngest partner in the history of Goldman Sachs; and GSO Capital Partners, a $25 billion hedge fund owned by the Blackstone Group. By October, GSO was the biggest headache. The firm had $115 million of notes, and it wanted its money back—right away.

Dreier, citing market conditions, pleaded for an extension until year-end. GSO executives reluctantly consented to a few weeks, but there was a catch. To grant the extension, they demanded to meet with top executives at Solow Realty. Unable to wriggle out of it, Dreier scheduled a meeting at Solow headquarters at 9 West Fifty-seventh Street for October 15. It was at that point that, desperate to extend the note, he staged his most elaborate charade to date. To pull it off, he brought in the odd little man who had helped him before: Kosta Kovachev.

The son of Serb-born doctors, Kovachev, fifty-seven, was a Wall Street refugee who had graduated from Harvard Business School and begun his career at firms such as Morgan Stanley, but, during the 1990s, for whatever reason, he spiraled downward through a series of increasingly obscure companies, eventually ending up selling time-shares in an alleged Missouri-based real-estate scam. He was sued by the S.E.C. and surrendered his broker's license in 2003 while admitting no wrongdoing. Kovachev was a shadowy figure in Dreier's life, a onetime client—Dreier says only that they met through a friend—with two ex-wives in Florida, six children, and a cell-phone number that rang at the Harvard Club. He wasn't quite the Igor to Dreier's Dr. Frankenstein, more a financial flunky. He had an electronic pass to Dreier

L.L.P. and court papers indicate he was paid as much as $100,000 for his role in Dreier's plan.

Dreier is maddeningly vague about Kovachev, who was also arrested last December; presumably he doesn't want to undermine Kovachev's defense. Kovachev did not respond to requests for comment, but from legal papers filed in the case, it appears he had carried out impersonations for Dreier before, at least once during a conference call with one of Dreier's hedge funds. That day in the Solow conference room, however, Kovachev delivered his performance in person, easily convincing a team from GSO that he worked for Solow; afterward, Dreier got his brief extension. A top Solow executive, Steven M. Cherniak, has said he actually noticed the meeting going on—the conference room has glass walls—and later told associates he wondered what Dreier was doing. Dreier, however, visited Solow's offices often enough that his unexplained appearance was shrugged off.

By the first week of November, it appeared Dreier had created some breathing space. That's when things really began to fall apart.

Game Over

As Dreier pieced it together for me, this is how it started. The small fund to which he had sold a $13.5 million note, Verition, was looking for ways to reduce its exposure. Verition executives reached out to another fund, Whippoorwill Associates, based in suburban Westchester County, to see if it might be interested in buying half the note. Whippoorwill, in turn, contacted Solow Realty's auditor, Berdon L.L.P., to obtain financial data. Berdon executives were confused; they didn't know anything about any Solow Realty notes. They called Sheldon Solow himself, who didn't either. A Berdon attorney named Thomas Manisero began investigating. One of the hedge funds turned over a Solow financial statement Dreier had supplied. It was clearly forged.

By the first week of November, Manisero and several Solow executives, including Solow himself, all suspected Dreier had committed fraud—a single act, but fraud nonetheless. Solow and Manisero telephoned Dreier and confronted him. "I tried to double-talk my way out of it, but I knew that would not work," Dreier recalls. "They accused me. I didn't acknowledge the extent of my wrongdoing. I acknowledged that what appeared to have happened had only happened once, with one small fund, and it had been rectified." Dreier said he was deeply "ashamed," and swore it would never again.

Neither Manisero nor Solow was satisfied, however. Manisero told Dreier that unless he could fully explain himself he was going to the authorities; Dreier assumed he would anyway. In fact, within days the U.S. Attorney's Office in New York became involved.

"I knew in that first week of November that unless I got extremely lucky I was going to get caught," Dreier says. He decided to do the only things he could: deny, delay, and obfuscate.

Just days later came a second shot across his bow. In concluding the Elliott deal, Dreier had given an Elliott executive a bogus e-mail address for Solow Realty—the address actually delivered any e-mail to Dreier's computer. When the Elliott executive attempted to use the address, he apparently made a typing error and was obliged to phone Solow Realty directly, as Dreier learned, to his horror, when he found himself c.c.'d on the man's e-mail exchanges with a Solow executive.

"From that point on, I knew I wouldn't get out of it," Dreier recalls. "I knew I couldn't talk my way out of that second one."

The clock was ticking. That same week Dreier flew to Dubai and Qatar, where he met with a group of Arab investors who he hoped might buy notes worth enough to bail him out. One evening, standing in the desert air, he finally began pondering what had once been unthinkable. Here he was, out of the country, with $100 million in cash. Why not run? Why not spend the rest of his days on some balmy Indian Ocean beach? For the moment, though, he just couldn't. He returned to New York for a day, then jetted to St. Martin, where he sat on his yacht, brooding. If he wanted, he could simply have his captain sail for Venezuela. He might be safe there.

But he couldn't do it. "I thought I would never see my kids," Dreier recalls. "I thought that, even if I did, they would be in danger. I guess I thought that, even more humiliating than coming home to face the music, would be a long life as a fugitive. I thought that, at fifty-eight years old, what was the point of living as a fugitive?"

For two more weeks Tom Manisero peppered Dreier with calls, demanding to know more about what he had done. Dreier says he assumed the authorities were recording Manisero's calls. They were. On the Friday after Thanksgiving, he asked Manisero if there was some kind of settlement he could offer to make Solow whole. Prosecutors would later characterize this as an attempt to bribe Manisero, a contention Dreier firmly denies.

That same Friday, Dreier received more worrisome news. One of his attorneys, Norman Kinel, needed to retrieve $38.5 million from one of Dreier L.L.P.'s escrow accounts; the money belonged to a bankrupt client who needed it to repay creditors. But to Kinel's surprise, less than half the money remained in the account. Dreier couldn't tell him the truth, that he had stolen it. He promised to get back to Kinel on Monday. Suddenly Dreier was consumed with replacing that money. He phoned Elliott Associates, which agreed to buy a new $40 million note. For a few hours, Dreier thought he was safe. Then, later that same day, an Elliott executive called to say the firm was backing out of the deal; he didn't say why, but Dreier thought they had become suspicious.

All that weekend Dreier frantically sought ways to replace the missing escrow funds. On Monday, December 1, he secured a commitment from Fortress for a new, $50 million note, this one to be "issued" by a firm whose name he had begun using, the

Ontario Teachers' Pension Plan, a massive, $100 billion fund based in Toronto that had once been a Dreier client. The new agreement, however, was struck with a different group inside Fortress, and this one insisted on signing the legal papers in a face-to-face meeting with an Ontario Teachers' executive.

Dreier knew what this meant: he would need to impersonate the executive, at the fund's offices in Toronto. That night Dreier telephoned Toronto and set up a meeting for the next day, Tuesday, with an Ontario Teachers' attorney, a man I'll call "Tom." He told Fortress to have one of its people come to the pension fund's offices to sign the papers. When the Fortress executive arrived, Dreier would need to be there, somehow masquerading as "Tom."

It was a dicey proposition at best, but as Dreier's private jet descended toward an Ontario commuter airport the next morning, he thought he could pull it off. Then, at the last moment, "Tom" telephoned and canceled their meeting. Dreier, fighting off panic, quickly set up a new meeting, this one with an Ontario Teachers' attorney named Michael Padfield, whom he did not know. He took a limousine downtown to the shimmering glass Xerox Tower. Inside, he boarded an elevator to the Ontario Teachers' third-floor offices, where he and Padfield held a quick meeting, ostensibly to discuss the sale of another bogus note; at one point, the two exchanged cards. Then Dreier asked if he might kill some time in a spare conference room. His jet back to New York was running late, he explained.

For the next hour or so, a receptionist watched as Dreier paced the pension fund's lobby, obviously waiting for someone. This is where things got strange. At one point, a man emerged from the elevators and moved toward the receptionist's desk. Before he could reach it, however, Dreier cut him off. The man was Howard Steinberg, the Fortress executive who had come to sign the note. He was to meet with Michael Padfield, the same attorney Dreier had just seen. Dreier introduced himself as Padfield, handed him

Padfield's business card, and guided Steinberg into the same conference room where he had been waiting.

Everything appeared to be going smoothly until Steinberg suddenly asked if Dreier knew "Tom"'s extension—apparently the two men were acquainted. Dreier reluctantly read off the number, at which point Steinberg rose, asked for a moment, and stepped outside. Dreier realized he was about to call "Tom," who of course knew nothing about the meeting or the note; if the two men spoke, it was all over. Dreier watched as Steinberg began dialing a phone in the lobby. As he did, Dreier yanked up a conference-room phone and, in a bid to somehow prevent the two from speaking, dialed "Tom" as well.

"He called the guy, I called the guy," Dreier recalls with a sigh. "He beat me to it."

He cut off his call, knowing the end was near. When Steinberg returned to the conference room, Dreier says, "I could see he was suspicious. It was the questions he asked me and the look he gave me. He asked several questions about personnel at Ontario Teachers', which indicated he was suspicious." Sensing the worst, Dreier hurriedly signed the legal papers, then excused himself for a moment. But instead of returning, he headed for the elevator and left the building.

After a few minutes, Steinberg emerged from the conference room.

"Was that Michael Padfield?" he asked the receptionist.

"No," she said.

Dreier's plane was waiting. He had just boarded when his phone rang. It was a Fortress executive, informing him there had been "some kind of problem" at Ontario Teachers'. The Fortress man, not knowing Dreier was in Canada, much less that he was behind the "problem," explained what little he knew. Dreier feigned astonishment. Moments later, his phone rang a second time. This time it was Peter Briger Jr., Fortress's co-chairman of the board. "We don't know what's going on," Briger told Dreier. "But we think there's some kind of impersonation going on."

"I played dumb," says Dreier, "and said I would look into it." When Dreier concluded the call, his mind raced. At that point, nine out of ten men would have simply fled back to New York. For some reason, Dreier returned to his limo and had the driver take him back to the pension fund's offices.

"I was 90 percent sure I would be caught when I went back," he says. "I was not thinking clearly. I was desperate. Clearly, there was a part of me that just wanted this to be over. I knew I was defeated. I went back knowing I would probably never leave that building [a free man]."

Once he was back in the Ontario Teachers' offices, an attorney asked him to wait in the conference room. By and by, security guards appeared and told him to wait for the police, who appeared not long after and arrested him. Dreier went without resistance.

There's a Moral to Draw

It was over. Canadian authorities held Dreier for four days, then put him on a plane back to New York's La Guardia Airport, where U.S. marshals took him into custody, just as Dreier suspected they would. He didn't bother with denials for long. He would admit everything: four long years of fraud, eighty or more bogus notes, thirteen hedge funds and four private investors, $380 million—everything. His glorious new life, the firm, the "Dreier Model"—it had all been built on lies. Within days, attorneys began resigning from Dreier L.L.P. At one point, Dreier's nineteen-year-old son, Spencer, barged into a meeting there and attempted to rally the assembled lawyers to his father's defense; he was hooted out of the room. Ten days after Dreier's New York arrest the firm declared bankruptcy. By that point almost every attorney had left. Dreier L.L.P. simply imploded.

Dreier was tossed into a dark cell on the ninth floor of the Metropolitan Correctional Center New York, a federal holding pen in downtown Manhattan. It was the shock of his life: Dreier, in fact, has quite a lot to say about the "M.C.C.," as it's known. He and his cellmate, the triple murderer, had no electric light, no reading materials, no heat, and a broken toilet, which left the floor covered in urine. Each night Dreier shivered beneath a thin blanket while other inmates yelled and screamed "like it was an insane asylum," he claims. He was allowed out of the cell for roof-top exercise once a day, at five A.M., for an hour. Meals were shoved through a slot. He showered twice a week, in cold water. "This was like *Midnight Express*," Dreier says in dismay. "I mean, it's beyond what people can imagine." (An M.C.C. New York spokesman disputes Dreier's account of his time there.)

It was certainly beyond anything Marc Dreier of Yale College and Harvard Law School had ever imagined. Finally, after eight days, he was released into the general population. Two months after that, following his indictment, a judge allowed him to return to his apartment under house arrest. During the period when we spoke, in April, Dreier was sleeping a lot, spending every available hour with his children, briefing lawyers tasked with sorting through the wreckage of Dreier L.L.P., and trying to come to grips with the end of life as he knew it.

"I expect to spend most of the rest of my life in prison," he tells me. "I hope I don't die there. I've been blessed with good genes, you know. My father died at ninety-one. So I think I have a few years left. I will try to have a meaningful life in prison. It won't be the life I anticipated. I won't attend my daughter's wedding. I will miss all the moments in life I assumed would be part of my life."

"This is a particularly sad case," Dreier's lawyer, Gerald Lefcourt, says. "Marc Dreier had everything going for him and essentially threw it away. To his credit, he realized early on that it was no one's fault but his own. When he went to prison, he was in many ways in a state of grace."

During twenty-five years of writing about financiers, I have spoken to several on their way to prison. Dreier was by far the most philosophical, and while his critique of America's material culture is no doubt self-serving, some of his final words were instructive.

"Many people," he observed, "are caught up in the notion that success in life is measured in professional and financial achievements and material acquisitions, and it's hard to step back from that and see the fallacy. You have to try and measure your life by the moments in your day. I see people my children's age first coming into finance, the working world, as having to make basic choices about how to define happiness and success. Obviously, I made the wrong choices.

"But they don't have to."

Esquire

Once the publisher of Ernest Hemingway and F. Scott Fitzgerald and later the home of the New Journalism, Esquire *is one of the leading general-interest magazines in the country. Edited since 1997 by David Granger, the magazine runs outstanding service journalism— just a year ago it won National Magazine Awards for both Personal Service and Leisure Interests (for its unforgettable "Almanac of Steak")—and in recent years has become known for print experiments like its whiz-bang seventy-fifth-anniversary cover and its December 2009 augmented-reality issue with Robert Downey Jr. But it is feature stories like "The Last Abortion Doctor" that for many readers will always be the strongest reminder of the power of print.*

John H. Richardson

The Last Abortion Doctor

The young couple flew into Wichita bearing, in the lovely swell of the wife's belly, a burden of grief. They came from a religious tradition where large families are celebrated, and they wanted this baby, and it was very late in her pregnancy. But the doctors recommended abortion. They said that with her complications, there were only two men skilled enough to pull it off. One was George Tiller, a Wichita doctor who specialized in late abortions.

They arrived in Wichita on Sunday, May 31. As they drove to their hotel, a Holiday Inn just two blocks from the Reformation Lutheran Church, they saw television cameras. They wondered what was going on, a passing curiosity quickly forgotten.

But when they got to their room, the phone was ringing. Her father was on the line. "There was some doctor who was shot who does abortions," he said.

They turned on CNN. Dr. Tiller had just been killed, shot in the head as he passed out church leaflets. In their shock, they mixed up the clinic and the church: *We were supposed to be there. What if it had happened while we were there? What if he couldn't complete the procedure?*

Now there is only one doctor left.

·   ·   ·

After the first two doors of bulletproof glass, a sign warns that cell phones, cameras, and PDAs will be confiscated. You put your ID into a turning wheel that spins it to the receptionist. She studies it and hits the buzzer that opens the third bulletproof door. In the waiting room, a sad woman with a tight perm waits for her daughter. The receptionist lets you through a fourth bulletproof door and leads you down a green hall decorated with lovely pictures of nature, leaving you in a small room stocked with tissues and free condoms.

Twenty minutes later, the abortionist enters. He's a tall man in green surgical scrubs, remarkably vigorous at seventy, emphatic in speech and impatient in manner. He has a long face and no lips, which gives him a severe look. He apologizes for having very little time. This is the day he sees patients for the first of three visits, giving them the seaweed laminaria, which slowly dilates the cervix, and his normal caseload has been doubled by Dr. Tiller's patients—including two with catastrophic fetal abnormalities and a fifteen-year-old who was raped, all in the second trimester, all traumatized by the assassin who calls himself pro-life, a phrase he cannot utter without air quotes and contempt. *They hate freedom*, he says. He says it again. He warns you not to use anyone's name or you will put them at risk.

Walking out, he leaves the door open. You hear voices drifting down the hall: *The worst picture of an abortion doctor ever. Is that Fox? Yes, Bill O'Reilly. Supposedly they were there to protect us.* You see a nurse you cannot name leading a middle-aged Indian woman to an examining room. *You'll need to undress completely from the waist down.* You hear one of the receptionists you cannot name speaking in the carefully modulated voice the abortionist prescribed in his first book, *Abortion Practice*, a classic in the field: "Truax and Carkhuff have described *empathy* as the counselor's ability to be sufficiently involved to make full use of his/her own emotional experience and *sufficiently detached* to differentiate his/her own emotional experience from those of the other."

Steps come down the hall. *I'm Dr. Hern. Where are you from? Lie down now. Put your hand on your chest.*

The phone rings. *Did you have an ultrasound? And they referred you here?*

Yesterday, the man arrested for Tiller's murder warned that more killings were on the way. All last week, the antiabortion groups put out statements denouncing the murder and praising the result. One called the killer a hero. As a result, a squad of U.S. marshals rushed out here last week on orders from the attorney general. One of them paces the hall. The second receptionist you cannot name asks him, *Did you see that guy out there smoking a cigarette?*

Yeah, I saw him.

The first receptionist keeps talking. *If you can fax us the amnio. We don't know, we'll have to wait to see what your body tells us. Do you want us to run your Amex now?*

Another phone rings and the second receptionist answers. *It's basically a three-day process. We require that you stay here in Colorado.*

The voices begin to overlap. *Are you on any medication? Have you had surgery in the last year? No, we don't have any genetics counselors to interpret that for you. We don't get a lot of protestors. It's a liberal and tolerant community. If that changes, we will contact you. No, you'll get up and get in your car and drive home. And Lisa, if you have a change of heart, please call us— our schedule is completely full and you'll be taking someone else's place.*

After another silence, a soft voice gets softer: *I also want you to know, we don't care what your reasons are. We're not going to judge you.*

·　　　·　　　·

In the kitchen of the Boulder Abortion Clinic, the abortionist bolts down two microwave tamales. He talks fast and doesn't smile. *It is my view that we are dealing with a fascist movement. It's a terrorist, violent terrorist movement, and they have a fascist ideology . . .*

He goes on like that for some time. Long before the first doctor got shot back in 1993, he was warning that it would happen. He was getting hate mail and death threats way back in 1970, just for working in family planning. They started up again in 1973, two weeks after he helped start the first nonprofit abortion clinic in Boulder. *I started sleeping with a rifle by my bed. I expected to get shot.* In 1985, someone threw a brick through his window during a protest by the *quote unquote* Pro-Life Action League. He put up a sign that said THIS WINDOW WAS BROKEN BY THOSE WHO HATE FREEDOM. In 1988, somebody fired five bullets through his window. In 1995, the American Coalition of *quote unquote* Life Activists put out a hit list with his name (and Tiller's name) on it. The feds gave them protection for about six months, then left them on their own.

People don't get it, he says. After 8 murders, 17 attempted murders, 406 death threats, 179 assaults, and 4 kidnappings, people are still in denial. They say, Well, this was just some wingnut guy who just decided to go blow up somebody. *Wrong.* This was a *cold-blooded, brutal, political assassination* that is the logical consequence of *thirty-five years of hate speech and incitement to violence* by people from the *highest levels of American society,* including but in no way limited to *George W. Bush, Ronald Reagan, Jesse Helms, Bill O'Reilly, Jerry Falwell, and Pat Robertson.* Reagan may not have been a fascist, but he was a tool of the fascists. George W. Bush was most certainly a tool of the fascists. They use this issue to get power. They seem civilized but underneath *you have this seething mass of angry, rabid anger and hatred of freedom that is really frightening,* and they support people like the guy who shot George—they're all pretending to be upset, issuing statements about how much they deplore violence, but it's just bullshit. This is *exactly what they wanted to happen.*

He goes on about Bill O'Reilly for a while. Over the course of twenty-nine separate shows, O'Reilly accused "Tiller the Baby Killer" of performing a late abortion for any reason at all, even so a girl could attend a rock concert—a charge that is blatantly untrue. O'Reilly is a *disgrace to American society,* he says.

But O'Reilly says he's just exercising his right to engage in vigorous debate, you point out.

He's full of shit. This is not a debate, it's a civil war. And the other people are using bullets and bombs. I think O'Reilly is a fascist, and he would fit right in in Nazi Germany as far as I'm concerned.

It's odd, you say, trying to be agreeable. They always go after the doctors. They never go after the moms.

His eyes snap up. *What moms? The patients?*

Yeah, the patients.

They're not moms until they have a baby.

.   .   .

By the way, he hates the word *abortionist.* Though it is a simple descriptive term like "podiatrist," the opponents of abortion have turned it into a *degrading and demeaning word that has the same negative connotations as the most despicable racial epithet.* All the same, it is the right word, an accurate word, and our discomfort with it is but a measure of how poisoned the language of abortion has become.

Late that night, he calls you at your hotel. You're reading one of his many scientific publications, which have titles like *Shipibo Polygyny and Patrilocality* or *Urban Malignancy: Similarity in the Fractal Dimensions of Urban Morphology and Malignant Neoplasms.* This one argues that man is a "malignant ecotumor" laying waste the planet. *One of the main characteristics of a cancerous growth is that it resists regulation. A cancer cell is a cell that reproduces without limits.*

He's sorry, he says, but he must turn down your request to ride in his car to the Tiller memorial in Denver. He has to go with four U.S. marshals in an armored car. Even his wife can't ride with him. Same with dinner in a restaurant. *I will never be safe*, he says. *I'm always looking over my shoulder.*

You use the term "partial-birth abortion" and he bristles. It's a *barbaric and grotesque* term for a procedure that was described at National Abortion Federation meetings in the early nineties by two doctors who *didn't take the deadliness of the psychological warfare seriously*, and then the Republicans took it up and it became *this obscene and basically pornographic anti-abortion pornography* with pictures that made it look like you were killing this beautiful Gerber baby—and when he tried to tell his colleagues, No, this is not the safest way to perform a delayed abortion, they accused him of working with the anti-abortion people and basically rode him out on a rail. The whole thing turned into a *tumultuous, writhing, tortured witch hunt*— an incredibly painful experience.

Nothing pains him more than the disdain of other doctors. Sometimes the young ones ask to come in for an afternoon so they can learn to make a little money while their careers get started— they think it's as simple as changing a tire. *There's no sense that this is an important operation that has to be done well, that a person's life depends on it.* But let's face it, abortion is the lowest-status activity in medicine. That's why they always call their clinics Family Planning Centers or Women's Wellness Facilities or some crap like that. Not his place. It's had the same name since 1975. *Because I felt that performing abortions was the most important thing I could do in medicine.*

The patients can be upsetting too. They're under terrible stress, of course, but sometimes they come in very angry. One had conjoined twins and would have died giving birth, but she exploded when he told her she couldn't smoke in the office. And some treat him with *contempt and disgust*, usually the ones who have been directly involved in antiabortion activities. They hate all abortion except for their special case. One even said they should all be killed. Only fourteen, she came with her mother. What brings you here? he asked. *I have to have an abortion.* Why? *I'm not old enough to have a baby.* But you told the counselor we should all be killed? *Yes, you should all be killed.* Why? *Because you do abortions.* Me too? *Yes, you should be killed too.* Do you want me killed before or after I do your abortion? *Before.*

He told her to leave. Her mother was very upset. But he isn't an abortion-dispensing machine. He's a physician. He's a person.

●   ●   ●

The abortionist's mother is ninety-two, but she still has a girlish smile and twinkling eyes that summon gingham skirts and radio serials. When you come in, she's sitting in an easy chair surrounded by her family. You bend down to shake her grandson's hand. So you're the one who wants to be a pirate. He nods and adds in a shy voice: *Or now maybe a doctor.*

The phone rings and the abortionist goes to answer. He speaks in a heated voice. Hanging up, he's visibly agitated. *That guy got your number off the Internet. He's a reporter. You have to change your number.*

Oh well, his mother says.

You have to change it. We'll talk about it later.

When he takes his family home, escorted by the U.S. marshals, she explains, almost apologetically, that her number hasn't been listed for almost forty years because the antiabortion people used to make nasty calls at two o'clock in the morning. Then there was a mix-up and it appeared in the phone book. *Warren kept saying, You have to change your number, and I said, I don't want to change my number. I've had it all these years.* Now she doesn't tell him about most of the calls. He's got enough to worry about.

As a boy? Always helpful. When he was just three, she'd give him a dust rag and let him dust. She'd set him on the counter and let him stir the cake. When he was ten, she and her husband, they went out one night and left the girls with a babysitter who spanked the oldest girl for refusing to go to sleep. When they got home, *Warren said, Mother, I don't want you to hire anybody else to take care of Cindy. I can take care of her.* So they never hired a babysitter again.

Warren sang in the choir. She felt it was important for the kids to go to church and Sunday school, and they didn't send them, they took them. They got involved in church activities. But politically, they were always on the liberal side. Warren likes to tell the story of how they cried when Roosevelt died. He was six, but he still remembers it.

He loved to go camping and fishing. He played clarinet in the Highlander Boys Band. He liked pranks—once he put an ad in the paper saying everybody could put their dead Christmas trees in a neighbor's yard.

His father was a carpenter, so they didn't have much money and couldn't afford to travel. But they always had exchange students from all over the world—Germany, Brazil, Italy, France, Pakistan, Japan, thirteen countries in all. That was a way the kids could learn how other people lived.

In fifth grade, Warren got interested in photography. Soon he was selling sports pictures to *The Denver Post*, staying up till midnight to develop the film, make prints, and rush them down to the paper. *I probably saved every one of those pictures.* He won second prize in Kodak's national contest for high school photography.

One thing that's probably important, she says: She had terrible migraines from as far back as she could remember. She'd get up in the morning and feel like her head was gonna roll down the hall. And one day she asked Warren what he wanted to be and he said, I really want to be a doctor, Mother. *He thought he'd be a neuro brain surgeon and maybe he could figure out what to do about my headaches.*

That same year, he read a book about Albert Schweitzer healing the sick in Africa and announced, Mother, I'm going to go to Africa before I go to medical school. And he did. He raised money from the Lions Club and the Rotary Club so he could be a community ambassador with the Experiment in International Living. She wasn't surprised. *Usually when he says he's going to do it, he's going to find a way to do it.*

At college, she says, he was the only white student in the African Club.

He worked three jobs to pay his tuition.

He began reading books like *The Golden Bough, Man and His Gods, A Man Against Fate.* He learned ancient Greek and studied the Bible in the original. Then he sat her down and said, *Mom, I don't believe in this stuff anymore.* She said, *Well, you don't have to believe in it. Maybe I don't believe in all of it either.* But she wasn't worried. She knew his heart.

In his last year of college, he went to a fundamentalist church to see an anticommunist movie called *Operation Abolition.* He came home and told his parents quite a story. *You want to hear the Word of the Lord, you've got to pay! And I don't mean that jigglin' money, I mean that foldin' money!* In an article he wrote for the school paper, he compared it to the "Two-Minute Hate" in George Orwell's *1984.*

In medical school, he saw his first botched abortions. Then he spent two years as a doctor for the Peace Corps in a Brazilian town so desperately poor, it wasn't unusual to see a dead baby on a trash heap. After that, he worked as a family-planning chief for the Nixon administration and spent some time in Appalachia, where he saw unintended pregnancies dragging families deeper and deeper into poverty. In an article for *The New Republic*, he quoted one exhausted mother: *Each one makes it harder on the ones we already got.*

But even after all that, there are still some family members who can't accept what he does. And other doctors too. It really hurts him terribly, she says. *In his mind, he's trying to help women who desperately need help. And why can't these doctors, of all people—*

In her opinion, he needs to retire. He has a dozen books he wants to write. And this just *takes his life.*

The shooting? He called her as soon as it happened. *He said, Jeanne just told me that George was shot in church.* He said MS-NBC wanted to interview him, told her what time to watch, trying to stay calm, but she could tell how upset he really was. It was all he could do to keep from losing it. *I could hear the terror in his voice.*

But when he was on TV that night, all you saw was his anger.

Well, you know, the people that really know Warren could see it, I'm sure. But not that many people probably.

You're a parent yourself, so you have to ask if she ever tried to get him to stop. Especially now that he's kind of making himself a target.

I know that, she answers. *I understand that. But that wouldn't do any good. He's got a mind of his own.*

The rims of her eyes are getting red. She moves her glasses and dabs at them with a balled-up tissue. You apologize for making her cry.

It's okay. It's all right.

Then she tries to be cheerful again, for the sake of her guest.

The next morning, you're just sitting down to breakfast when the phone rings. It's the abortionist's mother. She's been calling hotels looking for you. *Please don't mention that thing I told you,* she says. You know exactly what she means, a story so personal and revealing that she preceded it with the words *Don't use this in your story.* You try to convince her that it would be the perfect humanizing detail. *I was up all night worrying about it,* she says. *I would never forgive myself if anything happened.*

You promise.

.   .   .

The abortionist's wife likes good coffee. So you meet at an espresso bar where the menu is in Italian.

She has a strong Roman nose and black hair that breaks against her cheeks in an ebony wave. Her earrings are shaped like dolphin tails. In a charming mixture of English and Spanish, she tells you about growing up in Cuba, happy sun-filled days and good medical training until she started ducking the weekly "discussion" meetings and they told her she wasn't a good communist. But when she finally managed to leave, she saw the other side. *For example, when I going to Argentina, I have intrauterine device for anti-conception. When the ginecólogo attend to me, "You need take off this! This makes an abortion!"*

Later, working in a hospital, she saw women who tried to induce their own miscarriages bleed to death.

Then she got pregnant. At eighteen weeks, she went to her gynecologist for the blood test. *They say, The baby's no good. Have really problem.* She went to a geneticist and a specialist in prenatal diagnosis. The geneticist suggested an abortion, *but the prenatal diagnoser, for one hour he was making the sonogram high-resolution. When he finish, he say, What do you think about the baby? And I say, I think he is good. I feel it in my soul, and I want to take him. He say, Go and take your baby.*

Labor lasted thirty-six hours, intensive care a month. The specialists told her the baby might have lifelong seizures or learning disabilities. To lighten her workload, she moved to Barcelona and took a job in an abortion clinic. She sees no contradiction in this. *Because I am happy in my pregnancy and I have a beautiful relationship with my belly. For many reasons, I believe in God and my fate. It's true in myself. But I know that many women don't feel nothing when they're pregnant and many women feel sad, feel angry. In this situation, you never can judge who's God. You need to respect women.*

All that led to the man who would become her husband. She was at a medical conference in 2003 when he came up to her and said, You are so beautiful. He was sixty-four, she was thirty-seven. She was struck by his confidence. *I say, This man is really seguro de sí mismo—sure of himself. I say, I like this man.*

On the last night, he went to his knees and begged her to dance. Stand up, she said. *Stand up!* But she felt good dancing with him.

They began to send letters across the ocean and talk for hours on the phone. He was not one of these men who was just *para enamorarla.* He tried to know her, the woman and the professional and the mother. And he always showed to her his *miedos,* his fears and loneliness, especially the long grim years when he thought no woman could tolerate a life under siege by fanatics. She could relate. *When I was aborting in Spain, I finished the abortion to a young woman, first trimester. When I finish this procedure, she sit on the table, see me to my face, say, Oh, doctor, you are really nice, you are such angel, how do you kill babies? I say, I'm sorry, I don't kill any baby. I aspirate gestational sac. You kill your baby.*

But most important, he always asked about her son. Other men did not do that.

In March, he flew to Palma de Mallorca and they spent three beautiful days together.

In May, she noticed that her son had no grip in his left hand. She took him to the hospital and they discovered a brain tumor—a big one, nearly four centimeters.

Warren started calling her every day, sometimes twice a day. The hospital suggested high doses of chemotherapy, her doctor disagreed, Warren said to send him the MRIs. *He doesn't rest one second. He find find find information.* She decided to try surgery. She told Warren not to come and moved into the hospital to focus on her son. One by one, her other friends stopped calling. Warren called three times a day.

At Christmas, she took her son to Boulder and Warren introduced him to Santa Claus. *I think I totally fall in love with him.* Warren said, Will you marry me?

Warren is the most passionate man she has ever known, *apasionado* about everything he does. *He is the kind of people that he going up to the mountain and he see the beautiful sunset, he sit down, he don't want to speak, and he cry.*

In the summer of 2006, they were married.

But that was not their happy ending. At the end of May, when they were just back from a rafting trip in Utah, the wet clothes in a pile on the stairs, the phone rang. Warren took the call in his office. *I start to take the breakfast in and he don't have color in his face. I say what happen? He say, A shooter shoot George Tiller. I think it's crazy people, and he say, No Amor, these people killed him. But why? You know why. I go to close the window but he no move, he no speak. I say, Do you need my help? He say, No. I need a little time.*

When the shock passed, he called CNN. All day long the phones kept ringing. *I kept say, He's on the other line. He cannot speak with you now.*

Since that day, he hasn't relaxed one second.

·   ·   ·

The abortionist barely has time to eat. Reporters come and go, the phone rings constantly, he disappears to the hidden rooms where no outsider is allowed to go. Every so often he snatches a minute or two to drop into the counseling room. *I want to talk to you about this dustup with National Abortion Federation*, he says. *They're not going to like to see this dirty laundry, but you know, this was a witch hunt. Just hideous attacks on my character. And I think that it's frankly far more painful to me than the fucking antiabortion people.*

He suggests you read a paper he wrote, "Administrative Incongruence and Authority Conflict in Four Abortion Clinics." But he doesn't have time to say why. *I have a lot of stuff to do. You're welcome to hang out.*

You squeeze in another question. This idea about mankind being a "malignant ecotumor." Doesn't it just invite the hate? *I'm not inviting people to do anything. I'd like them to think. What a concept.*

But still.

I do think that helping people control their fertility is highly consistent with helping people be responsible citizens of the planet. If somebody misunderstands it or tries to distort it, I don't give a shit. I'm sorry, I'm living in this country because I can say what I think.

But you're seventy. You have ideas for a dozen books. Why not retire?

I have work to do here. I have important work to do here.

You wanted to cozy up to the next question but there's no time, so you just blurt it out: What are your limits? When would you tell a woman no?

There's no specific answer to that. I'm in the process of turning down somebody who's going to be thirty-four, thirty-five weeks, with an important reason for doing abortion. I'm not going to do it.

The phone rings. *Okay. I'll be right there*, and he's gone.

•   •   •

Hours pass. You've been moved to the nurses' office, where a soft felt sunflower weaves through the metal in-box. On the wall, a poster of female reproductive organs looks vaguely like the mother alien from *Aliens*. You are staring at a flyer advertising the clinic's services: "Specializing in late abortion for fetal disorders. Outpatient abortion over twenty-six menstrual weeks for selected patients with documented fetal anomaly, fetal demise, or medical indications."

The opponents of legal abortion often use the phrase "abortion on demand," implying there are no restrictions at all. This characterization is untrue. It has always been illegal, even under *Roe v. Wade*, to perform abortions after viability without a compelling medical reason. In Kansas, for example, where Dr. Tiller practiced medicine, the law for any abortion after twenty-two weeks requires two doctors to agree that failure to abort would put the mother at risk of "substantial and irreversible harm." But the abortionist's long list of fetal abnormalities that have led women to his clinic ranges from anencephaly to dwarfism, and you know a few dwarfs. You like to think you'd be happy with a dwarf child.

The abortionist comes in, remembers that the U.S. marshals don't like him to use this room because the window is too exposed, and walks right back out. You follow, asking about the patients who were supposed to see Dr. Tiller.

The patient I just finished was very unhappy to see me. I think they are very antiabortion. She had a fetal abnormality, and she and her husband are just devastated. Stuff like that.

What kind of fetal abnormalities are we talking about?

One was Down syndrome, another was a lethal brain abnormality along with a lethal heart abnormality. Another one had a catastrophic—we're not talking about cleft lip, we are talking about cleft face. There was no face.

Is there any chance of interviewing some of them?

Absolutely not.

·   ·   ·

The abortionist goes home, riding in the bulletproof car with three U.S. marshals. You follow in a separate car. Another set of marshals checks your credentials before they let you in. Inside there's a beautiful Bösendorfer piano with Beethoven on the stand and a primitive bow and arrow from the Amazon rain forest, where the abortionist has traveled to cure diseases and conduct ethnographic studies for more than forty years. There are books everywhere, and many of the nature photographs he has published in environmental books and magazines. Then he leads you to his office. *This is the descent into hell. I haven't had a chance to clean this up.*

It's an understatement. There's a narrow path between the books and papers. The stacks rise like the houses in *Horton Hears a Who!* You walk around reading titles: *Organization of Insect Societies. Sister Carrie. The Black Death. Cleansing the Fatherland. Abortion and Medical Ethics. Eve's Herbs. The Complete Idiot's Guide to MBA Basics.* There's a book on clutter control, which is obviously not doing much good. Even the bathroom is stuffed with boxes.

Don't go in there. It's pretty bad.

He sits down to bang out a letter to President Obama. *As you know, Dr. Tiller was unarmed, vulnerable, and acting as an usher for his fellow worshippers.* It's four in the afternoon and he still hasn't eaten his miserable microwave tamales. You can't help wondering if he's the abstemious type who doesn't take pleasure in simple things like food.

I enjoy food when I have a chance. I love to cook. Grown men lie down on the floor and cry with ecstasy over my paella.

What do the women do?

They watch the men.

In three days, it's the first light thing you've heard him say. So you take the opportunity to try to reach the emotional core everyone keeps telling you about. This woman you refused to treat, what was her reason?

She was raped. I'm very sympathetic, but I can't risk my medical license for someone who just didn't get around to doing anything about it. I've done some cases over thirty-six weeks, but very few.

For what cause?

For some catastrophic problems.

Like what?

Oh, anencephaly or lack of kidneys, you know. Lack of a brain.

The antiabortionists say that in those cases, the woman should just give birth naturally and let God take the baby.

The sharp tone comes back. *Having a delivery is not a benign procedure. When you are trying to keep the baby alive, that increases the risk for the woman. And Reagan put in a bunch of rules about requiring to keep babies alive no matter how hopeless it is. You have people going to Europe to get away from that.*

You mean the hospital requires them to save the baby?

The hospital requires full resuscitation measures, no matter what.

Also, his seaweed procedure is very slow and gentle on the cervix. The tissue dehydrates, the collagen starts to pull apart, the uterus gets softer. If you do a forceful dilation, you're going to tear the cervix. All around, his way is safer.

Safer for the mom?

Not for the mom, he snaps, *for the woman. Till she's had a baby, she's not a mom.*

·   ·   ·

While you wait, you try to chat up his staff. Most don't want to talk on the record, but Amanda says she's been working here for thirteen years. The abortionist is very caring with all of them, she says. Like all doctors, he wants things done exactly his way. But he doesn't tolerate them being treated poorly. He pays them well. He gives them insurance and 401(k)'s, which is not routine in the abortion trade. Once, he took them all rafting down the Green River. *That was delightful. He didn't care where anything was laid out in the camp.*

The pens in the counseling room are always diagonal to the pad of paper, you've noticed.

He'll move them, too. As he talks to you, he'll move them.

So what brings out his emotions?

Well, I think it is really difficult for him when women are experiencing pain and he's not able to control that for them. That really affects him.

How?

He becomes very introverted.

Have you ever seen him cry?

That's a question for Dr. Hern.

Does it bother him when the patients show disgust?

That's a question for Dr. Hern.

· · ·

The abortionist is on the phone, talking with the editor of a scientific journal. *Well, I went to George's funeral in Wichita, and I was probably the most heavily protected son of a bitch in the state. I was surrounded by rings of marshals and they might've been able to get me with a shoulder-mounted rocket or something. But the grief of this situation was pretty hard.*

He hangs up and dials another number. *Well, it's been a very tough week. You know, I liked the world a lot better the way it was a week ago Sunday morning—with George in it.*

Another line lights up. *Amor, cómo estás? Tengo mucho trabajo. No, no, está bien, Amor. Beso, beso, ciao.*

Back on the other line, he tells a reporter that he's just staggered by what happened last week and *grieving the loss of a wonderful friend and an excellent doctor.* Then a graphic designer comes in to chat about his latest book, an elaborate collage of photographs, stories, and poems:

> *I have resigned myself to temporary complicity with evil in order to accomplish certain strategic things for people whose suffering is more important than my need to maintain moral purity*

The poem is about his work in the Nixon administration, he says.

The phone rings again. This time it's the president of the National Society of Genetic Counselors, Steven Keiles. The abortionist wants him to issue a statement denouncing the murder, the sooner the better. *I'm sorry, this is not very complicated. You make a statement and you issue it to the press, a one-page statement condemning the brutal assassination of a conscientious and dedicated doctor who helped tens of thousands of women. As far as I'm concerned, it should have been issued last Monday. I don't know why you have to go through a PR firm. I'm sorry, but it just seems very, very bureaucratic to me. I know that abortion is controversial among the members, but I think that the statement by the NSGC would be very important.* He slams down the receiver. *That guy is a fucking clerk.*

It's ridiculous, the designer says.

I have no patience for this kind of bullshit. George gave them so much money and so much help.

Encouraged by the designer, he starts ranting about the time the militant antiabortion activist Randall Terry prayed for his death on national Christian radio. *These guys are just despicable. If anyone wants hope for the human species, don't talk to me.*

A receptionist comes to close the door so the patients don't hear him.

·   ·   ·

In passing, the abortionist says *you can never get used to this.* Next time he gives you a minute, you ask him to elaborate.

You can't, he says. *I think we're hardwired, biologically, to protect small, vulnerable creatures, especially babies. The fetuses may not be babies, but some of them are pretty close.*

Since you've become wary of even saying the word *baby* around him, always using *fetus* instead, this surprises you. But he refuses to say any more. He suggests you read an essay called "What About Us? Staff Reactions to D&E." *The antiabortion people quote the shit out of it. It's kind of antiabortion porn for them.* But the pro-choice people don't like it either. *They don't like it when you talk about how it really feels to do this work.* His voice is somewhere between bitter and proud.

So why did he write it? For that matter, why does he write so many papers and books? And why does he escape to the jungles of Peru every chance he gets? And what about this theory that man is a cancer? Is it all some kind of elaborate coping mechanism that makes it easier for him to do what he does?

I wrote it because, A, I'm a human being, and B, I'm a writer, and C and D, I'm a physician and I'm trying to understand what we're doing here.

You read the paper. He describes the reactions members of his staff have when they see residue of late abortions, which include *shock, dismay, amazement, disgust, fear, and sadness.* The later the pregnancy, the harder it is to accept. One assistant resented the patients for putting them through such a horrible experience. Two others described dreams where they vomited fetuses or felt an overwhelming urge to protect others from viewing the fetal parts. Common coping mechanisms were denial, projection, and rationalization. *For the senior author, rationalization has been shown by his intensive involvement in professional meetings, where this matter is discussed, and by his seeking peer support from colleagues who have similar experiences. Another great help was the relation-*

ships with the patients, which helped the senior author maintain his sense of commitment. It ended with the passage the antiabortionists love to quote, always out of context, words so honest they are almost as painful to read as they must have been to write:

> *We have reached a point in this particular technology where there is no possibility of denying an act of destruction. It is before one's eyes. The sensations of dismemberment flow through the forceps like an electric current. It is the crucible of a raging controversy, the confrontation of a modern existential dilemma. The more we seem to solve the problem, the more intractable it becomes.*

•　　　•　　　•

The abortionist is in the basement doing an abortion. Today is Thursday, operating day. He said you couldn't be here but he called at 7:30 A.M. and said he changed his mind. Now it's just after 8:00. It's very quiet. The waiting room is empty. So are the examining rooms. A receptionist tells you he just got done with a patient and should get back shortly.

A woman comes to the door. *Is it okay if I go outside for a minute?*

Sure. Knock on the door if you're starting to feel bad.

The phone keeps ringing. *If you have tissue samples,* says the receptionist you cannot name, *that makes it logistically easier. Can I put you on hold one second?*

She opens the door for the sad woman and her daughter. *Thank you,* the daughter says in an emphatic tone that suggests she's not just talking about the door.

A few minutes pass and the phone rings again. *Good morning, Dr. Hern's office. Okay, did you get any measurements from the ultrasound? Okay. And where was this done? Okay.*

Another line rings. *Could you hold for a second? Good morning, Dr. Hern's office. Okay, I can make an appointment. Can I have your last name and date of birth? Can you hold for a second?*

When the calls slow down, the receptionist tells you about the time a pro-life reporter pretended to be looking for information and then quoted her by name. *They do these things to scare you. They like to let you know they know where you live.*

The U.S. marshals keep walking up and down the hall, carrying black bags that look ominously tactical.

The abortionist comes upstairs and moves you to the nurses' office so he can do an interview with a reporter from *The Wichita Eagle*. Her husband was in the church when Tiller got killed. They're just getting started when he jumps up. *I'm sorry, I have to go see a patient.*

The receptionist you cannot name is on the phone again. *Is someone reading the results for you? Is there someone who can interpret them for you?*

The other receptionist lets a man in the door. *Thanks for being here*, she says. *You'll wait downstairs.*

The abortionist comes back to the reporter from Wichita. *The antiabortion movement is the face of fascism*, he says. *It cannot be separated from the ruthless and cynical manipulation of antiabortion rhetoric by the Republican party.*

The receptionist opens the door again. It's a woman in an ankle-length Amish dress. You've seen her before. She's usually with another woman in the same kind of dress. *She's waiting downstairs*, the receptionist says, hitting a button that rings an internal line. *Dr. Hern? Can you tell B—— her mother is coming down to be with her?*

While you wait, you read another one of the abortionist's essays. *It has been my practice to rupture membranes with ring forceps*, it says.

Another man comes to the door. *I'll tell her you're on your way down*, the receptionist says.

The phone rings. *Dr. Hern's office. I can check for you. He's with a patient. Are you sure you don't want me to take a phone number?*

The phone rings again. *Dr. Hern's office.*

.   .   .

At 11:30, the abortionist comes up in a cheerful mood. *I have to go check the level of molecular degeneration in my tamales.*

It's the second lighthearted thing you've heard him say this week. And when he comes back from the kitchen, he says another. *I identified a new species in my tamales. But I think with a gastroenterologist standing by . . .*

The receptionist smiles. *It's your risk.*

The two Amish women leave. The abortionist walks them to the door. *Have a safe trip home*, he says. *Give my regards to Dr. H——.*

In the counseling room, which the marshals have judged safe, he sits down with a weary sigh and picks up the phone. *Amor*, he says.

In the nurses' office, the soft felt sunflower weaves through the metal in-box. The poster that looks like the mother alien glares down at you. From the room next door, the abortionist's voice rises so high you can hear it through the wall. *I'm sorry, I'm sorry, I can't meet with every person who wants to talk to me.*

He stops in to say hello, forgetting the rule about not using this room for a moment. *I have to go downstairs and finish seeing a patient*, he says.

The phone rings. *June 24 is the first time we are seeing patients. At that time, based on the information you gave me, the fee will be $7,500.*

A young woman wearing a 1920s flapper scarf that Isadora Duncan might have worn comes up the stairs alone. At that very moment, you are reading page 83 of *Abortion Practice*, the section called Isolation: *One of the loneliest persons in the world is the woman who has not told anyone she is pregnant or considering an abortion. Some women have no one to whom they can turn; others insist on suffering alone as a form of self-punishment. The individual abortion counselor may, and frequently does, fill that gap for both kinds of patients.*

The woman in the flapper scarf stops at the receptionist's office. *Thank you so much*, she says. *You're so helpful. You're wonderful ladies.*

Another woman stops at the desk. She's a Latina with short black hair, here for her sister. *Can I wait? I want to say goodbye to everyone.*

The phone rings. *Who referred you to our office? And they did the ultrasound? Can you call them and have them send it to us? Do you have a pencil handy? You have a whole week. Don't give up.*

The phone rings. *Well, have you had an ultrasound? Okay. If it's between nineteen weeks and twenty-four weeks, it'll be between $5,000 and $7,500.*

Five minutes later, it rings again. *No, we need to know what the measurements are before you travel all the way to Colorado. It's a measurement in millimeters and centimeters. Fax it to us. Everything is based on the measurement.*

Three minutes later, it rings again. *Dr. Hern's office.*

Four minutes later, it rings again. *Dr. Hern's office.*

At 1:35, the sad woman emerges from the basement with her daughter, who is very tall for fifteen. The sad woman goes out the bulletproof doors and the daughter sits down in the waiting room. The receptionist goes out to check on her. *Are you waiting for your mom?*

She answers in a soft and girlish voice that makes you think of the army of Beanie Babies in your daughter's closet. *Yeah, she's coming.*

You'll get a good night's sleep tonight. Tomorrow, drink a lot of fluids and get rest.
At 1:43, the phone rings. *Dr. Hern's office.*

. . .

Now it's 1:47, and you're sitting down in the counseling room with the young couple who arrived in Wichita just in time to see the news cameras that surrounded the Reformation Lutheran Church. The woman has light-brown hair and wears conservative glasses. She is calm, somber, and depleted. Her husband sits in the opposite chair watching her carefully. He says he does not want her to talk for too long. She's feeling weak.

As gently as you can, you ask her to tell you why she chose abortion.

We had found out that something was wrong at twenty-eight weeks, seriously wrong. And they found out that it was going to put me, my health, perhaps in danger if I carried through to the end of the pregnancy.

And it was a planned pregnancy?

Oh yes. This was a wanted pregnancy, absolutely.

And when you arrived in Wichita?

We were caught between grieving about going through this and this awful situation.

And then what did you do?

I was scared to stay so close to where something like this could happen. We went home right away.

She corrects herself. *Well, we tried to call here to see if we could fly here, but they were already overbooked and obviously the whole emotional thing, so they recommended that we wait a week.*

And you couldn't find any other doctor close to home?

They do these kinds of procedures in Canada, where we come from, but because I was a very complicated case, and because I didn't feel comfortable with the way they wanted to do it, it was very high risk, and I wanted to come to someone who really knows and is an expert at this.

Do you mind explaining why it was so complicated?

Because of the abnormalities of the child. It was giving me health complications.

What was wrong?

It was severe abnormalities.

You change the subject, asking what was wrong with the Canadian doctors.

They do it very fast. They don't use the seaweed, they don't take their time, and it puts the woman at risk. And you're at risk of losing your uterus. I would like to have children, so I didn't want to have that risk.

And how did it go, the surgery?

Well Dr. Tiller said that—

Hern.

Oh, sorry, sorry, sorry. Dr. Hern said that I was a very complicated case. He said it went well, but it wasn't an easy thing to do.

Was it painful?

Yeah, it was painful physically and mentally.

You don't want to push it. So you ask if there's anything else they want to say. The husband answers.

It's important that people have a choice. At the end of the day, when things go bad, you know? I mean, God forbid something happens to Dr. Hern, where are we going to go next? Australia? China? It's important that people know that choice is very important when it comes to things like this.

Five minutes later, you catch the abortionist in the nurses' office, where the U.S. marshals don't want him to go, and ask him to tell you what was wrong with the couple's baby—excuse me, fetus. You're pretty sure it was the one with the lethal brain and lethal heart. But he won't say. So you ask him how it went.

It was very difficult.

Did it take a long time?

Yeah, it was a long time. Very long procedure.

How long is long?

Forty-five minutes. The average procedure is five minutes.

What was the problem?

Well, she was very far along. It was the position of the uterus, and she had a previous C-section, poor dilation, it was very difficult. I think any other procedure would have been very, very dangerous for her.

She was in danger of her life?

Oh yeah. She would have risked having a ruptured uterus in an induction procedure.

In surgery, or in birth?

Well, she's at risk, at this point, no matter what she decides to do. That's why I'm quite sure this was the safest option for her. No doubt about it.

.　　.　　.

The abortionist gives you directions to the Temple Emanuel in Denver. Later that evening, you will drive down with his wife and son, chatting about life under communism and brain surgery from the patient's point of view. You'll have a copy of the abortionist's speech, which he stayed up till 1:00 A.M. writing, but when he ascends to the dais, for reasons you feel more than understand, you will turn on your recorder anyway. He'll start to choke up when he says that Tiller was *gentle, considerate, and compassionate,* then recover and roll into the refuge of his annealing anger: *This brutal, cold-blooded, premeditated political assassination is the inevitable and predictable result of over thirty-five years of rabid antiabortion harassment, hate rhetoric, violence . . .*

When he comes off the stage to embrace the wife you cannot name, he will break down in racking sobs. The son you cannot name will stroke his shoulder. You will be standing right next to them, close enough to hear him say, *Amor, Amor, Amor,* close enough to hear members of the audience—who came by word of mouth, because the rabbi considered it too dangerous to advertise publicly—whisper their gratitude. *Thank you for your courage. Thank you for your commitment.* One woman squeezes his hand between hers. *It's because of people like you that my relatives survived the 1940s.*

But this comes later. Right now, it's 2:27 and the receptionist you cannot name is talking on the phone again. *No, he can't do it tonight. The soonest we can schedule it is the twenty-third.*

She cups her hand over the receiver. *This woman wants to come tonight—to fly in.*

Absolutely not, the abortionist says. *I absolutely can't do it.*

The receptionist takes her hand off the phone. *He can't do it until the twenty-third. He can't see you tonight.*

She pauses to listen. *He's trying to live his life as well,* she says. *The best we can do is the twenty-third.*

She pauses again. *I would say check with the doctor who referred you. Do you want to take a deep breath? Take a deep breath and call me back.*

Another pause, then the receptionist continues. *He can't change his mind. This is beyond his control. All you need to know is he can see you on the twenty-third. You need to plan a plane trip to Colorado on the twenty-second. Talk to your husband for a minute and call me back. My name is—*But you cannot say her name.

Three weeks later, the woman from Canada calls you on the phone. She says she has some things she wants to tell you. It was the most tragic and terrible experience of my life, she begins, speaking with force, the words rushing out. She has a son almost ready to start kindergarten, she was afraid she wouldn't survive to raise him, and she wants to have a big family, with lots of children, and the situation was so crazy with the marshals and the bulletproof glass and the constant fear of a mad killer with a gun. Dr. Hern was under so much pressure. She could see the stress in his face. *I didn't have a chance to tell you all this because after the procedure I just wanted to curl up in a ball, and I didn't know how I felt back then, to be honest. Now I'm still recovering and still sad and still mourning, and I realize how grateful I am that Dr. Hern was able to take me under such quick and terrible circumstances. That's what gets me so upset. He's a doctor who is trying to help people—it's shocking that people would want to hurt him.*

Without Dr. Hern, she says, she doesn't know what she would have done. It's crazy that he's the only one left. She is grateful, grateful, so grateful that she will be here to raise her son. And as the words tumble and repeat you hear, in the urgency unleashed by her deliverance, a love too sad for sermons, too personal for headlines, a private benediction, the abortionist's reward, the love song of Warren Martin Hern, M.D.

The New Yorker

WINNER—PUBLIC INTEREST

The National Magazine Award for Public Service "honors . . . magazine journalism that illuminates issues of public importance . . . and that has the potential to affect social or political debate." This piece did more than that. At a time when health care spending was the subject of a seemingly endless number of newspaper and magazine stories, Atul Gawande's reporting on the state of health care in McAllen, Texas, drew the attention of President Obama and, according to the New York Times, *"became required reading in the White House."*

Atul Gawande

The Cost
Conundrum

I t is spring in McAllen, Texas. The morning sun is warm. The streets are lined with palm trees and pickup trucks. McAllen is in Hidalgo County, which has the lowest household income in the country, but it's a border town, and a thriving foreign-trade zone has kept the unemployment rate below 10 percent. McAllen calls itself the Square Dance Capital of the World. *Lonesome Dove* was set around here.

McAllen has another distinction, too: it is one of the most expensive health-care markets in the country. Only Miami—which has much higher labor and living costs—spends more per person on health care. In 2006, Medicare spent $15,000 per enrollee here, almost twice the national average. The income per capita is $12,000. In other words, Medicare spends $3,000 more per person here than the average person earns.

The explosive trend in American medical costs seems to have occurred here in an especially intense form. Our country's health care is by far the most expensive in the world. In Washington, the aim of health-care reform is not just to extend medical coverage to everybody but also to bring costs under control. Spending on doctors, hospitals, drugs, and the like now consumes more than one of every six dollars we earn. The financial burden has damaged the global competitiveness of American businesses and bankrupted millions of families, even those with insurance. It's also devouring our government. "The greatest threat to America's fiscal health is not Social Security," President Barack Obama said in a March speech at the White House. "It's not the investments that we've made to rescue our economy during this crisis. By a wide margin, the biggest threat to our nation's balance sheet is the skyrocketing cost of health care. It's not even close."

The question we're now frantically grappling with is how this came to be, and what can be done about it. McAllen, Texas, the most expensive town in the most expensive country for health care in the world, seemed a good place to look for some answers.

.   .   .

From the moment I arrived, I asked almost everyone I encountered about McAllen's health costs—a businessman I met at the five-gate McAllen-Miller International Airport, the desk clerks at the Embassy Suites Hotel, a police-academy cadet at McDonald's. Most weren't surprised to hear that McAllen was an outlier. "Just look around," the cadet said. "People are not healthy here." McAllen, with its high poverty rate, has an incidence of heavy drinking 60 percent higher than the national average. And the Tex-Mex diet has contributed to a 38 percent obesity rate.

One day, I went on rounds with Lester Dyke, a weather-beaten, ranch-owning fifty-three-year-old cardiac surgeon who grew up in Austin, did his surgical training with the army all over the country, and settled into practice in Hidalgo County. He has not lacked for business: in the past twenty years, he has done some 8,000 heart operations, which exhausts me just thinking about it. I walked around with him as he checked in on ten or so of his patients who were recuperating at the three hospitals where he operates. It was easy to see what had landed them under his knife. They were nearly all obese or diabetic or both. Many had a family history of heart disease. Few were taking preventive measures, such as cholesterol-lowering drugs, which, studies indicate, would have obviated surgery for up to half of them.

Yet public-health statistics show that cardiovascular-disease rates in the county are actually lower than average, probably because its smoking rates are quite low. Rates of asthma, H.I.V., infant mortality, cancer, and injury are lower, too. El Paso County, eight hundred miles up the border, has essentially the same demographics. Both counties have a population of roughly 700,000, similar public-health statistics, and similar percentages of non-English speakers, illegal immigrants, and the unemployed. Yet in 2006 Medicare expenditures (our best approximation of overall spending patterns) in El Paso were $7,504 per enrollee—half as much as in McAllen. An unhealthy population couldn't possibly be the reason that McAllen's health-care costs are so high. (Or the reason that America's are. We may be more obese than any other industrialized nation, but we have among the lowest rates of smoking and alcoholism, and we are in the middle of the range for cardiovascular disease and diabetes.)

Was the explanation, then, that McAllen was providing unusually good health care? I took a walk through Doctors Hospital at Renaissance, in Edinburg, one of the towns in the McAllen metropolitan area, with Robert Alleyn, a Houston-trained general surgeon who had grown up here and returned home to practice. The hospital campus sprawled across two city blocks, with a series of three- and four-story stucco buildings separated by golfing-green lawns and black asphalt parking lots. He pointed out the sights—the cancer center is over here, the heart center is over there, now we're coming to the imaging center. We went inside the surgery building. It was sleek and modern, with recessed lighting, classical music piped into the waiting areas, and nurses moving from patient to patient behind rolling black computer pods. We changed into scrubs and Alleyn took me through the sixteen operating rooms to show me the laparoscopy suite, with its flat-screen video monitors, the hybrid operating room with built-in imaging equipment, the surgical robot for minimally invasive robotic surgery.

I was impressed. The place had virtually all the technology that you'd find at Harvard and Stanford and the Mayo Clinic, and, as I walked through that hospital on a dusty road in south Texas, this struck me as a remarkable thing. Rich towns get the new school buildings, fire trucks, and roads, not to mention the better teachers and police officers and civil engineers. Poor towns don't. But that rule doesn't hold for health care.

At McAllen Medical Center, I saw an orthopedic surgeon work under an operating microscope to remove a tumor that had wrapped around the spinal cord of a fourteen-year-old. At a home-health agency, I spoke to a nurse who could provide intravenous-drug therapy for patients with congestive heart failure. At McAllen Heart Hospital, I watched Dyke and a team of six do a coronary-artery bypass using technologies that didn't exist a few years ago. At Renaissance, I talked with a neonatologist who trained at my hospital, in Boston, and brought McAllen new skills and technologies for premature babies. "I've had nurses come up to me and say, 'I never knew these babies could survive,'" he said.

And yet there's no evidence that the treatments and technologies available at McAllen are better than those found elsewhere in the country. The annual reports that hospitals file with Medicare show that those in McAllen and El Paso offer comparable technologies—neonatal intensive-care units, advanced cardiac services, PET scans, and so on. Public statistics show no difference in the supply of doctors. Hidalgo County actually has fewer specialists than the national average.

Nor does the care given in McAllen stand out for its quality. Medicare ranks hospitals on twenty-five metrics of care. On all but two of these, McAllen's five largest hospitals performed worse, on average, than El Paso's. McAllen costs Medicare $7,000 more per person each year than does the average city in America.

But not, so far as one can tell, because it's delivering better health care.

.   .   .

One night, I went to dinner with six McAllen doctors. All were what you would call bread-and-butter physicians: busy, full-time, private-practice doctors who work from seven in the morning to seven at night and sometimes later, their waiting rooms teeming and their desks stacked with medical charts to review. Some were dubious when I told them that McAllen was the country's most expensive place for health care. I gave them the spending data from Medicare. In 1992, in the McAllen market, the average cost per Medicare enrollee was $4,891, almost exactly the national average. But since then, year after year, McAllen's health costs have grown faster than any other market in the country, ultimately soaring by more than $10,000 per person.

"Maybe the service is better here," the cardiologist suggested. People can be seen faster and get their tests more readily, he said.

Others were skeptical. "I don't think that explains the costs he's talking about," the general surgeon said.

"It's malpractice," a family physician who had practiced here for thirty-three years said.

"McAllen is legal hell," the cardiologist agreed. Doctors order unnecessary tests just to protect themselves, he said. Everyone thought the lawyers here were worse than elsewhere.

That explanation puzzled me. Several years ago, Texas passed a tough malpractice law that capped pain-and-suffering awards at $250,000. Didn't lawsuits go down?

"Practically to zero," the cardiologist admitted.

"Come on," the general surgeon finally said. "We all know these arguments are bullshit. There is overutilization here, pure and simple." Doctors, he said, were racking up charges with extra tests, services, and procedures.

The surgeon came to McAllen in the mid-nineties, and since then, he said, "the way to practice medicine has changed completely. Before, it was about how to do a good job. Now it is about 'How much will you benefit?' "

Everyone agreed that something fundamental had changed since the days when health-care costs in McAllen were the same as those in El Paso and elsewhere. Yes, they had more technology. "But young doctors don't think anymore," the family physician said.

The surgeon gave me an example. General surgeons are often asked to see patients with pain from gallstones. If there aren't any complications—and there usually aren't—the pain goes away on its own or with pain medication. With instruction on eating a lower-fat diet, most patients experience no further difficulties. But some have recurrent episodes, and need surgery to remove their gallbladder.

Seeing a patient who has had uncomplicated, first-time gallstone pain requires some judgment. A surgeon has to provide reassurance (people are often scared and want to go straight to surgery), some education about gallstone disease and diet, perhaps a prescription for pain; in a few weeks, the surgeon might follow up. But increasingly, I was told, McAllen surgeons simply operate. The patient wasn't going to moderate her diet, they tell themselves. The pain was just going to come back. And by operating they happen to make an extra $700.

I gave the doctors around the table a scenario. A forty-year-old woman comes in with chest pain after a fight with her husband. An EKG is normal. The chest pain goes away. She has no family history of heart disease. What did McAllen doctors do fifteen years ago?

Send her home, they said. Maybe get a stress test to confirm that there's no issue, but even that might be overkill.

And today? Today, the cardiologist said, she would get a stress test, an echocardiogram, a mobile Holter monitor, and maybe even a cardiac catheterization.

"Oh, she's *definitely* getting a cath," the internist said, laughing grimly.

To determine whether overuse of medical care was really the problem in McAllen, I turned to Jonathan Skinner, an economist at Dartmouth's Institute for Health Policy and Clinical Practice, which has three decades of expertise in examining regional patterns in Medicare payment data. I also turned to two private firms—D2Hawkeye, an independent company, and Ingenix, UnitedHealthcare's data-analysis company—to analyze commercial insurance data for McAllen. The answer was yes. Compared with patients in El Paso and nationwide, patients in McAllen got more of pretty much everything—more diagnostic testing, more hospital treatment, more surgery, more home care.

The Medicare payment data provided the most detail. Between 2001 and 2005, critically ill Medicare patients received almost 50 percent more specialist visits in McAllen than in El Paso, and were two-thirds more likely to see ten or more specialists in a six-month period. In 2005 and 2006, patients in McAllen received 20 percent more abdominal ultrasounds, 30 percent more bone-density studies, 60 percent more stress tests with echocardiography, 200 percent more nerve-conduction studies to diagnose carpal-tunnel syndrome, and 550 percent more urine-flow studies to diagnose prostate troubles. They received one-fifth to two-thirds more gallbladder operations, knee replacements, breast biopsies, and bladder scopes. They also received two to three times as many pacemakers, implantable defibrillators, cardiac-bypass operations, carotid endarterectomies, and coronary-artery stents. And Medicare paid for five times as many home-nurse visits. The primary cause of McAllen's extreme costs was, very simply, the across-the-board overuse of medicine.

· · ·

This is a disturbing and perhaps surprising diagnosis. Americans like to believe that, with most things, more is better. But research suggests that where medicine is concerned it may actually be worse. For example, Rochester, Minnesota, where the Mayo Clinic dominates the scene, has fantastically high levels of technological capability and quality, but its Medicare spending is in the lowest 15 percent of the country—$6,688 per enrollee in 2006, which is $8,000 less than the figure for McAllen. Two economists working at Dartmouth, Katherine Baicker and Amitabh Chandra, found that the more money Medicare spent per person in a given state the lower that state's quality ranking tended to be. In fact, the four states with the highest levels of spending—Louisiana, Texas, California, and Florida—were near the bottom of the national rankings on the quality of patient care.

In a 2003 study, another Dartmouth team, led by the internist Elliott Fisher, examined the treatment received by a million elderly Americans diagnosed with colon or rectal cancer, a hip fracture, or a heart attack. They found that patients in higher-spending regions received 60 percent more care than elsewhere. They got more frequent tests and procedures, more visits with specialists, and more frequent admission to hospitals. Yet they did no better than other patients, whether this was measured in terms of survival, their ability to function, or satisfaction with the care they received. If anything, they seemed to do worse.

That's because nothing in medicine is without risks. Complications can arise from hospital stays, medications, procedures, and tests, and when these things are of marginal value the harm can be greater than the benefits. In recent years, we doctors have markedly increased the number of operations we do, for instance. In 2006, doctors performed at least 60 million surgical procedures, one for every five Americans. No other country does anything like as many operations on its citizens. Are we better off for it? No one knows for sure, but it seems highly unlikely. After all, some hundred thousand people die each year from complications of surgery—far more than die in car crashes.

To make matters worse, Fisher found that patients in high-cost areas were actually less likely to receive low-cost preventive services, such as flu and pneumonia vaccines, faced longer waits at doctor and emergency-room visits, and were less likely to have a primary-care physician. They got more of the stuff that cost more, but not more of what they needed.

In an odd way, this news is reassuring. Universal coverage won't be feasible unless we can control costs. Policymakers have worried that doing so would require rationing, which the public would never go along with. So the idea that there's plenty of fat in the system is proving deeply attractive. "Nearly 30 percent of Medicare's costs could be saved without negatively affecting health outcomes if spending in high- and medium-cost areas could be reduced to the level in low-cost areas," Peter Orszag, the president's budget director, has stated.

Most Americans would be delighted to have the quality of care found in places like Rochester, Minnesota, or Seattle, Washington, or Durham, North Carolina—all of which have world-class hospitals and costs that fall below the national average. If we brought the cost curve in the expensive places down to their level, Medicare's problems (indeed, almost all the federal government's budget problems for the next fifty years) would be solved. The difficulty is how to go about it. Physicians in places like Mc-Allen behave differently from others. The $2.4 trillion question is why. Unless we figure it out, health reform will fail.

•   •   •

I had what I considered to be a reasonable plan for finding out what was going on in McAllen. I would call on the heads of its hospitals, in their swanky, decorator-designed, *churrigueresco* offices, and I'd ask them.

The first hospital I visited, McAllen Heart Hospital, is owned by Universal Health Services, a for-profit hospital chain with headquarters in King of Prussia, Pennsylvania, and revenues of $5 billion last year. I went to see the hospital's chief operating officer, Gilda Romero. Truth be told, her office seemed less *churrigueresco* than Office Depot. She had straight brown hair, sympathetic eyes, and looked more like a young school teacher than like a corporate officer with nineteen years of experience. And when I inquired, "What is going on in this place?" she looked surprised.

Is McAllen really that expensive? she asked.

I described the data, including the numbers indicating that heart operations and catheter procedures and pacemakers were being performed in McAllen at double the usual rate.

"That is *interesting*," she said, by which she did not mean, "Uh-oh, you've caught us" but, rather, "That is actually interesting." The problem of McAllen's outlandish costs was new to her. She puzzled over the numbers. She was certain that her doctors performed surgery only when it was necessary. It had to be one of the other hospitals. And she had one in mind—Doctors Hospital at Renaissance, the hospital in Edinburg that I had toured.

She wasn't the only person to mention Renaissance. It is the newest hospital in the area. It is physician-owned. And it has a reputation (which it disclaims) for aggressively recruiting high-volume physicians to become investors and send patients there. Physicians who do so receive not only their fee for whatever service they provide but also a percentage of the hospital's profits from the tests, surgery, or other care patients are given. (In 2007, its profits totaled $34 million.) Romero and others argued that this gives physicians an unholy temptation to overorder.

Such an arrangement can make physician investors rich. But it can't be the whole explanation. The hospital gets barely a sixth of the patients in the region; its margins are no bigger than the other hospitals'—whether for profit or not for profit—and it didn't have much of a presence until 2004 at the earliest, a full decade after the cost explosion in McAllen began.

"Those are good points," Romero said. She couldn't explain what was going on.

The following afternoon, I visited the top managers of Doctors Hospital at Renaissance. We sat in their boardroom around one end of a yacht-length table. The chairman of the board offered me a soda. The chief of staff smiled at me. The chief financial officer shook my hand as if I were an old friend. The C.E.O., however, was having a hard time pretending that he was happy to see me. Lawrence Gelman was a fifty-seven-year-old anesthesiologist with a Bill Clinton shock of white hair and a weekly local radio show tag-lined "Opinions from an Unrelenting Conservative Spirit." He had helped found the hospital. He barely greeted me, and while the others were trying for a how-can-I-help-you-today attitude, his body language was more let's-get-this-over-with.

So I asked him why McAllen's health-care costs were so high. What he gave me was a disquisition on the theory and history of American health-care financing going back to Lyndon Johnson and the creation of Medicare, the upshot of which was: (1) Government is the problem in health care. "The people in charge of the purse strings don't know what they're doing." (2) If anything, government insurance programs like Medicare don't pay enough. "I, as an anesthesiologist, know that they pay me 10 percent of what a private insurer pays." (3) Government programs are full of waste. "Every person in this room could easily go through the expenditures of Medicare and Medicaid and see all kinds of waste." (4) But not in McAllen. The clinicians here, at least at Doctors Hospital at Renaissance, "are providing necessary, essential health care," Gelman said. "We don't invent patients."

Then why do hospitals in McAllen order so much more surgery and scans and tests than hospitals in El Paso and elsewhere?

In the end, the only explanation he and his colleagues could offer was this: The other doctors and hospitals in McAllen may be overspending, but, to the extent that his hospital provides costlier treatment than other places in the country, it is making people better in ways that data on quality and outcomes do not measure.

"Do we provide better health care than El Paso?" Gelman asked. "I would bet you two to one that we do."

It was a depressing conversation—not because I thought the executives were being evasive but because they weren't being evasive. The data on McAllen's costs were clearly new to them. They were defending McAllen reflexively. But they really didn't know the big picture of what was happening.

And, I realized, few people in their position do. Local executives for hospitals and clinics and home-health agencies understand their growth rate and their market share; they know whether they are losing money or making money. They know that if their doctors bring in enough business—surgery, imaging, home-nursing referrals—they make money; and if they get the doctors to bring in more, they make more. But they have only the vaguest notion of whether the doctors are making their communities as healthy as they can, or whether they are more or less efficient than their counterparts elsewhere. A doctor sees a patient in clinic, and has her check into a McAllen hospital for a CT scan, an ultrasound, three rounds of blood tests, another ultrasound, and then surgery to have her gallbladder removed. How is Lawrence Gelman or Gilda Romero to know whether all that is essential, let alone the best possible treatment for the patient? It isn't what they are responsible or accountable for.

Health-care costs ultimately arise from the accumulation of individual decisions doctors make about which services and treatments to write an order for. The most expensive piece of medical equipment, as the saying goes, is a doctor's pen. And, as a rule, hospital executives don't own the pen caps. Doctors do.

•   •   •

If doctors wield the pen, why do they do it so differently from one place to another? Brenda Sirovich, another Dartmouth researcher, published a study last year that provided an important clue. She and her team surveyed some 800 primary-care physicians from high-cost cities (such as Las Vegas and New York), low-cost cities (such as Sacramento and Boise), and others in between. The researchers asked the physicians specifically how they would handle a variety of patient cases. It turned out that differences in decision making emerged in only some kinds of cases. In situations in which the right thing to do was well established—for example, whether to recommend a mammogram for a fifty-year-old woman (the answer is yes)—physicians in high- and low-cost cities made the same decisions. But, in cases in which the science was unclear, some physicians pursued the maximum possible amount of testing and procedures; some pursued the minimum. And which kind of doctor they were depended on where they came from.

Sirovich asked doctors how they would treat a seventy-five-year-old woman with typical heartburn symptoms and "adequate health insurance to cover tests and medications." Physicians in high- and low-cost cities were equally likely to prescribe antacid therapy and to check for H. pylori, an ulcer-causing bacterium—steps strongly recommended by national guidelines. But when it came to measures of less certain value—and higher cost—the differences were considerable. More than 70 percent of physicians in high-cost cities referred the patient to a gastroenterologist, ordered an upper endoscopy, or both, while half as many in low-cost cities did. Physicians from high-cost cities typically recommended that patients with well-controlled hypertension see them in the office every one to three months, while those from low-cost cities recommended visits twice yearly. In case after uncertain case, more was not necessarily better. But physicians from the most expensive cities did the most expensive things.

Why? Some of it could reflect differences in training. I remember when my wife brought our infant son Walker to visit his grandparents in Virginia, and he took a terrifying fall down a set of stairs. They drove him to the local community hospital in Alexandria. A CT scan showed that he had a tiny subdural hematoma—a small area of bleeding in the brain. During ten hours of observation, though, he was fine—eating, drinking, completely alert. I was a surgery resident then and had seen many cases like his. We observed each child in intensive care for at least twenty-four hours and got a repeat CT scan. That was how I'd been trained. But the doctor in Alexandria was going to send Walker home. That was how he'd been trained. Suppose things change for the worse? I asked him. It's extremely unlikely, he said, and if anything changed Walker could always be brought back. I bullied the doctor into admitting him anyway. The next day, the scan and the patient were fine. And, looking in the textbooks, I learned that the doctor was right. Walker could have been managed safely either way.

There was no sign, however, that McAllen's doctors as a group were trained any differently from El Paso's. One morning, I met with a hospital administrator who had extensive experience managing for-profit hospitals along the border. He offered a different possible explanation: the culture of money.

"In El Paso, if you took a random doctor and looked at his tax returns 85 percent of his income would come from the usual practice of medicine," he said. But in McAllen, the administrator thought, that percentage would be a lot less.

He knew of doctors who owned strip malls, orange groves, apartment complexes—or imaging centers, surgery centers, or another part of the hospital they directed patients to. They had "entrepreneurial spirit," he said. They were innovative and aggressive in finding ways to increase revenues from patient care.

"There's no lack of work ethic," he said. But he had often seen financial considerations drive the decisions doctors made for patients—the tests they ordered, the doctors and hospitals they recommended—and it bothered him. Several doctors who were unhappy about the direction medicine had taken in McAllen told me the same thing. "It's a machine, my friend," one surgeon explained.

No one teaches you how to think about money in medical school or residency. Yet, from the moment you start practicing, you must think about it. You must consider what is covered for a patient and what is not. You must pay attention to insurance rejections and government-reimbursement rules. You must think about having enough money for the secretary and the nurse and the rent and the malpractice insurance.

Beyond the basics, however, many physicians are remarkably oblivious to the financial implications of their decisions. They see their patients. They make their recommendations. They send out the bills. And, as long as the numbers come out all right at the end of each month, they put the money out of their minds.

Others think of the money as a means of improving what they do. They think about how to use the insurance money to maybe install electronic health records with colleagues, or provide easier phone and e-mail access, or offer expanded hours. They hire an extra nurse to monitor diabetic patients more closely, and to make sure that patients don't miss their mammograms and pap smears and colonoscopies.

Then there are the physicians who see their practice primarily as a revenue stream. They instruct their secretary to have patients who call with follow-up questions schedule an appointment, because insurers don't pay for phone calls, only office visits. They consider providing Botox injections for cash. They take a Doppler ultrasound course, buy a machine, and start doing their patients' scans themselves, so that the insurance payments go to them rather than to the hospital. They figure out ways to increase their high-margin work and decrease their low-margin work. This is a business, after all.

In every community, you'll find a mixture of these views among physicians, but one or another tends to predominate. McAllen seems simply to be the community at one extreme.

In a few cases, the hospital executive told me, he'd seen the behavior cross over into what seemed like outright fraud. "I've had doctors here come up to me and say, 'You want me to admit patients to your hospital, you're going to have to pay me.'"

"How much?" I asked.

"The amounts—all of them were over a hundred thousand dollars per year," he said. The doctors were specific. The most he was asked for was five hundred thousand dollars per year.

He didn't pay any of them, he said: "I mean, I gotta sleep at night." And he emphasized that these were just a handful of doctors. But he had never been asked for a kickback before coming to McAllen.

Woody Powell is a Stanford sociologist who studies the economic culture of cities. Recently, he and his research team studied why certain regions—Boston, San Francisco, San Diego— became leaders in biotechnology while others with a similar concentration of scientific and corporate talent—Los Angeles, Philadelphia, New York—did not. The answer they found was what Powell describes as the anchor-tenant theory of economic development. Just as an anchor store will define the character of a mall, anchor tenants in biotechnology, whether it's a company like Genentech, in south San Francisco, or a university like M.I.T., in Cambridge, define the character of an economic community. They set the norms. The anchor tenants that set norms encouraging the free flow of ideas and collaboration, even with competitors, produced enduringly successful communities, while those that mainly sought to dominate did not.

Powell suspects that anchor tenants play a similarly powerful community role in other areas of economics, too, and health care may be no exception. I spoke to a marketing rep for a McAllen home-health agency who told me of a process uncannily similar to what Powell found in biotech. Her job is to persuade doctors to use her agency rather than others. The competition is fierce. I opened the phone book and found seventeen pages of listings for home-health agencies—two hundred and sixty in all. A patient typically brings in between $1,200 and $1,500, and double that amount for specialized care. She described how, a decade or so ago, a few early agencies began rewarding doctors who ordered home visits with more than trinkets: they provided tickets to professional sporting events, jewelry, and other gifts. That set the tone. Other agencies jumped in. Some began paying doctors a supplemental salary, as "medical directors," for steering business in their direction. Doctors came to expect a share of the revenue stream.

Agencies that want to compete on quality struggle to remain in business, the rep said. Doctors have asked her for a medical-director salary of four or five thousand dollars a month in return for sending her business. One asked a colleague of hers for private-school tuition for his child; another wanted sex.

"I explained the rules and regulations and the anti-kickback law, and told them no," she said of her dealings with such doctors. "Does it hurt my business?" She paused. "I'm O.K. working only with ethical physicians," she finally said.

About fifteen years ago, it seems, something began to change in McAllen. A few leaders of local institutions took profit growth to be a legitimate ethic in the practice of medicine. Not all the doctors accepted this. But they failed to discourage those who did. So here, along the banks of the Rio Grande, in the Square Dance Capital of the World, a medical community came to treat patients the way subprime-mortgage lenders treated home buyers: as profit centers.

•   •   •

The real puzzle of American health care, I realized on the airplane home, is not why McAllen is different from El Paso. It's why El Paso isn't like McAllen. Every incentive in the system is an invitation to go the way McAllen has gone. Yet, across the country, large numbers of communities have managed to control their health costs rather than ratchet them up.

I talked to Denis Cortese, the C.E.O. of the Mayo Clinic, which is among the highest-quality, lowest-cost health-care systems in the country. A couple of years ago, I spent several days there as a visiting surgeon. Among the things that stand out from that visit was how much time the doctors spent with patients. There was no churn—no shuttling patients in and out of rooms while the doctor bounces from one to the other. I accompanied a colleague while he saw patients. Most of the patients, like those in my clinic, required about twenty minutes. But one patient had colon cancer and a number of other complex issues, including heart disease. The physician spent an hour with her, sorting things out. He phoned a cardiologist with a question.

"I'll be there," the cardiologist said.

Fifteen minutes later, he was. They mulled over everything together. The cardiologist adjusted a medication, and said that no further testing was needed. He cleared the patient for surgery, and the operating room gave her a slot the next day.

The whole interaction was astonishing to me. Just having the cardiologist pop down to see the patient with the surgeon would be unimaginable at my hospital. The time required wouldn't pay. The time required just to organize the system wouldn't pay.

The core tenet of the Mayo Clinic is "The needs of the patient come first"—not the convenience of the doctors, not their revenues. The doctors and nurses, and even the janitors, sat in meetings almost weekly, working on ideas to make the service and the care better, not to get more money out of patients. I asked Cortese how the Mayo Clinic made this possible.

"It's not easy," he said. But decades ago Mayo recognized that the first thing it needed to do was eliminate the financial barriers. It pooled all the money the doctors and the hospital system received and began paying everyone a salary, so that the doctors' goal in patient care couldn't be increasing their income. Mayo promoted leaders who focused first on what was best for patients, and then on how to make this financially possible.

No one there actually intends to do fewer expensive scans and procedures than is done elsewhere in the country. The aim is to raise quality and to help doctors and other staff members work as a team. But, almost by happenstance, the result has been lower costs.

"When doctors put their heads together in a room, when they share expertise, you get more thinking and less testing," Cortese told me.

Skeptics saw the Mayo model as a local phenomenon that wouldn't carry beyond the hay fields of northern Minnesota. But in 1986 the Mayo Clinic opened a campus in Florida, one of our most expensive states for health care, and, in 1987, another one in Arizona. It was difficult to recruit staff members who would accept a salary and the Mayo's collaborative way of practicing. Leaders were working against the dominant medical culture and incentives. The expansion sites took at least a decade to get properly established. But eventually they achieved the same high-quality, low-cost results as Rochester. Indeed, Cortese says that the Florida site has become, in some respects, the most efficient one in the system.

The Mayo Clinic is not an aberration. One of the lowest-cost markets in the country is Grand Junction, Colorado, a community of a 120,000 that nonetheless has achieved some of Medicare's highest quality-of-care scores. Michael Pramenko is a family physician and a local medical leader there. Unlike doctors at the Mayo Clinic, he told me, those in Grand Junction get piecework fees from insurers. But years ago the doctors agreed among themselves to a system that paid them a similar fee whether they saw Medicare, Medicaid, or private-insurance patients, so that there would be little incentive to cherry-pick patients. They also agreed, at the behest of the main health plan in town, an H.M.O., to meet regularly on small peer-review committees to go over their patient charts together. They focused on rooting out problems like poor prevention practices, unnecessary back operations, and unusual hospital-complication rates. Problems went down. Quality went up. Then, in 2004, the doctors' group and the local H.M.O. jointly created a regional information network—a community-wide electronic-record system that shared office notes, test results, and hospital data for patients across the area. Again, problems went down. Quality went up. And costs ended up lower than just about anywhere else in the United States.

Grand Junction's medical community was not following anyone else's recipe. But, like Mayo, it created what Elliott Fisher, of Dartmouth, calls an accountable-care organization. The leading doctors and the hospital system adopted measures to blunt harmful financial incentives, and they took collective responsibility for improving the sum total of patient care.

This approach has been adopted in other places, too: the Geisinger Health System, in Danville, Pennsylvania; the Marshfield Clinic, in Marshfield, Wisconsin; Intermountain Healthcare, in Salt Lake City; Kaiser Permanente, in Northern California. All of them function on similar principles. All are not-for-profit institutions. And all have produced enviably higher quality and lower costs than the average American town enjoys.

•   •   •

When you look across the spectrum from Grand Junction to McAllen—and the almost threefold difference in the costs of care—you come to realize that we are witnessing a battle for the soul of American medicine. Somewhere in the United States at this moment, a patient with chest pain, or a tumor, or a cough is seeing a doctor. And the damning question we have to ask is whether the doctor is set up to meet the needs of the patient, first and foremost, or to maximize revenue.

There is no insurance system that will make the two aims match perfectly. But having a system that does so much to misalign them has proved disastrous. As economists have often pointed out, we pay doctors for quantity, not quality. As they point out less often, we also pay them as individuals, rather than as members of a team working together for their patients. Both practices have made for serious problems.

Providing health care is like building a house. The task requires experts, expensive equipment and materials, and a huge amount of coordination. Imagine that, instead of paying a contractor to pull a team together and keep them on track, you paid an electrician for every outlet he recommends, a plumber for every faucet, and a carpenter for every cabinet. Would you be surprised if you got a house with a thousand outlets, faucets, and cabinets, at three times the cost you expected, and the whole thing fell apart a couple of years later? Getting the country's best electrician on the job (he trained at Harvard, somebody tells you) isn't going to solve this problem. Nor will changing the person who writes him the check.

This last point is vital. Activists and policymakers spend an inordinate amount of time arguing about whether the solution to high medical costs is to have government or private insurance companies write the checks. Here's how this whole debate goes. Advocates of a public option say government financing would save the most money by having leaner administrative costs and forcing doctors and hospitals to take lower payments than they get from private insurance. Opponents say doctors would skimp, quit, or game the system, and make us wait in line for our care; they maintain that private insurers are better at policing doctors.

No, the skeptics say: all insurance companies do is reject applicants who need health care and stall on paying their bills. Then we have the economists who say that the people who should pay the doctors are the ones who use them. Have consumers pay with their own dollars, make sure that they have some "skin in the game," and then they'll get the care they deserve. These arguments miss the main issue. When it comes to making care better and cheaper, changing who pays the doctor will make no more difference than changing who pays the electrician. The lesson of the high-quality, low-cost communities is that someone has to be accountable for the totality of care. Otherwise, you get a system that has no brakes. You get McAllen.

One afternoon in McAllen, I rode down McColl Road with Lester Dyke, the cardiac surgeon, and we passed a series of office plazas that seemed to be nothing but home-health agencies, imaging centers, and medical-equipment stores.

"Medicine has become a pig trough here," he muttered.

Dyke is among the few vocal critics of what's happened in McAllen. "We took a wrong turn when doctors stopped being doctors and became businessmen," he said.

We began talking about the various proposals being touted in Washington to fix the cost problem. I asked him whether expanding public-insurance programs like Medicare and shrinking the role of insurance companies would do the trick in McAllen.

"I don't have a problem with it," he said. "But it won't make a difference." In McAllen, government payers already predominate—not many people have jobs with private insurance.

How about doing the opposite and increasing the role of big insurance companies?

"What good would that do?" Dyke asked.

The third class of health-cost proposals, I explained, would push people to use medical savings accounts and hold high-deductible insurance policies: "They'd have more of their own money on the line, and that'd drive them to bargain with you and other surgeons, right?"

He gave me a quizzical look. We tried to imagine the scenario. A cardiologist tells an elderly woman that she needs bypass surgery and has Dr. Dyke see her. They discuss the blockages in her heart, the operation, the risks. And now they're supposed to haggle over the price as if he were selling a rug in a souk? "I'll do three vessels for thirty thousand, but if you take four I'll throw in an extra night in the I.C.U."—that sort of thing? Dyke shook his head. "Who comes up with this stuff?" he asked. "Any plan that relies on the sheep to negotiate with the wolves is doomed to failure."

Instead, McAllen and other cities like it have to be weaned away from their untenably fragmented, quantity-driven systems of health care, step by step. And that will mean rewarding doctors and hospitals if they band together to form Grand Junction–like accountable-care organizations, in which doctors collaborate to increase prevention and the quality of care, while discouraging overtreatment, undertreatment, and sheer profiteering. Under one approach, insurers—whether public or private—would allow clinicians who formed such organizations and met quality goals to keep half the savings they generate. Government could also shift regulatory burdens, and even malpractice liability, from the doctors to the organization. Other, sterner, approaches would penalize those who don't form these organizations.

This will by necessity be an experiment. We will need to do in-depth research on what makes the best systems successful— the peer-review committees? recruiting more primary-care doctors and nurses? putting doctors on salary?—and disseminate what we learn. Congress has provided vital funding for research that compares the effectiveness of different treatments, and this should help reduce uncertainty about which treatments are best. But we also need to fund research that compares the effectiveness of different systems of care—to reduce our uncertainty about which systems work best for communities. These are empirical, not ideological, questions. And we would do well to form a national institute for health-care delivery, bringing together clinicians, hospitals, insurers, employers, and citizens to assess, regularly, the quality and the cost of our care, review the strategies that produce good results, and make clear recommendations for local systems.

Dramatic improvements and savings will take at least a decade. But a choice must be made. Whom do we want in charge of managing the full complexity of medical care? We can turn to insurers (whether public or private), which have proved repeatedly that they can't do it. Or we can turn to the local medical communities, which have proved that they can. But we have to choose someone—because, in much of the country, no one is in charge. And the result is the most wasteful and the least sustainable health-care system in the world.

·　　·　　·

Something even more worrisome is going on as well. In the war over the culture of medicine—the war over whether our country's anchor model will be Mayo or McAllen—the Mayo model is losing. In the sharpest economic downturn that our health system has faced in half a century, many people in medicine don't see why they should do the hard work of organizing themselves in ways that reduce waste and improve quality if it means sacrificing revenue.

In El Paso, the for-profit health-care executive told me, a few leading physicians recently followed McAllen's lead and opened their own centers for surgery and imaging. When I was in Tulsa a few months ago, a fellow surgeon explained how he had made up for lost revenue by shifting his operations for well-insured patients to a specialty hospital that he partially owned while keeping his poor and uninsured patients at a nonprofit hospital in town. Even in Grand Junction, Michael Pramenko told me, "some of the doctors are beginning to complain about 'leaving money on the table.'"

As America struggles to extend health-care coverage while curbing health-care costs, we face a decision that is more important than whether we have a public-insurance option, more important than whether we will have a single-payer system in the long run or a mixture of public and private insurance, as we do now. The decision is whether we are going to reward the leaders who are trying to build a new generation of Mayos and Grand Junctions. If we don't, McAllen won't be an outlier. It will be our future.

Boston Review

FINALIST—PUBLIC
INTEREST

There is nothing glossy about
Boston Review. *Edited by Deborah
Chasman and Joshua Cohen and
published six times a year, it has a
print circulation of 10,000—a
fraction of the size of most of the
other magazines entered in the
National Magazine Awards. Yet
there is nothing small about its
ambitions, as shown by "A Death
in Texas," Tom Barry's
investigation of the for-profit
prisons where increasing numbers
of illegal immigrants are
incarcerated in conditions that kill.*

Tom Barry

A Death in Texas

County Clerk Dianne Florez noticed it first. Plumes of smoke were rising outside the small West Texas town of Pecos. "The prison is burning again," she announced.

About a month and a half before, on December 12, 2008, inmates had rioted to protest the death of one of their own, Jesus Manuel Galindo, thirty-two. When Galindo's body was removed from the prison in what looked to them like a large black trash bag, they set fire to the recreational center and occupied the exercise yard overnight. Using smuggled cell phones, they told worried family members and the media about poor medical care in the prison and described the treatment of Galindo, who had been in solitary confinement since mid-November. During that time, fellow inmates and his mother, who called the prison nearly every day, had warned authorities that Galindo needed daily medication for epilepsy and was suffering from severe seizures in the "security housing unit," which the inmates call the "hole."

I arrived in Pecos on February 2, shortly after the second riot broke out. I had driven 200 miles east from El Paso through the northern reaches of the Chihuahuan desert.

Pecos is the seat of Reeves County in "far west" Texas and home to what the prison giant GEO Group calls "the largest detention/correctional facility under private management in the world." The prison, a sprawling complex surrounded by forbidding perimeter fences on the town's deserted southwest edge, holds up to 3,700 prisoners. Almost all are serving time in federal lockup before being deported and are what the Departments of Justice and Homeland Security (DHS) call "criminal aliens."

Although the term "criminal aliens" has no precise definition, its broadening use reflects a trend in dealing with immigrants. With the post-9/11 creation of DHS and its two agencies—Immigration and Customs Enforcement (ICE) and Customs and Border Protection (CBP)—a wide sector of aliens increasingly became the focus of joint efforts by immigration and law enforcement officers. ICE's Criminal Alien Program, working with local police, began targeting for deportation both legal and illegal immigrants with criminal records. And CBP's Border Patrol began to turn over illegal border crossers to the justice system for criminal prosecution, instead of, as in the past, simply deporting them. Many criminal aliens are long-term legal residents of the United States and are also the parents, children, or siblings of U.S. citizens and lawful residents.

When the prison started burning again I was in the county clerk's office tracking down the agreements, contracts, and subcontracts that establish the paper foundation of the Reeves County Detention Complex, the oldest county-owned immigrant prison, constructed as a speculative venture and opened in 1988. Over the past eight years, immigration prisons such as Reeves have boomed along the border in Texas, New Mexico, and Arizona. Some hold ICE detainees, some U.S. Marshals Service (USMS) detainees, and others, like the one in Reeves, prisoners of the Federal Bureau of Prisons (BOP). But in the nine months I traveled along the Southwest border visiting eleven prison towns, all the prisons I saw had two common features: they were managed and operated by private-prison corporations—including two of the world's largest, Corrections Corporation of America (CCA) and GEO—and they were located in remote, rural areas, invariably described by locals as being "in the middle of nowhere."

These immigration prisons constitute the new face of imprisonment in America: the speculative public-private prison, publicly owned by local governments, privately operated by corporations, publicly financed by tax-exempt bonds, and located in depressed communities. Because they rely on project revenue instead of tax revenue, these prisons do not need voter approval. Instead they are marketed by prison consultants to municipal and county governments as economic-development tools promising job creation and new revenue without new taxes. The possibility of riots usually goes unmentioned.

Sirens blared outside the Complex as an array of law enforcement forces—county deputies, city police, Border Patrol agents, state police, and GEO's own security guards—rushed toward it. Inmates had set fire to a housing unit this time. David Galindo, Jesus's brother, told a reporter, "They're afraid somebody might die there again." According to one inmate, jailors placed a detainee, twenty-five-year-old Ramon Garcia, in solitary confinement after he complained of dizziness and feeling ill. "All we wanted was for them to give him medical care and because they didn't, things got out of control and people started fires in several offices," said the inmate, who declined to give his name for fear of reprisals by officials.

As smoke billowed up from the prison on that early February morning, officials and staff at the county building expressed more resentment than concern. Florez complained that the inmates can count on three meals a day and a television to watch while they idle their time away. Not to mention that their rent and electricity bills get paid, while Pecos residents have to work every day to make ends meet. (In September 2009 the unemployment rate in Reeves County—whose 13,300 residents have a per capita income of $10,800 a year—topped 14 percent.) Others worried for the jobs of more than 400 county residents who worked at the prison and the cost of repairing the damaged buildings.

"You can be sure that we will be paying for it," lamented one county employee.

·   ·   ·

The Pecos of the mythical Pecos Bill and the "Home of the World's First Rodeo" was a famous cowboy crossroads where the Pecos River met the Butterfield Route, Chisholm Trail, and Loving-Goodnight Trail. In the late 1800s, rowdy saloons began giving way to more wholesome establishments and hotels, and Pecos became a major transportation hub with the arrival of the Texas and Pacific Railroad. For almost a century, a progression of railway men, cotton farmers, ranchers, oil riggers, wildcatters, and B-1 pilots filled the streets.

But the oil riggers and wildcatters began leaving town in the early 1980s. Except for the county courthouse, the sheriff's office, and a few remaining retail stores, downtown Pecos is now dead. The old railway depots are shut down; the Santa Fe depot was sold off for its aged bricks and timber to a steak house in Odessa, an hour down the interstate. With the railroad companies long since gone and ranching, cotton, and oil booms collapsing, Pecos is valued today not as a transportation and distribution center but rather for its isolation and economic desperation.

Debbie Thomas, curator of the West of the Pecos Museum (commonly known as the cowboy museum), sighs when asked about the town's only steady business over the past two decades. "Well, we don't want to be known as a prison town, but it's better than being a ghost town," she says.

In 1985 Reeves County became the first of a few dozen Texas counties to get into the speculative prison business, when Judge

Jimmy Galindo (no relation to Jesus Manuel Galindo) persuaded the County Commissioners Court to take a bold step for Pecos's economic future. At the time, Judge Galindo and other county leaders argued that Pecos could cash in on the surge in incarceration rates that accompanied the war on drugs. Years later, for the prison's two expansions, the county and the private operators would rely on the federal government to send them immigrant inmates.

Indeed, immigrant detention has been central to the growth of the "privates" for more than two decades. The Immigration and Naturalization Service's (INS) 1983 decision to outsource immigrant detention to the newly established Corrections Corporation of America gave birth to the private-prison industry; GEO Group (formerly Wackenhut) got its start imprisoning immigrants in the late 1980s.

While the nation's nonimmigrant prison population has recently leveled off, the number of immigrants in ICE (formerly INS) detention has increased fivefold since the mid-1990s, and continues year after year to reach record highs. Assuming current trends hold, ICE will detain more than 400,000 immigrants in 2009.

The federal government's escalating demand for immigrant prison beds saved CCA and other privates that had overbuilt speculative prisons. Over the past eight years, the prison giants CCA ($1.6 billion in annual revenue) and GEO Group ($1.1 billion) have racked up record profits, with jumps in revenue and profits roughly paralleling the rising numbers of detained immigrants.

Initially, most speculative prisons were privately owned, a case of the federal government outsourcing its responsibilities. But prison outsourcing is rarely that simple anymore. The private-prison industry increasingly works with local governments to establish and operate speculative prisons. Prison-town officials have a mantra: "If you build a prison the prisoners will come."

Most of the time, these public-private prisons are speculative ventures only for bondholders and local governments, because agreements signed with federal agencies do not guarantee prisoners. For the privates, risks are low and the rewards large. Usually paid a set fee by local governments to operate prisons, management companies have no capital investment and lose little, other than hefty monthly fees, if inmate flows from the federal government decline or stop.

Prisons are owned by local governments, but local oversight of finances is rare, and the condition of prisoners is often ignored. Inmates such as those in Pecos are technically in the custody of the federal government, but they are in fact in the custody of corporations with little or no federal supervision. So labyrinthine are the contracting and financing arrangements that there are no clear pathways to determine responsibility and accountability. Yet every contract provides an obvious and unimpeded flow of money to the private industry and consultants.

In the case of immigration prisons, BOP, USMS, and ICE sign intergovernmental agreements and contracts with local governments, generally in remote, economically deprived communities. A prison consultancy such as Innovative Government Strategies (IGS), a Texas- based firm that specializes in selling private-prison projects to rural governments, coordinates the deal.

Most often, a team of private-prison intermediaries—bond brokers, design and construction firms, law firms—are brought together by the consultancy, which is fronting for a prison-management consultancy. The consultant and these private clients plant the idea of prison-led development with one or two key community officials, and then wine, dine, and fly them around to other prisons to sell and seal the deal. The lead official promotes the project in the community as his or her brainchild.

Once other county commissioners are also persuaded by the grand promises of prison-led development, the county commission sets up a paper "public facility corporation" for the sole purpose of issuing so-called project revenue bonds—secured not by the general revenues of the issuing government but by those from the bond-financed project—to fund the prison. This corporation then leases the project back to the county government, which signs an agreement with a federal agency that authorizes it to hold federal prisoners. The county, in turn, subcontracts the responsibility for managing and operating to the private-prison firm represented by the consultant. In many cases the rural government also subcontracts responsibility for medical services to a provider specializing in "correctional health services."

Project revenues are the per diems paid by the feds—BOP, USMS, or ICE—or by the corrections departments of the state governments. In the case of ICE, these per diems now average $87 for every "man day." But since the bondholders own the prison, the payments go not to the county but to a trustee established to manage the payments to the bondholders and all other parties in the prison project—county, consultants, builders, and prison operator.

County governments see a new revenue stream from the federal per diem—usually a mere $1–2 a day per inmate, depending on the terms of the agreement with the prison operator—but only after the bondholders and private operator have been paid. The privates receive hefty operating fees (normally $500,000–$750,000 a month) and salaries for their administrative team of wardens and assistants, while assuming none of the capital, operating, or maintenance costs. Because the prisons are public facilities, communities receive no property or sales tax revenue (from construction and maintenance) but are expected to provide the water and sewage services.

In Hudspeth County, Texas Judge Becky Dean-Walker signs the agreements and contracts that have, since 2003, made Sierra Blanca an immigrant prison-town. Situated ninety miles from El Paso, Sierra Blanca, population 650, hosts the West Texas

Detention Facility, a 500-bed immigrant prison with another 500 still-unoccupied beds in three adjoining structures awaiting overflow. The prison, a public-private complex, is owned by bond-holders until 2025.

In establishing the prison on the edge of town, Hudspeth, where one in three families survives under the poverty line, incurred a $23.5 million debt in revenue bonds. Six years after the prison opened for business, the county still has a debt of $21.8 million. According to the Texas Bond Review Board, the remaining principal on the prison bonds translates into a per capita debt ratio—debt divided by population—higher than the county's annual per capita income of $9,549, which is one of the lowest in the nation.

Emerald Corrections, a Shreveport, Louisiana–based corrections management company, and its intermediaries promoted the prison as an economic-development project, promising jobs and income growth. But only a few locals work at the facility, with most employees bused every morning from El Paso.

When the bonds mature in 2025, the facility will be a badly depreciated investment, a community eyesore, and a reminder of the delusional dreams of prison-based economic development. This is true in many parts of Texas, such as Encinal, a town even poorer than Sierra Blanca, with its very own Emerald-operated prison thanks to an identical arrangement of consultancies, bond brokers, contractors, and county officials. IGS walked away with a reported $700,000 in consultancy fees.

Bill Addington, who lives within easy sight of the prison in Sierra Blanca and who opposed the prison proposal, said the prison was approved by the county without any involvement in or specific knowledge of the bond agreement or operating agreements. In fact, no one in county government could find the agreement with USMS or the bond-issuing statement, or even remember their details.

Hudspeth is hardly alone in this regard. Local governments typically do not have anyone to keep track of the complex prison business—a high-finance enterprise involving tens of millions of dollars in bonds (more than $130 million in Reeves County) and millions of dollars in annual federal payments. Not only had contracts seemingly disappeared in the counties I visited, none could locate a full accounting of prison-related expenses and income.

At a public meeting to consider the proposal for the first immigrant prison in Otero County, New Mexico, county resident George Bussing captured the confusion. "I'm smarter than most average bears," he said, "but I honestly don't understand what I'm reading here."

Despite dubious benefits to local economies, new prisons continue to spring up. District chairman Austin Nuñez of the Tohono O'odham Nation is planning to use tax-exempt project revenue bonds to finance a prison for immigrants on tribal land south of Tucson, in the district of San Xavier. He describes it as an "economic-development project" that will bring jobs and revenue to this poor Native American community that spans the U.S.-Mexico border.

IGS is making the necessary arrangements. All the San Xavier District has to do is sign a contract agreeing to subcontract its imprisonment authority to a private-prison company.

The same team of private-prison intermediaries that interested the Tohono O'odham community in prison-based economic development also enticed a poor community in Montana. Two years after construction—with most of the bond fund depleted from payouts to the prison consultants, design and construction firms, and bond underwriters—the prison in Hardin, Montana, stands empty, and the local development authority that issued the bonds has defaulted and is pleading with the Obama administration to consider holding Guantánamo Bay detainees there.

There is no paper trail that explains how these speculative prisons secure federal contracts. But like most scenarios in which public governance meets private business, the partnerships are usually the product of connections and influence, highly paid friends in the right places.

That was the case in 2004 when Judge Galindo overrode the objections of a Reeves County auditor in his bid to hire Public-Private Strategies Consulting to represent the interests of the Reeves County Detention Center to the BOP. The firm's president, Randy DeLay, charged $120,000 a year plus expenses, but hiring him may have made good political sense. Randy's famous last name is no coincidence—his brother Tom, the Texas Republican, was the House majority leader at the time. Reeves County secured one of four BOP prison contracts for detaining criminal aliens the following year. Judge Galindo was unequivocal about Randy DeLay's usefulness, arguing that he was able to get meetings with people in Washington: "I think it's vital that we have a direct line into the inner workings," Galindo told the Commissioners Court.

•   •   •

Though speculative prisons come with no guarantees, all along the Southwest border—from Florence, Arizona, to Raymondville, Texas—business is good. Since early 2003, the criminal justice and immigration enforcement systems have merged, breaking the long-standing tradition of treating immigration violations as administrative offenses and creating hundreds of thousands of new criminal aliens.

While the growth in immigrant detention is in part due to the country's increased immigrant population, the shift in immigration policy away from regulation and toward enforcement, punishment, and deterrence is more significant. Unwilling to pass a reform bill that would effectively regulate immigration,

Congress and the executive branch have turned to the criminal justice and penal systems.

New anti-immigrant laws and practices by ICE and CBP subject immigrants, legal or illegal, to double jeopardy, punishing them twice for the same offense. In 1996 the Republican majority in Congress led approval of three anti-immigrant and anti-crime laws that spurred INS to start cracking down on and deporting immigrants. These laws, together with the executive branch's increased authority to devise repressive immigration procedures under the post-9/11 pretext of a war on terror, have created an enforcement regime in which noncitizen legal immigrants face immigration consequences (as well as criminal consequences) for past or present violations of criminal law. In other words, illegal immigrants and even noncitizen permanent residents may be jailed and deported for committing crimes or other offenses, whether violent or not. DHS and the Justice Department are not only combing the criminal justice system for legal and illegal immigrants to be detained and deported, but the departments are also working together to transfer illegal immigrants into federal courts and prisons.

Legal scholars have taken to calling this increasing merger of criminal and immigration law and the integration of the criminal justice and immigration systems "crimmigration."

The private-prison industry's executives are particularly upbeat about new criminal alien programs such as CBP's Operation Streamline and ICE's Secure Communities. GEO chairman George Zoley told Wall Street analysts in a July 2009 investment conference call: "The main driver for the growth of new beds at the federal level continues to be the detention and incarceration of criminal aliens." CCA's chief financial officer, Todd Mullenger, emphasized the importance of programs such as Operation Streamline to prison profits in a recent investment conference call:

> Border Patrol has consistently indicated from the planning
> stage of the initiative to the present that Operation Stream-
> line will require additional detain beds due to increased
> prosecution and length of stay anticipated by the initiative.

Operation Streamline was launched in 2005 as a pilot project
of the Del Rio sector of Texas and extends east to the southern
Rio Grande Valley and west to Yuma, Arizona. It is part of a
national immigrant crackdown that CBP and ICE variously call
"enhanced enforcement" and "zero tolerance." The program di-
rects Border Patrol agents to turn captured illegal border crossers over to the Marshals Service for prosecution, breaking with
the usual practice of simply returning Mexican immigrants to
Mexico or releasing non-Mexican immigrants with an order to
appear in immigration court.

A few mornings each week, detainees pack the federal courtroom in Del Rio, Texas, where they plead guilty to illegal entry
and are sentenced as criminals. The scene in Judge Dennis Green's
chamber is replicated along much of the border. While the
courtroom is quickly filling, Del Rio's nearby Main Street, which
once bustled with shoppers from Ciudad Acuña across the river,
is quiet, lined with empty and closed stores.

More than four dozen young men and eight young women
shuffle into the courtroom on April 17, 2009, occupying the
seats normally reserved for visitors and family members. Only
at the last minute do the security guards allow me in, after determining that the back row will not be occupied by the day's crowd
of criminal aliens.

The clinking of chains fills the room as the accused are ushered into their seats. Handcuffed, chained from waist to ankles,
they stand then sit in uniform when ordered by the attending
U.S. marshals.

The scene was shocking the first time, but now I have witnessed it in three courts of justice in the borderlands: shackled

immigrants filling up the courtrooms, and then, after an hour or two, shuffling out, where they are taken back to USMS detention centers or a BOP prison. At first I wondered if their laceless running shoes and work boots, with their tongues hanging loose, were a new style for young Mexicans. But later I understood that the marshals obligated them to surrender the laces (as possible weapons or suicide instruments) and that this, not the chains, explains why they walk without lifting their feet out of their shoes.

At these mass convictions and sentencings, I was in a small minority. The judges, the marshals, the lawyers, the security guards, and me—all white and older, with jobs and homes. And them: criminal aliens, all young and lean, most with strong arms and calloused hands, all with black hair and weathered brown skin. These courtrooms are where the South encounters the North, where the exclusionary institutions on one side of the global economic divide collide with collective desperation on the other. The power imbalance, so starkly visible, is startling.

· · ·

Before starting the overland journey north—sometimes from as far as Honduras, El Salvador, and Guatemala—each immigrant understood that he or she was an economic castoff, marginalized by national and global economic forces. But each hoped that the United States would be what so many claim: the land of opportunity, where class and circumstances are no barrier to economic security, as long as you are willing to work hard.

Judge Green enters—"All rise," intones the court sergeant at arms, and the immigrants stand up in unison, following the Spanish-language echo of their bilingual courtroom manager.

Over the past day or two, each prisoner has told his or her story in a few minutes to a paralegal who has organized a two-sentence defense.

Unlike the U.S. criminal justice system, immigration law provides no guarantees that all accused have the right to a court-appointed lawyer. Those facing criminal charges in federal court for immigration violations, however, do get free legal defense, but it is pro forma—a windfall for many regional attorneys who thrive on government fees for nominal defense work. The attorney representing the immigrants on April 17 in Del Rio was applauded publicly that day by the sitting judge for having recently been appointed to take his place on the bench. (Judge Green's congratulatory comment went untranslated.)

One by one, the defendants are escorted to the front of the court. A CBP lawyer tells the judge that the accused has crossed the border between the ports of entry without inspection (violating Title 8 USC 1325) and recounts any previous record of illegal entry or criminal conviction.

More than fifty individual criminal hearings are streamlined—a possible explanation of the operation's name—with the same judge, same public defender, and same outcome: guilty as charged and remanded for incarceration.

Before each case is heard and before each defendant is sentenced, Judge Green asks them en masse if they have had time to consult their attorney, if they have been forced or threatened to plead guilty, if they have knowingly violated the laws of the United States of America by crossing without inspection. They reply in a chorus of "*Sí*" and "*No*," bringing to mind an elementary school classroom.

Could one gather a group of unfamiliar U.S. citizens and see such cooperation, such compliance?

As each faces the judge, their collective defense attorney reads from a sheet his assistant has prepared with the abbreviated stories and pleas for mercy from this mass of immigrants.

No one has more than an eighth-grade education, three out of four cite medical emergencies, all crossed to seek work and food, and many hoped to reunite with families that need them.

Story after abbreviated story of fathers, mothers, wives, and children with brain tumors, heart conditions, crippling accidents, no work, and little to eat.

Judge Green occasionally expresses sympathy, encourages them to secure a visa the next time they want to come to the United States—a near impossibility for Latin Americans with no bank accounts and no property and utterly out of the question for these detainees, imprisoned and eventually deported for illegal entry—and then asks if they are guilty of breaking the laws of this country by entering without permission. One after another they say, "culpable" or "guilty."

Before sentencing, the judge warns those who have never been previously deported that they will be judged felons if they are caught in the future. Depending on the time they have already spent in jail, they are sentenced up to twelve days. Those with a record of previous illegal crossings get harsher sentences, routinely as much as 180 days and sometimes several years. Although the charge is always illegal entry or reentry, the sentence varies based on the number of illegal entries, whether the charged immigrant has a criminal record, and the judge's discretion.

The defense attorney and government prosecutors pack up their papers and leave the courtroom. Any hope on the part of an immigrant that the judge would find mercy is now dashed. Ordered to stand, the convicted and sentenced immigrants rise in unison, and, row by row, exit the courtroom, feet dragging in their laceless shoes. It's back to the GEO prison whence they came that morning.

Between apprehension and removal, an unauthorized immigrant who is criminally prosecuted is technically in the custody of, first, CBP or ICE, then the Marshals Service, and finally BOP or the Marshals Service again. Depending on how long it takes ICE to prepare the removal papers and to present its case before the DOJ's immigration court, immigrants may spend anywhere from a week to several years in detention before being deported.

With its staggering administrative, legal, and detention costs, Operation Streamline is certainly not quick and easy. But Operation Streamline is less about law than strategy. The idea is that, having suffered the humiliation of being branded a criminal and spending time in prison, these immigrants will not come back once deported and will tell others that the price of immigration is too high. As DHS Secretary Michael Chertoff explained in 2006, "We are working to get [Operation Streamline] expanded across other parts of the border" because "it has a great deterrent effect."

Measured by the number of immigrants apprehended in the Del Rio sector and others, immigration flows have decreased markedly, although no one can say to what extent the drop is a result of deterrence as opposed to recession. But nearly three years after the program's initiation, immigrants keep crossing the river at Del Rio. What strategy of deterrence could stop those forced to leave their families from attempting, even at the risk of increased jail time, to return to their loved ones back home in the United States?

.   .   .

Jesus Manuel Galindo, a native of Ciudad Juárez, had compelling reasons to come to the United States. His parents, originally from the Mexican state of Chihuahua, are both legal U.S. residents. They live in the border *colonia* of Anthony, New Mexico, just outside El Paso. They obtained legal residency for their younger son and daughter, and were in the process of getting papers for Jesus, their oldest. According to them, it was easier to get papers for younger children.

Jesus was twice married to legal U.S. residents; his children are American citizens.

In 2006 Jesus was picked up by the police when he had a seizure at a convenience store. When the deputies checked his records and saw that he had no legal status, they turned him over to immigration officials. He was deported to Juárez, where he remained a month or so, determined to come back to his second wife and children.

According to his mother, Graciela, he had the *"mala suerte,"* bad luck, to be caught by the Border Patrol. In the past the Border Patrol had just sent him back to Juárez. This time, he went first to the Otero County Prison Facility, and then spent three months in Sierra Blanca before being sent to Reeves County Detention Complex. Although he was convicted only of illegal entry, Galindo was sentenced to thirty months under a system of "penalty enhancement" that allows judges to add time for past crimes—in Galindo's case, writing a hot check (for which he had already spent time in other Texas prisons) and contacting his ex-wife in violation of a restraining order—even if prior sentences were served.

Graciela said he had been working hard at Sierra Blanca in the laundry trying to reduce his time for good behavior, but it did not count for anything. He did the same thing at Reeves until prison administrators told him he could no longer work because of his seizures.

On December 11 he wrote to his mother:

> Don't despair. . . . But tell the investigator [a paralegal sent by federal public defenders] that I get sick here by being locked up all by myself. They don't even know and I am all bruised up [from falling and thrashing during seizures]. . . . Tell the investigator that the medical care in here is no good and that I'm scared. Well, mom, I love you very much. I will write you on Monday. Kisses to everyone.

On the morning of December 12, Graciela called the prison to see how he was. "They didn't want to talk to me. But I kept calling and then they told me that my son was dead."

El Paso attorney Miguel Torres, who is preparing a wrongful death suit on behalf of Galindo's wife, three children, and parents, calls Galindo's death a "quintessentially avoidable tragedy." The suit will likely be filed against GEO, Reeves County, and Physicians Network Association (PNA), the contractor responsible for providing medical services at the Complex. According to Torres, both Graciela and fellow inmates repeatedly urged prison officials to give Galindo his medication and to get him out of the security housing unit (SHU)—solitary confinement—where he had been placed for medical observation in November after an emergency stay at an area hospital due to a severe seizure. Graciela mailed the prison her son's medical records, but they sent them back, instructing her not to send them again.

"The doctor said Jesus had an attitude problem because he was complaining about the lack of medical treatment that killed him three days later," Torres told a reporter. "When they found him at 7 A.M., December 12, rigor mortis had set in, which meant he had been dead for three to five hours."

Galindo's father broke down as he discussed the conditions in which his son was kept:

> We don't understand how there can be so little humanity there in the prison. Animals aren't even treated as badly as they treated our son, keeping him locked up in the hole so sick and without any company. It was so cruel, and he died sick and afraid.

In fact, lockdown in the SHU was Reeves's policy for all ailing inmates. The prison does not have an infirmary. After the riots, BOP requested that one be built as part of the prison reconstruction and upgrade. At a public discussion, County Judge Sam Contreras explained why the $1.8 million outlay was needed: "[The lack of infirmary beds is] what caused the disturbance—because [prisoners] were placed in the SHU when they didn't do nothing wrong. They are just sick."

Galindo is not the only casualty of a toxic mix of crackdown policies and a burgeoning public-private-prison complex. At least 104 immigrants have died in ICE custody since 2003. Given the lack of oversight and legal protections, the gains to be made from cost-cutting, and the apathy surrounding prisoner well-being, these deaths are predictable. Indeed, the county awarded the medical care subcontract to PNA primarily because the medical services provider boasted that it would reduce the county's expenses by cutting back on prescriptions, medical tests, and outside medical visits. And in this regard, according to former Reeves warden Rudy Franco, PNA did not fail.

. . .

PNA is the brainchild of a Lubbock, Texas physician, Vernon Farthing. In 1991, after working as a contract doctor for Lubbock's county jail, Farthing started PNA, which he calls "a leader in correctional healthcare."

From his base in Lubbock, Farthing oversees operations in dozens of prisons in Texas, Arizona, and New Mexico. PNA and prison operator Management and Training Corporation (MTC) were the subjects of a federal civil rights investigation into conditions at Santa Fe County Detention Center, which houses a large population of Native American inmates. The investigation was sparked by the suicide of pre-trial inmate Tyson Johnson, who suffered from severe claustrophobia and other mental illnesses.

In its report the Justice Department specified fifty-two actions needed "to rectify the identified deficiencies and to protect the constitutional rights of the facility's inmates to bring the jail into compliance with civil rights standards." Thirty-eight of the fifty-two identified deficiencies related to medical services. According to the report, the Detention Center, through PNA, provides inadequate medical services in the following areas: intake, screening, and referral; acute care; emergent care; chronic and prenatal care; and medication administration and management. As a result, inmates at the Detention Center with serious medical needs are at risk for harm.

In a story on the investigation, Suzan Garcia, Johnson's mother, explained that she had tried to contact the jail because she was concerned about her son's psychological condition. "I called the jail and asked to speak to a doctor, but they said they didn't have a doctor," Garcia said. "When I asked to speak to the warden, they just put me on hold and then the phone would disconnect."

According to the Justice Department's findings and associated reports, Johnson had asked to see a psychologist, but the 580-inmate jail did not have one. Johnson was placed in solitary confinement, and managed to hang himself from a sprinkler head in his windowless cell.

Soon after the Justice Department released the results of its investigation, PNA pulled out of its subcontract with MTC, claiming it could not continue because it was losing money. Within a year, MTC terminated its contract with the county, also claiming it was losing money.

Three years later, when seeking to renew its Reeves County contract, PNA submitted what was at best a misleading statement about its history of providing correctional health care. PNA told the county commission that it was "proud of its record of no substantiated grievances in any facility" and that it had "never had a contract canceled or been removed from a facility."

The riots at Reeves brought PNA's medical services to the attention of the Austin-based advocacy group Grassroots Leadership as well as the American Civil Liberties Union of Texas, both of which are now focusing on reform efforts. When asked about the liability that Reeves County may face if the inmates take their cases to court, County Attorney Alma Alvarez said she was not worried, noting that GEO and PNA had recently secured accreditation for the prison from both the American Correctional Association (ACA) and the Joint Commission on Accreditation of Healthcare Organizations. After visiting the prison herself, she said she was confident that the medical care was up to or above standards. She acknowledged, however, that she never spoke to any of the inmates about the quality of medical care, only to the administration.

Concerning the prisoner complaints made during the riots, Alvarez said, "They want to be media stars. They call the media from their cell phones and tell these stories because they want to be famous. It's like they want to be on *American Idol*."

A framed certificate of achievement from the ACA hangs on the wall of the prison's lobby. Awarded exactly a month after the December 12 riot, it honors the prison for "the attainment of excellence in adult correctional care."

Sheriff Andy Gomez said of Galindo's death, "We investigate all the deaths in the prison, but I can't remember every one." And Gomez summed up a common sentiment in Reeves County when it comes to prisoners' grievances about denial of medical attention: "These guys are criminals," he said. "They need to realize that they are in jail."

·　　·　　·

Soon after opening its first immigrant prison, MTC named Otero County Administrator Ruth Hooser a "Community Supporter of the Year," describing her as "The Best of the Best" and placing her among the most appreciated public officials involved in eleven MTC correctional operations in the United States, Australia, and Canada. In accepting the award, Hooser said, "I just kept pushing and helping with whatever they needed."

County officials play the role of smart economic developers and prison companies respond with accolades and awards. The mutual admiration is on display in the waiting rooms of the prisons, where plaques from local chambers of commerce praising companies' civic virtues, statements of appreciation from the high school marching band or football team, and award certificates from the prison operators plaster the walls. At least in prison towns along the border, there is nearly universal agreement that the prison business is like any other.

Yet, while most government officials passively accept the conditions of the prison deals, and hardly anyone harbors moral or ethical reservations about the business, in some towns, including Pecos, locals grumble that they should be getting a greater share of the revenue. In Reeves County, many believe that the county could do a better job of running the prison than GEO.

"We pay the same management fees and salaries to GEO no matter how many inmates are out there," said County Treasurer Linda Clark, who bemoaned the multiple riots and the millions paid GEO. County Auditor Lynn Owens observed that GEO has never received a merit-based increase in federal per diem payments, and both officials agreed that the county should be in charge at the Detention Center.

The prison industry occasionally runs into resident opposition of the not-in-my-backyard sort. In Otero County, residents of Alamogordo blocked a proposed GEO immigrant prison because the intended site was within the city limits. Several years later, a new proposal from MTC for a USMS immigrant prison seventy miles away on the far south side of the county was approved by the Otero County Commission with little protest. The county liked the business—a half-dollar a day per immigrant in the 630-bed prison—so much that it signed on with MTC in 2008 to build an ICE-fed, 1,100-bed detention center next to the existing prison.

Poverty partly explains the willingness to scrape a couple of dollars off federal per diem payments and in the process incur massive bond debt. The prison industry introduces the governments of desperate communities to what some call "backdoor financing": project revenue bonds in the tens of millions of dollars that suddenly make them feel like economic players.

Since funding is provided by project revenue bonds rather than general obligation bonds, the county faces no direct liability if the speculative prison fails. "Money for nothing" is a common refrain when county officers are asked about the advisability of prison deals. This answer, however, is as naïve as it sounds. Even though the bondholders cannot hold the issuing government responsible if the speculative prison fails, there are still real costs, as Reeves County is experiencing.

Its overall bond rating was downgraded in 2003 when the prison expansion went unfilled, and now, as residents and local officials predicted, the county must cover millions in repairs in the wake of the prisoner protests.

The full cost of the public-private immigrant prisons that now litter the Southwest and elsewhere is not yet known. Most counties and municipalities are still ten to fifteen years away from paying off the bonds. But poor rural governments worried that they may have been snookered into the prison business have some options. Last year Haskell County, Texas, sold its Rolling Plains Regional Jail & Detention Center for immigrants to the Inland Real Estate Group, a Chicago-based holding company specializing in shopping malls and government properties.

Beyond the false hopes and corporate greed that build immigrant prisons, their expansion, like that of other prisons that have mushroomed across the rural United States, seems fueled by something both sinister and uniquely American. The growing divide between citizens and immigrants is only partially responsible for what has befallen this new class of inmates. A wider sensibility about prisoners is also at work. The men and women held behind the perimeter fences are never seen, never discussed. The prison is treated as a waste dump, similarly placed on the community's edge, where property values are low and there are no neighbors. The prisoners themselves are society's refuse, its discards, outcasts, and outsiders who have lost their membership rights in the human community.

.   .   .

The United States's high incarceration rate—fives times greater than the average rate in the rest of the world—is evidence, says Virginia Democratic senator Jim Webb, that we are "doing something dramatically wrong in our criminal justice system." Senator Webb apparently sees no contradiction in advocating an end to mass incarceration while supporting legislation calling for increased immigration enforcement and the doubling of immigrant-detention beds.

Since the 1970s crime control has become a central theme in U.S. politics and society. In the words of Berkeley Law professor Jonathan Simon, we are "governing through crime"—isolation and exclusion in an expansive penal system is the dominant response to tough social problems. Although the immigrant crackdown raises its own special concerns, it largely mirrors and merges with the broader wars on drugs and crime in terms of increasing costs, expanding law enforcement, high incarceration rates, and dismal cost-benefit ratios. Immigration, a contentious social issue lacking any easy policy solution, has similarly been addressed through increased enforcement and incarceration.

Given that get-tough models are the basis for our current approach to immigration, it comes as little surprise that, like the war on crime, the immigrant crackdown has flooded the federal courts with nonviolent offenders, besieged poor communities, and dramatically increased the U.S. prison population, while doing little to solve the problem itself.

Enforcement practices like Operation Streamline (and its many cousins: Operation Jump Start, Operation Return-to-Sender, Operation Reservation Guaranteed) and such absurdities as the border wall are not the partisan initiatives of restrictionist forces in Congress. The post-9/11 commitments by DHS to "protect America against dangerous people and goods" and to "restore respect for immigration laws" by making immigration enforcement and border patrol "consistent" and "comprehensive" are central to the immigration positions of both major political parties. Indeed, it has been Democrats, such as U.S. Representative David Price of North Carolina, who have led the efforts to extend Operation Streamline and pursue criminal aliens. Visiting Del Rio, Price, who chairs the Homeland Security Subcommittee of the House Appropriations Committee, gushed, "It's just a great model we need to put to use everywhere."

But what works for Washington faces opposition in the trenches. Many of those living on the border are less enthusiastic about a strategy that turns immigrants seeking work into criminal aliens. Courts are clogged, the Marshals Service is severely taxed, and some in the Border Patrol are angered by the idea of sending workers to prison.

"This [criminalization] strategy pretty much has it backwards," T. J. Bonner, president of the National Border Patrol Council told the *Washington Post*. "It's going after desperate people who are crossing the border in search of a better way of life, instead of going after employers who are hiring people who have no right to work in this country."

In the same article, Heather Williams, first assistant to the federal public defender of Arizona, complained about "misdirection of resources," pointing out that the criminal crackdown on immigrants diverts attention from real crimes.

Williams also questions the fairness of the program. "[If U.S. citizens] were placed in any other country on the planet, and had to resolve a case in a day that could result in being deported and having a criminal record, we would be outraged, and so would our government," she said.

Federal prosecutions for immigration violations have steadily climbed. In June 2009, immigration accounted for 55 percent of federal prosecutions. Sixty-one percent of prosecutions referred to the Justice Department that month originated at DHS. The judicial districts with the highest number of prosecutions in June were all on the border: Southern California, New Mexico, west Texas, south Texas, and Arizona.

Thus far, immigration prosecutions in 2009 outpace those of 2008 by 14 percent. Prosecutions are up 139 percent compared to five years ago, 459 percent compared to 1999, and 973 percent compared to 1989.

The Obama administration has done nothing to stop this flood of prosecutions or contest the misperception that immigrants are disproportionately responsible for crime. Instead it has embraced Secure Communities, a new criminal aliens program; extended federal-local cooperation in immigration enforcement through the notorious 287(g) program, which allows DHS to delegate immigrant-detention authority to local law enforcement; and responded to alarmist calls about purported spillover violence from drug wars in Mexico by deploying more U.S. marshals, ICE agents, and federal prosecutors to the border.

Rather than rejecting the immigration enforcement regime installed during the Bush administration, Obama has finessed the existing system, which remains in full effect. Since 2003 the combined budgets of CBP and ICE have more than doubled, rising from $7.4 billion to $14.9 billion in 2009, with $17.2 billion requested for 2010. Companies such as CCA and GEO—and their subcontractors, including PNA—will see continuing profit, as federal immigrant-detention, imprisonment, and correctional services contracts account for 40 percent of their revenues.

.   .   .

Concern for immigrant rights and the deplorable, largely un-regulated conditions at public-private immigrant prisons may lead to better oversight. This past summer ICE announced a "major overhaul" of the detention system, including the creation of an Office of Detention Planning and Policy. However, while committing the agency to increased oversight of the nearly 400 facilities where immigrants are held for processing and deporta-tion, ICE director John Morton said that the numbers of detain-ees would not decrease and that the agency had no plans to end its relationships with its many partners in state and local gov-ernment and with prison contractors. Morton refused to sup-port legally binding and enforceable minimum standards for immigrant- detention centers, sorely disappointing immigrant-rights and prison-reform advocates.

Nor did recent announcements from DHS include any plan to review the ICE practices that drive the demand for immigrant prison beds. There is every indication that DHS will continue to criminalize immigration through ever-more expansive local-federal cooperation in immigration enforcement and by prose-cuting immigrants twice for crimes, once in criminal court and again in immigration court. These practices have not fueled only the growth of the ICE detention system, they have also sparked a dramatic expansion of USMS and BOP detention regimes, over which DHS exercises no direct authority. The failure of DHS and the White House to address the full range of players involved in immigrant detention indicates that the promised overhaul of the patchwork system will be no such thing.

The Obama administration has deftly deflected ethical argu-ments against mass detention with liberal rule-of-law logic. DHS, it argues, is simply upholding the rule of law by consis-tently and wholeheartedly enforcing immigration statutes and securing the border. Rather than echoing or shadowing the ideo-logical restrictionism of the right, as the Bush administration did, the Obama administration argues that enforcement-first immigration policy will establish the political foundation for immigration reform. But there is no sign yet that the administration or the Democratic leadership are willing to lead the way toward durable immigration reform that would address both the future structure of immigration and the failures of the existing immigration system.

Such a reform should be based on measurements of how immigration flows affect existing wages. Armed with these benchmarks, we can establish how much new immigration is sustainable. The goal is both to ensure that new immigration will not undermine wages or working conditions in the U.S. labor force, and, at the same time, to allow American society and the economy to benefit from regulated flows of unskilled and skilled labor. Reforms would need to account for unauthorized immigrants who for many years were tolerated or even welcomed in the United States. These immigrants and their families have integrated into this country, and should now be accorded a path to citizenship.

As the immigrant crackdown continues, hundreds of thousands of immigrants like Jesus Manuel Galindo will be caught in the profit-driven public-private-prison complex. In the end though, the human cost of the system is unlikely to bring it down. It may only be when citizens and politicians start questioning the financial cost of incarcerating immigrants that these public-private prisons will go bust.

Meanwhile, the twenty-six inmates identified by GEO as having been involved in the riot following Galindo's death will spend an additional year in detention. After the initial April 2009 count against them failed to elicit guilty pleas—there was little hard evidence—the U.S. Attorney's office added another count to the indictment under an obscure statute requiring a mandatory ten-year sentence for the use of fire in the commission of a federal crime. Under threat, all plead guilty to the first charge. More than one hundred inmates will be indicted for the second riot.

Reeves County recently approved another $15.5 million in project revenue bonds to pay for prison repairs and upgrades that will not be covered by insurance. If the county does not make the costly improvements, it may lose its BOP contract to imprison criminal aliens. County Attorney Alvarez knows what is at stake. "Without that prison," she told the Commissioners Court, "basically, Reeves County is going under."

Wired

FINALIST—FEATURE
WRITING

Who hasn't thought about running away, shucking responsibility, just plain disappearing? It's an American thing, as Huckleberry Finn says, "to light out for the Territory ahead of the rest." Or as we might say today, to drop off the grid. Evan Ratliff tried. This well-told narrative chronicles a month-long cat-and-computer-mouse game that pitted a resourceful writer against a horde of equally determined social networkers.

Evan Ratliff

Vanish

1

August 13, 6:40 P.M.: I'm driving East out of San Francisco on I-80, fleeing my life under the cover of dusk. Having come to the interstate by a circuitous route, full of quick turns and double backs, I'm reasonably sure that no one is following me. I keep checking the rearview mirror anyway. From this point on, there's no such thing as sure. Being too sure will get me caught.

I had intended to flee in broad daylight, but when you are going on the lam, there are a surprising number of last-minute errands to run. This morning, I picked up a set of professionally designed business cards for my fake company under my fake name, *James Donald Gatz*. I drove to a Best Buy, where I bought two prepaid cell phones with cash and then put a USB cord on my credit card—an arbitrary dollar amount I hoped would confuse investigators, who would scan my bill and wonder what gadgetry I had purchased. An oil change for my car was another head fake. Who would think that a guy about to sell his car would spend $60 at Oil Can Henry's?

I already owned a couple of prepaid phones; I left one of the new ones with my girlfriend and mailed the other to my parents—giving them an untraceable way to contact me in emergencies. I bought some Just for Men beard-and-mustache dye at a drugstore. My final stop was the bank, to draw a $477 cashier's check. It's payment for rent on an anonymous office in Las Vegas, which is where I need to deliver the check by midday tomorrow.

Crossing the Bay Bridge, I glance back for a last nostalgic glimpse of the skyline. Then I reach over, slide the back cover off my cell phone, and pop out the battery. A cell phone with a battery inside is a cell phone that's trackable.

About twenty-five minutes later, as the California Department of Transportation database will record, my green 1999 Honda Civic, California plates 4MUN509, passes through the tollbooth on the far side of the Carquinez Bridge, setting off the FasTrak toll device, and continues east toward Lake Tahoe.

What the digital trail will not reflect is that a few miles past the bridge I pull off the road, detach the FasTrak, and stuff it into the duffle bag in my trunk, where its signal can't be detected. Nor will it note that I then double back on rural roads to I-5 and drive south through the night, cutting east at Bakersfield. There will be no digital record that at 4 A.M. I hit Primm, Nevada, a sad little gambling town about forty minutes from Vegas, where $15 cash gets me a room with a view of a gravel pile.

2

"Author Evan Ratliff Is on the Lam. Locate Him and Win $5,000."

—wired.com/vanish, August 14, 2009 5:38 P.M.

Officially it will be another twenty-four hours before the manhunt begins. That's when *Wired*'s announcement of my disappearance will be posted online. It coincides with the arrival on newsstands of the September issue of the magazine, which contains a page of mugshot-like photos of me, eyes slightly vacant.

The premise is simple: I will try to vanish for a month and start over under a new identity. *Wired* readers, or whoever else happens upon the chase, will try to find me.

The idea for the contest started with a series of questions, foremost among them: How hard is it to vanish in the digital age? Long fascinated by stories of faked deaths, sudden disappearances, and cat-and-mouse games between investigators and fugitives, I signed on to write a story for *Wired* about people who've tried to end one life and start another. People fret about privacy, but what are the consequences of giving it all up, I wondered. What can investigators glean from all the digital fingerprints we leave behind? You can be anybody you want online, sure, but can you reinvent yourself in real life?

It's one thing to report on the phenomenon of people disappearing. But to really understand it, I figured that I had to try it myself. So I decided to vanish. I would leave behind my loved ones, my home, and my name. I wasn't going off the grid, dropping out to live in a cabin. Rather, I would actually try to drop my life and pick up another.

Wired offered a $5,000 bounty—$3,000 of which would come out of my own pocket—to anyone who could locate me between August 15 and September 15, say the password "fluke," and take my picture. Nicholas Thompson, my editor, would have complete access to information that a private investigator hired to find me might uncover: my real bank accounts, credit cards, phone records, social networking accounts, and e-mail. I'd give Thompson my friends' contact information so he could conduct interviews. He would parcel out my personal details online, available to whichever amateur or professional investigators chose to hunt for me. To add a layer of intrigue, *Wired* hired the puzzle creators at Lone Shark Games to help structure the contest.

I began my planning months in advance. I let my hair and beard grow out, got a motorcycle license, and siphoned off extra cash whenever I visited an ATM, storing it in a hollowed-out book. One day over lunch, a friend from Google suggested software to hide my Internet address—"but all of these things can be broken," he warned—and how best to employ prepaid phones. I learned how to use Visa and American Express gift cards, bought with cash, to make untraceable purchases online. I installed software to mask my Web searches and generated a small notebook's worth of fake e-mail addresses.

I shared my plans with no one, not my girlfriend, not my parents, not my closest friends. Nobody knew the route I was taking out of town, where I was going, or my new name. Not even a hint. If I got caught, it would be by my own mistakes.

Friday afternoon, August 14, I arrive in Vegas wearing a suit and sporting my normal brown hair, a beard, and a pair of rectangular tortoiseshell glasses. Carrying enough electronic equipment to stock a RadioShack, I drive straight to a dreary two-story office complex among the strip malls on South Pecos Road and hand over the cashier's check, securing a tiny windowless office. There I set up two laptops, flip on a webcam to track any activity in the office, and leave.

At CarMax, a used-auto outlet, I then sell my Civic for $3,000. The next day, the first official one of my disappearance, is spent dyeing my hair and goatee jet-black and locking down the security on my laptops—including a third one that I'll carry with me.

At 5 A.M. on Sunday morning, the graveyard shift clerk at the Tropicana hotel hands over my $100 cash deposit, barely looking up. If she had, she might have noticed that the man checking out of room 480—wearing a pair of oversize Harry Potter-style glasses, hazel-colored contact lenses, slicked-back hair, and a belt with $2,000 cash hidden in an underside pocket—bears surprisingly little resemblance to the one who checked in two days before.

3

> wayale *Found #vanish SF apt (http://bit .ly/6yvkR), talked to lady upstairs said he moved to NY. He can't be in NY apt, according to @wired. 8:27 pm aug 17th*
>
> moshi77 *#vanish Evan bought swim trunks for $78, + UPS of $12. 8/10/09 they had a sale on them at gilt.com 8:10 pm Aug 19th*
>
> Xov0x *another address: 166 GERMANIA ST SAN FRANCISCO, CA 94117 middle name Donald? ;) #vanish 8:27 pm Aug 19th*

When Sarah Manello heard from a friend about the search for Ratliff, she couldn't resist. A researcher based in Rochester, New York, Manello had long worked with private investigators, digging up information for defense attorneys and tracking down missing people. She quit a few years ago after growing increasingly dissatisfied with the industry's tactics. But her skills remained intact. The initial question she posted on Twitter, under the handle @menacingpickle, was private investigation 101: What was Ratliff's middle name?

The first trickle of discussion among Manello and other hunters appeared by the morning of August 16, thirty-six hours after news of the hunt was posted on Wired.com. The next day it had grown into a deluge. On Twitter, anonymous users dedicated to Ratliff's pursuit sprouted by the hour: @VanishingAct01, @Find EvanRatliff, @EvanOffGrid, @FinderofEvan, @FindThatMan, among others. They organized around the Twitter tag #vanish, which, when placed in a post, allowed the growing horde of investigators to exchange theories, clues, and questions. They created Web sites and blogs and flyers and even a telephone tip line. A programmer in St. Louis, Michael Toecker, started a Facebook group called "The Search for Evan Ratliff." A week later it would have nearly a thousand members. (A countergroup designed to help Ratliff, founded by a banker in Cincinnati named Rich Reder, garnered a few dozen.)

What drew all these people? Some of them were lured by the $5,000 bounty. Others were intrigued by the technical challenges of online tracking or the thrill of stakeouts. Some felt that a public dare needed to be answered. For many, Ratliff's flight evoked their own fleeting thoughts of starting over. "It was an adventure," says Matty Gilreath, a grant manager at UC San Francisco, referring to the dozens of hours he spent on the pursuit. "I'm grateful for my career. But there are other things I'd like to do, and this brought up a lot of issues about reinventing yourself."

From the *Wired* offices, Thompson began doling out information from Ratliff's accounts onto a blog—starting with the final credit card purchases and the FasTrak data. The would-be hunters dissected it as quickly as Thompson could post it. Using two FedEx tracking numbers from Ratliff's credit card bill, Manello managed, in a few aboveboard telephone calls, to find out where the packages had gone and who had signed for them. Hunters scoured the pictures on Ratliff's Flickr page, writing software code to extract information about the camera used and search for other photos it had taken. They combined the FasTrak data with other clues to build maps of possible routes.

Within days, they knew that Ratliff was a borderline-obsessive U.S. national soccer team fan and a follower of the English team Fulham. That he had celiac disease, a condition under which he ate a diet entirely free of gluten, a protein found in wheat. That he and his girlfriend had bought an apartment in Brooklyn (in fact, the hunters posted a scan of Ratliff's signature from the deed). That he had recently attended a wedding, sporting a beard, in Palo Alto. They knew of his purchases at Best Buy and Oil Can Henry's and bombarded both businesses with calls.

What had started as an exercise in escape quickly became a cross between a massively multiplayer online game and a reality show. A staggeringly large community arose spontaneously, splintered into organized groups, and set to work turning over every rock in Ratliff's life. It topped out at 600 Twitter posts a day. The hunters knew the names of his cat sitter and his mechanic, his favorite authors, his childhood nicknames. They found every article he'd ever written; they found recent videos of him. They discovered and published every address he'd ever had in the U.S., from Atlanta to Hawaii, together with the full name and age of every member of his family.

They discovered almost every available piece of data about Ratliff, in fact, except his current location.

4

The Search for Evan Ratliff Facebook wall

Michael P. Anderson (Dallas / Fort Worth, TX) wrote at 2:21 pm on August 19th, 2009 *Sooooo. If I am trying to disappear wouldn't it make sense to leave a misdirection? I would arrange in advance to have some packages mailed to someplace where I knew that I would not be. Likewise I would make sure that a tab turned up at a local bar somewhere. What we really need to see is an ATM where he takes cash out.*

Michael Toecker wrote at 7:27 pm on August 19th, 2009 *1999 Honda Civic—4MUN509 CA—Don't ask me how I found out, but it's solid and legal.*

If you are looking to launch a disappearance, I cannot recommend any location more highly than a big-city Greyhound bus station. A mode of transportation Americans have seemingly left to the poor and desperate, it reeks of neglect and disdain. But for anonymity in the post-9/11 world—when the words "I'll just need to see a photo ID" are as common as a handshake—bus travel remains a sanctuary untouched by security. At the station in Las Vegas, I paid cash for a ticket under the name

James Gatz, no ID required. Six cramped hours later I was in Los Angeles.

I hopped a city bus to Venice Beach and checked in to 15 Rose, a quaint European-style hostel that I'd found online. The laid-back day manager sympathized with my story of losing my credit cards and driver's license and showed me to a clean, spare room with free Wi-Fi. So began what I thought might be a few pleasant days on the beach: no phone calls to return, no deadlines to hit. Just my new life, stretching leisurely out before me.

When I flipped open my laptop and saw my private information spilling onto the Web, however, I got my first taste of a soon-to-be-permanent state of fitful anxiety. I'd signed up for it, of course. But actually living the new, paranoid reality felt different. Absurd ideas suddenly seemed plausible. They'd contacted my cat sitter; would they kidnap my cat?

Email was choking the inbox of the account Wired had made public, eratliff@atavist.net. Most of the messages consisted of efforts to subtly or not-so-subtly trick me into revealing my location by replying or visiting a Web site designed to trap my Internet protocol (IP) address, which maps to a physical location. I also started getting what I came to think of as little plea bargain offers: "Send me a picture and the code word and I'll split the $5K 50/50."

Fortunately, while I was shocked by the intensity of the pursuit, I had anticipated the tactics. To keep my Web surfing from being tracked I often used a piece of free software called Tor, designed to protect the Internet activities of dissidents and whistleblowers around the world. Tor masks a computer's IP address by diverting its requests through designated routers around the world. So when I logged in to Gmail from IP 131.179.50.72 in Los Angeles, the logs showed my request originating from 192.251.226.206 in Germany.

But as my friend from Google had reminded me, no security is unbreakable, so I'd added another layer: Vegas. I used the laptop I carried with me to log in remotely to my computers there, using free software from LogMeIn.com. The Vegas machines, in turn, were running Tor. Anyone clever enough to untangle those foreign routers would get only as far as a laptop sitting in an empty office on South Pecos Road.

Meanwhile, in L.A., I meticulously kept up my physical disguise. One afternoon, a few blocks from my hotel, I had a chance to test it. A camera crew, fronted by an Internet news correspondent named Amanda Congdon, was corralling passersby for man-on-the-street interviews about their views on swine flu. I volunteered myself as an interview subject. A few days later, I found my interview on the Sometimesdaily.com site, Venice Beach in the background. It was time to get out of LA.

5

socillion *@dimitrirose the only IP not part of the Tor network is in Los Angeles and is owned by Trit Networks #vanish* 5:33 pm Aug 20th

menacingpickle *@alanbly I personally would not hide out in Vegas as every single movement is captured on camera* 7:15 pm aug 2oth

evanoffgrid *Hunch Evan started growing out his hair/grew beard knowing his friends wld give out info, now he's bald or crewcut and blond #vanish* 6:06 pm aug 26th

labfly *on yet another evan stake out :) following a hunch #vanish* 6:27 pm Aug 27th

On August 20, a sixteen-year-old high school student in Portland, Oregon, named Jonathan Mäkelä saw a link to the story about the *Wired* contest on Hacker News. Mäkelä was a casual participant in the online community 4chan, whose pranks sometimes involved tracking down documents concerning unsuspecting targets. Mäkelä had grown fascinated by how much intel could be legally dug up online. Here was a guy, Ratliff, who invited people to use that same intel to find him. Now that was interesting.

Mäkelä began using a Twitter account under an anonymous handle, @socillion, and started pulling apart Ratliff's IP addresses. He quickly marshaled a collection of online tools with which he could peg IPs to a physical location and Internet service provider, often triangulating between several sites. By now, other hunters had determined that Ratliff's IPs—which Thompson published several times a day after logging in to Ratliff's e-mail—appeared to be useless nodes from the Tor network. But Mäkelä meticulously verified that each was indeed a Tor node. He shared his information with the crowd and then got feedback in return. Eventually, he figured, the target might make a mistake.

Mäkelä quickly became one of the most active investigators, posting ideas to Twitter at least a dozen times a day. But this public collaboration, he soon realized, was itself a problem. The hunters were benefiting from their collective brainpower, but Ratliff could follow their thoughts just as easily. "Groups need to take this private," he posted to Twitter on August 20, "otherwise we are guaranteed never to win." Mäkelä set up a secure chat room and gave the password to only those he could verify weren't Ratliff.

6

To eratliff@atavist.net
From Mike
Date Fri, Aug 21, 2009 1:47 AM
Subject Your Disappearance

I want you to know right now that this is not an attempt to track you down . . . I want to know firsthand from you, what is it like disappearing? How does it feel? Are you lonely? Do you miss life? Is it liberating to be free from everything? I ask these

*questions because the idea of leaving and starting a new life
entertains me.*

My plan involved leaving L.A. for good by midday Friday, August 21, and heading east. But before I left, I wanted to give my investigators a parting diversion, something to keep them fixated on the West Coast. So at 11:55 P.M. Thursday night, I inserted my bank card into an ATM in nearby Santa Monica, deposited the $3,000 car check, and took out $300 cash, the maximum single-day withdrawal. Figuring that as long as I was revealing my location to the world, I might as well pad my reserves, I withdrew another $300 at 12:01. Then I treated myself to a credit card purchase: a $13 vodka martini at the nearby Viceroy hotel.

Friday, I woke up at dawn and found the hostel Wi-Fi down. Blind to my pursuers, I decided to risk a last jog; I donned a baseball cap and trotted down along the water's edge. As I turned around to head back, a helicopter came up the beach from the opposite direction, flying low. It stopped and hovered between me and a group of surfers floating idly on their boards.

I'm not sure when the thought entered my head, but when it did, it lodged there: Was it possible that someone had seen my ATM transactions, called up a friend with a helicopter, and sent them out to scan the beach for me?

The correct answer was no. Deep down I knew this. But there the chopper was, hovering. I jogged a little bit farther, and it seemed to ease toward me, staying not-quite-directly overhead. I stopped to see if it would pass over. It didn't. The beach was empty. I jogged up to a lifeguard stand, putting it between me and the helicopter, and waited. A few seconds later, the nose crept around the building and back into my line of sight.

In that moment, reason evaporated. I took off toward the boardwalk, a lone figure sprinting across the sand at dawn. Seen from the air, I must have appeared, at this point, worth following.

Whatever the reason, the helicopter kept coming. I reached the pavement and turned down a side street, bolted up one alley and down another, and finally ducked under a tree, lungs burning. I could still hear the thump-thump of the blades. I waited, my thoughts spinning out into ever-wilder fantasies. Were they radioing a ground team to drive by and yell "fluke"? Had they already staked out my hotel? Really? All for $5,000?

A few minutes passed and I heard it drift away. I took off again down the alley and ducked into a convenience store. There was an old pay-by-the-minute Internet terminal, and I slipped in a dollar. The ATM transactions hadn't even posted to my account yet.

7

alanbly *he just hit an ATM in Santa Monica #vanish* 11:51 AM Aug 21st

lookingforevan *@combobulate #vanish. His phone has been off for days. I think he's using a prepaid.* 1:26 PM Aug 21st

labfly *okay now i'm walking up to 30 something guys that look anyting like evan & people r thinking i'm nutz* 4:14 PM Aug 21st

socillion *@RatliffPatrol According to the statements its at 1300 4TH ST SANTA MONICA CA whre thrs a wells fargo. street view blckd by bus tho #vanish* 1:23 AM Aug 22nd

When Thompson posted Ratliff's ATM transactions online, late the morning of August 21, the pursuit kicked into high gear. For the first time, Ratliff had pegged himself to a specific place, and hunters hit the streets to try to nab him. Mäkelä pinpointed the exact location of the ATM in Santa Monica. One man set about frantically calling restaurants in the area, asking whoever picked up the phone to scan the crowd for someone who met Ratliff's description. Manello called the car dealer in Vegas, then she found a bookstore owner who claimed to have seen him.

In the private chat room that Mäkelä ran as Socillion, however, the consensus seemed to be that Ratliff had moved on. They discussed and discarded strategies ranging from the clever to the outlandish to the completely illegal. Somehow, they had to figure out how to get ahead of him. "Right now, Evan is controlling us," a participant named AtavistTracker wrote. "Evan's had over two months to plan this. We need to alter that plan. I like disinformation."

"Me too," Socillion replied. "Fight with his tools."

8

EvanOffGrid *remember we can't trust messages from Evan.* 8:46 am Aug 27th

how2stalk *Latest Evan Google Earth file: http://bit.ly/nNh7K* *#vanish* 9:39 am aug 27th

TrackEvan *Update: "Evan's Reading List" now on http:// www.trackevan.com/ #vanish* 7:24 pm Aug 27th

bellyscratcher *#vanish Contacting more PIs, will update when done.* 12:13 am Aug 28th

By the end of the first week, the deception had already begun to wear me down. Lying about your identity involves more than just transgressing some abstract prohibition against deceit. It means overcoming a lifetime of built-up habits, from a well-rehearsed life story to the sound of your own name. When I convinced people that I really was James Donald Gatz, I occasionally felt a mischievous thrill. Most of the time, however, I felt awful. The people I encountered weren't credulous; they were just nice.

I left L.A. with a band called the Hermit Thrushes, trading gas money for a spot onboard a converted retirement-home shuttle van that served as their tour bus. An indie rock group composed of college grads from Philadelphia, they'd responded to an ad I posted on craigslist, under the name Don, needing a ride to Austin or New Orleans. We rattled along from show to show: L.A. to Tempe to Las Cruces, up to Lubbock and Tulsa, east to Fayetteville, then north toward Chicago. The band played whiskey bars, coffee shops, and rowdy house parties. We crashed on living room floors or crammed into the seats of the bus, and, once, on the grass at a rest stop in Texas.

The band was serious about its music but unperturbed about much else, and I settled into a role somewhere between lazy roadie and moneyed patron, pulling $100 bills from my belt at gas stations. On board, I staked out the bus's backseat, where I could use my laptop without anyone looking over my shoulder. With a $150 wireless broadband card from Virgin Mobile, the only nationwide service that didn't require a credit check, I had almost uninterrupted online access.

So I passed the long hours on the road building up an online life for my new identity. I'd opened a Facebook account under "GatzJD" and a Twitter account under @jdgatz (which I kept open to the world for days, cataloging my location for posterity, before panicking and locking it from public view). For the average person, populating an online social network account is as easy as finding your friends, connecting to their friends, and watching the virtual acquaintances pile up. As Gatz, though, I had no actual friends. Instead, I set about finding people who would accept my friendship automatically, and soon my profile was overrun with multilevel marketers and inspirational speakers. Enough, I thought, to convince potential real acquaintances who didn't look too hard that I wasn't friendless.

I'd been set to depart the tour in Lubbock, Texas, but the band was cool and I was safe, so I kept going. On the afternoon . of August 26, the bus finally pulled into St. Louis, where the band had a college radio gig scheduled and I had a plan to get to the train station. A half hour later, listeners to KWUR heard the Hermit Thrushes dedicate their show to a mysterious single-named traveler, Don, headed for New Orleans.

9

> I looked out my office window (about 6 floors up) about
> 11AM and spotted Evan walking up 1st avenue from the
> direction of Qwest Field—he was wearing a backpack and
> heading into downtown . . . My heart started to race as I ran
> out of the office and hit the elevator button. Once I got to
> the street Evan w/ backpack was nowhere to be found . . .
> Walking to the bus that evening I surveyed the faces of every
> stranger I walked past—looked at the eyes, the hair, finding
> at least 3 possible Evans on my 15 minute walk to the bus.
> I think I was going insane!
>
> —Jeremy Thompson aka @evan_ratliff

On August 24, a former Microsoft group program manager in Seattle named Jeff Reifman read about the hunt in *Wired*. Reifman, self-employed these days, had recently launched a series of grant-funded Facebook applications to study the engagement of young people with the news. From a technical standpoint, the contest seemed intriguing.

On August 27, working on a desktop in his living room, he created Vanish Team, a Facebook app dedicated to information and discussion about Ratliff. He announced it on Twitter, and people began clicking over to check it out. Reifman was late to the party, however; most of the real intel swap stayed on Twitter or in Mäkelä's secure chat room.

Down in Portland, Mäkelä was learning that it wasn't secure enough. One night, as a San Diego–based hunter was making the drive to Las Vegas—where the chat room believed Ratliff was headed—an insider e-mailed Ratliff to tip him off.

When Thompson posted the anonymous e-mail on the *Wired* blog, it was the hunters' turn to be paranoid. Mäkelä moved to another chat room, and then started another, jettisoning all but a few of his most trustworthy correspondents. One of the people he kicked out, after a set of heated exchanges, was Reifman.

10

SearchForEvan *Ok, best guesses . . . what is Evan doing RIGHT NOW? #vanish* 9:40 pm aug 28th

From St. Louis I took a bus to Carbondale, Illinois, and caught a train south to New Orleans. To get around Amtrak's mandatory government ID requirements, I booked online, using my real name, and picked up the ticket from a machine at the station. I still might need an ID on the train, so to obscure myself to anyone who might get into the Amtrak database, I booked under my middle name and misspelled my last name ever so slightly, leaving out the l.

I'd chosen New Orleans months before, distant enough from the coasts to provide obscurity but familiar to me from trips I'd taken years before. Showing up in a city with no friends, no contacts, no credit cards, and no ID is itself a discomfiting experience, and having a basic grip on the layout eases the alienation. After four days in a vacation condo, rented from an absentee landlord who accepted PayPal, I found a cheap one-bedroom apartment around the corner. The next day I signed my well-practiced J. D. Gatz scrawl on the lease. The landlord, after a friendly chat, was ready to hand over the keys. He would, he said, just need to see my driver's license.

I'd been working for months to establish James Donald Gatz as a separate identity. The name itself—the one that Jay Gatsby sheds to start over in *The Great Gatsby*—was easy for me to remember. More important, due to the prolific amount of Gatsby analysis online, it was basically un-Googleable. The middle name was my own, but Mr. Gatz received an entirely new birthday: July 1, 1976, shaving about a year off my age.

He also got a "research firm," Bespect LLC, registered in the state of New Mexico and complete with a logo—a bespectacled cartoon man with a mustache—and a Web site at Bespect.com. Gatz's PayPal account was funded using gift cards. I'd even ordered up a gift card with his name on it that looked to the casual eye like a real credit card.

My new landlord glanced at the business card and flimsy home-laminated "visiting scholar" credentials that I slid across the table. "Bespect.com, eh?" he said. "Interesting. These will do." He turned around, photocopied them, and dropped the copy in a folder along with my lease.

At this point, my new life seemed, superficially at least, satisfactory. My days were spent jogging along the Mississippi, haunting the coffee shops and jazz bars of my adopted neighborhood, and exploring the city by bike. I located a soccer bar and even got a one-night job selling beer and nachos for tips during a Saints game at the Superdome.

The gnawing flaw in the idyllic life of J. D. Gatz was that I did all of these activities alone. It wasn't just that I had no friends. It was that the interactions I did have were beyond superficial. They were fake. My online social networks were populated with strangers; my girlfriend was thousands of miles away; my family knew about me only from news reports and online speculation.

I'd always prided myself on being comfortable with solitude, but this wasn't normal solitude. It was everyone-is-out-to-get-me isolation. What to the hunters felt like an intricate puzzle felt real enough to me—and there was no one around to laugh and tell me otherwise. Instead there was just me, staring into my laptop all day, wondering if it was safe to go out and get the paper.

For the first time in my life, I couldn't sleep. One night I awoke at 4 A.M. drenched in sweat, having dreamed that a childhood friend turned me in.

11

vanishteam *Evan shaved his cat on Aug 19 http://bit.ly/ zrO86—after shaving his own head? It's the easiest and coolest way to chg appearance #vanish* 11:38 PM Aug 28th

    vanishteam *Am pretty certain @theatavist is openly blogging and posting photos of his travels somewhere on the net. #vanish* 2:57 PM Sep 1st

    vanishteam *Hope @theatavist returns safely or we're all suspects! #vanish* 6:41 PM Sep 2nd

Out in Seattle, Reifman wasn't generating solid leads. Through a convoluted set of clues, some of which later turned out to be inaccurate, he developed a theory that the target had headed to San Diego. Reifman posted it to the Vanish Team site, but nothing came of it.

He decided to try a different tack. Instead of using the Vanish Team application to gather news about Ratliff, he'd use it to track him. He installed thirty-eight lines of new code. It was rudimentary and unlikely to work if Ratliff had set up Tor, his anonymity software, correctly. But it gave Reifman a tool to easily pick out the IP addresses of Facebook visitors to Vanish Team. Ratliff might be among them. He'd be the guy without many friends.

12

jdgatz *Just arranged to sublet cool apt yesterday. Upstairs back of shotgun house, called a "camel back" apartment. Sounds dirty, but it's not.* 2:33 PM Aug 30th

> jdgatz *I'm not sure I've ever stayed up all night before in order to (partially) re-shave my head before a morning flight. But desperate times . . .* 12:51 AM Sep 5th
> jdgatz *I'm learning to love Amtrak, but anything over 5 hrs w/out sleeping car = yearning for the development of air travel. Wait, they have that?* 12:51 AM Sep 5th

In constructing a proper disguise, there is no place for vanity or pride. Altering your appearance, after all, is not about convincing people. It's about misdirection, diverting their attention from the physical features you are unable to change and toward the ones you can. Success often involves making yourself look older, fatter, nerdier, sleazier, or otherwise more unpleasant than you were before. The goal is to be overlooked, ignored, or, sometimes, noticed and then dismissed with a chuckle.

It was the last to which I aspired as I walked through security at the Memphis airport, on Saturday morning, September 5, barely resembling the face on the real ID I showed at the security line. My hair was shaved clean on top with a razor but left short-cropped on the sides and back, in the manner of advanced male pattern baldness. The bald spot had been enhanced with tanning cream, compensation for the sudden paleness of my newly shorn dome. I wore a borderline-creepy mustache, above which a new set of prescriptionless glasses were backed by brown prescription contacts. I twirled a fake wedding band on my finger. A hands-free cell phone headset dangled from my ear.

Unable to completely abandon the hobbies of my previous life, I was headed to Salt Lake City for the U.S. World Cup qualifying soccer match against El Salvador. The logistics had been complicated: a train to Memphis, followed by a flight to San Francisco (which needed to be under $250, the maximum gift card available) that stopped in Salt Lake.

The greater problem would be avoiding the hunters. They had long speculated that I might attend the game, and I'd seen stakeout rumors on Twitter. So I bought two fully refundable tickets to Salt Lake on my credit card for September 4, originating in LA and Portland—misdirections I knew they'd discover and that I hoped would lead them to the airport on the wrong day. I'd anonymously e-mailed a prominent hunter a link to the Venice Beach "swine flu video" to fix my previous appearance in their minds. Finally, I'd unmasked my computers' address in Las Vegas several times, turning off Tor while visiting Web sites that I knew were trapping IPs.

But it was my disguise that gave me confidence as I breezed off the plane in Salt Lake City, dressed in a suit and tie, jabbering loudly to imaginary business contacts on my hands-free. I met an accomplice, an old friend also dressed as a low-rent sales rep; we dodged a suspicious lurker at the baggage claim. Then we checked in to a downtown hotel and changed into our gameday disguises. For him: a red, white, and blue afro wig. For me: waving stars and stripes painted atop my head, augmented with a bulky pair of American flag sunglasses and a red clown nose.

Walking to the stadium, we passed several people who seemed to be doing nothing other than scanning the crowd. "I've already seen a few people that I thought could be him," one man murmured as we passed a few feet away.

13

socillion @nxthompson #vanish a Wired reader/tw telecoms hostmaster tells me that the LV IPs are from a biz @ 4760 S. Pecos Road, Las Vegas 89121 3:48 pm sEp 3rd

    viequense @EvanOffGrid We were pretty sure we saw Evan last nt but we were also pretty drunk. Got pick & password. #vanish 8:06 am sep 5th

viequense *@EvanOffGrid It was last night, maybe about
11pm at a bar in SLC where we were having a USMNT party for
the game tomorrow.* 8:16 am sep 5th

For the hunters, it was again time to put boots on the ground. But
where? Mäkelä, jumping on the real IP address, called a techni-
cian at an ISP in Las Vegas who happily revealed the address on
South Pecos Road. The hunters puzzled over the businesses listed
there, wondering if Ratliff somehow had a friend among them.

For now, though, the action was headed for Salt Lake City.
One woman bought a refundable ticket to get through security
and stake out departure gates at the Portland airport. A man did
the same for arrivals in Salt Lake City, waiting for seven hours
over two days. Mäkelä generated a map of all the known gluten-
free eateries in the area, and hunters hit pregame parties. All
that turned up were look-alikes.

That Friday afternoon in Seattle, Reifman was sorting through
more Facebook profiles. Recalling Thompson's statement that
Ratliff would not just be hiding but trying to make new friends,
Reifman had decided to expand his search to include Vanish
Team visitors with up to fifty Facebook friends. He pulled up the
profile for a James Donald Gatz, who seemed to be visiting Vanish Team regularly. The name didn't ring a bell, but the photo
looked familiar. Then he realized where he'd seen that look before: the swine flu video. He flipped back and forth between the
two, and soon he was positive. Gatz was Ratliff.

At first, he was giddy. All he needed to do was friend one of
Gatz's friends or convince one to reveal their new pal's location.
Looking through the profile, though, he realized that Ratliff had
populated his account with what amounted to Facebook auto-
matons. Reifman tried sending messages to a few, telling them
about the hunt. No luck.

He decided to try Twitter. Eventually, he typed in "jdgatz"
and found the account, locked from public view. Friends of

@jdgatz could see his posts, but the general public, including Reifman, couldn't. With a simple Google search for "jdgatz," Reifman located an archived, unprotected version of jdgatz's posts from the previous week. Gatz, at least at that point, had been revealing his location as he moved around. Maybe he'd do it again.

Currently, though, gaining access to Gatz's daily feed would require his permission. Not wanting to spook the target, Reifman tried to enlist the help of one of Gatz's current connections, who would already have access. Again, most were multilevel marketers or auto-reply bots. But he managed to find three real people among them: a Hawaii real estate agent, a Segway aficionado in New Zealand, and a blogger in Atlanta. Reifman convinced all three to keep him apprised of whatever Gatz wrote.

At 4 A.M. on Sunday morning, Reifman's girlfriend came downstairs and found him staring into the screen. "What are you doing?"

"I think I've found Evan."

14

The Search for Evan Ratliff Facebook wall

Landon Anderson (Salt Lake City, UT) wrote at 8:26pm on September 6, 2009 *EVERYBODY!!!!! I do not know how to use Twitter, so I am posting this information here so that someone can post it on Twitter. Evan is in ATLANTA. He landed there at about 8:10 pm Atlanta time today. He showed up to SLC airport this morning, canceled the itinerary from SLC to SFO, purchased a new ticket to Atlanta via Denver. I am sure my knowledge will soon be confirmed by Nicholas. I did nothing illegal . . . just have connections.*

The morning after the soccer game, I caught a flight to Atlanta via Denver. After landing at Hartsfield Airport, I rushed off the jetway, a businessman in a hurry. Safely a few gates away, I opened my laptop for a routine check of the Wired blog. Headline: "Evan Ratliff will arrive in Atlanta in 5 minutes." I slammed the laptop shut and took off.

All of the Hartsfield terminals funnel out to a single exit. But as a former Atlanta resident, I knew one other way out, a solitary revolving door from the T Gates leading to a remote part of baggage claim. It was eerily empty when I got there. I slipped out, hustled to the public transit station at the far end, and caught a train into town. Only later would I learn that a hunter in Atlanta arrived minutes after I'd left, sprinted to the trains, and frantically canvassed the passengers.

I crashed for a few hours at the house of a friend—one of only a few I was willing to reach out to, knowing that Thompson was posting interview transcripts of his talks with them. The next morning I caught the first Amtrak train out, sinking down in my seat for the twelve-hour ride back to New Orleans. A few times en route I opened my laptop to check on reports of the hunters scurrying furiously around Atlanta. On Twitter, the guy running the Vanish Team Facebook application kept announcing new scoops, exhorting people to check out his site. Each time, I'd click over to Facebook, using James Gatz's account. What scoops? Vanish Team seemed like all bluster.

At this point, I'd stopped logging in to my Vegas computers for anything but the riskiest Web surfing. This was partly out of a growing laziness; the whole process took longer than dialup circa 1993. I also figured that I could freely visit Facebook pages like Vanish Team. Anyone who built an application to use on a corporate site, I assumed, would need cooperation from the company to track their users.

Once back safely in New Orleans, I decided to redouble my efforts to socialize, both online and in real life. For starters, I opened up my @jdgatz Twitter feed to the public—maybe I could connect with some local friends. I searched for New Orleans businesses I might follow. One was a local gluten-free pizza place I'd wanted to go to called NakedPizza.

15

From Jeff Reifman
Date Mon, Sep 7, 2009 9:48 PM
    Subject Re: ALERT Evan in Jacksons Gap, Alabama—Got a clear lead just now

By Monday, Jeff Reifman had mentioned the @jdgatz account to a few active hunters, including Sarah Manello and Mäkelä, with whom he'd patched things up. When Ratliff opened his Twitter feed to the public, Reifman created two fake accounts of his own—crafted to look like automated Twitter bots, so as not to raise Ratliff's suspicion—and started following the account.

Then Monday night, Reifman noticed James Gatz logging in from a new IP address: 74.180.70.233. According to the database Reifman was using, the address pointed to Jacksons' Gap, Alabama. After he e-mailed his select group of trusted hunters, Mäkelä ran the address through his own little triangulated system and discovered where it actually originated from. Two minutes later he sent a one-line response to Reifman: "That IP is in New Orleans."

Reifman flipped over to the @jdgatz Twitter feed and noticed that the number of accounts Gatz was following had gone up by three—all New Orleans businesses. He looked up NakedPizza's Web site and fired off an e-mail explaining the hunt. "I have accurate information that Evan has arrived in New Orleans and plans to go to NakedPizza Tuesday or Wednesday," he wrote. A few minutes later, he followed up. "I forgot to mention," he said, "that we know Evan has shaved his head either partially (male pattern bald) or fully." Reifman informed his fellow hunters, and Manello spent the evening dialing fifty hotels near the restaurant, asking for a James Gatz.

The next morning when Jeff Leach, cofounder of NakedPizza and a tech-savvy entrepreneur, got the e-mail, he thought at first it was a scam. But he passed it along to his business partner, and after delving into the hunt information online, they concluded it was real. Leach decided to help.

16

To Jeff Reifman
From Jeff Leach
Date Tue, Sep 8, 2009 8:17 AM
    We will catch him.

Tuesday, September 8, 7 A.M.: Just seven days to go. I awake in my apartment in New Orleans, relieved to find no online indication of anyone wise to my location. Aside from a few random new followers to my Twitter feed, all of whom seem like automated bots, nobody seems to be paying attention to my fake accounts either.

I use a gift card to book a flight to New York City on September 15, the final day of my disappearance, and hatch plans to surprise Thompson in his office using a fake security badge. I've been communicating sporadically with my editor through a public blog—I'd post something, he'd read it, delete it, and then post his response. Before Salt Lake City, I'd boasted that I could survive the month, "just by keeping my head down and being careful with my phones and IPs."

Now *Wired* has decided to up the stakes, offering me $400 for each of a series of challenges I complete. And I could use it. As much as any other factor—personal gall, or endurance, or discipline—staying on the run requires an abundance of cash.

I've already nearly spent the three grand I brought with me. Besides, I made it through the Salt Lake City gauntlet and survived a near miss in Atlanta. I can do this.

The first two challenges—clues to which are embedded, with the help of Will Shortz and Lone Shark Games, for the hunters to find in the *New York Times* crossword puzzle—are to go to the fiftieth story of a building and to attend a book reading. Checking online, I identify only two buildings in downtown New Orleans of fifty stories or taller, and I choose One Shell Square. At the security desk, back in my businessman disguise, I step up and announce that I'm here to visit the law firm occupying the upper floors. "Just sign in here. And we'll need to see your ID."

"Well, I've lost mine. Will a business card and a credit card do?"

In two minutes, I'm on the fiftieth floor, video camera rolling. Later, as I wander home through the French Quarter, a street vendor sidles up beside me with some friendly unsolicited advice. "Hey buddy," he says, gesturing to my haircut. "You gotta shave the rest of that off, man."

That same morning, Leach, of NakedPizza, calls Reifman, and the two begin comparing notes. Leach searches through his Web site's logs, finding that IP address 74.180.70.233—aka James Gatz—visited NakedPizza.biz late the previous evening.

By 11 A.M., Leach has briefed all of his employees on the hunt. If they see the target, he explains, they need to say "fluke" and take a photo. He creates a folder on the company network with pictures for them to study. One is a Photoshopped mock-up of Ratliff, bald.

Brock Fillinger, also a cofounder, whose own pate is clean-shaven, heads over to stake out the tours at Old New Orleans Rum, another business Ratliff was following on Twitter and that Reifman had contacted. "Hey," the woman behind the desk says as Fillinger lingers nearby, "are you that *Wired* writer?"

Snide street comments aside, I've already decided to shave the rest of my head and mustache. My acquisition of actual friends will require looking less creepy. I change into casual clothes, grab a fedora, and ride my bicycle to the barber.

At 5:20 I'm completely bald, and I'll have to hustle to make it across town for the book reading I plan to attend.

At 5:48, Leach and Fillinger are watching both entrances to the Garden District BookShop. They're expecting someone "wigged up," someone who looks like he doesn't quite belong. But the reading started promptly at 5:30, and there is no sign of Ratliff.

Leach sends a text message to Fillinger. This looks like a bust. They meet up out front, ready to move on.

It's surreal, in those moments when I stop to think about it. Scores of people have studied my picture, stared into those empty eyes in the hopes of relieving me of thousands of dollars. They have stood for hours, trying to pick out my face in a crowd. They've come to know me like we've been friends for years. It's weirdly thrilling, in a narcissistic kind of way, but also occasionally terrifying.

I almost ride past the bookshop before I see the sign, tucked into a tiny shopping center. I stop at the corner and pull out my bike lock. Two men stand on the stairs outside, facing the street. They glance over at me.

My first impulse is to ride away. But at what point do I separate caution from self-delusion? Not every out-of-place person is looking for me.

Tired from the bike ride, tired of the corrosive suspicion, I decide to walk past them on the sidewalk, making no move toward the bookstore. Just a local, heading down the street to visit a friend.

"Hey," Leach calls out from the stairs, taking a hesitant step toward me. I freeze and stare back helplessly. "You wouldn't happen to know a guy named Fluke, would you?"

17

To Nicholas Thompson
From Laurie Ambrose
Date Wed, Sep 9, 2009 12:54 PM
Subject My #Vanish Story

Why would a middle-aged woman with virtually no technical knowledge be interested in following the Evan's Vanished story on Twitter? You see, my father walked out one morning in Sumter, South Carolina, kissed the wife and two young children good-bye as if he was going to work as always, and disappeared for 12 years. He was around Evan's age. He sent the family a telegraph a few days later asking them not to look for him. To this day, no one knows anything about his personal life during those years. I guess I'm hoping to have some clues to some of my questions.

At first I was angry: at myself for getting caught and losing the money, at *Wired* for tempting me with the challenges. But that was soon replaced by the thrill of being redeposited in my own identity, with a family, a partner, friends, and a past I didn't have to hide. I packed up my apartment, rented a car, and visited my parents in Florida. Then I bought a plane ticket home.

Leach and Reifman had agreed to split the prize money, but they both ended up giving it all to Unity of Greater New Orleans, a charity helping the city recover from Hurricane Katrina. Socillion started his junior year of high school. The online chatter dissolved as quickly as it had formed.

And what of our original questions? Had I shown that a person, given enough resources and discipline, could vanish from one life and reinvent himself in another? I thought I had, though only up to a point. Obviously the smarts and dedication of the hunters had overwhelmed my planning and endurance. Along the way they'd also proven my privacy to be a modern fiction. It turns out that people—ordinary people—really can gather an incredible dossier of facts about you. But a month later, life was back to normal and no one was taking any interest.

More than all that, I'd discovered how quickly the vision of total reinvention can dissolve into its lonely, mundane reality. Whatever reason you might have for discarding your old self and the people who went with it, you'll need more than a made-up backstory and a belt full of cash to replace them.

For weeks after the hunt ended, I still paused when introducing myself and felt a twinge of panic when I handed over my credit card. The paranoid outlook of James Donald Gatz was hard to shake. Even now, my stomach lurches when I think back to the night I got caught. "You wouldn't happen to know a guy named Fluke, would you?"

Right after it happened, I rode my bike back to my apartment and sat in the air-conditioning, unsure what to do. Finally I got online and logged in to the hunters' private chat room for the first time. Rich Reder, founder of the Facebook countergroup designed to help me stay hidden, had infiltrated the room and sent me the password. Just a little too late.

I found Mäkelä there, still logged in. I asked him why he was hanging around a chat room dedicated to catching a guy who'd already been caught. "Just lurking," he wrote. "Working out the moles."

After a while I signed off, closed my laptop, and walked down the street to J. D. Gatz's local dive bar. I ordered a whiskey and tried to tell the bartender the story of how I abandoned my life and then got it back. For the first time in weeks, someone didn't seem to believe my story.

Orion

FINALIST—ESSAYS

Published bimonthly in Great Barrington, Massachusetts, Orion *describes itself as a "magazine devoted to creating a stronger bond between people and nature." If that sounds idealistic to you, don't be fooled. The magazine received its first National Magazine Awards nomination for Joe Wilkins's "Out West," a tough piece of work the judges called "raw and richly descriptive." "It was all about the land," Wilkins writes about the Montana of his youth. "We didn't do right by it. And we lost it." "Out West" makes that loss ours.*

Joe Wilkins

Out West

Out on the Big Dry we had to kill to live:

Come October, we'd herd a yearling lamb into the west pen, throw it some good flakes of alfalfa hay. It'd be grass-fat by then, nearly tame, just chewing, and looking around, and chewing. My father, his black hair bright and wild in the early winter light, would put the rifle barrel in its soft ear and pull the trigger. We were nearly two hours away from the nearest supermarket. And even if we were closer, we couldn't afford it. We ate lamb all winter—lamb chops and leg of lamb and lamb stew with garden peas my mother canned. All kinds of lamb.

But on Sunday, we almost always pulled a fryer out of the freezer for dinner. Butchering chickens was an all-day affair, a late-summer festival of sorts, a kind of prairie celebration. We put on our old jeans and stained snap shirts and ate a big breakfast of hamburger steak, eggs, and potatoes. My mother and grandmother set up aluminum basins of hot water for the plucking. My father and grandfather sharpened knives and hatchets. And when everything was finally ready, they sent us children into the coop.

A moment later we scrambled out slicked with shit and feathers, holding squawking hens to our heaving chests. We gave those orange and brown and piebald hens over to my father or my grandfather, whoever happened to be kneeling behind the pine stump that day, and one-by-one they stretched the hens out on the stump and stroked their necks until they calmed and brought the hatchet down hard. They gave them back to us—still flapping and jerking, blood suddenly everywhere—by their bony feet. There'd be a line of us then, happy children holding headless chickens upside down, blood running out and all over the dust.

·   ·   ·

But to kill is not necessarily to do violence:

I remember my grandfather standing above me, his breath steaming out of him. He was telling me to take my knife and cut the throat of the first antelope I had ever shot. I was twelve years old and confused. This thing laid out on the snow before me was so fine and beautiful; I had no idea it would be like this. I was looking to my grandfather for help, for release from this duty—but he shook his head. I turned back to the buck, took up my eight-inch, bone-handled knife, and eased the bright blade through the skin of the buck's neck and the hollow beneath. There is so much blood in a thing.

After I gutted him and packed him on my back up the ridge and loaded him into the bed of the pickup, I stood in the clear, cold light of the morning, marveling at my blood-crusted jeans, my still blood-wet hands. All winter, I knew, we'd eat breakfasts of antelope steak and fried eggs, earthy-tasting antelope sausage mixed into cream gravy and poured over toast come dinner. My father was years dead by then, and my mother came home from work each day tired in the dark. This blood, I thought, will get us through.

My grandfather broke my reverie. He took me by the shoulders, told me I had done a good, hard thing and done it well. He told me to be careful that it always remained a hard thing to do. "Easy isn't any good," he said. "If it ever gets easy—quit."

. • •

Now you're thirteen, old enough to hunt by yourself, so you load an old, bolt-action .22 with shells. You walk north. There is little wind, the sun a white hole in the sky. Beneath your boots the bones of dry grass bend and crack. You feel good about this. Prairie dogs are bad for the fields. They spread disease. A sheep will snap a front leg in a doghole. Your father is dead, your grandfather is old, and you tell yourself you are just doing what a man does. You are taking care of the fields, keeping the stock safe. You tell yourself all kinds of things.

You lay your skinny body down over a pile of rotten fence posts. The prairie dogs run and dash and scamper to their little mounds, now stand and chirp at one another. You close your left eye and snug the butt up against your shoulder, the polished wood cool and smooth on the warm skin of your cheek. There's a fat one not fifty yards away. You steady yourself. There is the smell of creosote, the taste of dust and rank weeds. You sight along the blue barrel and pull the trigger. There is a small pop. The prairie dog flops over and rolls down its mound and is dead.

You are pleased with yourself. You stand for a better look. A cottontail rabbit zigzags out from beneath the pile of old posts some twenty yards and stops. You step back with your right foot and swing the rifle butt up to your shoulder again. There's no need to shoot rabbits. You close your left eye. Rabbits are no good to eat, they don't do any damage to the fields. You drop the open sights over the rabbit's spine. Its long ears twitch one, two, three times. You squeeze the trigger.

The rabbit bucks and jumps, screams. You didn't know rabbits could scream. You shoot again. And again. It's still screaming, back legs kicking at the empty air. You shoot again. The body bucks and jumps and is still.

Your breath comes back to you. That wasn't so bad, you think. But you won't tell your grandfather. He wouldn't like you killing rabbits. He's old, though, and what does he know and who really cares about rabbits anyway? All the older boys you run around with at school shoot them.

.   .   .

It's Saturday night. You are fourteen now, nearly grown, you think—your grandfather older and older yet, his once board-straight shoulders beginning to buckle and slump, and your mother still tired, voiceless and sad-eyed as you slam the screen door and screech the truck's tires on your way out.

You drive on into Melstone and park down by the Sportsman Bar. You get in with that bunch of older boys. They've got cigarettes, beer in the backseat, a bottle of whiskey they're passing around. Boy, they drive fast. They take the corners at a gravelly skid, they raise dust right through the middle of town. Now they race on out to the river. You all pile out and run and yell and knock down the sign that says primitive road, now the one that says narrow bridge. Someone starts throwing beer bottles at the old homesteader's shack off in the willows. They crash and shatter, the glass lovely in the light of the moon. One boy runs up on the bridge and strips off his clothes and jumps. Everyone cheers and swears. From somewhere down in the watery dark, he swears back.

You don't like this. You know this isn't any good. You're all drunk. It's dark. The water's fast and cold this spring. And who knows how deep it is here, anyway? Doesn't anyone remember the Dejagher boy? You've seen him, slouched in his wheelchair, sucking can after can of 7Up through a straw. But all of a sudden—you don't quite know how it happens—you're there with the other boys, in line, laughing right there behind them. Each jumps in turn, and now it's your turn. You don't know what to do about all this. The other boys cheer and holler. Someone passes you the whiskey bottle. You take a big swig, wing off your t-shirt, edge your toes over the rusted iron—into the dark, you leap.

.   .   .

And for a good while, that's how it goes: you drive fast and wild out into the dark, you coax girls down to your riverbottom bonfire parties, you stand on the beer cooler in the back of Adam's truck and flood the dark trees with a spotlight—your friend, Vinny, shoots and hits the coon between the eyes, hollers, sprays beer foam everywhere.

But then, late one night on your way back from Addie Mae's trailer, where you smoked Winstons and drank Bud Ice and laughed like you knew what you were doing, you come over Hougen's Hill out of Melstone headed west at about ninety miles an hour right down the middle of the road. As your headlights shift from sky to highway, there, straddling the double yellow line, is a big Angus. You're in the old Tercel; that cow's as big as you. You spin the wheel this way and that way and the night spins too around you.

You aren't scared. A little angry, maybe. But mostly it is like a thing coming down that you knew would always come down, the way you know your grandfather will soon die and that skinny sophomore you like will take up with some twenty-seven-year-old ranch hand and Adam will end up knocking over the liquor store in Roundup.

There goes basketball, you think. There goes just about everything.

.   .   .

And then everything is still: and I am in the middle of the road, facing east instead of west, headlights veering off into the dark. I turn the car around and drive slowly toward home. I make it nearly to our turnoff before the shaking starts. I fall into bed with my jeans on, my arms and shoulders and face and heart jerking, banging like a screen door slapped about in the wind. My breath runs from me in the dark. I don't sleep until I see the sun. Then I dream. Then, miraculously, I wake.

·   ·   ·

Ten-odd years later the night is dark and shot with stars, the red tracers of lit cigarettes, a scattered rainbow of light from the dance hall.

It's a cover band, mostly George Strait numbers, some old Eric Clapton. And this is the All-School Reunion. Melstone is so small there are no individual class reunions; instead, every ten years or so, anyone who ever graduated from the local high school shows up for two days of handshakes and hellos, Main Street bonfires, beer gardens, and big stories. So that's where I am, at the All-School Reunion, drunk and leaning up against someone's pickup. It's very late. My wife, Liz, has been asking to go. And we should. But maybe just one more beer. A friend of mine from college, who didn't graduate from Melstone but happened to be passing through Montana when we were passing through Montana, is even drunker than I am. He's telling me something, something sad, I think, but I'm not really listening. I'm staring at the stars.

Now two older men are in front of my friend and me. I try to concentrate on them. One is Kevin Kincheloe. I know him. He's a good guy. I used to play with his oldest daughter, Janna, during the noon recess up at school. She was small and dark-haired, and I thought she was beautiful. But when I was in the third grade, just after my father died, they had to move away. The bank foreclosed, and they lost their ranch and everything else. I think Kevin works some kind of wage job up around Billings now.

Anyway, Kevin's a good guy. He says hello, shakes my hand, offers us a pull off his fifth of Southern Comfort. But now the other man shoulders his way up to us. He's big and fat, his face wide and whiskered. His untucked shirt waves over the bulk of his belly. Kevin starts to introduce him, but the fat man cuts him off and says something stupid. My friend says something stupid back. The fat man thumps my friend in the chest with his meaty finger—and the air around us goes glass.

Kevin slides back half a step and quits talking, his mouth dropping into a hard line. This man is a father of two daughters, I think, drunkenly surprised to find Kevin readying himself, to find that I too am straightening up, my arms loose, my hands curling into fists at my sides. My friend, stepping toward the fat man, sneering at the fat man, slowly raises the bottle of Southern Comfort and takes a long drink. Then he takes another. He wipes his mouth with the back of his hand, shoves the bottle hard into the fat man's chest, says, "I want to see you drink."

The fat man stands there for a moment. Then drinks—one, two, three, four swallows. My friend, still rigid and pissed and sneering at the fat man, nods with each swallow. The fat man lowers the bottle and hands it to Kevin, who drinks and then hands the bottle to me. So I drink, the syrupy bourbon coating my throat, and somehow, for no decent reason at all, this solves the whole mess: the fat man belches and turns away; my friend laughs and stumbles a bit, sits on his ass in the gravel; I breathe and let my shoulders go soft; Kevin smiles drunkenly and steps back toward me and starts in again on whatever story he was telling in the first place.

I lean back up against the hard, cool steel of the truck to watch the stars open and close their bright and tiny mouths. I am surprised at myself. Here I am: a college professor going soft in the middle thinking I'm going to get into a fistfight. I've never been in a fistfight. Even when I was an idiot-hearted boy, drinking too much and driving too fast and doing stupid things out there in the night, I always stopped before I stepped into that kind of violence. I always turned away. What would I have done tonight? What would have Kevin done? What might have happened?

I'm still idiot-hearted, I think, and then try very hard to quit thinking. Kevin's saying something about how much he misses the people out here, the Sportsman Bar, the good land along the river they used to own.

·   ·   ·

The land out on the Big Dry was bad, but we tried hard to make it good:

We drained the river for irrigation, we sprayed the fields for knapweed and foxtail, we set out tubs of used motor oil for grasshopper traps. We ran electric fence up the hillsides to make the sheep eat right, we stayed all night in the shed to pull breech lambs, we vaccinated and de-horned and fed tons and tons of corn. And when none of it worked, when the wheat still burned and the grasshoppers came like a plague and the sheep went bone skinny in the sun, when that bad land still beat us, we prayed. And when that didn't work, we cursed. And then we slung the bodies to the boneyard and tried again—harder this time, the wheels greased with another layer of our bile.

Even done well, you couldn't call it a living; it was all a kind of ritualized dying. And that's not to demean a way of life. It's simply to call it like it is. Living off the land, any land, is hard. Living off that bad land, part of that stretch of high plains along the eastern front of the Rockies they used to call the Great American Desert, was nearly impossible. Especially when the rules of agriculture changed under Reagan, which was about the same time the summers got longer and the winters shorter and the creeks that once ran in all the coulees just dried up. And even then we didn't do anything different. We didn't advocate for ourselves or educate ourselves. We just doubled down and got tougher, worked harder—more loans from the bank, more acres grazed to the ground, more chemicals washed across the alfalfa.

We hurt the land, and it hurt us. Sometimes it hurt us physically: I didn't know a man in the valley who wasn't missing a couple of fingers, or maybe recovering from a broken leg after being thrown, again, by that ornery mare. There were boys in wheelchairs, girls with barbed-wire scars down their faces. Women who were forty looked sixty-five, and women who were sixty-five looked downright biblical. Clyde Brewer's heart blew up. Multiple sclerosis took hold of Butch Treible's straight spine and shook it crooked. And when I was nine, my father turned to the wall and died of cancer, probably exacerbated, they told us, by prolonged exposure to potent herbicides.

And sometimes it struck us in other, deeper ways: after my father died, my grandfather, who was one of the last of the old-time cowboys to ride the Comanche Flats before barbed wire, sold the family ranch. We were surprised and broken up about it—I remember my mother and my uncle Tom were especially questioning—but the important thing is my grandfather didn't go bankrupt. He had a choice. He was old but could have waited for me or for my brother, yet of his own will he sold, and then he told us boys a new story: he told us we would leave this place and go off to college. He only had an eighth-grade education, but that's the story he started telling, all about the things we could do if we only buckled down and kept at those books. It was a good story. So many of the other stories weren't working anymore, those ones other men told to their sons and grandsons, the ones about that good land along the river, about how some great-grandfather settled it way back when, about how it was hard going but they made it, about how even in the worst of times the land would see them through, about how the land was theirs and had been theirs and would always be theirs—but then when their boys got ready to start working that land, turned to that land, it was gone. Where'd it go? Ask the Crow, the Northern Cheyenne, the Sioux. See, out West all the old mistakes are new, and many men, good men like Kevin Kincheloe, had to sit at their kitchen tables and watch through the front window as the bank's auctioneer walked their acres, selling everything—from combines to skinny cattle, selling it all right down to the dry grass: imagine it for a moment. Imagine everything you love of the world taken from you. Now imagine it being taken from your child.

It was all about the land. We didn't do right by it. And we lost it: the phone rings, and my mother shakes her head, adds another name to the list of farm foreclosures. The neighbors, the few left, sit silently at the kitchen table, the clink of coffee cups saying all there is to say.

It was a slow, psychic violence. And many turned that violence inward: Over another shot of Rich & Rare at a roadside bar, men hatched a thousand plots for revenge. Boys drove hell-bent down gravel roads. Women left screen doors screeching on their hinges. Girls climbed in with whoever had a fast car headed somewhere else. That's mostly what folks did: they left. And they left like leaving is some kind of answer, like you're not carrying anyway your bad heart out into the hot night, loading into the one pickup the boss won't miss that much a saddle and some tack and that vodka box the kids packed lip-full of toys, and driving through the star-cut dark, trying to decide whether to try Harlowton or Big Timber or maybe up and do it, make for Spokane. On the television politicians talked about this program or that program to help rural America, but someone knew what it was really all about—they set up a suicide hotline strictly for farmers and ranchers who'd gone bankrupt and had to sell and found themselves stuck in a world they didn't recognize.

But too there were those who picked up their rifles and, instead of slipping the barrel under their own chins, shouldered them, drew a bead on that world. Like that bunch in Jordan, Montana, calling themselves The Freemen, barricading themselves in a place they dubbed Justus Township, and holding off the feds for weeks with a big arsenal and bigger threats. The press called them a militia group, a one-time thing, a bunch of crazies, but they were just ranchers who had lost their land, folks like so many who had fallen into reactionary politics. Others got fundamental, went back to the church in a big way, started thinking the books in the library or the new schoolteacher's ideas were to blame. And some just struck out at whoever or whatever happened to be in the way. When the bills piled up too high, my friend Justin's uncle used to take up a logging chain and beat whichever kid happened to be around.

It was historical: smallpox blankets and slaughtered buffalo gave our ancestors the land in the first place. Maybe more blood could get it back.

·   ·   ·

I was just sixteen the first time I saw a person try to kill another person.

I had parked at the café and was riding around with some older boys in a pickup. One of them had just been dumped by his girlfriend. And he was angry, really angry—swearing and sucking warm beer right from the can and telling us again and again what he ought to do, what he would do. When he spotted her car pulling onto Main Street, he yelled at the boy driving to follow her. Follow her!

So we did. We tailed her through town. We yelled when we got close, swore and said all kinds of things. And when she took off down the highway, we came after her. We cranked it up to a hundred and pulled even with her and threw beer cans at her windshield. We followed her when she turned off onto a gravel road, when she turned off into a field of sagebrush, when she skidded to a dusty stop in the middle of nowhere. I was drunk and scared, but I piled out of the pickup like the other boys, ready to yell, ready to stomp around and act mad, ready to do something. And when that girl threw open her car door and shouldered a rifle and started shooting, like the other boys I took off across the prairie.

She was yelling and crying, shaking something terrible. Her father, I knew, was a bad drunk. He'd sold off, leased or lost of most their land and a few months back left the family for a cocktail waitress and an abandoned trailer over near Jordan. I'd still see him sometimes, at ball games or in the café. He'd stumble over to me and shake my hand and try to tell me funny stories about my father, though he couldn't ever remember how they ended and always got them twisted up. Anyway, she must have shot five or six times, maybe more. After a moment, the last report still clanging along the hills, she dropped the rifle and collapsed there beside it in the dust.

We all ran back to the pickup and got in and drove away.

•   •   •

And I thought, as I left for college a few years later, I was getting clean away:

But when I start graduate school, instead of renting an apartment in town, we settle in a little white house down the highway near the crossroads of Bovill, Idaho. Out our backdoor the Bitterroot Mountains rise up with their blue faces of cedar and pine. In the mornings I run along the creek down to the log works, the smell of stone and water and sweet sap strong in the air. Liz brings home buckets of blackberries from the canyon. We make pancakes for dinner, cover them with berries and cream. We've been traveling for a few years, living here and there, and are happy to be back in the West, this place we feel we know, this wide open we both love.

Saturday night we head over to the Elk Bar. It's a one-room joint in the ground floor of the old Bovill Hotel, a pile of bricks that looks like it might collapse if you kicked it hard enough. I order two bottles of High Life and two shots of Jim Beam. We smile at one another, say, "Here's to the West!" Then clink our shot glasses and drink, seal our toast with a whiskey kiss. We take our beers and wander over to the jukebox and lean down to read the yellowing song titles. I pick a Hank Williams tune. Liz goes for Patsy Cline. I start to say something to her, but suddenly she turns and yells.

There are two men—shirtless, stains on their faces, one leaning on a pool cue, the other working a wad of snoose around his mouth. They seem built out of wires and boards, their stringy legs and thick chests and hands. Liz is yelling at them, stepping forward, pointing, her voice high and loud, her face hot. These men are half grinning, half pleading, saying they didn't know who she was, thought she was a girlfriend, a cousin. And suddenly, as the one with the snoose streak on his chin glances at me and wipes at his mouth, I get it. One of them has felt her up, grabbed her ass or something as we were bent over the jukebox. I feel my whole body go tight and ready. I step forward, in front of Liz, and say, "Leave my wife the fuck alone."

They grin at one another. They step forward too, their shoulders rolling back. The one wraps both hands around his pool stick. "Hey, man, I thought she was my girlfriend. She looks like my girlfriend. Honest mistake, right? No trouble, right? You don't want any trouble, do you?" It's an honest question. Because they do. They've forgotten Liz entirely. They're both staring right at me, the sweat shining on their bare chests. The stains, I see now, are blood bright on their faces. This is what they came for, this is what they wanted all along. And the rest of the bar knows this, too. They have quieted, hunkered down, turned ever so slightly our way. They're waiting, wondering. What will this man do, this skinny man who goes to the university, this man we don't know, this outsider? Will he do the right thing? Will he swing? He ought to swing. That's his wife there. He ought to bust that beer bottle right across that boy's face. He'll get the shit kicked out of him then. Those boys are twice as mean as he is.

You can see that plain as day. But that doesn't matter. He ought to swing.

I don't swing. I say, again, "Leave my wife the fuck alone," and I take her arm, and we leave. We walk down the street to the other bar in town, Bailey's, where I drink shot after shot of bourbon, where someone follows us from the Elk and tells us that it's a good thing we left because those boys just got laid off by the local logging company and have been strung out on meth for days and getting meaner each hour. But neither booze nor commiseration helps. I'm in a bad way. I'm in a darkness I haven't ever known. This is as close as I've ever been, and I'm furious that I didn't, furious that in that moment they could have done whatever they wanted, taken what I love most.

Later, as Liz sleeps, I go to the shed behind the house and stand in front of the rough cut boards of the back wall. I swing and swing and my fists crack against the wood and soon the skin of my knuckles is shredded, my fingers swollen and bleeding. I beat the boards with my open hands, my elbows, my chest, my face. At some point, I fall to my knees. I breathe. I stand and walk back with my broken hands into the house.

·   ·   ·

Go over it again: how it begins with the whims of wind and want, or maybe just some quick moment of stupidity; how failure and shame, even in an instant, become so impossibly heavy, a sack of stones you must shoulder; how this then is fear; and how fear someday detonates you—the slow implosion, the breakneck explosion.

But it doesn't have to be this way. We will fail, we will still act without good reason, we will always be burdened with failure and shame—but that, I think, is where things can change: There is a kind of awful and ready reverence that is some kin to fear but is not fear. It is when we understand the blood drying on our hands, the package of hand-wrapped meat we pull from the freezer. It is when we recognize how stories fail us and how stories save us. It is when we have heard them both and tell, in the moment of our greatest need, the story that will save us.

Like my grandfather. He knew and loved the way it had been, he saw the way it had to be. And always, even in the darkest of my days, my blood remembers his voice. I am here and mostly whole because of the stories he told me. We need to remember how it really was and is out West. And we need to tell those true, new stories.

Newsweek

WINNER—COLUMNS AND
COMMENTARY

More than any other medium, magazines have the power to explain, to define, to put things into perspective. Magazines display that power on every page—in their reporting, in their photography, but especially in their analysis of political issues. Here Fareed Zakaria, editor of Newsweek International, *explains the significance of the unrest that followed the 2009 presidential election in Iran. This column from June 20, 2009, was one of three by Zakaria (the others were "Worthwhile Canadian Initiative," published February 16, and "The Way Out of Afghanistan," published September 21) that won* Newsweek *the award for Columns and Commentary.*

Fareed Zakaria

Theocracy and Its Discontents

We are watching the fall of Islamic theocracy in Iran. I don't mean by this that the Iranian regime is about to collapse. It may—I certainly hope it will—but repressive regimes can stick around for a long time. We are watching the failure of the ideology that lay at the basis of the Iranian government. The regime's founder, Ayatollah Ruhollah Khomeini, laid out his special interpretation of political Islam in a series of lectures in 1970. In this interpretation of Shia Islam, Islamic jurists were presumed to have divinely ordained powers to rule as guardians of the society, supreme arbiters not only on matters of morality, but politics as well. When Khomeini established the Islamic Republic of Iran, this idea, *velayat-e faqih*, rule by the Supreme Jurist, was at its heart. Last week that ideology suffered a fatal blow.

When the current Supreme Leader, Ayatollah Ali Khamenei, declared the election of Mahmoud Ahmadinejad a "divine assessment," he was using the key weapon of *velayat-e faqih*, divine sanction. Millions of Iranians didn't buy it, convinced that their votes—one of the key secular rights allowed them under Iran's religious system—had been stolen. Soon Khamenei was forced to accept the need for an inquiry into the election. The Guardian Council, Iran's supreme constitutional body, promised to investigate, meet with the candidates and recount some votes. Khamenei has realized that the regime's existence is at stake and has now hardened his position, but that cannot put things back together. It has become clear that in Iran today, legitimacy does not flow from divine authority but from popular will. For three decades, the Iranian regime has wielded its power through its religious standing, effectively excommunicating those who defied it. This no longer works—and the mullahs know it. For millions, perhaps the majority of Iranians, the regime has lost its legitimacy.

Why is this happening? There have been protests in Iran before, but they always placed the street against the state, and the clerics all sided with the state. When the reformist president Mohammad Khatami was in power, he entertained the possibility of siding with the street after student riots broke out in 1999 and 2003, but in the end he stuck with the establishment. The street and state are at odds again—the difference this time is that the clerics are divided. Khatami has openly backed the challenger, Mir Hossein Mousavi, as has the reformist Grand Ayatollah Hussein Ali Montazeri. Even Parliament Speaker Ali Larijani, not a cleric himself but a man with strong family connections to the highest levels of the religious hierarchy, has expressed doubts about the election. Behind the scenes, former president Ali Akbar Hashemi Rafsanjani—the head of the Assembly of Experts, another important constitutional body—is reportedly waging a campaign against Ahmadinejad and even possibly the Supreme Leader. If senior clerics dispute Khamenei's divine assessment and argue that the Guardian Council is wrong, it would represent a death blow to the basic premise behind the Islamic Republic of Iran. It would be as though a senior Soviet leader had said in 1980 that Karl Marx was not the right guide to economic policy.

The Islamic Republic might endure but would be devoid of legitimacy. The regime could certainly prevail in this struggle; in fact, that would have to be the most likely outcome. But it will do so by using drastic means—banning all protests, arresting students, punishing senior leaders, and shutting down civil society. No matter how things turn out—crackdown, co-optation— it is clear that millions in Iran no longer believe in the regime's governing ideology. If it holds on to power, it will do so like the Soviet Union in the late Brezhnev era, surviving only through military intimidation. "Iran will turn into Egypt," says the Iranian-born intellectual Reza Aslan, meaning a regime in which guns, rather than ideas, hold things together behind a façade of politics.

The Islamic Republic has been watching its legitimacy dwindle over the past decade. First came Khatami, the reformist, who won landslide victories and began some reforms before he was stymied by the Guardian Council. That experience made the mullahs decide they had to reverse course on the only element of democracy they'd permitted in Iran—reasonably open elections. The regime's method of control used to be to select permissible candidates, favor one or two, but allow genuine, secret balloting. In the parliamentary elections of 2004, however, the Guardian Council decided that normal methods would not achieve acceptable results. So it summarily banned 3,000 candidates, including many sitting parliamentarians. Because public support was even less certain this time, the regime went further, announcing the election results in two hours and giving Ahmadinejad victory by such a wide margin that it would preclude any dispute. Khamenei revealed the strategy in his sermon last Friday. "A difference of 11 million votes—how can there be vote rigging?" he asked.

How should the United States deal with the situation in Iran? First, it is worth pointing out that Washington is dealing with it. By reaching out to Iran, publicly and repeatedly, President Barack Obama has made it extremely difficult for the Iranian regime to claim that it is battling an aggressive America, bent on attacking Iran. A few years ago, this was a perfectly plausible claim. George W. Bush had repeatedly declared that the Iranian regime was a mortal enemy, that Iran was part of the Axis of Evil and that a military assault on the country was something he was considering. Obama has done the opposite, making clear that he views the Iranian people with warmth and would negotiate with whichever leaders they chose to represent them. In his Inaugural Address, his Persian New Year greetings, and his Cairo speech, he has made a consistent effort to convey respect and friendship for Iranians. That is why Khamenei reacted so angrily throughout most of his response to the New Year message. It undermined the image of the Great Satan that he routinely paints in his sermons. (Of course, ever the ruthless pragmatist, he also carefully left open the door to negotiations with the United States.)

In his Friday sermon, Khamenei said that the United States, Israel, and especially Britain were behind the street protests that have roiled Tehran, an accusation that will surely sound ridiculous to many Iranians. But not all: suspicion of meddling by outside powers is deeply ingrained among even the most Westernized citizens in Iran. The fact that Obama has been cautious in his reaction makes it all the harder for Khamenei and Ahmadinejad to wrap themselves in a nationalist flag.

Neoconservatives are already denouncing Obama for his caution. Paul Wolfowitz, deputy defense secretary under Donald Rumsfeld, has compared the White House reaction to Ronald Reagan's reticence when Ferdinand Marcos's regime was challenged on the streets of the Philippines. But the analogy makes no sense. Marcos was an American client—he was in power courtesy of the United States. The protesters were asking Reagan to withdraw that support and let events take their course. Iran, on the other hand, is an independent, fiercely nationalistic country with a history of British and U.S. interference in its politics and economy. Britain essentially took over Iran's oil industry in 1901; the United States engineered a coup in 1953. The chief criticism of the Shah of Iran was that he was an American puppet. As in many such countries—India is another example—this anti-imperial sentiment is quite powerful. Iranians know this is their fight, and they want it to be.

The appropriate analogy is actually to George H. W. Bush's cautious response to the cracks that started to appear in the Soviet empire in 1989. Then, as now with Obama, many neoconservatives were livid with Bush for not loudly supporting those trying to topple the communist regimes in Eastern Europe. But Bush's concern was that the situation was fragile. Those regimes could easily crack down on the protesters, and the Soviet Union could send in its own tanks. Handing the communists reasons to react forcefully would help no one, least of all the protesters. Bush's basic approach was correct and has been vindicated by history.

But there is one statement that I wish Obama had not made. Discussing the events taking place in Iran, he said that there was no important difference between Ahmadinejad and Mousavi, since they would both defend the Islamic Republic's key foreign-policy choices, from its nuclear ambitions to its support for organizations like Hamas and Hizbullah. That viewpoint has actually been voiced by some in the neoconservative camp who have openly preferred Ahmadinejad: a more threatening foe would more clearly highlight the dangers of the regime to the rest of the world. But even if this were true before the election, it is no longer true. Mousavi has become a symbol of change, anti-Ahmadinejad sentiment, and even anti-regime aspirations. He is clearly aware of this and is embracing the support. A victory for him would mean a different Iran.

Even during the campaign, what did Mousavi say that resonated most with voters? That he would do a better job on the economy? That corruption had gotten out of hand? Perhaps, but every challenger says that, and Mousavi didn't really have many new ideas or an impressive recent record to make these claims credible. The theme that Mousavi constantly hit was that Ahmadinejad had isolated the country, engaged in an aggressive foreign policy, and needlessly turned Iran into a pariah state. For many of his supporters, this was the key issue: they craved more engagement with the world, not less. Ahmadinejad's willful rejection of the West and constant references to America's supposed decline were insults to their ambition to be included again in the world community.

President Obama could look at these events and simply say, "Iran has a proud and long history of being actively involved with the world, not being isolated from it. The world has long wanted to extend the hand of engagement with the Iranian people. Watching the elections and the remarkable, peaceful demonstrations that are ongoing, it is clear that the Iranian people also want engagement with the world. We hear your voices and wish you well." That way, in a careful fashion, Obama could turn Iranian nationalism on the regime itself.

But the real issue here is not a few words from Obama, but events on the ground in Iran. The faltering of the Islamic Republic will have repercussions all over the Muslim world. Although Iran is Shia and most of the Islamic world is Sunni, Khomeini's rise to power was a shock to every Muslim country, a sign that Islamic fundamentalism was a force to be reckoned with. Some countries, like Saudi Arabia, tried to co-opt that force. Others, like Egypt, repressed it brutally. But everywhere, Iran was the symbol of the rise of political Islam. If it now fails, a thirty-year-old tide will have turned.

The Atlantic

FINALIST—COLUMNS AND
COMMENTARY

The Atlantic *is one of the most
honored publications in the history
of the National Magazine Awards.
Now edited by James Bennet, the
magazine began winning Ellies in
1971 (it won for Reporting that
year—and the following year, too)
and has received a total of 110
nominations, including one this
year for the work of Megan
McArdle. Described by the
National Magazine Awards judges
as "offbeat and on target,"
McArdle's piece "Lead Us Not Into
Debt" brings the meaning of
deficit spending home.*

Megan McArdle

Lead Us Not Into Debt

D ave Ramsey looks nothing like a televangelist. He's a little on the short side, neither fat nor thin, and he wears jeans and a sports jacket, not a shiny suit and an oily smile. With his goatee and what's left of his graying hair trimmed close to his head, he looks mostly like what he is—a well-groomed, middle- to upper-middle-class American professional. But when he runs out onstage and starts dispensing financial advice, you realize that he could have been a great preacher.

On a fine summer day at the end of August, I paid $220 for front-row seats on the floor of a minor-league hockey rink in Detroit, just to hear Ramsey talk for five hours. The ostensible topic: getting your financial life in order. Afterward, my fiancé, who grew up in the Bible Belt, called me to ask what I'd thought.

"I think I just attended my first prayer meeting," I told him.

There was, of course, a great deal of talk about money, and what to do with it. But the format was more tent revival than accounting seminar, with the first ninety minutes or so mostly devoted to Ramsey's personal story of ruin and redemption. We heard how, during the second half of the 1980s, a young Ramsey built up a multimillion-dollar real-estate empire—then lost it all as the bank got nervous and called his loans, ultimately forcing him and his wife into bankruptcy. How, searching for help in his hour of need, he turned to the Bible and discovered Proverbs 22:7: "The rich rule over the poor, and the borrower is slave of the lender." At that moment, he told an audience so hushed that we could hear the ice squeak, Ramsey decided to never borrow another dollar again.

By all accounts, he hasn't—a commitment that many business owners would like to catch him out on, since his disciples routinely shun lucrative financing deals at car dealerships, furniture stores, and electronics warehouses. The merchants' loss is Ramsey's gain: he has become rich spreading his debt-free gospel. The Dave Ramsey program got traction in evangelical churches, which are still one of the biggest distribution networks for his thirteen-week video program, Financial Peace University. Ramsey is not the first evangelical to sell financial advice to his co-religionists, of course. Jim Sammons, Crown Financial Ministries, and others all offer similar messages to get out of debt, tithe, and so on—not to mention the far more numerous proponents of the so-called prosperity gospel, who encourage consumption rather than restraint because they believe that God will shower the faithful with riches.

But although other evangelical financial advisers flourish mostly within their religious communities, Ramsey has made himself the breakout act, bringing his basic message to the wider world. His programs are available in high schools and on military bases, and Ramsey himself can be heard through his daily radio show, his nightly Fox Business broadcast, his Web sites, his live events, and his many books, including a special line of children's stories. His company, the Lampo Group, now has hundreds of employees.

Ramsey offers some investment advice (much of which would have struck horror in my business-school professors), but for most of his followers, the main attraction is a simple program: give 10 percent of your income to charity, save 15 percent for retirement, build up a sizable emergency stash and a college fund for your kids, and above all, stop borrowing money. Ramsey devotees pay cash for everything they can. They are allowed only one exception to the no-more-debt rule: a fifteen-year fixed-rate mortgage. He is so serious about shunning debt that his Web site takes only debit cards; try to pay with a Capital One Visa, and the system rejects the card, then tut-tuts at you. These simple, austere, unbreakable rules are, as Ramsey likes to say, "the advice that God and Grandma gave you."

Most things sound a lot crazier from the outside, and so once I'd decided to write about the friendly, slightly bombastic man on the television screen, I thought I should try his program, as outlined in his book *The Total Money Makeover*. At the beginning of August, I had dutifully sat down with Peter, my fiancé, to draft a budget. Once we'd given every dollar a name (as the book puts it), I drove to the bank and withdrew 1,800 of them. Huddled over the wheel to hide this stupendous wad of cash from prying eyes, I doled out the money among various envelopes for groceries, parking, entertainment, clothing, and so on, as recommended by Ramsey—and, funnily enough, by my grandmother, who invented a nearly identical system to manage my grandfather's meager earnings from delivering groceries during the Great Depression.

When you pay for something with a credit card, or even a debit card, you can easily spend a few extra dollars here and there. But as Ramsey explained—while waving a handful of hundred-dollar bills to illustrate the point—if you have to actually hand over some of your dwindling cash supply, you tend to ponder every purchase. That impulsive latte buy becomes a little less enjoyable when every time you haul out your wallet, a quavering voice inside your head asks, "You want to send Uncle Abe *away*?" And sure enough, though we thought we'd budgeted conservatively for just the necessities, we nonetheless finished the month with extra money in every envelope.

It's also hard to spend cash, because so many people look at you funny when you try. The very first day, I spent almost twenty minutes trying to check out in the "better dresses" section of a department store. The saleslady stared at the hundred-dollar bill in her palm as if I'd just handed her an eel. After a series of plaintive looks at my obviously card-free wallet, she started stabbing at the cash-register keyboard with a sort of bleak despair. To my immense surprise and relief—and clearly, also to hers—the cash drawer eventually opened.

Ramsey calls this "being weird." The phrase came up over and over again in his five-hour spiel, always punctuated with the same rejoinder: "Normal is broke." During our first month on the Dave Ramsey program, I was startled to find out how true this is. When I described my project, a really shocking number of people, many of them married professionals with good incomes, confessed that they had no control over their money.

They aren't much different from most of America. According to a recent survey from CareerBuilder, six of every ten workers "always" or "usually" live paycheck to paycheck. Affluent, educated people do a little better, but they certainly aren't immune— three in ten of those with salaries above $100,000 also report that they're spending it as fast as they make it.

In fact, in some ways, education makes living above your means easier. In business school, my fellow students and I became big fans of the idea of "consumption smoothing," as laid out in the work of economic luminaries like Milton Friedman and Laurence Kotlikoff. At least as we read it, the theory told us to do what we wanted, which was to spend money on stuff we didn't quite need. After all, we'd be making good money when we graduated, so why not borrow a little against that future income to buy a car or go to Cancun?

Ramsey could have told me why not, but I doubt I would have listened; it's a lesson you can perhaps learn only firsthand. I graduated into the teeth of the 2001 recession $100,000 in debt. My six-figure job offer evaporated when the consulting firm fell on hard times. It took me two years to find a permanent job, and when I did, that job was in journalism, which paid about a third of what I'd been expecting.

Just like me, our nation has experimented with the "educated" overuse of leverage, aka debt. Homeowners who believed that they would have been fools to rent when a mortgage-interest tax deduction was available have poured their savings and their hearts into homes they are now losing to foreclosure. M.B.A.'s are shuttering the companies they leveraged to the hilt as they chased tax deductions and higher returns. Even our politicians speak of deficit spending as a sort of investment opportunity. In industries from autos to housing, even as the private sector has retreated to repair its balance sheets, the government has dangled money it has borrowed in front of potential buyers to tempt them to further purchases.

Debt magnifies our fortunes, whichever way they're going. When incomes are rising, debt helps us live even better. When incomes are falling, fixed debt payments can push us into the abyss. If you have substantial assets, you can lose a lot more than your sterling FICO score in a bankruptcy, and bankruptcy makes it hard to save, or start over. Even if you don't go bankrupt, debt payments make it difficult for you to accumulate wealth, or to take the kind of risks that can make your life better, like switching jobs, starting a business, or getting married. And of course, if everyone takes on too much leverage at once, the whole system can collapse.

Really, we know all this. We knew it before. Just as G. K. Chesterton once remarked of Christianity, the Grandma Plan hasn't been tried and found wanting, so much as found difficult and left untried. It's hard to make a collective decision to delay gratification—and even harder to "get your grandma on" when everyone else is out charging the good life to MasterCard.

After all, many people who got caught out in the housing bubble didn't exactly want to take out an adjustable-rate mortgage with a 3 percent down payment. But there was no other way they could afford even a modest-size house in a decent school district. Houses were being priced, not on some notion of intrinsic value, but on the maximum payment that likely buyers could afford. As other buyers and many bankers became more willing to take absurd risks, even previously prudent consumers felt they had to follow suit. They couldn't get "weird" without sacrificing their children's education.

Dave Ramsey has little patience with this sort of argument. Some of his most scathing mockery is reserved for people who take out loans to pay tuition at an expensive private college. No school, he avers, is so much better than the local college that it's worth gambling with your financial future.

There's some evidence that he's right about this; a study by the economists Stacy Berg Dale and Alan Krueger famously found that students who were accepted by schools with high average SAT scores, but chose to go somewhere else, earn about the same as those who actually attend the higher-ranked school. But there is also evidence to the contrary; and what nice upper-middle-class family is willing to, well, gamble with their child's financial future?

This may be why Ramsey and the other evangelists for a debt-free existence have thrived most in a subculture that offers something even more sacred than a Harvard education. Though Ramsey's television and radio shows have attracted a large secular audience, his hard-core followers still seem to be overwhelmingly evangelical. Ramsey closed his talk in Detroit with a sober lecture on taking care of yourself mentally, physically, emotionally, and of course, spiritually. "Bluntly," he said, "I'm talking about this man named Jesus, and if you don't know him, *you need to be introduced.*" The arena erupted in a joyous roar.

Though I did take the audio CD of Ramsey's personal witness being handed out free at the exit, I'm afraid that Jesus and I aren't really any better acquainted than we were before. Nonetheless, Ramsey has made a convert out of a secular journalist with one of the pricey M.B.A.'s he likes to poke fun at. I have never felt as serenely in control of my finances as I have during these months of knowing that every single dollar is where it is supposed to be: either in the bank, or on a well-chaperoned date with our envelope organizer. The process has been surprisingly painless but, even more surprisingly, pleasant.

Of course, both my fiancé and I have already acquired our expensive educations and a pair of decent cars. We don't have any kids, we don't own a home, and it won't hurt us to rent a few extra years until we have paid off the last of our student loans and can afford a 20 percent down payment on a house. It is easier for us to be weird than for most of our peers.

On the other hand, Americans aren't going to fix our national financial problems until a lot more people decide to drop out of the "normal" competition to see who can borrow the most money in order to bid on a fixed number of homes in affluent school districts and places at selective colleges. You don't need to be a Christian to look for a better way. Even an unbeliever knew enough to listen up when he saw the bright light on the road to Damascus.

Popular Science

FINALIST—COLUMNS AND COMMENTARY

The National Magazine Award judges described Theodore Gray's monthly column, "Gray Matter," in Popular Science, *as "a concise tutorial on the science of how things work . . . an argument for awe, for a sense of wonder." When the video for this piece appeared on the Pop Sci website, one visitor's comment was a bit more succinct: "that's freaking awesome!!!" But what else can you say when someone shows you how to use bacon to melt metal? What follows is a 500-word explanation of why readers love magazines.*

Theodore Gray

Bacon: The Other White Heat

I recently committed myself to the goal, before the weekend was out, of creating a device entirely from bacon and using it to cut a steel pan in half. My initial attempts were failures, but I knew success was within reach when I was able to ignite and melt the pan using seven beef sticks and a cucumber.

No, seriously. The device I built was a form of thermal lance. A thermal lance, typically made of iron instead of bacon, is used to cut up scrap metal and rescue people from collapsed buildings. It works by blowing pure oxygen gas through a pipe packed with iron and magnesium rods. These metals are surprisingly flammable in pure oxygen, releasing a huge amount of heat as they are consumed. The result is a jet of superheated iron plasma coming out of the end of the pipe. For sheer destructive force, few tools match a thermal lance. But iron isn't the only thing that's flammable in a stream of pure oxygen.

Bacon is fattening because it contains a lot of chemical energy tied up in its proteins, and especially in its fat. You can release that energy either by digesting it or by burning it with a healthy supply of oxygen. The challenge isn't creating the heat; it's engineering a bacon structure strong enough to withstand the stress of a 5,000°F bacon plasma flame.

I used prosciutto (Italian for "expensive bacon") because it is a superior engineering grade of meat. I wrapped slices of it into thin tubes and baked them overnight in a warm oven to drive off all the water. Then I bundled seven of those together, wrapped them in additional slices, and baked the bundle again until it was hard and dry.

To make an airtight, less-flammable outer casing, I wrapped this fuel core with uncooked prosciutto before attaching one end of it to an oxygen hose. You can't imagine the feeling of triumph when I first saw the telltale signs of burning iron: sparks bursting from the metal, and then a rush of flame out of the other side as I witnessed perhaps the first-ever example of bacon-cut steel. And the lance kept on burning for about a minute.

It turns out there are much easier ways to do this. For example, while researching how to build a vegetarian lance, I hit on the perfect pipe material—hollowed-out cucumbers. The pressure-containment capacity of a standard cucumber is remarkable, and the smooth skin makes it easy to create an airtight seal with the pipe delivering oxygen to the device. A cucumber packed with beef sticks will burn for almost two minutes, and a completely vegetarian version stuffed with breadsticks, though not quite as long-lasting, still produces a very impressive flame.

The lesson here is that food is a source of serious amounts of energy. Pure oxygen helps release it in a much shorter time than usual, but it's really the chemical energy in the bacon that makes the steel pan burn. Whether it's worth building a bacon lance to demonstrate this—well, only you can be the judge of that.

Travel & Leisure

FINALIST—COLUMNS AND
COMMENTARY

If you go out of your way to avoid tourists—even if it means missing out on the best cannoli in town or hearing a sizzling band in New Orleans—then read this. "In Defense of the Tourist" was one of three pieces by Jon Peter Lindberg nominated for the National Magazine Award for Columns and Commentary; the others were "Unhappy to Serve You" (published in the September Travel & Leisure), *about the mysterious attraction rude waiters exert on some diners, and "Stop the Music!" (November) about—what else?—Muzak.*

Peter Jon Lindberg

In Defense of Tourism

Once I got into an argument with a friend over the hot-button issue of cannoli. We were standing in Mike's Pastry, a popular stop for bus tourists and presidential candidates in Boston's North End. My friend's problem was not so much with the cannoli (which he called "flaky" and "cheesy") as with a prominently displayed photograph of Bill Clinton gobbling one up. "How can you like this place?" Alex ranted. "It's like a funnel siphoning the souls out of hapless tourists."

"Really? And I thought the filling was ricotta."

My side of the argument was also less about Mike's cannoli (which I call "Proustian" and "delicious") than Alex's counterintuitive conviction to boycott Mike's Pastry because Bill Clinton and bus tours went there. When his own grandparents had come to town asking about "that bakery the president likes," Alex shanghaied them across Hanover Street to Modern Pastry—a shop serving an adequate cannoli and not one head shot. God forbid they be suckered into the sublime, "touristy" rendition at Mike's.

I admit, though, that I'm prone to thinking like Alex when I travel. Maybe you are too. We'll come upon this fabulous Japanese *izakaya* or Czech jazz club or Parisian zinc bar—some corner of the universe that seems to have been created to our own specifications—and then, suddenly, all these other people show up. And then more of them. And then still more. *Ohhhhhh, this is all wrong*, we think; our beloved discovery is a tourist trap.

Yet recently I got to wondering: maybe it was my worrying that was all wrong. What did I really care about the presence or absence of fellow travelers, or the character thereof? Was this precious zinc bar so fragile it couldn't withstand the affection of a hundred other like-minded visitors? Perhaps it wasn't the place that needed saving, but my outlook. Doesn't every traveler start out as a tourist?

You know how politicians are always saying this is no time to engage in politics? Well, what *politician* is to politics, *tourist* is to tourism. And *touristy* has devolved from "of or relating to tourists" to "ignoble, tacky, cloying, ersatz." For travel writers, *touristy* is the ultimate slander. Even *flea-ridden flophouse* seems less damning. We're forever distinguishing between hip travelers and sheeplike tourists. We parse the world's offerings into things tourists do versus things "locals" do, as if the mere act of residing somewhere confers a sense of style. For all the times I've indulged that facile distinction, I offer my apologies. Because frankly, this ridiculous fixation on what is and what isn't "touristy"—and who is or isn't a "tourist"—can ruin a vacation.

In the age of mass tourism, high-end travel becomes increasingly about exclusivity—seeking out isolated places and rarefied encounters that only a lucky few can enjoy. (It was easier back in the day: when Delacroix visited Tangier, there were no bus tours to flee from.) By this equation, the merit of an experience corresponds inversely to the number of people we're obliged to share it with. In the urge to legitimize, singularize, and privatize our travel experiences, we trade the proverbial hell of other people for the hell of trying in vain to avoid other people. That's a terribly cool way to travel, and when I say *cool* I mean *chilly*, and when I say *chilly* I mean obnoxious.

Sure, certain places are so extraordinary we forgive them their teeming hordes. No traveler could honestly dismiss as tourist traps the terra-cotta warriors at Xi'an, Machu Picchu, the Taj Mahal, or the British Museum. But when it comes to choosing what other sites to visit, where to have dinner, or which show to see that evening, we go out of our way to leave the hoi polloi behind. Exclusivity threatens to become an end in itself, wherein we base our itineraries not on what's actually worth seeing but on where other Americans aren't.

For most of my life, I believed independent travel was the only route to the real unfiltered stuff. I eschewed group experiences like the plague, running from cruises, luaus, dinner shows, and, most of all, anything incorporating the word tour: carriage tours, walking tours, eight-seat tandem-bike tours, gondola tours, duck-boat tours, harbor tours, sunset harbor tours, ghost tours, foliage tours. . . . To me they all sounded silly and artificial. Why would I actually plan to put other people between me and what I'd come to see?

My mistake. Since being cajoled into what turned out to be a brilliant London Walks ramble through Hampstead Heath, I've gained some of my best travel memories from being herded around with a bunch of strangers—on a Big Onion Walking Tour of Irish New York; on a twenty-person nature trek in the Malaysian jungle; on a National Park Service stroll through New Orleans's French Quarter under the tutelage of an erudite ranger in a funny hat. It struck me that independent travelers, so adamant about seeing the world on their own terms, tend not to line up to listen to People Who Know Things, and therefore tend not to learn about, say, the Great Boston Molasses Flood of 1919. Seriously, Google that. I lived in Boston for years, yet the first time I heard of this sticky and surreal episode was on a Boston Duck Tours boat with my nephew.

Being a tourist can give you access to experiences you wouldn't have otherwise—experiences that aren't so much exclusive as *inclusive*, drawing their appeal from the company of other people. Independent travel may offer the tantalizing possibility of disappearing into a place, name-tagless, and acting the part of the vaunted native, but that rarely pans out. Traveling solo through India, I always expected some local shopkeeper or templegoer to invite me home for chai and divulge all the secrets of the culture. Never happened. Last year a couple I know took a Road Scholar tour of Rajasthan with a dozen other Americans; every day they shared tea or a home-cooked meal with Rajasthanis, several of whom they still correspond with. If that's "touristy," somebody strap a Nikon around my neck.

Snooty travelers would instinctively dismiss a place like Bukhara as a feedlot for tourist cattle. Every New Delhi guidebook recommends this boisterous kebab restaurant, which is why it's always packed to its exposed rafters. Whole planeloads of tour groups come through Bukhara each evening, and guess what: they're having a way better meal than you are tonight. The chicken and lamb kebabs are easily the best I've tasted (and not a word to my Iranian mother-in-law). After one visit, Bukhara shot to the top of my Really Is list—as in, "No, no, it *really is* that good." I laughed and thought of my old friend Alex as I scanned the house specialties: the "presidential" platter and the "Chelsea" platter, the former named after Alex's North End cannoli nemesis, who dined here during a state visit to India in 2000. Judging from the proportions of their namesake dishes, Bill and Chelsea Clinton not only took a village, they devoured most of its livestock. Yet the crowd at Bukhara is so consumed with enjoying themselves that one can imagine the Clintons hardly making a stir. British honeymooners, Elderhostel groups from Sarasota, Kuwaiti businessmen, Indian clans with toddlers in tow—all are having a blast. And in the ultimate mark of a proud tourist haunt, every last patron is wearing a gingham bib.

The problem with the term *touristy* is that it broadly applies to—and condemns—a whole lot of things that are merely guilty of being popular with out-of-towners. The leather-bound guest directory at New Orleans's Ritz-Carlton recommends a night at

Vaughan's Lounge with Kermit Ruffins & the Barbecue Swingers. If I were a hotel guest directory, I would too: Ruffins's Thursday sets at Vaughan's are incendiary, and a favorite even among (ahem) locals. Should it matter that a bunch of people from Minneapolis and Osaka are there too? When something inherently cool is adopted by tourists, does that render it uncool? In Reykjavík, Iceland, the Islandia shop is exactly what you'd expect of a state-sponsored tourist emporium, packed with souvenir puffin dolls, die-cast Viking figurines, and overpriced wool sweaters for your dad. They also sell the complete discographies of Björk, Sigur Rós, and the Sugarcubes. So: Is Björk "touristy"? Is Kermit Ruffins? No. The answer is no.

Considering that only 28 percent of Americans have passports, you sort of have to hand it to anyone who leaves home in the first place, no matter how often they show up in your photos of the Pont Neuf. Rather than resenting your compatriots for the audacity of choosing the same vacation spot as you, why not tip your hat to them for having found their way there at all? Would that more of us had the time and money to travel. As for cynical travelers, they can arguably learn, or relearn, something from the wide-eyed "tourist"—from the sense of wonder and unmitigated joy he brings to those top-of-the–Eiffel Tower, crest-of-the-Cyclone, edge-of-the–Grand Canyon moments that all travelers, no matter how jaded, long for. This involves surrendering to the inherent awkwardness of being a stranger in a foreign land, yet somehow losing yourself—and your self-consciousness—at the same time. It means letting go of the suspicion, letting down the defenses, and allowing for a genuine response, even if that response is simply "*Wow.*" It means enjoying a Central Park carriage ride or a London walking tour or a sunset cruise on San Francisco Bay without second-guessing whether you should be doing so. It means finally quieting—or ignoring—that nagging inner voice that asks, Do I dare to eat a peach? Or are peaches just a little too . . . touristy?

New York

Not every magazine story is a feature story or an opinion piece. In fact, magazines publish more stories about taking care of your family, managing your finances, and staying healthy and happy than anything else. As a sample of this work, here is an outstanding piece of service journalism: a package on, yes, circumcision. Of course, these kinds of things usually include photographs, illustrations, diagrams, listings, sidebars—this package originally had them all, but, hey, this is a book, not a magazine.

Michael Idov,
Christopher Bonanos,
and Hanna Rosin

Excerpts from

For and Against Foreskin

Would You Circumcise This Baby?

Michael Idov

To cut or not to cut. The choice loomed the moment New Yorkers
Rob and Deanna Morea found out, three months into Deanna's
pregnancy, that their first child was going to be a boy. Both had
grown up with the view of circumcision as something automatic,
like severing the umbilical cord. To Rob—white, Catholic, and
circumcised—an intact foreskin seemed vaguely un-American.
Deanna, African American and also Catholic, dismissed the parents who don't circumcise their children as a "granola-eating,
Birkenstock-wearing type of crowd." But that was before they
knew they were having a son.

Circumcision is still, as it has been for decades, one of the
most routinely performed surgical procedures in the United
States—a million of the operations are performed every year.
Yet more Americans are beginning to ask themselves the same
question the Moreas did: Why, exactly, are we doing this? Having peaked at a staggering 85 percent in the sixties and seventies, the U.S. newborn-circumcision rate dropped to 65 percent
in 1999 and to 56 percent in 2006. Give or take a hiccup here

and there, the trend is remarkably clear: Over the past thirty years, the circumcision rate has fallen 30 percent. All evidence suggests that we are nearing the moment (2014?) when the year's crop of circumcised newborns will be in the minority.

Opposition to circumcision isn't new, of course. What is new are the opponents. What was once mostly a fringe movement has been flowing steadily into the mainstream. Today's anti-circumcision crowd are people like the Moreas—people whose religious and ideological passions don't run high either way and who arrive at their decision through a kind of personal cost-benefit analysis involving health concerns, pain, and other factors. At the same time, new evidence that circumcision can help prevent the spread of AIDS, coupled with centuries-old sentiments supporting the practice, are touching off a backlash to the backlash. Lately, arguments pro and con have grown fierce, flaring with the contentious intensity of our time.

The idea of separating the prepuce from the penis is older than the Old Testament. The first depiction of the procedure exists on the walls of an Egyptian tomb built in 2400 B.C.—a relief complete with hieroglyphics that read, "Hold him and do not allow him to faint." The notion appears to have occurred to several disparate cultures, for reasons unknown. "It is far easier to imagine the impulse behind Neolithic cave painting than to guess what inspired the ancients to cut their genitals," writes David L. Gollaher in his definitive tome *Circumcision: A History of the World's Most Controversial Surgery*. One theory suggests that the ritual's original goal was to simply draw blood from the sexual organ—to serve as the male equivalent of menstruation, in other words, and thus a rite of passage into adulthood. The Jews took their enslavers' practice and turned it into a sign of their own covenant with God; 2,000 years later, Muslims followed suit.

Medical concerns didn't enter the picture until the late nineteenth century, when science began competing with religious belief. America took its first step toward universal secular circumcision, writes Gollaher, on "the rainy morning of February 9, 1870." Lewis Sayre, a leading Manhattan surgeon, was treating an anemic five-year-old boy with partially paralyzed leg muscles when he noticed that the boy's penis was encased in an unusually tight foreskin, causing chronic pain. Going on intuition, Sayre drove the boy to Bellevue and circumcised him, improvising on the spot with scissors and his fingernails. The boy felt better almost immediately and fully recovered the use of his legs within weeks. Sayre began to perform circumcisions to treat paralysis—and, in at least five cases, his strange inspiration worked. When Sayre published the results in the *Transactions of the American Medical Association*, the floodgates swung open. Before long, surgeons were using circumcision to treat all manner of ailments.

There was another, half-hidden appeal to the procedure. Ever since the twelfth-century Jewish scholar and physician Maimonides, doctors realized that circumcision dulls the sensation in the glans, supposedly discouraging promiscuity. The idea was especially attractive to the Victorians, famously obsessed with the perils of masturbation. From therapeutic circumcision as a cure for insomnia there was only a short step toward circumcision as a way to dull the "out of control" libido.

In the thirties, another argument for routine circumcision presented itself. Research suggested a link between circumcision and reduced risk of penile and cervical cancer. In addition to the obvious health implications, the finding strengthened the idea of the foreskin as unclean. On par with deodorant and a daily shower, circumcision became a means of assimilating the immigrant and urbanizing the country bumpkin—a civilizing cut. And so at the century's midpoint, just as the rest of the English-speaking world began souring on the practice (the British National Health Service stopped covering it in 1949), the U.S.

settled into its status as the planet's one bastion of routine neo-natal circumcision—second only to Israel.

That belief held sway for decades. Men had it done to their sons because it was done to them. Generations of women came to think of the uncircumcised penis as odd. To leave your son uncircumcised was to expose him to ostracism in the locker room and the bedroom. No amount of debunking seemed to alter that. As far back as 1971, the American Academy of Pediatrics declared that there were "no valid medical indications for circumcision in the neonatal period." The following year, some 80 percent of Americans circumcised their newborns.

What changed? The shift away from circumcision is driven by a mass of converging trends. For one, we live in an age of child-centric parenting. New research suggests that the babies feel and process more than previously thought, including physical pain (see "How Much Does It Hurt?"). In a survey conducted for this story, every respondent who decided against circumcision cited "unwillingness to inflict pain on the baby" as the main reason. The movement toward healthier living is another factor. Just as people have grown increasingly wary of the impact of artificial foods in their diets and chemical products in the environment, so too have they become more suspicious of the routine use of preventive medical procedures. We've already rejected tonsillectomy and appendectomy as bad ideas. The new holistically minded consensus seems to be that if something is there, it's there for a reason: Leave it alone. Globalization plays a part too. As more U.S. women have sex with foreign-born men, the American perception of the uncut penis as exotic has begun to fade. The decline in the number of practicing Jews contributes as well. Perhaps as a reflection of all of these typically urban-minded ideas, circumcision rates are dropping in big coastal cities at a faster rate than in the heartland. In 2006, for example, a minority of male New York City newborns were circumcised—43.4 percent. In Minnesota, the rate was 70 percent. Circumcision, you could say, is becoming a blue-state-red-state issue.

The Moreas considered all of this and more, having imbibed more information about both the pros and cons of circumcision during the last four months of Deanna's pregnancy than they care to recall. They still hadn't decided what to do until the day after their son, Anderson, was born. Then, when a nurse came to take the boy to be circumcised, the decision came clear to them. "We didn't want to put him through that—we didn't want to cut him," says Deanna. "It's mutilation. They do it to girls in Africa. No matter how accepted it is, it's mutilation."

And yet, the pendulum is already swinging back. Earlier this year, the *New York Times* published a front-page story noting that the Centers for Disease Control was considering recommending routine circumcision to help stop the spread of AIDS. The idea was based largely on studies done in Africa indicating that circumcised heterosexual men were at least 60 percent less susceptible to HIV than uncircumcised ones. The story promptly touched off a firestorm, with pro- and anti-circumcision commenters exchanging angry barbs. The CDC will now say only that it's in the process of determining a recommendation.

Caught at the crossroads of religion and science, circumcision has proved to be a free-floating symbol, attaching itself to whatever orthodoxy captures a society's imagination. Its history is driven by wildly shifting rationales: from tribal rite of passage to covenant with God to chastity guarantor to paralysis cure to cancer guard to unnecessary, painful surgery to a Hail Mary pass in the struggle with the AIDS pandemic. There's no reason to think a new rationale won't come down the pike when we least expect it. Our millennia-long quest to justify one of civilization's most curious habits continues.

Anatomy of a Circumcision

Christopher Bonanos

No matter who performs a circumcision—an obstetrician at the hospital, or a mohel at a bris—the operation is more or less the same every time. So how does it work?

First comes anesthetic, at least in the hospital. Some mohels use none, and simply work fast. Others administer a few drops of sugary syrup or sweet wine to help distract and sedate the baby. Still others use a topical cream. Doctors, as well as some medical-school-trained mohels, sometimes administer a penile block, a set of anesthetic injections. The first needle goes in under the pubic bone, where the nerves are. One or more injections follow, and those subsequent needles "go into numbed areas," says Dr. Jed Kaminetsky, a urologist.

Now the cutting begins. The opening at the tip of the foreskin is stretched and held open, usually with surgical clamps. Then the doctor or mohel makes a snip up the center of the foreskin with a pair of surgical scissors, peeling the two halves back to make a flat sheet of skin. At this early stage of life, the foreskin is attached to the underlying skin by thin membranes, and has to be picked away, typically with a little sticklike tool.

From there, most circumcisions are performed with one of three instruments. *The Mogen clamp*—similar to the traditional rabbi's tool known as a Mogen shield—clasps the flattened foreskin between two wide, flat pieces of metal, and a scalpel is run along their face to trim away the foreskin.

Another option, *the Plastibell*, is a small sleeve that's slipped over the tip of the penis, under the foreskin. The cutter simply ties a tight suture all the way around the base of the foreskin, cinching it against the plastic cylinder. Then the excess skin is trimmed off with surgical scissors, and the Plastibell's handle is snapped off and discarded. The tie stays in place; so does the

Plastibell. Over the next several days, the remaining bit of fore-skin withers and falls off, taking the string and Plastibell with it.

Then there's a more complex device called *the Gomco clamp*. It's a stainless-steel gizmo that allows the doctor or mohel to pull up the foreskin around a steel cap, tie it taut, and then slice neatly around the penile head.

After the procedure, parents should check for bleeding every half-hour for the first few hours. There's usually some swelling, which goes down after a week or so. Parents should also check for fevers, which can indicate an infection, and keep an eye out for yellowish pus or any other evidence that the wound isn't healing properly. Most important, though, is plain old hygiene. Change diapers frequently, to keep the wound from getting con-taminated, and add a dab of Vaseline to the scab each time so it doesn't stick to the diaper.

How Much Does It Hurt?

Michael Idov

Conventional wisdom once held that because an infant's nervous system was not yet fully developed, he wasn't fully capable of ex-periencing pain. Modern research, however, suggests otherwise.

In a study conducted at Rochester General Hospital in 1994, researchers used heart rate, breathing, and reactions like crying and making eye contact to quantify infant pain. They came to the conclusion that infant *Tylenol, the customary pain reliever* used in most hospitals, was not nearly enough to do the job.

Three years later, a University of Toronto study suggested that the pain experienced in the course of a neonatal circumcision may even have long-lasting behavioral effects. During a trial of a numbing cream, the scientists discovered that *circumcised babies show stronger pain response to subsequent routine vacci-nation* than uncircumcised ones, even after four or six months.

(This study employed a technique called neonatal facial coding, which gauges pain from such indicators as "brow bulge," "naso-labial furrow," and "eyes squeezed shut.") The paper concluded that the findings might "represent an infant analogue of a post-traumatic-stress disorder." The American Academy of Pediatrics has since formally recommended the use of anesthetic in circumcisions.

Advocates of circumcision insist that the above studies rely on circumstantial evidence. They note that many medical procedures are painful, and that infants' kicking and screaming comes as much from being restrained as it does from the cut.

All that may be true, but the scientific community seems to have reached a new consensus: While the consequences of infant pain are still not fully understood, circumcision hurts plenty.

What Can Go Wrong?

Christopher Bonanos

Circumcision is, by and large, one of the safest surgical procedures one can perform on a human. But complications do happen. Estimates of their frequency vary dramatically, from 0.01 percent of cases up to 10 percent or more. *A paper by the American Academy of Family Physicians claims that there are two deaths per million circumcisions. Not a lot—but not zero, either.*

Trouble mostly falls into two categories: general surgical issues like infections and excessive bleeding, and flat-out errors. The medical literature includes, for example, the story of a wound that became infected with staphylococcus bacteria, which spread, fatally, to the lungs. As for accidents, they are exceedingly infrequent, but they're unnerving all the same. Most of those involve slightly misplaced cuts: *If there's too much foreskin left, it can adhere to the penis as the scar forms. If there's too little, a skin graft may be necessary to fill in the gap.*

Perhaps the ultimate nightmare scenario is the so-called John/ Joan story. In 1966, after an eight-month-old named Bruce Reimer lost his penis to a horribly botched circumcision, doctors persuaded his family to allow gender-reassignment surgery and raise him as a girl. Reimer later re-declared himself male, and eventually took his own life, at thirty-eight, in 2004.

What About Cancer and AIDS?

Christopher Bonanos

One of the trump cards in the pro-circumcision argument has been this: Men who are circumcised rarely get penile cancer and have a markedly lower incidence of AIDS and other sexually transmitted diseases. Studies have appeared to prove, disprove, and qualify both questions. So what are we to believe?

When it comes to cancer, an intact *foreskin tends to trap bacteria against the delicate and permeable skin of the glans.* That can create an environment that breeds infections and, over time, raises cancer risk. That said, penile cancer is already extremely rare, constituting just 0.2 percent of all cancers in U.S. men. Simply keeping clean may be nearly as effective as circumcising.

In terms of AIDS, scientists have found that the inner surface of the *foreskin contains a large number of immune cells that attract the virus.* Add to that the fact that the foreskin tends to trap germs, and you have a well-defined means of infection. In one of the largest randomized controlled studies on AIDS and circumcision in sub-Saharan Africa, *researchers found that widespread mass circumcision could cut HIV infection rates by 60 percent* or more. The prevailing science, in other words, suggests that universal male circumcision would probably significantly decrease the spread of AIDS in Africa. Whether the same benefits are enough to justify the procedure in the West remains an open question.

One Man, Both Ways

As told to Molly Bennet

I wasn't circumcised because my father felt it wasn't medically necessary. He was born in Europe and wasn't circumcised, and I think fathers have an almost primal urge for their sons to look like them. I was teased about my penis as a kid, but by high school it had mostly stopped. The bigger problems started when I become sexually active. Sometimes when I would have sex, the foreskin would tear. I had to go to the hospital once in my twenties, and the doctor recommended circumcision. I was horrified. It seemed like the classic example of the remedy being worse than the problem. And by that point I was proud of my uncircumcised penis. A few women thought it was weird, but in general I got positive feedback. I decided it was one of those defining features that no one should want to get rid of, like Cindy Crawford's mole.

My mind started to change for a number of reasons. For one, the foreskin tearing didn't get better, and I started to develop scar tissue. But the bigger issue was that I was in a relationship with the woman (at that time, she was my fiancée) who would go on to become my wife. Before her, I'd had something of a promiscuous past. I wanted to feel as if I was starting over sexually. No matter how many people I'd been with, she would be the only woman to see me like this.

Of course I was apprehensive about the surgery. I read some horror stories about surgical mistakes, that there would be a loss of sensation, the sex wouldn't be as good, the healing process could be agonizing. But then I contacted a couple guys who had been circumcised as adults, largely because they were converting to Judaism, and I heard good things from them. The hardest part was the anesthesia: They take a needle and make a circle all around the base of the penis. That hurt. And then there is a tiny pinprick right around the head of the penis, but after that, the surgery is painless. It is an outpatient procedure: I was in and out of there in less than two hours. The first night was very painful, but 800 milligrams of ibuprofen got me through it, and after that I didn't take anything. It was just sore.

Obviously the no. 1 question is, what's sex like? One thing that's different is that I always used to beg out of oral sex. Even from women who were very good at it. It was too much sensation, too intense. After the circumcision, oral sex became a whole lot easier; the pain was gone but the pleasure remained. Plus there are other little things that I used to take for granted. I'd been sexually active for twenty years—from when I was seventeen until I was circumcised at thirty-seven—which is a long time to acclimate yourself: This is how I do it, this is how my body works. I hadn't realized how many compromises I'd made, just little shifts of flesh, to feel comfortable. The things that I can do now are totally different. When I'm with my wife, I don't have to have that moment of, *Uh oh, is this going to hurt?* That is an enormous relief. There haven't been any complications either. You hear stories about men who turn into premature ejaculators or have difficulty ejaculating. Neither of those things turned out to be true. My wife says she doesn't notice any difference.

If I were to have a son, I don't see why I wouldn't have him circumcised, given the potential benefits, in terms of cleanliness and what we're finding about HIV and STDs. As I see it, there really are very few negatives. After my procedure I did feel a twinge of loss when I thought about my father—that I was different from him now. He died in 2006, but he knew about the surgery, and was a little perplexed by it. He gave me that look of *Why on Earth would you want to do that?* But my dad was a good liberal dad—do what you want to do. For me, circumcision made sense on every level: medically, sexually, and emotionally. I have never regretted it for a single day.

What Your Sex Partners Think

Sarah Bernard

"The first time I saw an uncircumcised penis, I was turned off by it. I was young, like twenty-one. It didn't look like it was clean. It's totally different with my husband. The first guy had a lot of foreskin—even with an erection it was still hooded—whereas my husband is never hooded. The skin moves. I didn't even know he was uncut until he told me. There are varying degrees of foreskin, I now realize."

—32-year-old woman, married to an uncut Englishman

"Oral sex is more interesting with uncircumcised. There's just more there; you get to engage with it. Every other girl I've talked to about it said she thought uncut penises were gross, but to me it's just a little turtleneck. What's the big deal?"

—28-year-old single woman

"Circumcised penises are definitely more attractive. Uncircumcised tends to look like there's been a lot of wear and tear on them after a while, because the foreskin stretches. Not that that hurts the sex."

—50-year-old woman, divorced from an uncut man, dating a cut man

"The first time I saw an uncircumcised penis, I was twenty-one. It was my first trip to Europe alone, and I hooked up with a French guy for a week. I was fascinated by it, because I didn't have the same equipment. It's fetishized in the gay community, I think, for that reason. You want what you don't have. I also feel like uncircumcised men have more intense orgasms than I have."

—42-year-old circumcised gay man

"My husband, who is circumcised, is impossible to get off. Like, impossible! The only other person I have been with wasn't circumcised. To get him aroused, I could just take the outer casing and peel it back, and I could tell by his face that the feeling was like, holy shit, that is good. You never get that with circumcised."

—32-year-old married woman

"The thing about having sex with an uncircumcised guy is you don't get dry. There's not as much friction involved, so you can go on for a lot longer. I absolutely prefer uncircumcised. Only thing is, guys with foreskins really don't like having a condom on, because it's more suffocating. And that can be a problem."

—26-year-old single woman

"I've had sex with sixteen guys, eight circumcised and eight not. In general, the cleanliness thing was an issue for me. I'd rather have circumcised, just because you never have to worry about that."

—31-year-old married woman

The Anti-Circumcision Reader

Four high-profile authors' objections and misgivings.

Railing against circumcision, or at least seriously questioning it, has become something of a voguish chattering-class obsession. Andrew Sullivan, author, journalist, and writer of *The Atlantic*'s Daily Dish blog, and Christopher Hitchens, author and *Vanity Fair* contributor, have both called the practice barbarism and say it should be banned for infants. Despite being Jewish and ultimately circumcising their sons, Michael Chabon, the novelist best known for *The Amazing Adventures of Kavalier and Clay*, and Shalom Auslander, whose memoir, *Foreskin's Lament*, tells you a lot just in its title, have expressed grave reservations of their own. Here, a sampling of their thoughts.

ANDREW SULLIVAN, AUTHOR, *THE CONSERVATIVE SOUL*

If parents tore the skin off their infants in any other part of the body, they'd be arrested for abuse. The great unmentionable, of course, is that religion, not medicine, is behind this practice—Judaism and Islam, to be precise. Many secular men, in other words, bear the scars of someone else's religion on their own bodies for life . . .

My own view is that forcing boys to have most of their sexual pleasure zones destroyed without their express permission is a form of child abuse . . .

CHRISTOPHER HITCHENS, AUTHOR, *GOD IS NOT GREAT: HOW RELIGION POISONS EVERYTHING*

As to immoral practice, it is hard to imagine anything more grotesque than the mutilation of infant genitalia. . . . In some animist and Muslim societies it is the female babies who suffer the worst, with the excision of the labia and the clitoris. . . . In other cultures, notably the "Judeo-Christian," it is the sexual mutilation of small boys that is insisted upon.

MICHAEL CHABON, AUTHOR, *MANHOOD FOR AMATEURS*

The stated reason for this minutely savage custom is that God—the God of Abraham—commanded it. . . . Nothing having to do with this particular version of God and His supposed Commandments could ever satisfactorily explain my willingness to subject my sons . . . to mutilation: the only honest name for this raw act that my wife and I have twice invited men with knives to come into our house and perform, in the presence of all our friends and family, with a nice buffet and a Weekend Cake from Just Desserts.

SHALOM AUSLANDER, AUTHOR, *FORESKIN'S LAMENT*

I found myself . . . sitting across the way from Patricia, a formerly Orthodox, currently Buddhist, macrobiotic, pro-Palestinian, animal-rights-activist art director. "I can't believe you're even considering it," she said "Why don't you just cut off his finger or slice off his nose? Stab him—knife him—for God" . . . I was beginning to feel a bit like a foreskin myself. "Why don't you just punch him in the face?" she suggested ". . . Wait eight days, invite the family over, put out some wine and kugel, and just punch him in the fucking face."

The Case Against the Case Against Circumcision

Hanna Rosin

Anyone with a heart would agree that the Jewish bris is a barbaric event. Grown-ups sit chatting politely, wiping the cream cheese off their lips, while some religious guy with minimal medical training prepares to slice up a newborn's penis. The helpless thing wakes up from a womb-slumber howling with pain. I felt near hysterical at both of my sons' brisses. Pumped up with new-mother hormones, I dug my nails into my palms to keep from clawing the rabbi. For a few days afterward, I cursed my God and everyone else for creating the bloody mess in the diaper. But then the penis healed and assumed its familiar heart shape and I promptly forgot about the whole trauma. Apparently some people never do.

I am Jewish enough that I never considered not circumcising my sons. I did not search the web or call a panel of doctors to fact-check the health benefits, as a growing number of wary Americans now do. Despite my momentary panic, the words "genital mutilation" did not enter my head. But now that I have done my homework, I'm sure I would do it again—even if I were not Jewish, didn't believe in ritual, and judged only by cold, secular science.

Every year, it seems, a new study confirms that the foreskin is pretty much like the appendix or the wisdom tooth—it is an evolutionary footnote that serves no purpose other than to incubate infections. There's no single overwhelming health reason to remove it, but there are a lot of smaller health reasons that add up. It's not critical that any individual boy get circumcised. For the growing number of people who feel hysterical at the thought, just don't do it. But don't ruin it for the rest of us. It's perfectly clear that on a grand public-health level, the more boys who get circumcised, the better it is for everyone.

Twenty years ago, this would have been a boring, obvious thing to say, like feed your baby rice cereal before bananas, or don't smoke while pregnant. These days, in certain newly enlightened circles on the East and West Coasts, it puts you in league with Josef Mengele. Late this summer, when the *New York Times* reported that the U.S. Centers for Disease Control might consider promoting routine circumcision as a tool in the fight against AIDS, the vicious comments that ensued included references to mass genocide.

There's no use arguing with the anti-circ activists, who only got through the headline of this story before hunting down my e-mail and offering to pay for me to be genitally mutilated. But for those in the nervous middle, here is my best case for why you should do it. Biologists think the foreskin plays a critical role in the womb, protecting the penis as it is growing during the third month of gestation. Outside the womb, the best guess is that it once kept the penis safe from, say, low-hanging thorny branches. Nowadays, we have pants for that.

Circumcision dates back some 6,000 years and was mostly associated with religious rituals, especially for Jews and Muslims. In the nineteenth century, moralists concocted some unfortunate theories about the connection between the foreskin and masturbation and other such degenerate impulses. The genuinely useful medical rationales came later. During the World War II campaign in North Africa, tens of thousands of American GIs fell short on their hygiene routines. Many of them came down with a host of painful and annoying infections, such as phimosis, where the foreskin gets too tight to retract over the glans.

Doctors already knew about the connection to sexually transmitted diseases and began recommending routine circumcision.

In the late eighties, researchers began to suspect a relationship between circumcision and transmission of HIV, the virus that causes AIDS. One researcher wondered why certain Kenyan men who see prostitutes get infected and others don't. The answer, it turned out, was that the ones who don't were circumcised. Three separate trials in Uganda, Kenya, and South Africa involving over 10,000 men turned up the same finding again and again. Circumcision, it turns out, could reduce the risk of HIV transmission by at least 60 percent, which, in Africa, adds up to 3 million lives saved over the next twenty years. The governments of Uganda and Kenya recently started mass-circumcision campaigns.

These studies are not entirely relevant to the U.S. They apply only to female-to-male transmission, which is relatively rare here. But the results are so dramatic that people who work in AIDS prevention can't ignore them. Daniel Halperin, an AIDS expert at the Harvard School of Public Health, has compared various countries, and the patterns are obvious. In a study of twenty-eight nations, he found that low circumcision rates (fewer than 20 percent) match up with high HIV rates, and vice versa. Similar patterns are turning up in the U.S. as well. A team of researchers from the CDC and Johns Hopkins analyzed records of over 26,000 heterosexual African American men who showed up at a Baltimore clinic for HIV testing and denied any drug use or homosexual contact. Among those with known HIV exposure, the ones who did turn out to be HIV-positive were twice as likely to be uncircumcised. There's no causal relationship here; foreskin does not cause HIV transmission. But researchers guess that foreskins are more susceptible to sores, and also have a high concentration of certain immune cells that are the main portals for HIV infection.

Then there are a host of other diseases that range from rare and deadly to ruin your life to annoying. Australian physicians give a decent summary: "STIs such as carcinogenic types of human papillomavirus (HPV), genital herpes, HIV, syphilis and chancroid, thrush, cancer of the penis, and most likely cancer of the prostate, phimosis, paraphimosis, inflammatory skin conditions such as balanoposthitis, inferior hygiene, sexual problems, especially with age and diabetes, and, in the female partners, HPV, cervical cancer, HSV-2, and chlamydia, which is an important cause of infertility." The percentages vary in each case, but it's clear that the foreskin is a public-health menace.

Edgar Schoen, now a professor emeritus of pediatrics at the University of California San Francisco, has been pushing the pro-circumcision case since 1989, when he chaired an American Academy of Pediatrics Task Force on the practice. The committee later found insufficient evidence to recommend routine circumcision, but to Schoen, this is the "narrow thinking of neonatologists" who sit on the panels. All they see is a screaming baby, not a lifetime of complications. In the meantime, sixteen states have eliminated Medicaid coverage for circumcision, causing the rates among Hispanics, for one, to plummet. For Schoen and Halperin and others, this issue has become primarily a question of "health-care parity for the poor." The people whom circumcision could help the most are now the least likely to get it.

This mundane march of health statistics has a hard time competing with the opposite side, which is fighting for something they see as fundamental: a right not to be messed with, a freedom from control, and a general sense of wholeness. For many circumcision opponents, preventive surgery is a bizarre, dystopian disruption. I can only say that in public health, preventive surgery is pretty common—appendix and wisdom teeth, for example. "If we could remove the appendix in a three- or four-minute operation without cutting into the abdomen, we would," says Schoen. Anesthesia is routine now, so the infants don't suffer the way they used to. My babies didn't seem to howl more than they did in their early vaccines, particularly the one where they "milk" the heel for blood.

Sexual pleasure comes up a lot. Opponents of circumcision often mention studies of "penile sensitivity regions," showing the foreskin to be the most sensitive. But erotic experience is a rich and complicated affair, and surely can't be summed up by nerve endings or friction or "sensitivity regions." More-nuanced studies have shown that men who were circumcised as adults report a decrease in sexual satisfaction when they were forced into it, because of an illness, and an increase when they did it of their own will. In a study of Kenyan men who volunteered for circumcision, 64 percent reported their penis to be "much more sensitive" and their ease of reaching orgasm much greater two years after the operation. In a similar study, Ugandan women reported a 40 percent increase in sexual satisfaction after their partners were circumcised. Go figure. Surely this is more psychology than science.

People who oppose circumcision are animated by a kind of rage and longing that seems larger than the thing itself. Websites are filled with testimonies from men who believe their lives were ruined by the operation they had as an infant. I can only conclude that it wasn't the cutting alone that did the ruining. An East Bay doctor who came out for circumcision recently wrote about having visions of tiny foreskins rising up in revenge at him, clogging the freeways. I see what he means. The foreskin is the new fetus— the object that has been imbued with magical powers to halt a merciless, violent world—a world that is particularly callous to children. The notion resonates in a moment when parents are especially overprotective, and fantasy death panels loom. It's all very visual and compelling—like the sight of your own newborn son with the scalpel looming over him. But it isn't the whole truth.

GQ

FINALIST—REVIEWS AND CRITICISM

The National Magazine Award judges said it best: "With dazzling skill, Tom Carson uses popular culture as a lens on our country's obsessions, charging his work with both relevance and revelation." This piece, on our never-dying love affair with vampires, was one of three nominated for the Ellie in Reviews and Criticism; the others were "One Glorious 'Basterd,'" on a different kind of gorefest, and "The Great White Hype," on the documentary Tyson.

Tom Carson

There's a
Sucker Born
Every Minute

Wake up and smell the coffin, gang. Not only is America's vampire crush outdoing "I Can Has Cheezburger?" as our time's defining meme, but Bela Lugosi wouldn't recognize himself. When Glenn Beck compared Obama to *Twilight*'s lead bloodsucker, he didn't realize he risked making Forty-Four look sexier to millions of nubiles who will soon be old enough to vote.

Lucky for the rest of us, the *Twilight* phenomenon is just the Kids Meal edition of jugular fever, with the CW's *The Vampire Diaries* doing its best to cash in while the cashing's good. At the other extreme is HBO's *True Blood*, juicing up the same premise—nice 98.6 girl meeting undead Mr. Right—with radlib double entendres, southern-fried kookiness, and Anna Paquin as the cutest naked lunch a vampire could crave. No contest which of them draws the happiest male crossover audience, yours truly included. Can *The Vampire Cookbook* (big type, wide margins, one succinct recipe) be far behind?

At one level, the variety just goes to show that what Bram Stoker wrought has become pop Esperanto. Since we all speak Vampire, TV and movies can use it to talk about whatever they like—not only here but abroad, where the topics are predictably different. (See: Sweden's top-notch *Let the Right One In* and South Korean auteur Chan-Wook Park's delirious *Thirst*.) What's done the most to transform the American variant, however, is the way vampires themselves—traditionally Hollywood's favorite exaggeration of old-world cosmopolitans whose ways were not our ways—have gotten as Americanized as Arnold Schwarzenegger.

Not coincidentally, they've also gone from representing our darkest fears to personifying attributes we envy. Both *Twilight* and *True Blood* feature humans eager to be "turned," an inversion of the classical vampire myth that's unmistakably a fantasy of Cinderella-style upward mobility. The unabashed title of one current vampire-fiction serial—*Blue Bloods*—pretty much gives the game away, since aspiring to join clubs like these used to be un-American by definition. Remember, Lugosi got famous playing Count Dracula.

Even Anne Rice—the most influential vampire novelist since Stoker himself—gave her elegant night people European bloodlines. But all that changed with director Kathryn Bigelow's terrific 1987 redneck thriller, *Near Dark*. As home-brewed as Pabst Blue Ribbon, Bigelow's wild-bunch antiheroes were also rowdy enough to fit right in at a town hall on health care. Even so, their indigenous successors didn't stay low-class for long.

Twenty-odd years later, not even meaning to be satiric, *Twilight* has given us vampires living the American Dream. Since dark comes early in November, the undead Cullen clan may even vote—and they probably vote Republican, since they've got a cushy lifestyle to protect. If their Frank Lloyd Wrong pad in the Pacific Northwest doesn't look a lot like the house original author Stephenie Meyer dreamed of buying with her book's royalties, I miss my bet.

It may go without saying that Meyer—Mormonism's drippiest gift to pop culture since the Osmonds—doesn't have an ironic bone in her body, let alone an ironic buck in her bank account. That's why the only irresistible scene in last year's Twilight movie was the nutso one that featured her pasty-faced crew taking advantage of a thunderstorm's cover to play a high-powered version of our national pastime. Vlad Durham, meet Yogi the Impaler.

Vampire baseball, can you dig it? If the old SCTV gang had thought that one up, they'd have knocked off early for the day to celebrate. But sometimes ninnies express truths that smart alecks couldn't think up at gunpoint. Thanks not least to its eerie echo of Camelot's touch-football games, the image of Lugosi's star-spangled descendants shagging flies in ball caps had the one pop-cult virtue that can't be faked: accidental profundity.

Or maybe it's just that I can relate to baseball, which gave me a welcome break from pondering girlie America's latest pinup. If you ask me, *Twilight* star Robert Pattinson was born to play the first teen heartthrob with no pulse. But my preference for acting that involves mutable facial expressions and such isn't likely to stop legions of ululators from crowding the multiplex this month for the *Twilight* sequel, *New Moon*, undaunted that Pattinson's character—hundredsome-year-old high schooler Edward Cullen, the River Styx dreamboat to Kristen Stewart's lachrymose Bella Swan—doesn't get too much screen time this go-round.

Saying I saw the first *Twilight* only out of duty is an understatement on a par with calling Miley Cyrus no great shakes as a pole dancer. But even though no one over twenty should care, director Catherine Hardwicke—who isn't on board for the sequel—was impressively smart about what would get her target audience tingly. The camera's awe whenever Pattinson deigned to so much as blink was any sane grown-up's cue to chortle, yet the hyperbole was as shrewdly judged as Josh Hartnett's magic-man entrance in *The Virgin Suicides*—in hindsight, a more pivotal movie than it appeared to be at the time. The sex-equals-death spin on girliness that haunted Sofia Coppola's directorial debut has taken exactly a decade to go from being the perturbing stuff of an art flick to providing eye candy for simps.

For loyal *Buffy the Vampire Slayer* boosters like me, the real marvel is that Joss Whedon's girl-power agit-pop needed even less time to get regurgitated as retro glop. Yet mass culture's genius isn't what it discovers—it's what it domesticates. Within limits, of course: If you enjoy truth in advertising, *Twilight*'s wittiest touch is that the Cullens are fangless, something so important to Meyer that she had it written into her contract when she sold the movie rights.

If that's her idea of avoiding clichés, not only has that ship already sailed; she might as well be rearranging dentures on the *Titanic*. Still, the grassy-knoll types who spent months dissecting *The Dark Knight* and *300* as pro-Bush allegories could do worse than get cracking on *Twilight*. It's not just that Edward Cullen is a virtuous vampire who only unleashes his powers to save Bella's bacon. His competition for her affections is a Native American shape-shifter—that's "D-e-m-o-c-r-a-t," Stephenie—who's kind of a wuss. See what I mean about pop Esperanto?

By contrast, *True Blood*'s anti-Bush glee makes subtext as archaic as laser discs. Before Anne Rice ruined everything for her fans by going Christer on them, she won a vast gay following by creating sympathetic vampires whose nonmainstream tastes made them mournful but special. Now Alan Ball has junked the mournfulness—about time, too—while reworking the parallel to send up homophobia.

Better yet, he's discovered that turning vampires into an interest group is a great way to crack wise about all the other smackdowns that keep God's favorite country so lively. Smug subcultures versus heartland straight arrows, ostracism versus tolerance, assimilation versus exclusivity—yep, the whole bazaar. Subtle he isn't, but you can't say it's not a joke we're all in on.

In case you don't know already, *True Blood*'s nifty premise is that vampires have become socialized. They're "out of the coffin," thanks to a synthetic blood substitute that keeps their teeth off our necks come chowtime. But they aren't quite accepted in red-state country, letting the obvious gags write themselves—from god hates fangs on a roadside sign to libruls' ongoing campaign to pass the Vampire Rights Amendment. To Ball's credit, some of his best gotchas zing his own in-group's vanities: I especially liked "breathers" for "breeders" as a term of abuse.

Despising *American Beauty* as I did, I never thought I'd have a good word for its Oscar-winning scenarist. Even Ball's *Six Feet Under* never wiggled my toes, but don't forget he used to write sitcoms. With *True Blood*, he's pulled off the trick of making vampirism funny without destroying its mystique, something the humor-challenged Rice not only wouldn't have attempted but couldn't have seen the point of.

Keeping the cleverness from turning too arch is six-ways-to-Sunday plotting that delivers the melo, abetted by the most enjoyable cast on TV. As the spunky heroine, Paquin combines acute concentration with giddy spontaneity; she's had this character nailed ever since she cracked up at the idea of a vampire named Bill when she met her future love interest in the premiere. She's also the smart half of an ace sibling act, with Ryan Kwanten putting the stud back in stupid as her well-meaning bro—a dude so susceptible he can go from volunteering for the "Fellowship of the Sun," the show's Christian Coalition parody, to embarrassing Vampire Bill (Stephen Moyer) with an "I love you, man" hug.

Since Bill is pretty democratic for a vampire—a believer in "mainstreaming," *TB*-speak for "Can we all just get along?"—his shudder spoke volumes. No matter how you transfuse it, the vampire myth will always be a fantasy of aristocracy. Those elegant but gloomy creeps snuffing the candles on their 300th birthdays were just the supernatural edition of all the Turner Classic Movie staples featuring rich folk who learn that wealth and fame can't buy happiness. But relocation to the New World and modern times has made snobbery central to vampirism's appeal.

In a society short on pedigrees, being undead gives them, y'know, roots. It's a virtue *True Blood* made merry with by having Bill talk to a club of Confederate idolaters about his firsthand Civil War experiences and that *Twilight*'s Bella is predictably impressed by. Maybe it does take a couple of centuries' practice for an American to learn how to be suave.

Lots of viewers must covet life in these covens the same way *Godfather* fans used to wish they could be the Corleones. Not only do vampires belong to a ritzy community that takes care of its own, but they've got traditions. They're a little blood-soaked, sure, but you know the old saying about omelets. If gangsters-as-metaphors are fading these days, that might be because vampires-as-metaphors have taken their place—not as a projection of go-getting capitalism but wishful privilege.

No wonder the bloodsuckers' main competition in pop circles is a renewed craze for zombies, the ultimate fantasy of mindless egalitarianism turned comic nightmare. Funny enough, they were always American: Defined a scant forty years ago by George A. Romero's *Night of the Living Dead*, they could be the only genuinely original contribution to monster lore we've ever made.

As a given—we may be dumb, but we've got working brains—zombies feed on their superiors. But I can't think of a vampire tale in which that's been true, which is the sickest reason we can sneakily imagine ourselves being one. Not exactly a pretty picture of our secret lives in 2009, is it? Go vampire or go zombie, America: It's your choice. Just don't say this great country doesn't offer you one.

Los Angeles

FINALIST—REVIEWS AND CRITICISM

Linking, blogging, tweeting—these days anyone with a laptop is a movie critic. Yet some people still like to hear what magazine writers who know what they're talking about have to say. For those people, there is Steve Erickson. "War Games" was one of three pieces by Erickson nominated for the National Magazine Award for Reviews and Criticism; the others were "The Next Frontier," about Battlestar Galactica, and "No Ordinary Fad," about those new videogame stars, the Beatles.

War Games

I f you love movies where any minute a bomb is going to go off and everything teeters on whether the red or green wire gets snipped in time—even though you sit through the whole thing peeking at the screen through your fingers—then Kathryn Bigelow's *The Hurt Locker* is for you. Not only is there one such situation after another, each more ominous than the last, but the bombs are in Iraq, a country caught in its own countdown to the detonation everyone knows is coming yet no one knows when. An unidentified number of days or months or years into the American occupation, the head of a special army detail dedicated to disarming mass explosives is killed and replaced by Sergeant William James (Jeremy Renner), who's defused more than 800 bombs through know-how and sheer force of attitude. Showing the anarchy of Iraq no respect, James swaggers into uncertainty like a gunslinger kicking in the swinging doors of the saloon. To his fellow soldiers he's one more element of craziness in a crazy place, ratcheting up an insanity they already can barely stand. The two specialists immediately under James's command, who have a month remaining in their rotation, openly contemplate blowing him up before he gets them killed.

Clearly inspired by the Iraq war, the British comedy *In the Loop* is about London and Washington bureaucrats maneuvering both capitals into a conflict the public would never tolerate if it spent five minutes paying attention. When a weaselly foreign minister for "international development" (Tom Hollander) characterizes the prospect of imminent war as "unforeseeable" in a television interview, alarm bells ring in the corridors of power—though to those of us in the audience watching (not through our fingers anymore), it's not altogether evident why. Is it because "unforeseeable" sounds like there *will* be a war or because it sounds like there won't? To those making policy, the very vagueness of the word represents an unacceptable instability, a loss of control of the spin. The international development minister thinks he's against the war, but a lot of other people think he's for it and soon he is, whatever he happens to really think, assuming he really thinks anything or knows what it is if he does. Soon everyone else around him, from pols to generals who understand the war is a big mistake, is swept up, as though the war is starting itself.

The Hurt Locker and *In the Loop* are the first two Iraq films to have gotten their tone right. For a couple of years movies have been circling the subject of the war, occasionally taking it head on—such as in Paul Haggis's *In the Valley of Elah*, which still felt compelled to masquerade as a thriller—but more often brushing up against it. If Iraq wasn't the explicit landscape of such features as *Rendition*, *Redacted*, *Lions for Lambs*, *Syriana*, *Charlie Wilson's War*, *The Kite Runner*, *The Kingdom*, and *Body of Lies*, most of the important points made by those movies were directed at the war, and the failure of these movies commercially and critically was born out of an unsolvable dilemma not unlike that of the war itself. Both the war and its films have taken place in the shadow of 9/11, which obscured the purpose and perception of the war exactly as anticipated by those who plotted it, including those who were planning it before 9/11 and who then used 9/11 to justify it. The movies were no less confused about this than everyone else. Filmmakers avoided Iraq while the war was popular; by the time they caught up with the public sentiment that shifted so rapidly, what the movies had to say was so obvious the audience didn't feel they needed to hear it.

A cult filmmaker in the '80s, Bigelow in the early '90s seemed on the cusp of some breakthrough to a mass audience. That never came to pass, and while you can argue that her crime thrillers *Blue Steel* and *Point Break*, as well as the future-noir *Strange Days*, were underrated, there was something grim about them, even slightly nasty, as there was about the desert vampire flick *Near Dark* that put Bigelow on the map. As *The Wild Bunch* did for westerns, *Near Dark* escalated the violence of its genre and imparted to it poetry, which made the violence that much more horrifying. Since then, Bigelow, who began as a painter, has filled her work with unforgiving imagery that insists on beauty in what otherwise verges on the unwatchable. If for Bigelow it's about the visuals, for *In the Loop*'s Scottish director, Armando Iannucci, who started in radio and TV, it's about the words, most spectacularly delivered with lacerating panache by Peter Capaldi as a Whitehall spinmeister trying to rein in hapless ministers who don't know how to zip it when words escape them. Like their movies, Bigelow and Iannucci couldn't be more different on the face of it. *The Hurt Locker* reminds you of *Full Metal Jacket*, and *In the Loop* recalls *Dr. Strangelove*, and it may take a moment to realize that both touchstones are by Stanley Kubrick, who seems more different still. What these directors do share with Kubrick, and with each other, is a pervasive and finally overwhelming sense of folly, something that eluded the earlier Iraq movies in all their sobriety and sorrow.

It's a cliché that war is folly. Treating World War II as folly would not only ignore history but betray the moral majesty of that war, the scale of its cost, the breathtakingly unambiguous evil that so distinguished one side from the other. It's why World War II has been so facilely analogized by the proponents of every war since, including the invasion of Iraq, a country where the ruling dictator was routinely compared to Adolf Hitler whenever other arguments having to do with 9/11, terrorism, and amazing weapons that threatened us from 8,000 miles away showed signs of faltering. Ever since Vietnam, however, our wars have become more confounding, which probably is a good thing, and as the subject of a movie, even Vietnam never lent itself to the theme of folly as easily as does Iraq. What neither *The Hurt Locker* nor *In the Loop* is quite bold enough to do, though the latter certainly comes closer, is implicate its audience in that folly. The best Vietnam War movies, Francis Ford Coppola's 1979 *Apocalypse Now* being the most obvious example, are infused with the tragic because they implicitly acknowledge how smart men could reasonably have believed Southeast Asia falling to communism might be a matter of mortal American peril. But while the human cost of Iraq is tragic, the experience itself hasn't earned tragedy's grandeur because the dimensions of its blunder were so evident to anyone who paused long enough to ask even the most slightly skeptical of questions. We can try to convince ourselves we were duped, we can protest that the "intelligence" was irresistible, we can insist on connections between the Iraq debacle and 9/11, terrorism, radical Islam; but too many weapons inspectors coming back from Iraq two months before the invasion were unable to find any of these weapons that supposedly were so massive and imposing they could be delivered halfway across the planet. On the eve of that war to justify all wars, Hitler had the biggest military machine in the world, and it wasn't buried in dunes but was out on the boulevards of Berlin for the world to see. Iraq never had the biggest military machine in the Arab world, let alone the Middle East, let alone the rest of the world.

An epigraph at the outset of *The Hurt Locker* alludes to the intoxication of war, the addiction to its rush by those like Sergeant James who fight it most mercilessly and successfully. But by the end of the movie we realize it's in no small part the absurdity of the war that James revels in, and by comparison the absurdity of standing in the cereal aisle of the supermarket trying to choose among the Cheerios is trivial, not worth living for as much as he finds Iraq's folly worth dying for. There may be nothing to do but either peek through our fingers at movies like *The Hurt Locker* and *In the Loop* or laugh at them; both get close enough to a truth that the responses could be interchangeable. Think long enough about the buffoonery of *In the Loop* and you may find you can barely watch, whereas the scene in *The Hurt Locker* when James digs from out of the parched desert ground the chains and cables of one bomb only to find he's pulled up half a dozen, sufficient to blow Baghdad off the earth, is in its own way the most hysterical of all. Cracked cowboy that he is, James himself might guffaw, if only the sound of his laughter wouldn't shake the bombs from their sleep. Sooner or later, of course, when more is at risk than merely his own life, there's a bomb James can't defuse. "I'm sorry" is all he can say to the Iraqi man strapped to it. But not sorry enough never to come back for more.

Harper's Magazine

FINALIST—REVIEWS AND CRITICISM

When he died, John Cheever was eulogized—in Jonathan Dee's words—as "a sagacious optimist and family man who sat among the commuters like Tolstoy in the village square"; later, Cheever came to be remembered as a closeted critic of the empty forms of middle-class respectability. Neither was the case. In this 5,000-word essay for Harper's Magazine, *Dee explores the contradictions that bedeviled Cheever's life—and enriched his fiction.*

Jonathan Dee

Suburban Ghetto

Nineteen sixty-eight wasn't the most wretched year in the life of John Cheever, but it was close. On poor terms with his three children, bitterly angry with his wife for daring to initiate a career outside the home, and having recently had the last of his teeth removed, he spent his mornings struggling weakly to postpone his first drink of the day. Even though he was set to publish his third novel, *Bullet Park*—which he suspected, correctly, wasn't very good—his alcoholism had so crippled his ability to write that he was in the midst of a creative drought that would see him complete only one short story in three years. Tortured by the self-loathing his homosexuality engendered, increasingly estranged from his neighbors' social circle by his drunken excesses, he was so lonely that he not only answered all the fan letters he received but would frequently invite their authors, total strangers to him, to come to his house. He was just a couple of years away from touching bottom—living alone and all but insensate in a Boston apartment, where he would come so close to drinking himself to death that his brain function was permanently impaired.

And then, as 1969 began, *Life* magazine called. Would Cheever consent, they wondered, to a feature article on his privileged life in the Westchester suburbs? Would he agree to host a cocktail party for his neighbors, which the magazine might photograph, and perhaps also a touch-football game on the lawn? Would he pose standing at the bottom of a neighbor's drained swimming pool? The author, of course, complied, though he later boasted that he got his interviewer, Wilfred Sheed, so plastered that Sheed had to return on a subsequent day to ask the last of his questions.

In the years before his death in 1982, John Cheever was arguably America's most famous living writer, and yet for all the attention we paid him, his public image could hardly have been more misleading. Obituaries referred to him as "a celebrant of sunlight," a Prospero of suburbia; his persona—shaped, in large measure, by extraordinary appearances (more than a decade apart) on the covers of *Time* and *Newsweek*—was that of a sagacious optimist and family man who sat among the commuters like Tolstoy in the village square, diagnosing the verities of the upper-middle-class heart. Cheever himself—a terrible snob with an exaggerated Back Bay accent, who lied compulsively about his own WASP pedigree and who so valued conformity that as a young man he put on a suit every morning just to ride the elevators with the businessmen living in his New York apartment building—did nothing to discourage this hagiography during his lifetime.

Almost immediately after his passing, it began to fall apart. With the publication of his letters, his daughter's memoirs, and, most astonishingly, selections from the vast, unforeseeably dark journals he kept all of his adult life, readers learned the extent to which his interior life was contorted by alcohol and depression and the guilty struggle to repress his homosexual longings. Blake Bailey's thorough new biography completes the total revolution our image of the man has undergone in the quarter century since his death. Disabusing ourselves of old notions about Cheever's happiness might seem like a pointless exercise, were it not for the accompanying suspicion that all the time we were celebrating him we were doing him the disservice of misreading his work too.

•   •   •

His childhood was a not-unfamiliar tale of lapsed aristocracy, of the eccentricity spawned by distinguished lineage and reduced circumstances. It wasn't until late in his writing career that he began mining his past for anything other than comedy; in *The Wapshot Chronicle,* for instance, he found lighthearted use for the fact that when his mother had been pregnant with him, his father had expressed his opinion of this development by inviting a local abortionist over for dinner. Their distinguished forebear Ezekiel Cheever may have been eulogized by Cotton Mather for "his untiring abjuration of the Devil," but by the time John was born there was little left of the past's dignities, and those his father still clung to—for instance, the fact that his Massachusetts license plate had only four digits on it, which he felt marked him as "a man of substance"—were mostly pathetic. As a lad, Cheever was short and unathletic, and his father took no pains to conceal his fear that he had "sired a fruit." John retained vivid memories of his father, a men's-clothing salesman, weeping at the breakfast table during the Depression, and then came the development that in some respects saved the family and in others dealt it a mortal blow: his mother opened up a gift shop, a rare enough enterprise for a woman, and one at which she had the temerity to succeed. This was the end of the marriage. Cheever's father became an unemployable alcoholic and local eccentric who spent his days writing epic letters to friends and public figures alike, living in an unheated Massachusetts farmhouse, stoking its five fireplaces to such an extraordinary glow in wintertime that drivers on the nearby highway frequently thought it was on fire. Cheever dealt with this heritage mostly via dissimulation, later citing in his journal "the familiar clash between my passionate wish to be honest and my passionate wish to possess a traditional past."

But the strangest of his family relationships had to have been with his older brother, Frederick, with whom he lived after the situation at home with his parents became intolerable, and with whom, one is startled to learn, he had, as a young man, a sexual relationship. (To be fair, Bailey himself writes that it is "hard to say" whether this relationship crossed the border into explicit sexual activity, but Cheever's journal entries on the subject, as well as his documented remarks to others, seem less ambiguous.) It is typical of Cheever's tragically convoluted thinking on the subject of homosexuality that this incestuous relationship between adults seemed to him so natural and incorruptible that it became in his mind a kind of model of purity, one that he longed to re-create his entire life.

His ejection from prep school gave him the material for his first published fiction, the precociously accomplished "Expelled," which appeared in *The New Republic* when he was just eighteen. Not that success was assured; he survived a chastening decade or so as a young writer in New York, scrounging for money, eating so little he would sometimes feel faint at his typewriter. He also had a brief sexual relationship with the photographer Walker Evans, among others; in those bohemian years, before marriage, Cheever's desires seem to have been somewhat less repressed. Still, the notion that sex with men tended ultimately toward anything other than self-destruction was a long way away: "If I followed my instincts," he wrote in his journal, "I would be strangled by some hairy sailor in a public urinal. Every comely man, every bank clerk and delivery boy, was aimed at my life like a loaded pistol." The guilt he suffered in the wake of such encounters—which were rare enough, even in those early years—was such that he referred to himself as "the walking bruise."

Despite, or perhaps because of, this sense of the toxicity of his own desires, he married the well-born Mary Winternitz (granddaughter of Thomas A. Watson, co-inventor of the telephone) in 1941. It is hard to do justice to the marriage of John and Mary, other than to say that it appears to have been one of the worst in recorded history, not least because neither of them could summon the fortitude to get out of it. Cheever was a narcissistic, closeted alcoholic with a chronic impotence problem and an absurdly conservative view of a woman's domestic role, all of which was exacerbated by the fact that, unlike his businessman peers in both city and suburbs, he was always at home. But every time you're ready to feel sorry for Mary and her forty-year martyrdom, Bailey supplies some reminder that, when it came to derision, she could give as good as she got. In 1958, when Cheever returned home from several days in the hospital after being treated for a viral pneumonia that was briefly thought to be a case of tuberculosis, his wife greeted him with the wistful observation that "it was nice while you were away to have a dry toilet seat"—a remark so memorably cutting that he used it verbatim, twenty years later, in his novel *Falconer.*

At least there were roses in his hospital room while he waited for his pneumonia to clear. They had been sent by William Maxwell, his editor for decades at *The New Yorker*, and a man whose own literary afterlife seems destined to be that of hero in every biography and memoir in which he appears. Maxwell makes an amusing bête noire for Cheever not only by virtue of his seemingly effortless courtliness but because, as Bailey points out, Maxwell, too, had a wealth of homosexual experience in his youth yet had managed to do two things Cheever found impossible: first, to move beyond those youthful indiscretions and lead a "normal" life as a loving husband and father; and second, to write honestly about it, as Maxwell did in his early novel *The Folded Leaf.* (Bailey does tarnish Maxwell's halo somewhat: acting on behalf of his employers at *The New Yorker*, Maxwell appears to have screwed Cheever out of a fair amount of money, and he also stands guilty of having initially rejected some of Cheever's greatest and most unconventional work, including, unfathomably, "The Death of Justina," one of the three or four best stories Cheever ever wrote.)

Although Cheever published 121 stories in the magazine during his lifetime, it is worth remembering that *The New Yorker* was long regarded as a compromisingly middlebrow place to publish, and the insecure Cheever was always vulnerable to the canard that serious fiction only came in the form of a novel. His New Year's resolution for 1960, which fortunately he failed to keep, was to write no more short stories. In the end, he produced five novels (he didn't finish his first until he was forty-five, after almost three decades of story-writing), and even though he was virtually incapable of writing a bad sentence—Bailey tells of his own glimpse of one of the first drafts of *Falconer*: unpunctuated, unparagraphed, and yet word for word almost identical to the published version—none of the novels approaches the mastery of the stories. The novels are noteworthy for the amount of autobiographical material they contain, and for repeatedly playing out the theme of two "brothers" as different sides of one personality; from a technical perspective, however, they are little more than a series of set pieces strung together until a more or less satisfactory length is reached. The many prizes they received seem, in retrospect, more like indirect acknowledgments of how great a short-story writer he was. "One never, of course, asks is it a novel?" he once wrote, more than a little defensively. "One asks is it interesting and interest connotes suspense, emotional involvement and a claim on one's attention."

.   .   .

But of course it is the stories whose claim on readers' attention will outlive us all. He worked in two distinct modes, and templates for both appeared early in his career. "Goodbye, My Brother" (1951) thematically prefigures most of the novels with its portrait of two adult brothers at the crumbling family beach house that is their inheritance, and with the lesson one teaches the other about the perils of excessive gloom by nearly murdering

him. Its tale of optimism and social ritual triumphing, if somewhat perversely, over the forces of depression and self-doubt is a
tale about the two sides of one man's nature; to put it as Cheever
himself did in a letter to Malcolm Cowley, "There was no brother,"
which overstates the case, but not by much. Though essentially
realistic, its first-person narration pulls off lyrical flourishes (particularly in its famous last paragraph) that in another writer's
work might easily curdle into sentimentality. Cheever's other
narrative mode was that of moralistic fantasist, a contemporary
Ovid or Aesop, as first evidenced in "The Enormous Radio"
(1947), in which a Manhattan couple buys an expensive new radio that turns out to play a sordid audio feed of the lives of the
fellow residents in their apartment building. This ancient style, to
which he turned now and then for his entire career, helped make
his reputation—in part, one sees now, because the stories he
wrote in this fabulist vein were the easiest to apprehend: their
every detail is pointed like a flight of arrows to the same moral
target. With one or two glorious exceptions, principally the
darkly ambiguous "The Swimmer," they have not improved with
age. Even the celebrated "O Youth and Beauty!" —the story of the
man who re-creates his high school track-star days by drunkenly
hurdling the host's furniture at the end of every cocktail party—
seems at this distance to strive for a kind of unmistakability. We
expect great writers to be wise, but there is too much of an air of
moral surety about these pieces; as in the case of most other great
artists—and, certainly, as evidenced by "Goodbye, My Brother"—
Cheever was at his boldest when advancing into the precincts of
self-doubt.

What is newly interesting about the fabulist stories is the
claim—put forth by Cheever himself, and echoed by both Bailey
and Maxwell—that the author was more or less ghettoized by
his association with suburban cocktail parties and thus never
received his critical due as a literary forefather of John Barth,
Thomas Pynchon, Donald Barthelme, and other disrupters of

narrative convention. Indeed, the last of those names was a particular aggravation: "The stuntiness of Barthelme disconcerts me. One can always begin: 'Mr. Frobisher, returning from a year in Europe, opened his trunk for the customs officer and found there, instead of his clothing and souvenirs, the mutilated and naked body of an Italian sailor.' Blooey. It's like the last act in vaudeville and anyhow it seems to me that I did it fifteen years ago." Bailey calls this a "legitimate aesthetic grievance," which is not quite the same as saying he thinks Cheever was right. In fact, the "suave and witty narrator" (as Bailey puts it) of Cheever's work, who drops occasional meta-fictional reminders of his own presence, seems more a throwback than a postmodern subversion. And then there is the unavoidable fact that some of his most daringly surrealistic stories are also his worst, such as "The Geometry of Love"—about a man who employs Euclidean theorems to try to overcome the mercurial hatefulness of his wife—a story so lazily schematic that Maxwell, concerned that alcohol was starting to strip Cheever of his powers, drove out to the author's suburban home to reject it in person.

·   ·   ·

Bailey's biography is artfully organized and highly readable; its tone, though, is one of pained detachment, which might seem odd until one remembers that his chief source is the author's own lifelong, 4,300-page, typed, single-spaced journal, and the journal, to put it bluntly, has a pretty high bullshit quotient. When long excerpts were first published in *The New Yorker* in 1990, and later in book form, they seemed almost unbearably honest and intimate; but at this distance it is easier to see how Cheever's confessions create ample room for mythmaking and self-pity. Take this entry, written during the family's year in Rome, after a drunken Cheever has made his nine-year-old son cry by mocking the boy's friends in front of company:

I speak to him, stupidly perhaps—I was too drunk to remember what I said—and this morning when I wake him he takes
one look at me and buries his face in the pillows. He does not
want to see me, touch me, he does not like my house or my
friends. And standing in the Piazza Venezia beside a dirty
beggar I get a crushing visitation of the shabbiness of my life.

One doubts the suspiciously literary existence of that "dirty
beggar"—but then why invent him at all? Why not just remain
standing next to the young son whom Cheever has reduced to
tears for no reason? His penitence after he misbehaves is so
gussied up that it doesn't read like penitence at all—more like a
man striking penitential faces in a mirror. Even his remorse
tends toward the narcissistic. Bailey is thus forever patiently cor-
recting the exaggerations—sometimes emotional, sometimes
literal—in his subject's own record, mostly by comparing it with
the more sober reminiscences of Cheever's friends and family.

In discussing Cheever's work, though, Bailey's detachment is a
little harder to fathom. Several pages of analysis are given over to
each of the novels and to the more significant stories, but even
here he tends to turn the microphone over to others, quoting not
just contemporaneous reviewers such as Benjamin DeMott and
Alfred Kazin but tributes from the likes of Michael Chabon and
Rick Moody, whose inclusion seems a little less organic to the
story he's telling. The opinions Bailey does express do very little
to challenge the conventional thinking about Cheever's work—
"The Swimmer" is "his greatest story," *Bullet Park* is "a strange
performance," and so on—and at the end of the book he neglects
to answer his own question as to whether the decline in Cheever's
reputation is deserved, venturing only to "hazard a few guesses"
rather than to argue the case, as one might expect a literary bio-
grapher to do, for his own subject's continued vitality.

Most egregiously, Bailey parrots the received wisdom that
Cheever was engaged in some sort of "corrosive criticism" of the

privileged bedroom communities in which he lived, that his was a "vision of suburban alienation." But if a revisit to Cheever's oeuvre shows us anything, it's that his art, and his alienation, had nothing to do with the suburbs per se. Cheever was, in his wife's phrase, a split personality—not only alienated from himself but also fearful of being otherwise—and that vision, which drove all his work, was something he took with him wherever economic circumstances forced him to go.

.　　　.　　　.

One night toward the end of 1950, the lights went out in the Cheevers' New York apartment, owing to his inability to pay the electric bill; this embarrassing augur of the cost of living in Manhattan induced him to move his family upstate to a rented house—a converted machine shop, actually, on the grounds of a much larger estate—in the town of Scarborough-on-Hudson, in Westchester County. (In what must have struck Bailey as an auspicious coincidence, the house itself had been occupied a few years earlier by the thirteen-year-old Richard Yates—the subject of Bailey's previous biography—and his mother, who were booted out for nonpayment of rent.) "The suburbs of the Northeast were still an experiment of sorts," Bailey writes, "and [Cheever] was quite earnestly curious about things: given the cultural vacuum, what sort of traditions would be established by such a diverse [*sic*] group of educated, affluent people?"

Certain traditions, not to say prejudices, were unfortunately likely to endure, and thus living among the "dauntingly normal" citizens of Scarborough only ratcheted up Cheever's fear of his own sexuality. He even worried that his appearance on the cover of *Time* in 1964 would "expose" him somehow. Crucially, though, it was never really the opprobrium of others that he most feared; acting on his impulses, he wrote, "would so damage the health of my self-esteem that I would be dealing with the obscenities of death." On the exceedingly rare occasions when he did give in, the guilt he suffered afterward was brutal. At one point, though urgently in need of money, he agonized over a lucrative offer to spend a few weeks writing a screenplay in Hollywood because he feared falling prey to the "sexual corruption" there.

He was to some degree an outsider—he dressed so shabbily, at least in the local context, that the town police once stopped him on suspicion of vagrancy. And he reserved some vitriol in the journals for those neighbors he considered less cultured than himself. But he wanted to belong. He was embarrassed when his brother, Fred—a full-blown alcoholic now, and something of a boor—moved to the same town and began turning up at the same cocktail parties. In 1960, John bought a house in Ossining, which, characteristically, he insisted on telling journalists had a distinguished colonial history, notwithstanding the fact that it was actually built in 1928. In the suburban "experiment" in self-invention and instantly conferred nobility (Scarborough-on-Hudson itself was less than half a century old, established by the fiat of a bank tycoon), he saw something that not only appealed to him but synced up quite naturally with the way he had been living all along.

"The village hangs, morally and economically, from a thread," goes a line in "The Country Husband." "But it hangs by its thread in the evening light." He meant not to expose that thread but to exalt and protect it. He got the idea for "O Youth and Beauty!" at a local civil-defense meeting during which he sensed that everyone's mind was much more on the touch-football game scheduled to follow than on their own sober discussions of what to do when the A-bomb dropped. But he didn't see their distraction as shallowness or hypocrisy—on the contrary, he approved of it: "This, he concluded, was as it should be—a childish, larky escapism had its uses, at least when the alternative was contemplating Doomsday," Bailey relates, drawing on the journals. "He didn't have to write an 'excoriation of the suburbs' after all, adopting instead a tone of detached gaiety—a tone most characteristic of Cheever's mature greatness."

And yet critics needed to believe he was writing censoriously about the suburbs. (When we talk about "the suburbs" in American art, we are almost always talking about an arrogantly small slice of humanity—two counties, really: Westchester and Fairfield—that is presumed to bear all the sins of American conformity.) But the stories are full of minor characters who mouth just the sort of indictments of suburban life Cheever himself is presumed to have supplied, and to a man they are portrayed as tiresome, humorless, and unattractive—figures of fun. Attacking the pretensions of social and economic strivers is best left to lesser writers like Yates, whose *Revolutionary Road* uses its characters as punching bags and dares to call them representative of anything more than their author's desire to feel superior to them. Cheever's characters, though, aspire to live—even to feel—not in a way that challenges social expectations but in a way that is worthy of them; and when they are expelled from their closed society, it is always reflective of their own failings. In their corruption the characters are guilty not of exposing the pretentious strictures of their social existence but of letting those strictures down.

"The Country Husband" is exemplary of a Cheever story that is prized without really being understood. Its famous last line—"Then it is dark; it is a night where kings in golden suits ride elephants over the mountains"—is often read as a reminder of eternity, a heroic invocation of greatness in sharp contrast to the pettiness on display in the story itself, in which Francis Weed, upset that his family does not care enough that he has just nearly died in a plane crash, falls in love with the teenage babysitter. But the correct reading, which Bailey manages to miss, is much more concrete. Midway through the story, as the Weeds' marriage is falling apart, Francis says goodbye to the host of a cocktail party they attend: "'She's my girl,' the host said, squeezing his wife. 'She's my blue sky. After sixteen years, I still bite her shoulders. She makes me feel like Hannibal crossing the Alps.' " In Cheever's world, the happy, well-married man is king. His suburban ordinariness is not a prison; it is Francis's own inability to partake in that ordinariness that dooms him.

The suburbs may have provided an apotheosis of this idea, but the idea itself was Cheever's subject all along. We tend to forget how much of his best work is set outside that narrow world. Near the end of "The Bus to St. James's," a father picks up his daughter at her Upper East Side dancing school, having just come from a hotel assignation with the mother of another young student. In this most mannered and rarefied of settings, listen to where the indictment falls:

> Two by two the children bowed, or curtsied, and joined the grown people at the door. Then Mr. Bruce saw Katherine. As he watched his daughter doing obediently what was expected of her, it struck him that he and the company that crowded around him were all cut out of the same cloth. They were bewildered and confused in principle, too selfish or too unlucky to abide by the forms that guarantee the permanence of a society, as their fathers and mothers had done. Instead, they put the burden of order onto their children and filled their days with specious rites and ceremonies.

The forms that guarantee the permanence of a society—that is the "thread" Cheever found so beautiful and tried to set in an evening light. He loved and celebrated the social and economic mainstream, its arbitrary strictures and faux traditionalism notwithstanding, and lived in constant fear of falling from its favor and into the underworld he imagined lay beneath it. It is hard to think of another American writer who maintained that social restraints were to be valued as a kind of salvation, that salvation itself was a collective matter rather than an individual one, and the story of Cheever's own life, his desperate attempts to stave off depression by living the life he believed we are all meant to live, only amplifies the terrible beauty of that particular vision. "I would like to live in a world in which there are no homosexuals," he wrote, "but I suppose Paradise is thronged with them."

·   ·   ·

It is startling to consider, as Bailey points out, that the very idea of a major, alcoholic American writer getting sober and continuing to write was, before Cheever, without precedent. One of the keys to Cheever's renaissance, even before he stopped drinking for good in 1974, was the decision—difficult to account for, on its face—to accept a job teaching creative writing to the inmates of Sing Sing prison, right there in Ossining, New York. Bailey compares it to Chekhov's own late-career pilgrimage (of which Cheever spoke admiringly) to the penal colony on the island of Sakhalin. Ignoring the fact that one of these pilgrimages involved life-threatening hardships and a trip of thousands of miles across Asia whereas the other involved ten or fifteen minutes in the car, we can be generous and admit the similarities. It seems fair to speculate as well that part of the attraction for Cheever may have been the notion of a closed society in which homosexual relationships were not taboo.

At any rate, the inspiration provided by Sing Sing led to the satisfying final act of Cheever's life and career, in which the publication of *Falconer*—by far his best novel, centering on a homosexual love affair in prison and a fratricide that makes good on the remarkably similar act of violence in "Goodbye, My Brother"—was followed by the publication of Cheever's collected stories, the latter a main event, as the late John Leonard wrote at the time, not just in the particular publishing season but in the history of twentieth-century literature. The frankness of *Falconer* was either the cause or the effect of a similar relaxation of Cheever's censorious attitude toward his own sexuality, and he had a number of affairs with men in these final, sober years that his younger self would never have risked.

It would be a pleasure to be able to report that the unfettering of his sexual impulses turned him into a less egocentric person, but the sad fact is that he exhibited remorseless selfishness in hitting on younger men, often his own students. Much of the biography's last chapters is given over to the story of an unfortunate aspiring writer named Max Zimmer, whose emotional well-being Cheever was willing to ruin in exchange for the occasional sexual favor. (One anecdote will suffice: affecting to believe that sexual stimulation improved his eyesight, Cheever insisted that his own reading of any of his lover's manuscripts be preceded by a hand job in order to "clear [his] vision.") Others, like his Iowa student Allan Gurganus, were saved from the full force of Cheever's attentions by being, in the older writer's estimation, too "like a woman."

· · ·

In his epilogue, Bailey inventively calls an unlikely witness: Larry David, the co-creator of *Seinfeld* and writer of a landmark episode of that TV series in which a trove of letters found after a fire reveal Cheever as the secret lover of George Costanza's soon-to-be father-in-law. Why Cheever? No special reason, David says; he was just looking for "a well-known writer who was gay."

Thus the revolution is complete: whereas once we saw Cheever as a happy and enviable Westchester family man, now, in the course of reading about that life, there are long stretches during which the knowledge of the agony caused by his closeted status is the only thing that enables us to work up any sympathy for him at all. He projected onto his sons his most crippling anxieties about the clichés of masculinity, such as making the varsity football team; he hectored his young daughter constantly about being fat and, despite her many precocious accomplishments, became most giddy when she brought home a young man named Cabot. He bragged at the dinner table about his affairs, even when the physical effects of his drinking made these indiscretions mostly emotional, as in his affair with the actress Hope Lange—a great subject of the journals, which turns out to have been barely consummated.

John Updike (another bête noire, whom Cheever tried his best to like despite the envy Updike's fame and skill aroused) wrote of the journals that they "posthumously administer a Christian lesson in the dark gulf between outward appearance and inward condition." Fair enough. But our own construction of that "outward appearance" stemmed, it seems now, from a misreading of the work. That the suburbs are a false veneer, that they crush free spirits and steamroll dissent, is one of the most tired tropes in American narrative art. It is unfair and reductive that Cheever should be tarred as the father of all this, especially since he never really believed it himself. His work is far more idiosyncratic than that. His constant exhortations, in the fiction and in the journals, toward "valor" and "cleanliness" and "good cheer" are all easily identifiable now as code for his desire to enter the matrix of heterosexual respectability; but he's neither the first nor the last artist to turn private demons into oblique, extended metaphor. "That one is in conflict with oneself," he told a presumably bemused audience of Yale undergraduates in 1977, "that one's erotic nature and one's social nature will everlastingly be at war with one another, is something I am happy to live with on terms as hearty and fleeting as laughter." We can now see that the laughter itself was a sham, a construction born primarily of desperation and fear, but the work, and our literature, is still the richer for it.

The Economist

FINALIST—COLUMNS AND COMMENTARY

The Economist describes itself as a newspaper. Its editor-in-chief, John Micklethwait, works in London. Its columns are unsigned. Yet these three obituaries were nominated for the National Magazine Award ("National" as in "American") for Columns and Commentary. What gives? Simply put, The Economist—*whatever it calls itself, wherever it comes from—is one of the most widely admired magazines published in the United States today. These three obituaries—of a female impersonator, a famous fish, and an American journalist—by the not-so-anonymous Ann Wroe clearly and briefly demonstrate some of the reasons for its success.*

Ann Wroe

Obituary Columns: Danny La Rue, Benson, William Safire

Danny La Rue

Daniel Carroll (Danny La Rue), female impersonator, died on
May 31, aged eighty-one

He was tall, dark and handsome, with broad shoulders and a
crushing handshake. His turned-up nose once annoyed him so
much that for a while he slept with a peg on it. He could growl
"Ol' Man River" like Harry Belafonte, and once defended the
honor of Barbara Windsor, a well-endowed Cockney comedi-
enne, by socking a man on the jaw. On board ship, no storm ever
bothered him; he was practical and calm, even when pianos
toppled and chinaware smashed all round him.

She was tall and handsome also, but there the resemblance
ended. Her hair was blonde, brunette, raven-black, silver minx,
as the mood took her. However coiffed, she looked stunning.
Fabulous loops of glitter-beading hung from her arms; sun-
bursts of diamanté snaked round her hips; fluorescent feather-
boas kissed her neck. One day she was Marlene Dietrich in a
silver sheath, the next Joan Collins in a deep blue gown, the next
Carmen Miranda, in nine-inch platform shoes and with three
tons of fruit on her head. She was probably never more herself
than when descending the grand staircase at London's Palace
Theatre, where she played for two unbroken years, with huge

pink plumes bobbing on her head and twenty feet of ostrich feathers slithering behind her.

He was well-mannered and rather shy, schooled in respect by his Irish mother and reinforced in fatalism by his fervent Catholic faith. Hard work was his cardinal virtue; in fifty years of cabaret, theater, and music hall he never missed a show. She was a lady of leisure who, under her inimitable elegance, could be lewd, rude, and blue. He called her a tart, which she was. In fact, a whole array of tarts: Nell Gywnne, Lady Hamilton, Cleopatra (to tiny Ronnie Corbett's Caesar). She was Lady Cynthia Grope, political hostess ("Life's better under the Tories, and I should know"), as well as "the girl with a little bit more." Nudge, wink. What she could never be was ugly, clumsy, or just a man in drag.

His beginnings were clear enough: born in Cork, brought up in Soho, undistinguished schooldays, a wartime in the navy. Hers were more misty. She emerged in Juliet at school, with a costume of colored crepe paper, and then in a navy production of *White Cargo*, a pouting beauty wearing nothing but a tan and a sheet she had pinched from the officers' quarters. Once out in public, she caused a sensation. Bob Hope called her the most glamorous woman in the world. Ingrid Bergman said no one could walk down a staircase like her. From 1964 to 1973 her allure alone packed out his night club in Hanover Square with Hollywood stars and the crowned heads of Europe. Women deluged her with requests for advice on how to move, how to stand, and what to do with their hands. Every woman longed to look like her (he said), but didn't dare.

In certain ways, their characters coincided. Both knew they were stars, no question. Both adored clothes. As a child, he once laid newspaper down the street to keep his new shoes clean. In the navy, lined up on his ship with 1,199 other seamen in pure white, he affected navy and white because it looked nicer. He could happily have stayed as a window-dresser at J. V. Hutton's

General Outfitters (Exeter and London), but the limelight called him, as it did her.

Lace and Jockstraps

Looking fabulous was all her money was for. A cool £10,000 was budgeted for her frocks at the Palace, and £30,000 when she played Widow Twankey in *Aladdin*. One mirrored train cost £7,000; one wrap involved £8,500-worth of fox-fur. He spent his earnings on houses, a stately home with seventy-six bedrooms, a Rolls Royce, and fine porcelain. Fire, and a fraud into which he innocently stumbled in 1983, destroyed almost all he had saved for. He started again, doggedly doing the rounds of clubs, pier-ends, and provincial theatres, the outposts of a disappearing world.

Over half an hour each night in the dressing room, he slowly became her. First, a shave (the face only, leaving a touch of stubble for shading; his legs he left alone). Then the pan make-up, powder on face and eyes, mascara and false lashes. Her foam-rubber bosoms were built into each dress; more pan-stick painted a cleavage. "I can hang my tits up when it's hot!" she once boasted to another envious girl. Last came the wig, made especially for her.

He allowed no one else to see this process. He was still Dan, and she was "whoever"; they were always two. Under her lace and glitz, he wore a jockstrap. When she was ready, resplendent in her glitter and feathers, Dan said his prayers and let her sail out of the wings. At the end of the show, he locked the frocks and wigs away. To appear in them off-stage, with a pint grasped in his manly hand, would destroy the vision of woman he had created.

He never married. He said he regretted it, and talked of near-misses that never seemed too convincing. There was already more than enough femininity in his life. His manager, Jack Hanson, was all the close companionship he needed. He shuddered at camp, and at men who wanted to be women or wear women's clothes. Not he; his act was just a wonderful, glamorous, beautiful, elegant joke.

He was the person, he always said. She was the illusion. In practice, it didn't seem quite as simple as that.

Benson

Benson, England's best-loved fish, died on July 29, aged about twenty-five.

Peterborough, in the English Midlands, is a red-brick town, best known as the midway point on the line between King's Cross and York. But from the bottom of Kingfisher Lake, just outside it, urban toil seems far away. There, all is most delightful silt and slime. A push of your probing nose sends up puffs and clouds of fine mud through the water. A riff of bubbles rises, silvery, towards the surface. The green reeds quiver, and sunlight ripples down almost to the depths where you are lurking, plump and still.

Such was mostly the life, and such was the address, of Benson, England's most famous fish. Her actual place of birth, as a wriggling, transparent fry prey to every frog, pike, and heron, was never known. But at ten, when she was stocked in Kingfisher, she was already a bruiser. And there, among the willow-shaded banks, she grew. And grew. At her peak weight, in 2006, she was 64lb 2oz (29kg), and was almost circular, like a puffed-up plaice. Bigger carp have been seen in Thailand and in France; but she still amounted to a lot of gefilte fish.

In her glory days she reminded some of Marilyn Monroe, others of Raquel Welch. She was lither than either as she cruised through the water-weed, a lazy twist of gold. Her gleaming scales, said one fan, were as perfect as if they had been painted on. Some wag had named her after a small black hole in her dorsal fin which looked, to him, like a cigarette burn. It was as beautiful and distinctive as a mole on an eighteenth-century belle. Her lips were full, sultry or sulking, her expression unblinking; she seldom smiled. Yet the reeds held fond memories of her friend Hedges, her companion in slinky swimming until she, or he, was carried away in 1998 by the waters of the River Nene.

Abandoned, she ate more. She devoured everything. Worms, plankton, crayfish, lily roots, disappeared down her toothed, capacious throat. She was a one-fish Hoover, motoring through the food-packed sludge and through rich layers of sedimentary smells. But she was offered daintier and more exotic fare. Cubes of cheese, scraps of luncheon meat, bread crusts, Peperami, dog biscuits, and tutti-frutti balls all came down invitingly through the water. She sampled most of them.

Of course, she was not fool enough to think they came from heaven. Carp are cunning, a very fox of the river, as Izaak Walton said. She could see the lines, and at the end of them the trembling shadows of Bert, or Mike, or Stan, spending an idle Sunday away from the wife with a brolly and a can of beer. Often she continued to lurk, roiling the mud to conceal herself and basking in her own scaled beauty, as carp will. On hot days she would rise to the surface, glowing and tantalizing, with a lily-leaf shading her like a parasol. She played hard-to-get, or the One That Got Away, nudging the line before drifting down towards the dark serene. But then, just for the hell of it, she would take the bait.

The first hookings hurt like hell, the whole weight of her body tearing her tongue like a razor blade. But over the years she got used to it, and her leathery mouth would seize the bait as a prize. Hauled to the limelight, she was admirably unphased. This was, after all, the homage beauty was owed. She would submit to the scales and then pose for the photographer, unmoving, holding her breath. She had her picture taken with Tony, owner of her lake, who confessed to the *Wall Street Journal* that he had "quite a rapport" with her; with Ray, who caught her at two in the morning, disturbing her beauty sleep; with Matt, of the shy smile and the woolly hat; with bearded Kyle, for whom she looked especially dark and pouting; and with Steve, who ungallantly told *Peterborough Today* that she felt like "a sack of potatoes" and was "available to everyone." She was not, but at least fifty others held her, or gripped her, for a moment or so. Uncomplainingly, she nestled in their arms before she was lowered to her element again.

These men had a knowledgeable air about them. They might have been a secret society, meeting at odd hours in hidden nooks around the lake. Each had his spot for anoracked meditation. When they spoke, it was of wagglers and clips, spods and back-biters, size 14s and number 8 elastic. Dates and weights were bandied about, an arcane code. For a while, Benson imbibed the philosophy of a gaudier and more complex sphere, heard the tinny music of their radios, and stared into the dazzle of the day. There was much that she herself might have imparted, of the mystery of reflected and inverted things. But her anglers needed to get home to the football and their tea.

The Fatal Nut

Greed probably undid her in the end. She was said to have taken a bait of uncooked tiger nuts, which swelled inside her until she floated upwards. Telltale empty paper bags were found on the bank of the river. Or she may have been pregnant, with 300,000 eggs causing complications, or stressed after so much catching and releasing, those constant brushes with extinction. On the line between life and death, at Kingfisher Lake, she breathed the fatal air and did not sink again. And there she lay, like Wisdom drawn up from the deep: as golden, and as quiet.

William Safire

William Safire, pundit and lexicographer, died on September 27, aged seventy-nine.

Had William Safire written his own obituary, he would have laid down a few simple rules. First, use the active, not the passive voice, no matter how inert the corpse. Second, taking the bull by the hand, nix those mixed metaphors. Third, kill all sentences starting with conjunctions, or ending in "by," "with," or "on." *De mortuis nil nisi bonum*? Preferably not; *swaydo-intellectual* Latinisms cut no ice with him, unless he allowed himself a silkily Catulline *ave atque vale*.

As a practiced scribbler—never truly a hack, for that word, borrowed from England, denoted a broken-down horse let out for hire—he also knew better than to squander a good nugget in the lede. Not until halfway through his article would grieving readers learn, for example, that he used to buy the unknown Ariel Sharon breakfast each time he came to New York; that Barbara Bush would wink at him on grand occasions, while her husband froze him out; or that he once wrote a spoof interview with Richard Nixon languishing in purgatory, his entry into heaven having been delayed because . . . he had imposed wage and price controls.

Mr. Safire was a *pundit*, or wise man, a word derived from the Hindi via Henry R. Luce at *Time* magazine (source also of the words *tycoon*, *moppet*, and *socialite*, to none of which Mr. Safire either ascended or aspired). As such, he wrote political and lexicological columns for the *New York Times* for more than thirty years. He was also, in a nod to his Jewish ancestry, a *maven*, meaning "he who understands," a Hebrew-Yiddish word slipped into English in the 1960s in an ad for herring in cream sauce. He was of the old school, and had been so long in the commentary dodge that he sometimes called his *computer* his *typewriter* (though keeping up, as nimbly as any twenty-something, with the *blargon* and *cellphoney-baloney* of the age). He wore *plaid*. An Englishman would have called it *tweed*, originally a misreading of *tweel*, the Scots form of *twill*. Either way, the check was loud, and rarely matched his tie.

He stood out at the *Times*, though, less for his clothes than his views. These were to the fiercely libertarian right, a stance rarely seen at the *Gray Lady*. That was exactly why Punch Sulzberger hired him. He arrived in 1973 fresh from a job as speechwriter and campaign strategist for Nixon and his veep, Spiro Agnew, after an energetic earlier career as a *flack*, or public-relations man. The word came from the Second World War, describing the smoke from German anti-aircraft shells, and hence the puffed-up information or exaggerated shows Mr. Safire and his sort provided. He liked battlefield coinings. His favorite word of all, his friend Daniel Schorr thought, was *zap*, as in "Let me *zap* him." Failing that, *snappers* and *zingers* were regularly landed on his foes: Hillary Clinton, Lee Kuan Yew, the startled John Ashcroft when attorney general, and anyone using singular verbs with plural nouns.

Hold That Prognostication

Nixon he did not dislike. (Nor backwards sentences, neither.) To him he was not *Tricky Dick*, a name first coined in 1950 by a rival in a race for junior senator from California, but rather *Mr. Nice Guy*. Mr. Safire did him a large favor, in 1959, by engineering a conversation between him and Nikita Khrushchev (Nik heated, Dick cool) at a trade fair in Moscow. Once he had joined the *Times*, though, Mr. Safire was shocked to find himself the victim of a Nixonian *wiretap*. It was made no better, but much more interesting, when one of his Lexicographic Irregulars found an early usage from the Civil War, a *tap* into the telegraph *wires* at Lebanon Junction during Morgan's raid of 1863 that discovered the Louisville garrison to be "much alarmed."

The most famous phrase from his speechwriting days was *nattering nabobs of negativism*, written for Agnew as a joke to describe "defeatists who thought we could never win in Vietnam." Agnew liked alliteration. (So did Mr. Safire; though asinine alliteration was best avoided, when pounding out the punditry he could rarely resist.) In his *Political Dictionary* he later explained that *negativism* was the key word; that *nabob*, from the Urdu, meaning governor, hence self-important potentate, was the ideal practitioner of a *negative* outlook (see the use by John Adams in 1776); and that *nattering* was meant to denote complaining, but that Stewart Alsop, his pundit-mentor, had told him that the British use was closer to *chattering*. Neither Agnew nor Vietnam victory-thoughts lasted too much longer.

He saw himself, mixing the metaphor only slightly, as a *lone wolf* gazing at the horizon. Since world politics was his beat as well as the English language, he loped off on wild excursions into both. He became obsessed with Iraqi spymasters meeting al-Qaeda operatives in Prague, and remained a cheerleader for the Iraq war when most folk had fallen quiet. (It was neither a *total* war nor quite a *limited* war, just a *quick* war, he wrote, after which joyful Iraqis would thank their liberators, and *freed scientists* would reveal giant stacks of weapons of mass destruction.) His legions of lefter-leaning fans wondered whether he also believed in the *tooth fairy*. They could look it up, in perhaps the most pleasing cross-reference from his *Political Dictionary*: "TOOTH FAIRY, See SANTA CLAUS, NOBODY SHOOTS AT."

National Geographic

WINNER—ESSAYS

Here is one American institution looking at another: National Geographic on the state fair. Actually, there's a third at work here: Garrison Keillor, whose magazine writing has unjustly, if understandably, come to be overshadowed by his long association with A Prairie Home Companion. *This is what the National Magazine Awards judges had to say about the piece: "From the breadbasket of our country comes a deep-fried, deliciously revealing essay on the peculiarly American ritual of the state fair." But don't worry—there's no fat here.*

Garrison Keillor

Top Ten State Fair Joys

The state fair is a ritual carnival marking the end of summer and gardens and apple orchards and the start of school and higher algebra and the imposition of strict rules and what we in the north call the Long Dark Time. Like gardening, the fair doesn't change all that much. The big wheel whirls and the girls squeal and the bratwursts cook on the little steel rollers and the boys slouch around and keep checking their hair. It isn't the World's Columbian Exposition, the Aquarian Exposition, the Great Exhibition of the Works of Industry of All Nations, the Exposition Universelle, the Gathering of the Tribes, or the Aspen Institute. It's just us, taking a break from digging potatoes.

The Ten Chief Joys of the State Fair are:

1. To eat food with your two hands.
2. To feel extreme centrifugal force reshaping your face and jowls as you are flung or whirled turbulently and you experience that intense joyfulness that is indistinguishable from anguish, or (as you get older) to observe other persons in extreme centrifugal situations.
3. To mingle, merge, mill, jostle gently, and flock together with throngs, swarms, mobs, and multitudes of persons slight or hefty, punky or preppy, young or ancient,

wandering through the hubbub and amplified razzmatazz and raw neon and clouds of wiener steam in search of some elusive thing, nobody is sure exactly what.

4. To witness the stupidity of others, their gluttony and low-grade obsessions, their poor manners and slack-jawed, mouth-breathing, pop-eyed yahootude, and feel rather sophisticated by comparison.

5. To see the art of salesmanship, of barking, hustling, touting, and see how effectively it works on others and not on cool you.

6. To see designer chickens, the largest swine, teams of mighty draft horses, llamas, rare breeds of geese, geckos, poisonous snakes, a two-headed calf, a 650-pound man, and whatever else appeals to the keen, inquiring mind.

7. To watch the judging of livestock.

8. To observe entertainers attempt to engage a crowd that is moving laterally.

9. To sit down and rest amid the turmoil and reconsider the meaning of life.

10. To turn away from food and amusement and crass pleasure and to resolve to live on a higher plane from now on.

The Midwest is State Fair Central, and it thrives here because we are the breadbasket of America, Hog Butcher, Machine-maker, Stacker of Particleboard, Player With Chain Saws, Land of the Big Haunches. And also because Midwesterners are insular, industrious, abstemious, introspective people skittish about body contact, and a state fair is liberation from all of that, a plunge into the pool of self-indulgence, starting with a thick pork chop hot off the grill and served on a stick with a band of crisp brown fat along one side. The fat is not good for you. You eat the pork chop, fat and all, and your child eats her pork chop, and then you score a giant vanilla shake from the Dairy Bar to cushion the fall of a bagful of tiny doughnuts. Now you're warmed up and ready to move on to the corn dog course.

But first here is a flume ride your child is agitating for, so you climb onto a steel raft and plunge into a concrete gorge and over a waterfall, and a two-foot wave washes over the gunwales, and now your pants are soaked. You disembark. You look like a man who could not contain his excitement. For cover, you hide in the crowd. You walk close behind people. You join the throng at the hot-corn stand and comfort yourself with a salty ear of buttered corn. Your pants chafe. You wander among booths of merchandise looking for men's pants and find encyclopedias, storm windows, lawn mowers, vegetable peelers and choppers, humidifiers, log splitters, and home saunas.

Your search for dry pants leads you through buildings where champion jams and jellies are displayed on tables draped with purple, blue, red, yellow ribbons, and also champion cakes (angel food, Bundt light, Bundt dark, chiffon, chocolate, chocolate chiffon, German chocolate, jelly roll, pound, spice, sponge, vegetable, or fruit) and pickles (beet, bean, bread-and-butter, cucumber sweet, dill without garlic, dill with garlic, peppers sweet, peppers hot, watermelon). And through an education pavilion where headhunters lie in wait for you to pause and make eye contact, and they leap on you and make you hear about the benefits of beautician training, the opportunities in the field of broadcasting.

The way to dry out your pants is to get on a motorized contraption that whirls you through the air. Your child suggests you ride the giant Slingshot that is across the street. A long line of dead-end kids wait to be strapped into a cage and flung straight up in the air. The mob of onlookers waiting for the big whoosh looks like the crowds that once gathered to watch public executions.

You pass up the Slingshot for the double Ferris wheel. An excellent clothes dryer, lifting you up above the honky-tonk, a nice breeze in your pants, in a series of parabolas, and at the apex you look out across the gaudy uproar and the blinking lights, and then you zoom down for a close-up of a passing gang of farm boys in green letter jackets and then back up in the air. You tell your child that this Ferris wheel is the ride that, going back to childhood, you always saved for last, and so riding it fills you with nostalgia. She pats your hand. "You'll be all right, Dad," she says. After ten minutes you come down nice and dry, and also the food has settled in your stomach, and you're ready for seconds.

Of the Ten Joys, the one that we Midwesterners are loath to cop to is number three, the mingling and jostling, a pleasure that Google and Facebook can't provide. American life tends more and more to put you in front of a computer screen in a cubicle, then into a car and head you toward home in the suburbs, where you drive directly into the garage and step into your kitchen without brushing elbows with anybody. People seem to want this, as opposed to urban tumult and squalor. But we have needs we can't admit, and one is to be in a scrum of thinly clad corpulence milling in brilliant sun in front of the deep-fried-ice-cream stand and feel the brush of wings, hip bumps, hands touching your arm ("Oh, excuse me!"), the heat of humanity with its many smells (citrus deodorant, sweat and musk, bouquet of beer, hair oil, stale cigar, methane), the solid, big-rump bodies of Brueghel peasants all around you like dogs in a pack, and you—yes, elegant you of the refined taste and the commitment to the arts—are one of these dogs. All your life you dreamed of attaining swanhood or equinity, but your fellow dogs know better. They sniff you and turn away, satisfied.

Some state fairs are roomier, some gaudier, but there is a great sameness to them, just as there is a similarity among Catholic churches. No state fair can be called trendy, luxurious, dreamy—none of that. Nothing that is farm oriented or pigcentric is even remotely upscale.

Wealth and social status aren't so evident at the fair. The tattooed carnies who run the rides have a certain hauteur, and of course if you're on horseback, you're aristocracy, but otherwise not. There is no first-class line, no concierge section roped off in the barns. The wine selection is white, red, pink, and fizzy. Nobody flaunts his money.

The state fair, at heart, is an agricultural expo, and farming isn't about getting rich, and farmers discuss annual income less than they practice nude meditation on beaches. Farming is about work and about there being a Right Way and a Wrong Way to do it. You sit in the bleachers by the show ring and see this by the way the young women and men lead their immaculate cows clockwise around the grumpy, baggy-pants judge in the center. They walk at the cow's left shoulder, hand on the halter, and keep the animal's head up, always presenting a clear profile to the judge's gaze, and when he motions them to get in line, the exhibitors stand facing their cows and keep them squared away.

You and I may have no relatives left in farming, and our memory of the farm, if we have any, may be faint, but the livestock judging is meaningful to us—husbandry is what we do, even if we call it education or health care or management. Sport is a seductive metaphor (life as a game in which we gain victory through hard work, discipline, and visualizing success), but the older metaphor of farming (life as hard labor that is subject to weather and quirks of blind fate and may return no reward whatsoever and don't be surprised) is still in our blood, especially those of us raised on holy scripture. The young men and women leading cows around the show ring are relatives of Abraham and Job and the faithful father of the prodigal son. They subscribe to the Love Thy Neighbor doctrine. They know about late-summer hailstorms. You could learn something from these people.

Twilight falls on the fairgrounds, and a person just suddenly gets sick of it all. You've spent hours gratifying yourself on deep-fried cheese curds, deep-fried ice cream, testing one sausage against another, washing them down with authentic American sarsaparilla, sampling your child's onion rings, postponing the honey sundae for later, and now it is later, and the horticulture building and the honey-sundae booth are four blocks and a river of humanity away. You and the child stand at the entrance to the midway, barkers barking at you to try the ringtoss, shoot a basketball, squirt the water in the clown's mouth and see the ponies run, win the teddy bear, but you don't want to win a big blue plush teddy bear. You have no use for one whatsoever. There is enough inertia in your life as it is. And now you feel the great joy of revulsion at the fair and its shallow pleasures, its cheap tinsel, its greasy food. You are slightly ashamed of your own intake of animal fats. Bleaugh, you think. Arghhhh. OMG. You have gone twice to ATMs to finance this binge, and you regret that. No more of this! You take the child's hand. There will be no honey sundae tonight, honey. We got all that out of our system. We are going home and sober up and get busy.

You hike toward where you recollect you parked your car this morning, and by a stroke of God's grace you actually find it, and your child does not have to watch a father roaming around pitifully, moaning to himself. You get in, and you drive back to the world that means something, the world of work. The Long Dark Time is coming, and you must gather your herds to shelter and lay in carrots and potatoes in the cellar.

The fair is gone the next day, the rides disassembled, the concessions boarded up, the streets swept clean. Dry leaves blow across the racing oval, brown squirrels den up in the ticket booths, the midway marquee sways in the wind. You drive past the fairgrounds a few days later on your way to work. It looks like the encampment of an invading army that got what booty it wanted and went home. And now you are yourself again, ambitious, disciplined, frugal, walking briskly, head held high, and nobody would ever associate you with that shameless person stuffing his face with bratwurst and kraut, mustard on his upper lip, and a half-eaten deep-fried Snickers in his other hand. That was not the real you. This is. This soldier of the simple declarative sentence. You have no need for cheap glitter and pig fat and pointless twirling. You have work to do. Onward.

Esquire

WINNER—PROFILE WRITING

Todd Marinovich was once on his way to being the greatest quarterback ever to play the game of football. His father planned it that way. But after winning the Rose Bowl at USC and playing two seasons with the Los Angeles Raiders, his career in the NFL ended when he failed his third drug test. The boy who was trained to be a star was never taught to be a man. The National Magazine Award judges called this story "a beautifully balanced portrait that avoids both mawkish sentiment and moral condescension."

Mike Sager

The Man Who
Never Was

Fallbrook Midget Chiefs are fanned out across the field on a sunny autumn day in southern California, two dozen eighth graders in red helmets and bulbous pads. Whistles trill and coaches bark, mothers camp in folding chairs in the welcoming shade of the school building, younger siblings romp. Fathers hover on the periphery, wincing with every missed tackle and dropped pass.

Into this tableau ambles a tall man with faded-orange hair cropped close around a crowning bald spot, giving him the aspect of a tonsured monk. His face is all angles, his fair skin is sunburned and heavily freckled, his lips are deeply lined, the back of his neck is weathered like an old farmer's. He is six foot five, 212 pounds, the same as when he reported for duty twenty-one years ago as a redshirt freshman quarterback at the University of Southern California, the Touchdown Club's 1987 national high school player of the year. The press dubbed him Robo Quarterback; he was the total package. His Orange County high school record for all-time passing yardage, 9,182, stood for more than two decades.

Now he is thirty-nine, wearing surfer shorts and rubber flip-flops. He moves toward the field in the manner of an athlete, loose limbed and physically confident, seemingly unconcerned, revealing nothing of the long and tortured trail he's left behind.

A coach hustles out to meet the party. He is wearing an Oakland Raiders cap. "Todd Marinovich!" he declares. "Would you mind signing these?" He produces a stack of bubble-gum cards. As Todd signs, everybody gathers and cops a squat. Somebody tosses him a football, like a speaking stick.

"Hi, my name is Todd. I played *waaaay* before you guys were even born." Without his sunglasses, resting now atop his head, his blue eyes look pale and unsure. Raised much of his life on the picturesque Balboa Peninsula, he speaks in the loopy dialect of a surfer dude. He once told a reporter in jest that he enjoyed surfing naked at a spot near a nuclear power plant. Thereafter, among his other transgressions—nine arrests, five felonies, a year in jail—he would be known derisively for naked surfing. "One thing that I am today and that's completely honest," he tells the Chiefs. "I wouldn't change anything for the world."

As he speaks, Todd fondles and flips and spins the ball. It seems small in his hands and very well behaved, like it belongs there. When he was born, his father placed a big plush football in his crib. Marv Marinovich was the cocaptain of John McKay's undefeated USC team of 1962. He played on the line both ways. The team won the national championship; Marv was ejected from the Rose Bowl for fighting. After a short NFL career, Marv began studying Eastern Bloc training methods. The Raiders' colorful owner, Al Davis, made him one of the NFL's first strength-and-conditioning coaches. Before Todd could walk, Marv had him on a balance beam. He would stretch the boy's little hamstrings in his crib. Years later, an ESPN columnist would name Marv number two on a list of "worst sports fathers." (After Jim Pierce, father of tennis player Mary, famous for verbally abusing opponents during matches.)

At the moment, Marv is sitting at the back of the Chiefs gathering, resting his bum knee, eating an organic apple. Nearly seventy, he has bull shoulders and a nimbus of curly gray hair.

His own pale-blue eyes are focused intently on his son's performance, as they have been from day one.

"I was the first freshman in Orange County to ever start a varsity game at quarterback," Todd continues. "I broke a lot of records. Then I chose to go to USC. We beat UCLA. We won a Rose Bowl. It's quite an experience playing in front of a hundred thousand people. It's a real rush. Everyone is holding their breath, wondering, *What's he gonna do next?* After my third year of college, I turned pro. Here's a name you'll recognize: I was drafted ahead of Brett Favre in the 1991 draft. I played for three years for the Raiders. I made some amazing friends—we're still in touch."

Todd surveys the young faces before him. In about a minute, he has summarized the entire first half of his life. He looks down at the football. "Any questions?"

One kid asks Todd if he fumbled a lot. Another wants to know how far Todd can throw. The coach in the Raiders cap—they call him Raider Bill—asks Todd how he got along with his coaches, eliciting a huge guffaw from both Todd and Marv, which makes everybody else crack up, too.

Then Todd points the football at a boy with freckles.

"You said you only played three years in the NFL," the boy says, more a statement than a question.

"Correctamundo," Todd replies, at ease now, playing to the crowd, not really thinking about what's coming next—which has always been his biggest strength and maybe also his biggest weakness.

"What ended your career?" the boy asks.

"What *ended* my career . . ." Todd repeats. His smile fades as he searches for the right words.

·   ·   ·

The Newport Beach Cheyennes were scrimmaging the best fourth-grade Pop Warner team in Orange County. It was

September 1978. Todd was nine years old, playing his first year of organized tackle football.

Todd was the quarterback, a twig figure with flaming-orange hair. The opposing team was anchored by its middle linebacker, one of those elementary-school Goliaths, physically mature for his age. With time waning and the score close, the game on the line, the Cheyennes' coach opted to give his second-string offense a chance. In this scheme, Todd moved to fullback. Over in his spot near the end zone, Marv's eyes bugged. *Why isn't this idiot going for the win?*

The Marinovich family had recently returned from living in Hawaii, where Marv, after coaching with the Raiders and the St. Louis Cardinals, had done a stint with the World Football League's Hawaiians. As Marv sorted out his work status, his family of four was living with the maternal grandparents in a little clapboard house on the Balboa Peninsula. Once a summer beach shack, it had been converted over the years into two stories, four bedrooms. The Pacific Ocean was two long blocks from the front deck; Newport Harbor was two short blocks from the back door, its docks crowded with yachts and pontoon party boats. In summer came the throngs: a nonstop party.

Todd's mom is the former Trudi Fertig. In high school, she held several swimming records in the butterfly. A prototype of the late-fifties California girl, Trudi was a Delta Gamma sorority sister at USC; she quit college after her sophomore year to marry the captain of the football team. Trudi's father, C. Henry Fertig, was the police chief of nearby Huntington Park. German-Irish, the son of a blacksmith, he was the one who'd passed down the carrot top. The Chief, as he was known to all, was the "most visible of all the Trojan alums," according to *The Orange County Register.* Before every USC game you'd find him, wearing his cardinal-colored shirt and bright gold pants, tailgating in his regular spot in front of the L. A. Coliseum, where the Trojans play their games. (After the Chief's death in 1997, at the age of eighty, the alumni laid a brass plaque on the hallowed spot.)

The Chief's son was Craig Fertig, a former USC quarterback, responsible for one of the greatest Trojan victories of all time, a comeback against undefeated Notre Dame in 1964. He was associated with the program for nearly fifty years as a coach, assistant athletic director, TV commentator, and fan until his death, the result of organ failure due to alcoholism.

Marv Marinovich grew up with his extended family on a three-thousand-acre ranch in Watsonville, in northern California. The spread was owned by his Croatian grandfather, J. G. Marinovich. According to family lore, J. G. was a general in the Russian army, a cruel man who'd overseen the battlefield amputation of his own arm. After high school, Marv played football for Santa Monica City College. The team went undefeated and won the 1958 national junior-college championship. From there Marv transferred to USC. He was known for foaming at the mouth. After the championship, he was named Most Inspirational Player. He still has the trophy.

Drafted by the L.A. Rams of the NFL and by the Oakland Raiders of the AFL, Marv "ran, lifted, pushed the envelope to the nth degree" in order to prepare for the pros. One exercise, he says: eleven-hundred-pound squats, with the bar full of forty-five-pound plates, with hundred-pound dumbbells chained and hanging on the ends because he couldn't get any more plates to fit. "And then I would rep out," he recalls. "I hadn't yet figured out that speed and flexibility were more important than weight and bulk. I overtrained so intensely that I never recovered."

After a disappointing three-year career with the Raiders and Rams, Marv turned to sports training. Over time, he would develop his own system for evaluating athletes and maximizing their potential. Much of the core- and swimming-pool-based conditioning programs in use today owe nods to Marv's ideas.

His latest reclamation project: Pittsburgh Steelers safety Troy Polamalu.

With the birth of his own two children, Traci and Todd, came the perfect opportunity for Marv to put his ideas into practice. "Some guys think the most important thing in life is their jobs, the stock market, whatever," he says. "To me, it was my kids. The question I asked myself was, How well could a kid develop if you provided him with the perfect environment?"

For the nine months prior to Todd's birth on July 4, 1969, Trudi used no salt, sugar, alcohol, or tobacco. As a baby, Todd was fed only fresh vegetables, fruits, and raw milk; when he was teething, he was given frozen kidneys to gnaw. As a child, he was allowed no junk food; Trudi sent Todd off to birthday parties with carrot sticks and carob muffins. By age three, Marv had the boy throwing with both hands, kicking with both feet, doing sit-ups and pull-ups, and lifting light hand weights. On his fourth birthday, Todd ran four miles along the ocean's edge in thirty-two minutes, an eight-minute-mile pace. Marv was with him every step of the way.

Now, late in one of Todd's first games in Pop Warner, the coach sent a play into the huddle, a handoff to the halfback. As fullback, Todd's job was to be lead blocker.

The ball was snapped. Todd led the halfback through the hole.

He'd just cleared the line of scrimmage when Goliath-boy stepped into the gap and delivered a forearm shiver very much like the one that had gotten Marv ejected from the Rose Bowl. Todd crumpled to the ground. Blood flowed copiously from his nose.

The whistle blew. As Todd was being cleaned up, Marv convinced the coach that Todd needed to go back in the game. Immediately. At quarterback.

Todd stood over center, his nose still bleeding. Part of him felt like crying. The other part knew that it was the last few seconds of the scrimmage and the team was down by only a few points. For as long as he could remember, no matter what sport he played, he always had to win.

He took the snap and faded back, threw a perfect pass into the back corner of the end zone. "That has always been my favorite route," he says now, sitting outside a little coffee shop on Balboa Boulevard, drinking a large drip with six sugars and smoking a Marlboro Red. He tells the story from a place of remove, as if describing something intimate that happened to someone else. "I remember seeing the ball. It was spiraling and there was blood just flying off of it, splattering out into the air."

When the catch was made, there was silence for a beat. "And then I remember the parents cheering."

.   .   .

Six years later, on the opening night of the 1984 football season, Todd once again gathered himself as best he could, rising to one knee on the turf at Orange Coast College. There were 7,000 fans in the stadium. He'd just been blasted by two big studs from the celebrated front line of the Fountain Valley High School Barons.

Three days before he'd even set foot in a ninth-grade classroom, the six-three, 170-pound freshman was the starting quarterback for the varsity team at Mater Dei High School in Santa Ana, the largest Catholic high school west of Michigan. In a sports-mad county known for its quarterbacks—from John Huarte and Matt Leinart to Carson Palmer and Mark Sanchez—Todd's freshman start was a first.

Todd fought for breath. His head was ringing, his vision was blurred, he wanted to puke. Later he would recognize the symptoms of his first concussion. Marv's conditioning was designed to train the body and the mind to push beyond pain and fear. Throughout his career, Todd would be known for his extraordinary focus and will—qualities that would both enable and doom him. Two years from now, the left-hander would lead a fourth-quarter rally with a broken thumb on his throwing hand. Five years from now, he would throw four college touchdowns with a fractured left wrist. Sixteen years from now, he'd throw ten touchdowns in one game, tying an Arena Football League record, while suffering from acute heroin withdrawal.

Acting on instinct, fifteen-year-old Todd rose to his feet and peered out of the echoing cavern of his helmet. He searched the sideline, looking for the signal caller, his next play. A teammate grabbed him by the shoulder pads, spun him around to face the Mater Dei bench. "We're over *here*, dude," he told Todd.

Back in seventh grade, Todd had set his goal: to start on a varsity team as a ninth grader. Marv made a progress chart and put it up in the garage; they worked every day. "It was brutal," Todd recalls. "Sometimes I didn't want anything to do with it. He'd give me the look, like, 'Well, fine, but you're gonna get your ass kicked when you start to play.'" Along the way, Marv consulted a series of experts: Tom House, the Texas Rangers' innovative pitching coach, found Todd's throwing motion to be 4.53 inches too low. A vision specialist in Westwood made Todd wear prism glasses, stand on a balance beam in a dark room, and bounce a ball while reciting multiplication tables.

By the summer before ninth grade, Todd was penciled in as Mater Dei's fifth-string quarterback. His typical week, as reported by the *Register*: Four days of weight lifting, three days of light work and running. Daily sessions with Mater Dei's assistant basketball coach. Twice weekly with a shooting coach. Two hours daily throwing the football. Twice weekly with a quarterback coach. Thrice-weekly sprint workouts with a track coach. There were also Mater Dei basketball club games and twice-daily football workouts.

"I don't think any of the kids were ever jealous of Todd, because they knew that when they left that field or court or gym,

Todd was still going to be there for many, many hours," Trudi recalls. When Todd and Traci were growing up, Trudi worked as a waitress during the periods when Marv wasn't employed. Sometimes she secretly took Todd to McDonald's. The Chief fed him pizza and beer. Though Traci once wrote of hearing Todd cry in his room, nobody wanted to butt heads with Marv. Like an obsessed scientist, he had tunnel vision. "He didn't do reality too well," Trudi says.

Todd lost that first game against Fountain Valley, 17-13, but he showed promise. Shut down completely after that blow in the first quarter, he gained composure as the evening progressed, completing nine of seventeen passes for 123 yards and two interceptions, the second of which foiled a fourth-quarter drive that could have won the game. The *Register* would report: "If not for Marinovich . . . the Monarchs wouldn't have had an offense to speak of."

After the final gun, Todd stood with his parents. His new teammates drifted over and surrounded him. "When I was growing up, the term my mom used was 'terrifyingly shy,'" Todd says. "That's why I always loved being on a team. It was the only way I could make friends. It was really amazing to have these guys, these upperclassmen, come over. And they're like, 'Hey, Todd, let's go! Come out with us after the game. It's party time!'"

Todd looked at Marv. The old man didn't hesitate. "He just gave me the nod, you know, like, 'Go ahead, you earned it.'

"We went directly to a kegger and started pounding down beers," Todd recalls.

·   ·   ·

It was January 1988, opening night of basketball season. With fifty-eight seconds left, the score was 61-all. Todd flashed into the key, took a pass from the wing. He made the lay-up and drew the foul. Whistle. Three thousand fans in the arena at the

University of California, Irvine, went nuts. The six-five, 215-pound high school senior pumped his fist in celebration.

During his two years at Mater Dei, Todd had thrown for nearly 4,400 yards and 34 touchdowns. But the Monarchs' record was mediocre; they had no blocking to protect Todd. So Marv had engineered his son's transfer to Capistrano Valley High, a public school in Mission Viejo. The team's head football coach, Dick Enright, was a USC alum and longtime friend of Marv's. As head coach at the University of Oregon, Enright had groomed quarterback Dan Fouts. Under Enright, Todd would go on to break the all-time Orange County passing record. He was named a *Parade* magazine All-American and the National High School Coaches Association's offensive player of the year.

Then the January 1988 issue of *California* magazine hit the stands with Todd's picture on the cover. The headline: ROBO QB: THE MAKING OF A PERFECT ATHLETE. A media onslaught ensued. They called Todd the bionic quarterback, a test-tube athlete, the boy in the bubble. All over the world, people were talking about Todd's amazing story. In truth, he was leading a double life.

"I really looked forward to giving it all I had at the game on Friday night and then continuing through the weekend with the partying. It opened up a new social scene for me—liquid courage. I wasn't scared of people anymore," Todd says.

At Mater Dei, Todd had also begun smoking marijuana. By the time his junior year rolled around, he says, "I was a full on loady." His parents had divorced just before his transfer, and he was sharing a one-bedroom apartment with Marv near Capistrano. "Probably the best part of my childhood was me and Marv's relationship my junior and senior years," Todd says. "After the divorce, he really loosened up. It was a bachelor pad. We were both dating."

Every day before school, Todd would meet a group at a friend's house and do bong hits. They called it Zero Period. Some of the guys were basketball players, others were into surfing, skateboarding, and music—the holy trinity of the OC slacker lifestyle.

"Pot just really relaxed me. I could just function better in public," he says. "I never played high or practiced high. It wasn't as hard on my body as drinking. I thought, Man, I have found the secret. I was in love."

Now it was January of his senior year, the opening game of basketball season. Todd was a swingman, the high scorer. The Capo Cougars were one of the top-ranked teams in the county. The contest against archrival El Toro High School had come down to the wire. Todd had just broken the tie with a layup. Then he hit the foul shot: 64-61.

El Toro inbounded the ball; Capo stole it. Pass to Todd. Hard foul in the paint. Todd went to the line again, two shots. Thirty-seven seconds left to play.

The crowd was screaming, pounding the floor. Behind the basket, dozens of El Toro students were wearing orange wigs to mock the carrot-topped Robo Quarterback. As Todd went through his foul-shot ritual, something broke his focus. The opposing fans were chanting: "Marijuana-*vich!* Marijuana-*vich!* Marijuana-*vich!*"

"I was supposed to be shooting free throws, but I was really glancing into the stands. I was trying to see if my father noticed," Todd told the *Los Angeles Times* later.

He put it out of mind and nailed both shots. Game over.

• • •

No matter what the teams' record or national ranking, UCLA versus USC is always the biggest game of the year. The sixtieth meeting occurred in November 1990. From the opening kickoff, the advantage seesawed. With less than a minute to go, the score was 42-38 in favor of UCLA. Todd and his Trojan squad began operating on their own twenty-three. A field goal wouldn't do.

On third down, Todd completed a twenty-seven-yard pass to his favorite target, five-foot-nine Gary Wellman, a future Houston Oiler. On the next play he hit Wellman again for twenty-two yards.

With sixteen seconds left, the football was spotted on the UCLA twenty-three-yard line. USC coach Larry Smith called for a time-out. Todd and his corps of receivers jogged to the sideline. A hush fell over the Rose Bowl crowd of 98,088.

Although he was recruited by every notable college, no other school really had a chance over USC. Todd's sister was a senior and his first cousin was planning on attending. His uncle Craig Fertig was an assistant athletic director. When Todd had visited USC that year, he'd been taken down onto the field of the empty Coliseum—where he'd watched games with the Chief his entire life—and they put his name up on the scoreboard, complete with piped-in crowd noise. After that, Todd was taken by his All-American escort to a party on campus. "There was a three-and-a-half-foot purple bong. I was like, 'I'm home.' I even had my own weed on me," Todd recalls.

Todd redshirted his first year at USC. His second year he started every game, completing 62 percent of his passes for 2,600 yards and 16 touchdowns, leading the 1989 Trojans to a 9-2-1 record, a Pac-10 title, and a Rose Bowl victory over Michigan. Todd was named freshman player of the year. There was Heisman talk, speculation he'd leave early for the NFL.

At the opening of the next season, however, Coach Smith told reporters he wasn't yet decided on his starting quarterback. Smith was a flinty Ohio native who stressed discipline. Of all the coaches he'd ever had, Todd says, he hated Smith the most. Smith seemed determined to break the kid, going so far as to outlaw flip-flops on road trips. Smith told Marv privately he suspected Todd was using drugs. During the two months leading up to the UCLA game, Todd had been repeatedly drug tested but never failed. He'd been suspended from the team for missing classes. He'd been benched as a starter for one set of downs. (When he returned to the game, the crowd booed; he threw a seventy-seven-yard touchdown pass.)

Now Todd and his receivers reached the sideline. "What do you want to do?" Coach Smith asked his quarterback.

Todd's face flushed to hot pink. "You're asking *me* what *I* want to do? Why start *now*?"

Todd turned to his receivers standing behind him. They believed in him. They'd seen his magic. His last-minute comeback against Washington State the previous season is still remembered as "the Drive": A textbook ninety-one-yard march downfield—with eleven crucial completions, including a touchdown pass and a two-point conversion—it prompted a call from former President Ronald Reagan.

Todd turned back to his coach. "This is what we're gonna do," he told Smith, yelling over the crowd. "*You're* gonna stay the fuck over here while *we* go win this game."

Todd and his boys jogged back to the huddle. Todd called the play. The ball was on the twenty-three; sixteen seconds left. Wellman was in the slot. The pass was designed to go to him. But as Todd took the snap, he saw Wellman get jammed at the line.

"Whenever a receiver doesn't get a clean release," Todd recalls, "you got to go away from him, 'cause it just screws up the timing. So I looked back to the other side, and I saw Johnnie Morton on his corner route. He was supposed to run an eighteen-yard comeback, but we'd changed it at the line of scrimmage. Now he was making his move. When Johnnie went to the post, I saw the safety just drive on it, thinking I was throwing there. That's when I knew I had it."

Morton caught the ball deep in the left corner of the end zone, in front of the seats occupied by the Chief and his wife, Virginia. "It's been my favorite pass since Pop Warner," Todd said. "You really can't stop it."

.　　　.　　　.

On the evening of Saturday, January 19, 1991, Todd hit the bars on Balboa with his cousin Marc Fertig, a former USC baseball player, and two Trojan footballers. Coming home at 4:00 A.M., the boys were less than ten yards from the family beach house when two cop cars came screeching through the alley.

"I had a little nug on me," a marijuana bud, Todd says. "And a bindle of coke this guy had given me, this fan. It was half a gram. The cop went right for the drugs. Somebody must have tipped somebody off."

Todd was charged with two misdemeanors and allowed into a program for first-time offenders, but his USC career was finished. He declared himself eligible for the NFL draft and signed with IMG, a big agency. For the first time since freshman summer, Todd went back into training with Marv.

Six weeks later, Todd walked onto the field at East Los Angeles College to show NFL scouts what he could do. His long locks had been sacrificed in favor of a bright-orange Johnny Unitas buzz cut, an image makeover suggested by his agent. There were representatives from eighteen teams. Trudi set up a table with lemonade and pastries. Todd was in the best shape of his life. With the help of a former NFL receiver, Todd says, "We put on an aerial show."

The only NFL owner in attendance was Al Davis of the Los Angeles Raiders. Arriving late, Davis climbed up into the stands and sat between his old friends Marv and Trudi. "I kind of knew right then that the Raiders were gonna pick me," Todd says. "I was totally psyched."

At the conclusion of Raider training camp that summer, as tradition dictated, the first draft pick threw a party. Todd had gone twenty-fourth in the first round and signed a three-year, $2.25 million deal, including a $1 million signing bonus. He rented a ranch and hired a company that did barbecue on a huge grill on a flatbed truck. He turned the barn into a stadium with haybale seating. He hired strippers, ten white and ten black. The grand finale: three porn stars with doubleheaded dildos. "They say in the history of the Raiders, it was the best rookie party ever," Todd says.

He made his first professional appearance on no smaller stage than *Monday Night Football*, an exhibition against Dallas on August 12, 1991. Entering the game with fifteen minutes remaining, he moved the Raiders crisply downfield, completing three of four passes for sixteen yards and a touchdown.

As the season opened, to reduce the pressure on the rookie, coach Art Shell made Todd the third-string quarterback. Seeing little action on the field, he seemed determined to live up to his reputation as an epic partier off it. Arriving at a hotel for an away game, he'd go with the rest of the players to a club. When they returned, he'd go out again. There were women, raves, Ecstasy, coke. Vets would save him a seat at the pregame meal just to hear his stories of the night before. "The cities started running into one another," Todd recalls.

Sometimes, for fun or hangover relief, Todd took pharmaceutical speed before the games. "I wasn't playing, so the warm-ups were my game. They'd have these great stereo systems in the stadiums; they'd be blasting the Stones or whatever. I'd take some black beauties and be throwing the ball seventy-five yards, running around playing receiver, fucking around—and then I was done for the day. I never played. Some guys did play on speed. Or they mixed with Vicodin. They could run through a fuckin' wall and not feel a thing."

The fifteenth week of the season, Todd made his first trip to New Orleans. After a long night of rum drinks in the Quarter, he ended up in bed with two stewardesses; he barely made it back for the pregame meal. The Superdome held seventy thousand screaming fans. "The noise was deafening. My *head*. I was in hell," Todd remembers now. "I was barely able to make it through warm-ups. I was sweating profusely, trying not to vomit."

Midway through the game, the Raiders' first-string quarterback, Jay Schroeder, was hit simultaneously from both sides, injuring an ankle. "Coach Shell looks at me, like, *Are you ready to go?*" Todd recalls. "I shook him off like a pitcher on the mound. I was like, *Are you fucking kidding me?*"

•   •   •

The following week, with Schroeder still sidelined for the final game of the regular season, Todd made his official debut against the Kansas City Chiefs. Marv was reported to have arrived at the stadium before the gates opened, waiting in line with the other fans to see his boy get his first start. Though the team lost 27-21, Todd completed twenty-three of forty passes for 243 yards. Crowed *Los Angeles Times* sports columnist Mike Downey: "Sunday was Marinovich's football bar mitzvah. The boy became a man."

The next day was a Monday—five days before the Raiders were due to appear in the AFC wild-card game, also against the Chiefs. Ready to leave home for practice, Todd went to his refrigerator and discovered that he'd run out of clean urine.

As a consequence of his arrest, the NFL had been requiring Todd to take frequent urine tests. Todd felt he couldn't function without marijuana. "It just allowed me to be comfortable in this loud, chaotic world. Especially the world I was living in. I couldn't fathom being sober," he says. To reconcile these conflicting realities, he kept Gatorade bottles of clean urine, donated by non-pot-smoking friends, in the refrigerator at his Manhattan Beach townhouse, one block from the ocean, which he'd purchased for $900,000.

All season long, this had been his pre-test routine: Pour the refrigerated pee into a small sunscreen bottle. Go to practice.

Put the bottle in a cup of coffee and leave it in his locker to warm up while attending a team meeting. Come back, stash the bottle inside his compression shorts, beneath his package. Usually he'd ask the supervisor to turn on the water in the sink to aid his shy bladder. "I got it down to a science," he says.

But now he was out of clean pee, another critical responsibility blown off—like the time at USC when he couldn't be bothered to fill out his housing paperwork and ended up a homeless scholarship athlete. Like Marv, the real world wasn't really his thing.

Luckily, on this Monday morning, one of Todd's former USC teammates was still at his house, left over from the weekend's partying. He didn't do drugs. Unbeknownst to Todd, however, he'd been drinking nonstop since his own game on Saturday.

Soon after, the Raiders got a call from the NFL: Todd's urine sample had registered a blood-alcohol level of .32—four times the legal limit. "They're like, 'This guy is a fucking full-blown alcoholic,'" Todd says. "They made me check into Centinela Hospital in Inglewood for alcohol detox—and I hadn't even been drinking." The team left without him; he flew later. This time the Chiefs were ready for Todd. He threw four interceptions, fumbled once.

After the season the team held an intervention. Todd spent forty-five days at a rehab facility. The next season, Todd tried to stop smoking pot. Instead, for six weeks, he took LSD after every game—acid didn't show up on the tox screen. After one poor performance, coaches complained that he wasn't grasping the complex offense. Finally, he failed an NFL drug test. Strike two. Back to rehab.

The next August, 1993, near the end of his third training camp, Todd failed a third drug test for marijuana. Al Davis brought the kid into his office. After two seasons, eight games, eight touchdown passes, Todd's NFL playing days were over.

"I was like, Fuck it. I'd been playing my whole life. I'd accomplished my goals. I never said I wanted to play forever. I just wanted to play at the highest level. Even in college, it felt like the shit you had to put up with in order to play wasn't worth it. Those few amazing hours on Sunday were being outweighed by all the bullshit."

Todd packed up his Land Cruiser and drove to Mexico to camp and surf. "I thought I had a ton of money," he says.

.   .   .

It was shortly after Swallows Day in San Juan Capistrano, March 24, 1997. Todd lived in a small house near the beach; a few friends were hanging out. At one point, somebody got the idea to go to the grammar school next door and play dunk hoops on the low baskets.

As the game got going, the motley crew of loadies transformed themselves into ballers. As always, Todd couldn't miss. He was by now twenty-seven. After traveling the world for two years, he'd attempted to return to football, only to blow out his knee on his first day of training camp with the Winnipeg Blue Bombers of the Canadian Football League. During his recovery, an old buddy from Zero Period at Capo had introduced him to the guitar and then later to heroin. Their band, Scurvy, achieved modest success playing at clubs on the Sunset Strip. Then the bassist was busted, ruining hopes for a record deal. For the past three years, Todd had been a full-blown addict.

Going up for a rebound, one guy hurt his back. John Valdez was twenty-nine and weighed about 275 pounds: He went down like a slab of beef. With much difficulty, the guys hauled him back to Todd's bed. In agony, he appealed to his host: "You got anything to help the pain?"

Todd left the room and retrieved his stash of Mexican blacktar heroin. "I fixed myself first," he says. "I remember it being strong stuff, so I just gave him a fraction of the amount." A few minutes later, returning from a cigarette break on the front porch, he checked on Valdez. "He's frothing from the mouth. He's fuckin' blue."

Todd ran outside and retrieved the garden hose—it was easier than lugging Valdez to the shower, as he'd seen in movies. When that didn't help, Todd started slapping him in the face.

"I'm fucking hitting this guy with everything I've got," he recalls. "And I swear, I could see his spirit struggling to leave his body. I don't tell this story much; people think I was hallucinating.

"But on heroin you don't hallucinate. You do *not* fucking hallucinate on fucking heroin. The only way I could describe it is like when you see heat waves on the beach—when the heat waves eddy up and warp your vision. It was like that, and it was colorful. I actually saw it, the life force or whatever, as it would leave the top of his head, and he'd become this fleshbag, and then I would smack the shit out of him and I would see it actually coming back into him."

The friends had scattered; there was one guy left with them in the house. Todd yelled, "Call fuckin' 911!"

As the other guy cleaned up the drugs and the syringe, the dispatcher coached Todd through CPR. Finally the paramedics arrived, along with sheriff's deputies.

The day before, Todd had helped a buddy harvest his marijuana crop. As a thank-you, he'd gotten a trash bag full of cuttings, not bud but still smokable. He'd stashed the bag in his garage rafters with his surfboards and promptly forgotten about it. As the paramedics wheeled out Valdez on a gurney, one of the deputies came into the room holding the trash bag of pot. "Where are the plants?" he demanded.

"I'm not a grower," Todd tried to explain. "See, this buddy of mine—"

Just then, another deputy entered the room. He was carrying two half-dead pot plants that Todd had set up in his laundry room with a drugstore-variety grow light.

Todd was charged with felony marijuana cultivation. He served two months in jail and a third at a minimum-security facility in OC known as the Farm.

●　　　●　　　●

In April 1999, just shy of his thirtieth birthday, Todd was finally cleared to play again by the NFL. He promptly herniated a disk playing pickup hoops. That summer, he worked out for several teams. The Chargers and the Bears showed real interest, but he failed the physical; no deals could be made. He ended up signing as a backup quarterback with the B.C. Lions of Vancouver, in the Canadian Football League.

Except for a little pot, Todd was drug free for the first time in years. His roomie was Canadian. About two weeks into his stay, he asked Todd if he wanted to go with him "to check his babies."

It turned out he was growing potent BC bud. On the way home, Todd stopped at a head shop to buy a bong. There were little vials scattered everywhere on the ground. His junkie warning system sounded a shrill alarm.

Todd had arrived in his own personal land of Oz, a place were junkies bought and used heroin openly and cops only got involved if somebody OD'd. The heroin was called China White. It was infinitely more potent than the black tar Todd had used before—and relatively cheap. He got into a routine: "The day before every game, we would do a walk-through in the dome—that was my day for needle exchange. All my years of being a dope fiend, the hardest part was always getting needles. I was getting good coke and really pure heroin and combining them. That's all I wanted to do. I woke up, fixed, went to practice. Thank God I was just backing up. I was just the clipboard guy, playing the opposing quarterback in practice."

Once, during halftime at a home game, Todd retrieved a premade rig out of his locker and went to the bathroom to shoot up.

Sitting on the toilet, half listening to the chalk talk, he slammed the heroin. As the team was leaving the locker room for the second half, he struggled with the screen in his glass crack pipe—he wasn't getting a good hit. Then the pipe broke, and he lacerated his left thumb. By the time he got out onto the field, his thumb wrapped in a towel, the game had already started. He took up the clipboard, his only duty. "I didn't even know what play they were calling," Todd says. "Nobody looked at the shit I wrote down anyway."

At the end of the season, the team had a party. Todd was "gowed out of my mind," meaning that he was "somewhere between a nod and full-on slumber." His weight had dropped to 176 pounds. "I was a celibate heroin monk. I would go downtown, cop, come back to my pad, and not leave till the drugs were gone," he says. "There was no furniture in my place, just a bed and a TV. I wasn't eating. I spent a lot of time in this Astro minivan I had. I'd just climb into the back and fix. My life revolved around dope and my dog."

Now, at the party, Todd became aware that the general manager of the Lions was motioning for him to come over. The GM was a good guy who'd recruited him to come to BC. He shook Todd's hand. "I know we signed you for one year with an option for another year—" he said pregnantly, looking grave.

And then he issued a toothy, *gotcha* grin: "We'd like to pick up that option!"

"You have to be fuckin' crazy," Todd said. "I can't stay here."

•   •   •

Todd returned to football for the last time in the spring of 2000—a mercurial stint with the Los Angeles Avengers in the Arena Football League. His first year, he tied the record for most touchdowns in a single game despite undergoing severe heroin withdrawal; after shitting his pants during warm-ups, he came out and threw ten touchdowns to win a game against the Houston Thunderbears. That same year, at age thirty-one, he was named to the all-rookie team. The next season, he became L.A.'s franchise player. The day he picked up his signing bonus, he was busted buying heroin. With him in the truck was $30,000 cash in an envelope. Toward the end of the season, he was ejected from successive games for throwing a clipboard and a hand towel at officials. Finally, he was suspended from the team.

"At that point, heroin became my full-time job," Todd says.

By 2004, he was broke and living again on the Balboa Peninsula, haunting the beaches and alleyways of his youth. In the summers, he often lived on the beach, washing at the bathhouse. Sometimes he couch-surfed with friends. Different from many junkies, he seemed to have a knack for being a good guest. Even at his worst, he maintained the sweet and vulnerable quality that makes people want to embrace him. He didn't go to his family's place often. He hated the way Trudi looked at him. At some point, his uncle Craig would accuse him of stealing and Trudi would change the locks.

Because he'd lost his car and license, Todd had trouble scoring heroin. He couldn't afford it, anyway. There was a ton of speed around Newport Beach, though. "People were practically giving it away," he recalls.

When he was high, he loved to skateboard. "It was a way to burn off all that energy that I had from the meth. It was like surfing on fucking concrete. I would skate for eight hours a day. I'd be just carving up and down the street for miles and miles. It was probably the most fun I've ever had on drugs. That and sex. Meth makes you just fucking perv. It turns normal people with some morals into just fucking sick perverts. That's all I wanted to do, you know, is look at porn or create my own."

A ghostly, six-five redhead living on the same tiny peninsula where he grew up so prominently, Todd was an easy mark. In

August 2004, he was arrested by Newport Beach police for skateboarding in a prohibited zone. Police found meth and syringes on him. In May 2005, he was rousted from a public bathhouse by police; he fled on his beach cruiser and was apprehended fifteen blocks away. Police found drug paraphernalia in his toiletry kit but no drugs. One of the cops was an old Capo Valley teammate. Todd was charged with violating probation. In June 2005, thanks to twenty-three of his former USC teammates who put up the $4,600 required for him to enter an inpatient treatment program, Todd avoided going back to jail. For the next year, he was in and out of rehab facilities.

At a little past one in the morning on August 26, 2007, a pair of Newport police officers riding in an unmarked minivan spotted Todd, by now thirty-eight years old, skateboarding on the boardwalk. He was carrying a guitar case and wearing a backpack; he had just been to his hook spot. As Todd knew well, skating is not permitted on the boardwalk.

"One cop started running at me. The other one's crossing the boulevard, trying to head me off. I popped off my skateboard, dropped my guitar case, and fucking ran down this alley. One of them yelled: 'Todd! Freeze!' I heard a *pop pop pop*. I thought they were fucking *shooting*!" It turned out to be a Taser. The projectile imbedded itself in the lower part of his backpack. "My leg started spasming, but it wasn't too bad. I just kept running." He ended up on a second-floor balcony. "I saw the fucking light come on, and a guy came out, looked at me, and shut the door real fast. I was like, *Oh fuck!*"

By then there were helicopters with spotlights. He could hear the dogs. "That's when I gave up. I've seen too many people come into fucking jail tore up from dogs. So I just laid down on the fucking ground and they found me."

It was his ninth arrest. He was charged with felony possession of a controlled substance and misdemeanor counts of unauthorized possession of a hypodermic needle and resisting a police officer. He did his second stint at the Farm, where he picked vegetables and repaired irrigation equipment.

•　　　•　　　•

Evening in the suburbs, September 2008. The dishes have been put away, the washer in the garage is cycling through another load. A fifteen-year-old boy sits at the dining- room table, doing his honors geometry homework.

Todd saunters into the room. He stands over the kid for a moment, places his large freckled mitt on his shoulder. The knuckles are raw from his part-time job scraping barnacles off the bottoms of boats. It is a tough, physical job. He likes that it tires him out; he always seems to be a little jittery and on edge, generally ill at ease in the world. He wears a wet suit and goggles, uses a long air hose, makes his rounds from motor yacht to sailboat in a dinghy. He'll be down there all alone for a half hour at a time, his bubbles slowly circling the hull, lost in repetitious physical effort, cocooned by the silent, salty water. He compares it to the soothing feeling of heroin.

As of tonight, he's been sober thirteen months. Following his last arrest, he was diverted to a special drug court run by a county judge. Hanging over Todd's head is a suspended sentence of two years in jail. His schedule is nearly as crowded as it was during the summer before ninth grade. Pee testing three times a week. Weekly drug-court sessions, one-on-one therapy, group therapy, sessions with his probation officer, thrice-weekly AA meetings. If he completes the program, in another eighteen months, he could have his felonies dismissed or reduced, opening up his opportunity for coaching at a public school. With all the responsibilities, he is expected to cobble together a new life. It is a difficult task.

Besides the barnacle scraping, for which he makes about forty dollars a boat, Todd leads a weekly group meeting at a rehab facility; people seem to respond to both his celebrity status and his easygoing manner. He's also been painting murals in people's houses. There is a local gallery that wants to show his work; a Web site is planned for direct buying. His other source of income is private coaching. Over the past year, he's become known as somewhat of a "quarterback whisperer." This past summer he worked with Jordan Palmer, brother of Carson; both Palmers are on the roster at Cincinnati. USC coach Pete Carroll recently told him he'd try to get Todd some work next summer at a football camp. There will be an interview for a job as offensive coordinator at a local junior college. Right now, Todd has four students, kids of varying ages. All of them have promise; Jordan Greenwood is one of his most talented.

"Dude. You got a minute?"

Jordan looks up attentively. He is five foot eleven and a half, 150 pounds. He's a freshman at Orange Lutheran, one of the schools that competes in the Trinity League against Todd's old team Mater Dei. Jordan started playing tackle football at age eight. He has always been a super athlete. One time in a soccer game, he had three goals in the first ten minutes.

About a year ago, Jordan was referred to Marv. Todd was brought in on day two. Though he hadn't been sober long, Todd watched Jordan throw and thought to himself, *I could really help this kid.* The first order of business: completely remake Jordan's throw—which nearly gave Jordan's father a heart attack. For the next six months, every night, Jordan had to stand in front of the mirror and repeat the new motion a thousand times. Each rep had to be perfect. It was up to Jordan; nobody could do it for him.

The first three exhibition games of the new season, the freshman-team coach rotated four quarterbacks. Fleet of foot, Jordan was perfect for the veer offense; he scored fifteen touchdowns, including a seventy-yard run against an inner-city team. Then came the fourth exhibition. The entire extended Greenwood family was on hand to watch. Jordan did not play.

Now, after a nice dinner of strip steaks and salmon and double-stuffed potatoes, with all the other adults out of the room, Todd folds himself into the chair next to Jordan. His orange hair is not so bright anymore, like a colorful curtain faded over the years by the sun.

"What's the worst part of your experience over there at Orange?" Todd asks. Jordan drums his pencil on the open pages of his math book. "I don't know," he says.

"Not playing?"

Jordan makes eye contact. "Yeah, mostly."

"What else?"

Shrug. "I dunno." This is the biggest thing in his life. You can tell he's trying not to cry.

"Listen, dude," Todd says, as warm a *dude* as was ever uttered. "Things can look pretty overwhelming right now because you're so young, but believe me, you can have a great career—possibly at Orange Lutheran. I wouldn't cash my chips and be bitter just yet. Some days, stuff just looks all wrong—take it from me. You're gonna be fine. You just have to believe in yourself."

Jordan nods his head, brightening.

Todd gives him a little shove. Next game, Jordan will run for three touchdowns and throw for another. Before the season is over, he'll be promoted to JV and win the team's most valuable offensive player award.

• • •

Todd and Marv Marinovich are at a self-storage facility in San Juan Capistrano. Most of Marv's equipment is inside, odd-looking machines and exercise stuff. Somehow, in the haste of the initial rental, the key was lost. After attempting to drill out the lock—it looks so easy in the movies—they await a locksmith.

Todd is squatting on the hot asphalt like a gang member in a prison yard. Marv is standing against the building in a sliver of shade. Ending his seventh decade, he looks twenty years younger. He lives alone, eats only organic food. Despite his ferocious reputation, he seems a sweet man who loves Todd very much. After two divorces, he has only Todd and Traci, who lives a couple hours away, and Mikhail, his son with his second wife, a former dancer. Mikhail is a six-foot-four sophomore defensive end at Syracuse, about as far as you can get from OC. Last year Mikhail made news when he was arrested for getting drunk and breaking into the college's gym equipment room with a friend. Todd advised: "Don't be stupid. You're a Marinovich. You have a target on your back."

Marv's stuff is in storage because he was asked to leave the private high school out of which he'd been working for nearly two years. There was a beef with his young partner. After a display of temper, Marv was asked to vacate by school authorities. The partner stayed. Todd and a friend went with a U-Haul to claim Marv's equipment.

Now, because it's the end of the month, they have to pay or move. A friend of Todd's has volunteered a garage. Todd has taken care of everything. Since he's been straight, he's spent a lot of time helping Marv. He's helping him get his driver's license back—a long tale of red tape. He helped him buy a computer. He's helping with visits to the doctor; there are indications of heart arrhythmia. "All those years I was so out of it. It feels good to be the one helping," Todd says. "He's always been there for me."

When Todd was born, he was listed as Marvin Scott Marinovich on his birth certificate. Trudi changed it a few years later to Todd Marvin. Later—an inside joke after a long day of training—Marv started calling his son Buzzy, after Buzzie Bavasi, the legendary Dodgers general manager. For some reason, Todd began calling Marv Buzzy, too. Nowadays, when Marv calls Todd's cell phone—Todd's ringtone is the opening bars of the *Monday Night Football* theme song—Todd will pick up and say, "Hey, Buzzy, what's up?"

Now, waiting for the locksmith, needing talk to fill the time, Todd begins telling Marv about the art-history course he's taking at Orange Coast College. The other night in class, Todd explains, they were learning about dadaism, the anti-art movement born in Switzerland during World War I. One of the icons of the movement was this dude named Marcel Duchamp. He did a cool painting called *Nude Descending a Staircase.* "When he was coming up, his older brothers and his friends were the ones recognized as the famous painters. They thought Marcel sucked," Todd explains. "But in the end, everybody recognized that Marcel was the true master."

"After he was dead, I'm sure," Marv says.

"When I heard that," Todd continues, ignoring his father's comment, "the first thing I thought of was you, Buzzy. Someday people will realize what a genius *you* are."

Marv looks at him. He's not sure if Todd is goofing or serious. He raises his thick eyebrows archly. "Have you been drinking something?" he asks.

And then the two of them, Buzzy and Buzzy, share a big laugh.

.   .   .

Driving north on I-5, past the rugged mountains of Camp Pendleton, Todd and I are returning from off-loading Marv's stuff. The large U-Haul truck judders wildly on the uneven asphalt. Even at fifty miles per hour in the slow lane, the ride is torturous. It has been a full day; the mood in the cab could rightfully be called slaphappy. Todd has noticed that if he sings a note and holds it, the pounding of the road will make his voice quaver rhythmically. It is a silly, joyful thing that turns the discomfort of the ride upside down. I remember my son doing the same on this stretch of road when he was about five.

You could say Todd missed his childhood. Sports took away his first twenty years. Then drugs took the second twenty, the decades of experience and personal growth that shape most men as they near forty, which Todd will turn this upcoming July 4. When Todd was young, Trudi used to tell him that the Independence Day fireworks were all for him. Today she estimates that since he's been straight, these past thirteen months, Todd has matured from an emotional age of about sixteen to maybe twenty-five, the same age as his fiancée.

Alix is an OC girl with pretty blue eyes. She is pregnant. They are expecting a boy. They plan to name him Baron Buzzy Marinovich. They have cleaned out the Chief's trophy room on the first floor of the beach house and made a little nest for themselves, complete with a new mini kitchen where the bar used to be.

Todd says he's finished with drugs—the frantic hustle, the lies, the insidious need, the way the world perceives you as a loser. Each time he went to jail, he walked the gantlet of deputies, many of them former high school football players. "You had everything and you threw it away," they said. It was hard to hear. He knows they were telling the truth.

Three months from now, in early February, feeling pressure from all directions—the deaths within two weeks of his uncle Craig and grandma Virginia, the upcoming gallery show, Marv's health problems, a new life with his fiancée, questions about his future—he will drive on a Sunday afternoon to his old hook spot in Santa Ana and buy some black tar. As soon as he smokes the first hit, he will throw the dope out the window and call his probation officer, then drive directly to the county offices to give himself up. Sixteen months of sobriety lost in an instant. His penalty will be one week at the Farm; it could have been two years. As he drives across town to surrender, he will see in his mind a picture of Alix, the swell of her belly. He wants to be a father to his son.

"I'm gonna get through this program," he says now, his voice quavering comically as we bounce up the road in the U-Haul.

"The day is coming when I'm not gonna have to piss in a fucking cup."

From the driver's seat, sensing his good mood, I ask: "How much effect do you think that Marv and sports and all contributed to you turning to drugs?" I'd been saving this line of questioning since our first interview, six months earlier. "If you look at your life, it's interesting. It appears that to get out of playing, you sort of partied away your eligibility. It's like you're too old to play now, so you don't have to do drugs anymore. Has the burden been lifted?"

Todd looks out the windshield down the road. The truck bounces. Thirty full seconds pass.

"I don't know how to answer that," Todd says at last. "I really have very few answers."

"That's kind of what it seems like. A little."

Twenty seconds.

"No thoughts?"

"I think, more than anything, it's genetic. I got that gene from the Fertigs—my uncle, the Chief. They were huge drinkers. And then the environment plays a part in it, for sure."

He lights another Marlboro Red, sucks down the first sweet hit. He rides in silence the rest of the way home.

The New Yorker

FINALIST—REPORTING

Did the state of Texas execute an innocent man in 2004? Texas has long been known for its willingness to use the death penalty—since the reintroduction of capital punishment, the state has put to death more men and women than any other—but no matter where you stand on the subject, there can be no greater injustice than the execution of the innocent. And so for many readers, David Grann's account of the trial and conviction of Todd Willingham for setting the fire that killed his three children and his execution by lethal injection twelve years later was the most unforgettable story of 2010. Grann's meticulous reporting and careful prose makes "Trial by Fire" all the more haunting.

David Grann

Trial by Fire

The fire moved quickly through the house, a one-story wood-frame structure in a working-class neighborhood of Corsicana, in northeast Texas. Flames spread along the walls, bursting through doorways, blistering paint and tiles and furniture. Smoke pressed against the ceiling, then banked downward, seeping into each room and through crevices in the windows, staining the morning sky.

Buffie Barbee, who was eleven years old and lived two houses down, was playing in her back yard when she smelled the smoke. She ran inside and told her mother, Diane, and they hurried up the street; that's when they saw the smoldering house and Cameron Todd Willingham standing on the front porch, wearing only a pair of jeans, his chest blackened with soot, his hair and eyelids singed. He was screaming, "My babies are burning up!" His children—Karmon and Kameron, who were one-year-old twin girls, and two-year-old Amber—were trapped inside.

Willingham told the Barbees to call the fire department, and while Diane raced down the street to get help he found a stick and broke the children's bedroom window. Fire lashed through the hole. He broke another window; flames burst through it, too, and he retreated into the yard, kneeling in front of the house. A neighbor later told police that Willingham intermittently cried, "My babies!" then fell silent, as if he had "blocked the fire out of his mind."

Diane Barbee, returning to the scene, could feel intense heat radiating off the house. Moments later, the five windows of the children's room exploded and flames "blew out," as Barbee put it. Within minutes, the first firemen had arrived, and Willingham approached them, shouting that his children were in their bedroom, where the flames were thickest. A fireman sent word over his radio for rescue teams to "step on it."

More men showed up, uncoiling hoses and aiming water at the blaze. One fireman, who had an air tank strapped to his back and a mask covering his face, slipped through a window but was hit by water from a hose and had to retreat. He then charged through the front door, into a swirl of smoke and fire. Heading down the main corridor, he reached the kitchen, where he saw a refrigerator blocking the back door.

Todd Willingham, looking on, appeared to grow more hysterical, and a police chaplain named George Monaghan led him to the back of a fire truck and tried to calm him down. Willingham explained that his wife, Stacy, had gone out earlier that morning, and that he had been jolted from sleep by Amber screaming, "Daddy! Daddy!"

"My little girl was trying to wake me up and tell me about the fire," he said, adding, "I couldn't get my babies out."

While he was talking, a fireman emerged from the house, cradling Amber. As she was given C.P.R., Willingham, who was twenty-three years old and powerfully built, ran to see her, then suddenly headed toward the babies' room. Monaghan and another man restrained him. "We had to wrestle with him and then handcuff him, for his and our protection," Monaghan later told police. "I received a black eye." One of the first firemen at the scene told investigators that, at an earlier point, he had also held Willingham back. "Based on what I saw on how the fire was burning, it would have been crazy for anyone to try and go into the house," he said.

Willingham was taken to a hospital, where he was told that Amber—who had actually been found in the master bedroom—had died of smoke inhalation. Kameron and Karmon had been lying on the floor of the children's bedroom, their bodies severely burned. According to the medical examiner, they, too, died from smoke inhalation.

News of the tragedy, which took place on December 23, 1991, spread through Corsicana. A small city fifty-five miles northeast of Waco, it had once been the center of Texas's first oil boom, but many of the wells had since dried up, and more than a quarter of the city's twenty thousand inhabitants had fallen into poverty. Several stores along the main street were shuttered, giving the place the feel of an abandoned outpost.

Willingham and his wife, who was twenty-two years old, had virtually no money. Stacy worked in her brother's bar, called Some Other Place, and Willingham, an unemployed auto mechanic, had been caring for the kids. The community took up a collection to help the Willinghams pay for funeral arrangements.

Fire investigators, meanwhile, tried to determine the cause of the blaze. (Willingham gave authorities permission to search the house: "I know we might not ever know all the answers, but I'd just like to know why my babies were taken from me.") Douglas Fogg, who was then the assistant fire chief in Corsicana, conducted the initial inspection. He was tall, with a crew cut, and his voice was raspy from years of inhaling smoke from fires and cigarettes. He had grown up in Corsicana and, after graduating from high school, in 1963, he had joined the navy, serving as a medic in Vietnam, where he was wounded on four occasions. He was awarded a Purple Heart each time. After he returned from Vietnam, he became a firefighter, and by the time of the Willingham blaze he had been battling fire—or what he calls "the beast"—for more than twenty years, and had become a certified arson investigator. "You learn that fire talks to you," he told me.

He was soon joined on the case by one of the state's leading arson sleuths, a deputy fire marshal named Manuel Vasquez, who has since died. Short, with a paunch, Vasquez had investigated more than 1,200 fires. Arson investigators have always been considered a special breed of detective. In the 1991 movie *Backdraft*, a heroic arson investigator says of fire, "It breathes, it eats, and it hates. The only way to beat it is to think like it. To know that this flame will spread this way across the door and up across the ceiling." Vasquez, who had previously worked in army intelligence, had several maxims of his own. One was "Fire does not destroy evidence—it creates it." Another was "The fire tells the story. I am just the interpreter." He cultivated a Sherlock Holmes–like aura of invincibility. Once, he was asked under oath whether he had ever been mistaken in a case. "If I have, sir, I don't know," he responded. "It's never been pointed out."

Vasquez and Fogg visited the Willinghams' house four days after the blaze. Following protocol, they moved from the least burned areas toward the most damaged ones. "It is a systematic method," Vasquez later testified, adding, "I'm just collecting information. . . . I have not made any determination. I don't have any preconceived idea."

The men slowly toured the perimeter of the house, taking notes and photographs, like archeologists mapping out a ruin. Upon opening the back door, Vasquez observed that there was just enough space to squeeze past the refrigerator blocking the exit. The air smelled of burned rubber and melted wires; a damp ash covered the ground, sticking to their boots. In the kitchen, Vasquez and Fogg discerned only smoke and heat damage—a sign that the fire had not originated there—and so they pushed deeper into the 975-square-foot building. A central corridor led past a utility room and the master bedroom, then past a small living room, on the left, and the children's bedroom, on the right, ending at the front door, which opened onto the porch. Vasquez tried to take in everything, a process that he compared to entering one's mother-in-law's house for the first time: "I have the same curiosity."

In the utility room, he noticed on the wall pictures of skulls and what he later described as an image of "the Grim Reaper." Then he turned into the master bedroom, where Amber's body had been found. Most of the damage there was also from smoke and heat, suggesting that the fire had started farther down the hallway, and he headed that way, stepping over debris and ducking under insulation and wiring that hung down from the exposed ceiling.

As he and Fogg removed some of the clutter, they noticed deep charring along the base of the walls. Because gases become buoyant when heated, flames ordinarily burn upward. But Vasquez and Fogg observed that the fire had burned extremely low down, and that there were peculiar char patterns on the floor, shaped like puddles.

Vasquez's mood darkened. He followed the "burn trailer"—the path etched by the fire—which led from the hallway into the children's bedroom. Sunlight filtering through the broken windows illuminated more of the irregularly shaped char patterns. A flammable or combustible liquid doused on a floor will cause a fire to concentrate in these kinds of pockets, which is why investigators refer to them as "pour patterns" or "puddle configurations."

The fire had burned through layers of carpeting and tile and plywood flooring. Moreover, the metal springs under the children's beds had turned white—a sign that intense heat had radiated beneath them. Seeing that the floor had some of the deepest burns, Vasquez deduced that it had been hotter than the ceiling, which, given that heat rises, was, in his words, "not normal."

Fogg examined a piece of glass from one of the broken windows. It contained a spider-web-like pattern—what fire investigators call "crazed glass." Forensic textbooks had long described the effect as a key indicator that a fire had burned "fast and hot," meaning that it had been fuelled by a liquid accelerant, causing the glass to fracture.

The men looked again at what appeared to be a distinct burn trailer through the house: it went from the children's bedroom into the corridor, then turned sharply to the right and proceeded out the front door. To the investigators' surprise, even the wood under the door's aluminum threshold was charred. On the concrete floor of the porch, just outside the front door, Vasquez and Fogg noticed another unusual thing: brown stains, which, they reported, were consistent with the presence of an accelerant.

The men scanned the walls for soot marks that resembled a "V." When an object catches on fire, it creates such a pattern, as heat and smoke radiate outward; the bottom of the "V" can therefore point to where a fire began. In the Willingham house, there was a distinct "V" in the main corridor. Examining it and other burn patterns, Vasquez identified three places where fire had originated: in the hallway, in the children's bedroom, and at the front door. Vasquez later testified that multiple origins pointed to one conclusion: the fire was "intentionally set by human hands."

By now, both investigators had a clear vision of what had happened. Someone had poured liquid accelerant throughout the children's room, even under their beds, then poured some more along the adjoining hallway and out the front door, creating a "fire barrier" that prevented anyone from escaping; similarly, a prosecutor later suggested, the refrigerator in the kitchen had been moved to block the back-door exit. The house, in short, had been deliberately transformed into a death trap.

The investigators collected samples of burned materials from the house and sent them to a laboratory that could detect the presence of a liquid accelerant. The lab's chemist reported that one of the samples contained evidence of "mineral spirits," a substance that is often found in charcoal-lighter fluid. The sample had been taken by the threshold of the front door.

The fire was now considered a triple homicide, and Todd Willingham—the only person, besides the victims, known to have been in the house at the time of the blaze—became the prime suspect.

. . .

Police and fire investigators canvassed the neighborhood, interviewing witnesses. Several, like Father Monaghan, initially portrayed Willingham as devastated by the fire. Yet, over time, an increasing number of witnesses offered damning statements. Diane Barbee said that she had not seen Willingham try to enter the house until after the authorities arrived, as if he were putting on a show. And when the children's room exploded with flames, she added, he seemed more preoccupied with his car, which he moved down the driveway. Another neighbor reported that when Willingham cried out for his babies he "did not appear to be excited or concerned." Even Father Monaghan wrote in a statement that, upon further reflection, "things were not as they seemed. I had the feeling that [Willingham] was in complete control."

The police began to piece together a disturbing profile of Willingham. Born in Ardmore, Oklahoma, in 1968, he had been abandoned by his mother when he was a baby. His father, Gene, who had divorced his mother, eventually raised him with his stepmother, Eugenia. Gene, a former U.S. marine, worked in a salvage yard, and the family lived in a cramped house; at night, they could hear freight trains rattling past on a nearby track. Willingham, who had what the family called the "classic Willingham look"—a handsome face, thick black hair, and dark eyes—struggled in school, and as a teen-ager began to sniff paint. When he was seventeen, Oklahoma's Department of Human Services evaluated him, and reported, "He likes 'girls,' music, fast cars, sharp trucks, swimming, and hunting, in that order." Willingham dropped out of high school, and over time was arrested for, among other things, driving under the influence, stealing a bicycle, and shoplifting.

In 1988, he met Stacy, a senior in high school, who also came from a troubled background: when she was four years old, her stepfather had strangled her mother to death during a fight. Stacy and Willingham had a turbulent relationship. Willingham, who was unfaithful, drank too much Jack Daniel's and sometimes hit Stacy—even when she was pregnant. A neighbor said that he once heard Willingham yell at her, "Get up, bitch, and I'll hit you again."

On December 31, the authorities brought Willingham in for questioning. Fogg and Vasquez were present for the interrogation, along with Jimmie Hensley, a police officer who was working his first arson case. Willingham said that Stacy had left the house around 9 A.M. to pick up a Christmas present for the kids, at the Salvation Army. "After she got out of the driveway, I heard the twins cry, so I got up and gave them a bottle," he said. The children's room had a safety gate across the doorway, which Amber could climb over but not the twins, and he and Stacy often let the twins nap on the floor after they drank their bottles. Amber was still in bed, Willingham said, so he went back into his room to sleep. "The next thing I remember is hearing 'Daddy, Daddy,'" he recalled. "The house was already full of smoke." He said that he got up, felt around the floor for a pair of pants, and put them on. He could no longer hear his daughter's voice ("I heard that last 'Daddy, Daddy' and never heard her again"), and he hollered, "'Oh God—Amber, get out of the house! Get out of the house!'"

He never sensed that Amber was in his room, he said. Perhaps she had already passed out by the time he stood up, or perhaps she came in after he left, through a second doorway, from the living room. He said that he went down the corridor and tried to reach the children's bedroom. In the hallway, he said, "you couldn't see nothing but black." The air smelled the way it had when their microwave had blown up, three weeks earlier—like "wire and stuff like that." He could hear sockets and light switches popping, and he crouched down, almost crawling. When he made it to the children's bedroom, he said, he stood and his hair caught on fire. "Oh God, I never felt anything that hot before," he said of the heat radiating out of the room.

After he patted out the fire on his hair, he said, he got down on the ground and groped in the dark. "I thought I found one of them once," he said, "but it was a doll." He couldn't bear the heat any longer. "I felt myself passing out," he said. Finally, he stumbled down the corridor and out the front door, trying to catch his breath. He saw Diane Barbee and yelled for her to call the Fire Department. After she left, he insisted, he tried without success to get back inside.

The investigators asked him if he had any idea how the fire had started. He said that he wasn't sure, though it must have originated in the children's room, since that was where he first saw flames; they were glowing like "bright lights." He and Stacy used three space heaters to keep the house warm, and one of them was in the children's room. "I taught Amber not to play with it," he said, adding that she got "whuppings every once in a while for messing with it." He said that he didn't know if the heater, which had an internal flame, was turned on. (Vasquez later testified that when he had checked the heater, four days after the fire, it was in the "Off" position.) Willingham speculated that the fire might have been started by something electrical: he had heard all that popping and crackling.

When pressed whether someone might have a motive to hurt his family, he said that he couldn't think of anyone that "cold-blooded." He said of his children, "I just don't understand why anybody would take them, you know? We had three of the most pretty babies anybody could have ever asked for." He went on, "Me and Stacy's been together for four years, but off and on we get into a fight and split up for a while and I think those babies is what brought us so close together . . . neither one of us . . . could live without them kids." Thinking of Amber, he said, "To tell you the honest-to-God's truth, I wish she hadn't woke me up."

During the interrogation, Vasquez let Fogg take the lead. Finally, Vasquez turned to Willingham and asked a seemingly random question: had he put on shoes before he fled the house?

"No, sir," Willingham replied.

A map of the house was on a table between the men, and Vasquez pointed to it. "You walked out this way?" he said.

Willingham said yes.

Vasquez was now convinced that Willingham had killed his children. If the floor had been soaked with a liquid accelerant and the fire had burned low, as the evidence suggested, Willingham could not have run out of the house the way he had described without badly burning his feet. A medical report indicated that his feet had been unscathed.

Willingham insisted that, when he left the house, the fire was still around the top of the walls and not on the floor. "I didn't have to jump through any flames," he said. Vasquez believed that this was impossible, and that Willingham had lit the fire as he was retreating—first, torching the children's room, then the hallway, and then, from the porch, the front door. Vasquez later said of Willingham, "He told me a story of pure fabrication. . . . He just talked and he talked and all he did was lie."

Still, there was no clear motive. The children had life-insurance policies, but they amounted to only $15,000, and Stacy's grandfather, who had paid for them, was listed as the primary beneficiary. Stacy told investigators that even though Willingham hit her he had never abused the children—"Our kids were spoiled rotten," she said—and she did not believe that Willingham could have killed them.

Ultimately, the authorities concluded that Willingham was a man without a conscience whose serial crimes had climaxed, almost inexorably, in murder. John Jackson, who was then the assistant district attorney in Corsicana, was assigned to prosecute Willingham's case. He later told the *Dallas Morning News* that he considered Willingham to be "an utterly sociopathic individual" who deemed his children "an impediment to his lifestyle." Or, as the local district attorney, Pat Batchelor, put it, "The children were interfering with his beer drinking and dart throwing."

On the night of January 8, 1992, two weeks after the fire, Willingham was riding in a car with Stacy when SWAT teams surrounded them, forcing them to the side of the road. "They pulled guns out like we had just robbed ten banks," Stacy later recalled. "All we heard was 'click, click.' . . . Then they arrested him."

Willingham was charged with murder. Because there were multiple victims, he was eligible for the death penalty, under Texas law. Unlike many other prosecutors in the state, Jackson, who had ambitions of becoming a judge, was personally opposed to capital punishment. "I don't think it's effective in deterring criminals," he told me. "I just don't think it works." He also considered it wasteful: because of the expense of litigation and the appeals process, it costs, on average, $2.3 million to execute a prisoner in Texas—about three times the cost of incarcerating someone for forty years. Plus, Jackson said, "What's the recourse if you make a mistake?" Yet his boss, Batchelor, believed that, as he once put it, "certain people who commit bad enough crimes give up the right to live," and Jackson came to agree that the heinous nature of the crime in the Willingham case—"one of the worst in terms of body count" that he had ever tried—mandated death.

Willingham couldn't afford to hire lawyers, and was assigned two by the state: David Martin, a former state trooper, and Robert Dunn, a local defense attorney who represented everyone from alleged murderers to spouses in divorce cases—a "Jack-of-all-trades," as he calls himself. ("In a small town, you can't say 'I'm a so-and-so lawyer,' because you'll starve to death," he told me.)

Not long after Willingham's arrest, authorities received a message from a prison inmate named Johnny Webb, who was in the same jail as Willingham. Webb alleged that Willingham had confessed to him that he took "some kind of lighter fluid, squirting [it] around the walls and the floor, and set a fire." The case against Willingham was considered airtight.

Even so, several of Stacy's relatives—who, unlike her, believed that Willingham was guilty—told Jackson that they preferred to avoid the anguish of a trial. And so, shortly before jury selection, Jackson approached Willingham's attorneys with an extraordinary offer: if their client pleaded guilty, the state would give him a life sentence. "I was really happy when I thought we might have a deal to avoid the death penalty," Jackson recalls.

Willingham's lawyers were equally pleased. They had little doubt that he had committed the murders and that, if the case went before a jury, he would be found guilty, and, subsequently, executed. "Everyone thinks defense lawyers must believe their clients are innocent, but that's seldom true," Martin told me. "Most of the time, they're guilty as sin." He added of Willingham, "All the evidence showed that he was 100 percent guilty. He poured accelerant all over the house and put lighter fluid under the kids' beds." It was, he said, "a classic arson case": there were "puddle patterns all over the place—no disputing those."

Martin and Dunn advised Willingham that he should accept the offer, but he refused. The lawyers asked his father and stepmother to speak to him. According to Eugenia, Martin showed them photographs of the burned children and said, "Look what your son did. You got to talk him into pleading, or he's going to be executed."

His parents went to see their son in jail. Though his father did not believe that he should plead guilty if he were innocent, his stepmother beseeched him to take the deal. "I just wanted to keep my boy alive," she told me.

Willingham was implacable. "I ain't gonna plead to something I didn't do, especially killing my own kids," he said. It was his final decision. Martin says, "I thought it was nuts at the time—and I think it's nuts now."

Willingham's refusal to accept the deal confirmed the view of the prosecution, and even that of his defense lawyers, that he was an unrepentant killer.

In August 1992, the trial commenced in the old stone courthouse in downtown Corsicana. Jackson and a team of prosecutors summoned a procession of witnesses, including Johnny Webb and the Barbees. The crux of the state's case, though, remained the scientific evidence gathered by Vasquez and Fogg. On the stand, Vasquez detailed what he called more than "twenty indicators" of arson.

"Do you have an opinion as to who started the fire?" one of the prosecutors asked.

"Yes, sir," Vasquez said. "Mr. Willingham."

The prosecutor asked Vasquez what he thought Willingham's intent was in lighting the fire. "To kill the little girls," he said.

The defense had tried to find a fire expert to counter Vasquez and Fogg's testimony, but the one they contacted concurred with the prosecution. Ultimately, the defense presented only one witness to the jury: the Willinghams' babysitter, who said she could not believe that Willingham could have killed his children. (Dunn told me that Willingham had wanted to testify, but Martin and Dunn thought that he would make a bad witness.) The trial ended after two days.

During his closing arguments, Jackson said that the puddle configurations and pour patterns were Willingham's inadvertent "confession," burned into the floor. Showing a Bible that had been salvaged from the fire, Jackson paraphrased the words of Jesus from the Gospel of Matthew: "Whomsoever shall harm one of my children, it's better for a millstone to be hung around his neck and for him to be cast in the sea."

The jury was out for barely an hour before returning with a unanimous guilty verdict. As Vasquez put it, "The fire does not lie."

II

When Elizabeth Gilbert approached the prison guard, on a spring day in 1999, and said Cameron Todd Willingham's name, she was uncertain about what she was doing. A forty-seven-year-old French teacher and playwright from Houston, Gilbert was divorced with two children. She had never visited a prison before. Several weeks earlier, a friend, who worked at an organization that opposed the death penalty, had encouraged her to volunteer as a pen pal for an inmate on death row, and Gilbert had offered her name and address. Not long after, a short letter, written with unsteady penmanship, arrived from Willingham. "If you wish to write back, I would be honored to correspond with you," he said. He also asked if she might visit him. Perhaps out of a writer's curiosity, or perhaps because she didn't feel quite herself (she had just been upset by news that her ex-husband was dying of cancer), she agreed. Now she was standing in front of the decrepit penitentiary in Huntsville, Texas—a place that inmates referred to as "the death pit."

She filed past a razor-wire fence, a series of floodlights, and a checkpoint, where she was patted down, until she entered a small chamber. Only a few feet in front of her was a man convicted of multiple infanticide. He was wearing a white jumpsuit with "DR"—for death row—printed on the back, in large black letters. He had a tattoo of a serpent and a skull on his left biceps. He stood nearly six feet tall and was muscular, though his legs had atrophied after years of confinement.

A Plexiglas window separated Willingham from her; still, Gilbert, who had short brown hair and a bookish manner, stared at him uneasily. Willingham had once fought another prisoner who called him a "baby killer," and since he had been incarcerated, seven years earlier, he had committed a series of disciplinary infractions that had periodically landed him in the segregation unit, which was known as "the dungeon."

Willingham greeted her politely. He seemed grateful that she had come. After his conviction, Stacy had campaigned for his release. She wrote to Ann Richards, then the governor of Texas, saying, "I know him in ways that no one else does when it comes to our children. Therefore, I believe that there is no way he could have possibly committed this crime." But within a year Stacy had filed for divorce, and Willingham had few visitors except for his parents, who drove from Oklahoma to see him once a month. "I really have no one outside my parents to remind me that I am a human being, not the animal the state professes I am," he told Gilbert at one point.

He didn't want to talk about death row. "Hell, I live here," he later wrote her. "When I have a visit, I want to escape from here." He asked her questions about her teaching and art. He expressed fear that, as a playwright, she might find him a "one-dimensional character," and apologized for lacking social graces; he now had trouble separating the mores in prison from those of the outside world.

When Gilbert asked him if he wanted something to eat or drink from the vending machines, he declined. "I hope I did not offend you by not accepting any snacks," he later wrote her. "I didn't want you to feel I was there just for something like that."

She had been warned that prisoners often tried to con visitors. He appeared to realize this, subsequently telling her, "I am just a simple man. Nothing else. And to most other people a convicted killer looking for someone to manipulate."

Their visit lasted for two hours, and afterward they continued to correspond. She was struck by his letters, which seemed introspective, and were not at all what she had expected. "I am a very honest person with my feelings," he wrote her. "I will not bullshit you on how I feel or what I think." He said that he used to be stoic, like his father. But, he added, "losing my three daughters . . . my home, wife and my life, you tend to wake up a little. I have learned to open myself."

She agreed to visit him again, and when she returned, several weeks later, he was visibly moved. "Here I am this person who nobody on the outside is ever going to know as a human, who has lost so much, but still trying to hold on," he wrote her afterward. "But you came back! I don't think you will ever know of what importance that visit was in my existence."

They kept exchanging letters, and she began asking him about the fire. He insisted that he was innocent and that, if someone had poured accelerant through the house and lit it, then the killer remained free. Gilbert wasn't naïve—she assumed that he was guilty. She did not mind giving him solace, but she was not there to absolve him.

Still, she had become curious about the case, and one day that fall she drove down to the courthouse in Corsicana to review the trial records. Many people in the community remembered the tragedy, and a clerk expressed bewilderment that anyone would be interested in a man who had burned his children alive.

Gilbert took the files and sat down at a small table. As she examined the eyewitness accounts, she noticed several contradictions. Diane Barbee had reported that, before the authorities arrived at the fire, Willingham never tried to get back into the house—yet she had been absent for some time while calling the Fire Department. Meanwhile, her daughter Buffie had reported witnessing Willingham on the porch breaking a window, in an apparent effort to reach his children. And the firemen and police on the scene had described Willingham frantically trying to get into the house.

The witnesses' testimony also grew more damning after authorities had concluded, in the beginning of January 1992, that Willingham was likely guilty of murder. In Diane Barbee's initial statement to authorities, she had portrayed Willingham as "hysterical," and described the front of the house exploding. But on January 4, after arson investigators began suspecting Willingham of murder, Barbee suggested that he could have gone back inside to rescue his children, for at the outset she had seen only "smoke coming from out of the front of the house"—smoke that was not "real thick."

An even starker shift occurred with Father Monaghan's testimony. In his first statement, he had depicted Willingham as a devastated father who had to be repeatedly restrained from risking his life. Yet, as investigators were preparing to arrest Willingham, he concluded that Willingham had been *too* emotional ("He seemed to have the type of distress that a woman who had given birth would have upon seeing her children die"); and he expressed a "gut feeling" that Willingham had "something to do with the setting of the fire."

Dozens of studies have shown that witnesses' memories of events often change when they are supplied with new contextual information. Itiel Dror, a cognitive psychologist who has done extensive research on eyewitness and expert testimony in criminal investigations, told me, "The mind is not a passive machine. Once you believe in something—once you expect something—it changes the way you perceive information and the way your memory recalls it."

After Gilbert's visit to the courthouse, she kept wondering about Willingham's motive, and she pressed him on the matter. In response, he wrote, of the death of his children, "I do not talk about it much anymore and it is still a very powerfully emotional pain inside my being." He admitted that he had been a "sorry-ass husband" who had hit Stacy—something he deeply regretted. But he said that he had loved his children and would never have hurt them. Fatherhood, he said, had changed him; he stopped being a hoodlum and "settled down" and "became a man." Nearly three months before the fire, he and Stacy, who had never married, wed at a small ceremony in his home town of Ardmore. He said that the prosecution had seized upon incidents from his past and from the day of the fire to create a portrait of a "demon," as Jackson, the prosecutor, referred to him. For instance, Willingham said, he had moved the car during the fire simply because he didn't want it to explode by the house, further threatening the children.

Gilbert was unsure what to make of his story, and she began to approach people who were involved in the case, asking them questions. "My friends thought I was crazy," Gilbert recalls. "I'd never done anything like this in my life."

One morning, when Willingham's parents came to visit him, Gilbert arranged to see them first, at a coffee shop near the prison. Gene, who was in his seventies, had the Willingham look, though his black hair had gray streaks and his dark eyes were magnified by glasses. Eugenia, who was in her fifties, with silvery hair, was as sweet and talkative as her husband was stern and reserved. The drive from Oklahoma to Texas took six hours, and they had woken at three in the morning; because they could not afford a motel, they would have to return home later that day. "I feel like a real burden to them," Willingham had written Gilbert.

As Gene and Eugenia sipped coffee, they told Gilbert how grateful they were that someone had finally taken an interest in Todd's case. Gene said that his son, though he had flaws, was no killer.

The evening before the fire, Eugenia said, she had spoken on the phone with Todd. She and Gene were planning on visiting two days later, on Christmas Eve, and Todd told her that he and Stacy and the kids had just picked up family photographs. "He said, 'We got your pictures for Christmas,'" she recalled. "He put Amber on the phone, and she was tattling on one of the twins. Todd didn't seem upset. If something was bothering him, I would have known."

Gene and Eugenia got up to go: they didn't want to miss any of the four hours that were allotted for the visit with their son. Before they left, Gene said, "You'll let us know if you find anything, won't you?"

Over the next few weeks, Gilbert continued to track down sources. Many of them, including the Barbees, remained convinced that Willingham was guilty, but several of his friends and relatives had doubts. So did some people in law enforcement. Willingham's former probation officer in Oklahoma, Polly Goodin, recently told me that Willingham had never demonstrated bizarre or sociopathic behavior. "He was probably one of my favorite kids," she said. Even a former judge named Bebe Bridges—who had often stood, as she put it, on the "opposite side" of Willingham in the legal system, and who had sent him to jail for stealing—told me that she could not imagine him killing his children. "He was polite, and he seemed to care," she said. "His convictions had been for dumb-kid stuff. Even the things stolen weren't significant." Several months before the fire, Willingham tracked Goodin down at her office, and proudly showed her photographs of Stacy and the kids. "He wanted Bebe and me to know he'd been doing good," Goodin recalled.

Eventually, Gilbert returned to Corsicana to interview Stacy, who had agreed to meet at the bed-and-breakfast where Gilbert was staying. Stacy was slightly plump, with pale, round cheeks and feathered dark-blond hair; her bangs were held in place by gel, and her face was heavily made up. According to a tape recording of the conversation, Stacy said that nothing unusual had happened in the days before the fire. She and Willingham had not fought, and were preparing for the holiday. Though Vasquez, the arson expert, had recalled finding the space heater off, Stacy was sure that, at least on the day of the incident—a cool winter morning—it had been on. "I remember turning it down," she recalled. "I always thought, Gosh, could Amber have put something in there?" Stacy added that, more than once, she had caught Amber "putting things too close to it."

Willingham had often not treated her well, she recalled, and after his incarceration she had left him for a man who did. But she didn't think that her former husband should be on death row. "I don't think he did it," she said, crying.

Though only the babysitter had appeared as a witness for the defense during the main trial, several family members, including Stacy, testified during the penalty phase, asking the jury to spare Willingham's life. When Stacy was on the stand, Jackson grilled her about the "significance" of Willingham's "very large tattoo of a skull, encircled by some kind of a serpent."

"It's just a tattoo," Stacy responded.

"He just likes skulls and snakes. Is that what you're saying?"

"No. He just had—he got a tattoo on him."

The prosecution cited such evidence in asserting that Willingham fit the profile of a sociopath, and brought forth two medical experts to confirm the theory. Neither had met Willingham. One of them was Tim Gregory, a psychologist with a master's degree in marriage and family issues, who had previously gone goose hunting with Jackson, and had not published any research in the field of sociopathic behavior. His practice was devoted to family counseling.

At one point, Jackson showed Gregory exhibit no. 60—a photograph of an Iron Maiden poster that had hung in Willingham's house—and asked the psychologist to interpret it. "This one is a picture of a skull, with a fist being punched through the skull," Gregory said; the image displayed "violence" and "death." Gregory looked at photographs of other music posters owned by

Willingham. "There's a hooded skull, with wings and a hatchet," Gregory continued. "And all of these are in fire, depicting—it reminds me of something like Hell. And there's a picture—a Led Zeppelin picture of a falling angel. . . . I see there's an association many times with cultive-type of activities. A focus on death, dying. Many times individuals that have a lot of this type of art have interest in satanic-type activities."

The other medical expert was James P. Grigson, a forensic psychiatrist. He testified so often for the prosecution in capital-punishment cases that he had become known as Dr. Death. (A Texas appellate judge once wrote that when Grigson appeared on the stand the defendant might as well "commence writing out his last will and testament.") Grigson suggested that Willingham was an "extremely severe sociopath," and that "no pill" or treatment could help him. Grigson had previously used nearly the same words in helping to secure a death sentence against Randall Dale Adams, who had been convicted of murdering a police officer, in 1977. After Adams, who had no prior criminal record, spent a dozen years on death row—and once came within seventy-two hours of being executed—new evidence emerged that absolved him, and he was released. In 1995, three years after Willingham's trial, Grigson was expelled from the American Psychiatric Association for violating ethics. The association stated that Grigson had repeatedly arrived at a "psychiatric diagnosis without first having examined the individuals in question, and for indicating, while testifying in court as an expert witness, that he could predict with 100-per-cent certainty that the individuals would engage in future violent acts."

.   .   .

After speaking to Stacy, Gilbert had one more person she wanted to interview: the jailhouse informant Johnny Webb, who was incarcerated in Iowa Park, Texas. She wrote to Webb, who said that she could see him, and they met in the prison visiting room. A man in his late twenties, he had pallid skin and a closely shaved head; his eyes were jumpy, and his entire body seemed to tremble. A reporter who once met him described him to me as "nervous as a cat around rocking chairs." Webb had begun taking drugs when he was nine years old, and had been convicted of, among other things, car theft, selling marijuana, forgery, and robbery.

As Gilbert chatted with him, she thought that he seemed paranoid. During Willingham's trial, Webb disclosed that he had been given a diagnosis of "post-traumatic stress disorder" after he was sexually assaulted in prison, in 1988, and that he often suffered from "mental impairment." Under cross-examination, Webb testified that he had no recollection of a robbery that he had pleaded guilty to only months earlier.

Webb repeated for her what he had said in court: he had passed by Willingham's cell, and as they spoke through a food slot Willingham broke down and told him that he intentionally set the house on fire. Gilbert was dubious. It was hard to believe that Willingham, who had otherwise insisted on his innocence, had suddenly confessed to an inmate he barely knew. The conversation had purportedly taken place by a speaker system that allowed any of the guards to listen—an unlikely spot for an inmate to reveal a secret. What's more, Webb alleged that Willingham had told him that Stacy had hurt one of the kids, and that the fire was set to cover up the crime. The autopsies, however, had revealed no bruises or signs of trauma on the children's bodies.

Jailhouse informants, many of whom are seeking reduced time or special privileges, are notoriously unreliable. According to a 2004 study by the Center on Wrongful Convictions, at Northwestern University Law School, lying police and jailhouse informants are the leading cause of wrongful convictions in capital cases in the United States. At the time that Webb came forward against Willingham, he was facing charges of robbery and forgery. During Willingham's trial, another inmate planned to testify that he had overheard Webb saying to another prisoner that he was hoping to "get time cut," but the testimony was ruled inadmissible, because it was hearsay. Webb, who pleaded guilty to the robbery and forgery charges, received a sentence of fifteen years. Jackson, the prosecutor, told me that he generally considered Webb "an unreliable kind of guy," but added, "I saw no real motive for him to make a statement like this if it wasn't true. We didn't cut him any slack." In 1997, five years after Willingham's trial, Jackson urged the Texas Board of Pardons and Paroles to grant Webb parole. "I asked them to cut him loose early," Jackson told me. The reason, Jackson said, was that Webb had been targeted by the Aryan Brotherhood. The board granted Webb parole, but within months of his release he was caught with cocaine and returned to prison.

In March 2000, several months after Gilbert's visit, Webb unexpectedly sent Jackson a Motion to Recant Testimony, declaring, "Mr. Willingham is innocent of all charges." But Willingham's lawyer was not informed of this development, and soon afterward Webb, without explanation, recanted his recantation. When I recently asked Webb, who was released from prison two years ago, about the turnabout and why Willingham would have confessed to a virtual stranger, he said that he knew only what "the dude told me." After I pressed him, he said, "It's very possible I misunderstood what he said." Since the trial, Webb has been given an additional diagnosis, bipolar disorder. "Being locked up in that little cell makes you kind of crazy," he said. "My memory is in bits and pieces. I was on a lot of medication at the time. Everyone knew that." He paused, then said, "The statute of limitations has run out on perjury, hasn't it?"

Aside from the scientific evidence of arson, the case against Willingham did not stand up to scrutiny. Jackson, the prosecutor, said of Webb's testimony, "You can take it or leave it." Even the refrigerator's placement by the back door of the house turned out to be innocuous; there were two refrigerators in the cramped kitchen, and one of them was by the back door. Jimmie Hensley, the police detective, and Douglas Fogg, the assistant fire chief, both of whom investigated the fire, told me recently that they had never believed that the fridge was part of the arson plot. "It didn't have nothing to do with the fire," Fogg said.

After months of investigating the case, Gilbert found that her faith in the prosecution was shaken. As she told me, "What if Todd really was innocent?"

III

In the summer of 1660, an Englishman named William Harrison vanished on a walk, near the village of Charingworth, in Gloucestershire. His bloodstained hat was soon discovered on the side of a local road. Police interrogated Harrison's servant, John Perry, and eventually Perry gave a statement that his mother and his brother had killed Harrison for money. Perry, his mother, and his brother were hanged.

Two years later, Harrison reappeared. He insisted, fancifully, that he had been abducted by a band of criminals and sold into slavery. Whatever happened, one thing was indisputable: he had not been murdered by the Perrys.

The fear that an innocent person might be executed has long haunted jurors and lawyers and judges. During America's colonial period, dozens of crimes were punishable by death, including horse thievery, blasphemy, "man-stealing," and highway robbery. After independence, the number of crimes eligible for the death penalty was gradually reduced, but doubts persisted over whether legal procedures were sufficient to prevent an innocent person from being executed. In 1868, John Stuart Mill made one of the most eloquent defenses of capital punishment, arguing that executing a murderer did not display a wanton disregard for life but, rather, proof of its value. "We show, on the contrary, most emphatically our regard for it by the adoption of a rule that he who violates that right in another forfeits it for himself," he said. For Mill, there was one counterargument that carried weight—"that if by an error of justice an innocent person is put to death, the mistake can never be corrected."

The modern legal system, with its lengthy appeals process and clemency boards, was widely assumed to protect the kind of "error of justice" that Mill feared. In 2000, while George W. Bush was governor of Texas, he said, "I know there are some in the country who don't care for the death penalty, but . . . we've adequately answered innocence or guilt." His top policy adviser on issues of criminal justice emphasized that there is "super due process to make sure that no innocent defendants are executed."

In recent years, though, questions have mounted over whether the system is fail-safe. Since 1976, more than 130 people on death row have been exonerated. DNA testing, which was developed in the eighties, saved seventeen of them, but the technique can be used only in rare instances. Barry Scheck, a cofounder of the Innocence Project, which has used DNA testing to exonerate prisoners, estimates that about 80 percent of felonies do not involve biological evidence.

In 2000, after thirteen people on death row in Illinois were exonerated, George Ryan, who was then governor of the state, suspended the death penalty. Though he had been a longtime advocate of capital punishment, he declared that he could no longer support a system that has "come so close to the ultimate nightmare—the state's taking of innocent life." Former supreme court justice Sandra Day O'Connor has said that the "execution of a legally and factually innocent person would be a constitutionally intolerable event."

Such a case has become a kind of grisly Holy Grail among opponents of capital punishment. In his 2002 book *The Death Penalty*, Stuart Banner observes, "The prospect of killing an innocent person seemed to be the one thing that could cause people to rethink their support for capital punishment. Some who were not troubled by statistical arguments against the death penalty—claims about deterrence or racial disparities—were deeply troubled that such an extreme injustice might occur in an individual case." Opponents of the death penalty have pointed to several questionable cases. In 1993, Ruben Cantu was executed in Texas for fatally shooting a man during a robbery. Years later, a second victim, who survived the shooting, told the *Houston Chronicle* that he had been pressured by police to identify Cantu as the gunman, even though he believed Cantu to be innocent. Sam Millsap, the district attorney in the case, who had once supported capital punishment ("I'm no wild-eyed, pointy-headed liberal"), said that he was disturbed by the thought that he had made a mistake.

In 1995, Larry Griffin was put to death in Missouri, for a drive-by shooting of a drug dealer. The case rested largely on the eyewitness testimony of a career criminal named Robert Fitzgerald, who had been an informant for prosecutors before and was in the witness-protection program. Fitzgerald maintained that he happened to be at the scene because his car had broken down. After Griffin's execution, a probe sponsored by the N.A.A.C.P.'s Legal Defense and Educational Fund revealed that a man who had been wounded during the incident insisted that Griffin was not the shooter. Moreover, the first police officer at the scene disputed that Fitzgerald had witnessed the crime.

These cases, however, stopped short of offering irrefutable proof that a "legally and factually innocent person" was executed. In 2005, a St. Louis prosecutor, Jennifer Joyce, launched an investigation of the Griffin case, upon being presented with what she called "compelling" evidence of Griffin's potential innocence. After two years of reviewing the evidence, and interviewing a new eyewitness, Joyce said that she and her team were convinced that the "right person was convicted."

Supreme Court Justice Antonin Scalia, in 2006, voted with a majority to uphold the death penalty in a Kansas case. In his opinion, Scalia declared that, in the modern judicial system, there has not been "a single case—not one—in which it is clear that a person was executed for a crime he did not commit. If such an event had occurred in recent years, we would not have to hunt for it; the innocent's name would be shouted from the rooftops."

. . .

"My problems are simple," Willingham wrote Gilbert in September 1999. "Try to keep them from killing me at all costs. End of story."

During his first years on death row, Willingham had pleaded with his lawyer, David Martin, to rescue him. "You can't imagine what it's like to be here, with people I have no business even being around," he wrote.

For a while, Willingham shared a cell with Ricky Lee Green, a serial killer, who castrated and fatally stabbed his victims, including a sixteen-year-old boy. (Green was executed in 1997.) Another of Willingham's cellmates, who had an I.Q. below seventy and the emotional development of an eight-year-old, was raped by an inmate. "You remember me telling you I had a new celly?" Willingham wrote in a letter to his parents. "The little retarded boy. . . . There was this guy here on the wing who is a shit sorry coward (who is the same one I got into it with a little over a month ago). Well, he raped [my cellmate] in the 3 row shower week before last." Willingham said that he couldn't believe that someone would "rape a boy who cannot even defend himself. Pretty damn low."

Because Willingham was known as a "baby killer," he was a target of attacks. "Prison is a rough place, and with a case like mine they never give you the benefit of a doubt," he wrote his parents. After he tried to fight one prisoner who threatened him, Willingham told a friend that if he hadn't stood up for himself several inmates would have "beaten me up or raped or"—his thought trailed off.

Over the years, Willingham's letters home became increasingly despairing. "This is a hard place, and it makes a person hard inside," he wrote. "I told myself that was one thing I did not want and that was for this place to make me bitter, but it is hard." He went on, "They have [executed] at least one person every month I have been here. It is senseless and brutal. . . . You see, we are not living in here, we are only existing." In 1996, he wrote, "I just been trying to figure out why after having a wife and 3 beautiful children that I loved my life has to end like this. And sometimes it just seems like it is not worth it all. . . . In the 3 ½ years I been here I have never felt that my life was as worthless and desolate as it is now." Since the fire, he wrote, he had the sense that his life was slowly being erased. He obsessively looked at photographs of his children and Stacy, which he stored in his cell. "So long ago, so far away," he wrote in a poem. "Was everything truly there?"

Inmates on death row are housed in a prison within a prison, where there are no attempts at rehabilitation, and no educational or training programs. In 1999, after seven prisoners tried to escape from Huntsville, Willingham and 459 other inmates on death row were moved to a more secure facility, in Livingston, Texas. Willingham was held in isolation in a sixty-square-foot cell, twenty-three hours a day. He tried to distract himself by drawing—"amateur stuff," as he put it—and writing poems. In a poem about his children, he wrote, "There is nothing more beautiful than you on this earth." When Gilbert once suggested some possible revisions to his poems, he explained that he wrote them simply as expressions, however crude, of his feelings. "So to me to cut them up and try to improve on them just for creative-writing purposes would be to destroy what I was doing to start with," he said.

Despite his efforts to occupy his thoughts, he wrote in his diary that his mind "deteriorates each passing day." He stopped working out and gained weight. He questioned his faith: "No God who cared about his creation would abandon the innocent." He seemed not to care if another inmate attacked him. "A person who is already dead inside does not fear" death, he wrote.

One by one, the people he knew in prison were escorted into the execution chamber. There was Clifton Russell Jr., who, at the age of eighteen, stabbed and beat a man to death, and who said, in his last statement, "I thank my Father, God in Heaven, for the grace he has granted me—I am ready." There was Jeffery Dean Motley, who kidnapped and fatally shot a woman, and who declared, in his final words, "I love you, Mom. Goodbye." And there was John Fearance, who murdered his neighbor, and who turned to God in his last moments and said, "I hope He will forgive me for what I done."

Willingham had grown close to some of his prison mates, even though he knew that they were guilty of brutal crimes. In March 2000, Willingham's friend Ponchai Wilkerson—a twenty-eight-year-old who had shot and killed a clerk during a jewelry heist—was executed. Afterward, Willingham wrote in his diary that he felt "an emptiness that has not been touched since my children were taken from me." A year later, another friend who was about to be executed—"one of the few real people I have met here not caught up in the bravado of prison"—asked Willingham to make him a final drawing. "Man, I never thought drawing a simple Rose could be so emotionally hard," Willingham wrote. "The hard part is knowing that this will be the last thing I can do for him."

Another inmate, Ernest Ray Willis, had a case that was freakishly similar to Willingham's. In 1987, Willis had been convicted of setting a fire, in west Texas, that killed two women. Willis told investigators that he had been sleeping on a friend's living-room couch and woke up to a house full of smoke. He said that he tried to rouse one of the women, who was sleeping in another room, but the flames and smoke drove him back, and he ran out the front door before the house exploded with flames. Witnesses maintained that Willis had acted suspiciously; he moved his car out of the yard, and didn't show "any emotion," as one volunteer firefighter put it. Authorities also wondered how Willis could have escaped the house without burning his bare feet. Fire investigators found pour patterns, puddle configurations, and other signs of arson. The authorities could discern no motive for the crime, but concluded that Willis, who had no previous record of violence, was a sociopath—a "demon," as the prosecutor put it. Willis was charged with capital murder and sentenced to death.

Willis had eventually obtained what Willingham called, enviously, a "bad-ass lawyer." James Blank, a noted patent attorney in New York, was assigned Willis's case as part of his firm's pro-bono work. Convinced that Willis was innocent, Blank devoted more than a dozen years to the case, and his firm spent millions, on fire consultants, private investigators, forensic experts, and the like. Willingham, meanwhile, relied on David Martin, his court-appointed lawyer, and one of Martin's colleagues to handle his appeals. Willingham often told his parents, "You don't know what it's like to have lawyers who won't even believe you're innocent." Like many inmates on death row, Willingham eventually filed a claim of inadequate legal representation. (When I recently asked Martin about his representation of Willingham, he said, "There were no grounds for reversal, and the verdict was absolutely the right one." He said of the case, "Shit, it's incredible that anyone's even thinking about it.")

Willingham tried to study the law himself, reading books such as *Tact in Court, or How Lawyers Win: Containing Sketches of Cases Won by Skill, Wit, Art, Tact, Courage, and Eloquence.*

Still, he confessed to a friend, "The law is so complicated it is hard for me to understand." In 1996, he obtained a new court-appointed lawyer, Walter Reaves, who told me that he was appalled by the quality of Willingham's defense at trial and on appeal. Reaves prepared for him a state writ of habeas corpus, known as a Great Writ. In the byzantine appeals process of death-penalty cases, which frequently takes more than ten years, the writ is the most critical stage: a prisoner can introduce new evidence detailing such things as perjured testimony, unreliable medical experts, and bogus scientific findings. Yet most indigent inmates, like Willingham, who constitute the bulk of those on death row, lack the resources to track down new witnesses or dig up fresh evidence. They must depend on court-appointed lawyers, many of whom are "unqualified, irresponsible, or overburdened," as a study by the Texas Defender Service, a nonprofit organization, put it. In 2000, a *Dallas Morning News* investigation revealed that roughly a quarter of the inmates condemned to death in Texas were represented by court-appointed attorneys who had, at some point in their careers, been "reprimanded, placed on probation, suspended or banned from practicing law by the State Bar." Although Reaves was more competent, he had few resources to reinvestigate the case, and his writ introduced no new exculpatory evidence: nothing further about Webb, or the reliability of the eyewitness testimony, or the credibility of the medical experts. It focused primarily on procedural questions, such as whether the trial court erred in its instructions to the jury.

The Texas Court of Criminal Appeals was known for upholding convictions even when overwhelming exculpatory evidence came to light. In 1997, DNA testing proved that sperm collected from a rape victim did not match Roy Criner, who had been sentenced to ninety-nine years for the crime. Two lower courts recommended that the verdict be overturned, but the Court of Criminal Appeals upheld it, arguing that Criner might have worn a condom or might not have ejaculated. Sharon Keller, who is now the presiding judge on the court, stated in a majority opinion, "The new evidence does not establish innocence." In 2000, George W. Bush pardoned Criner. (Keller was recently charged with judicial misconduct, for refusing to keep open past five o'clock a clerk's office in order to allow a last-minute petition from a man who was executed later that night.)

On October 31, 1997, the Court of Criminal Appeals denied Willingham's writ. After Willingham filed another writ of habeas corpus, this time in federal court, he was granted a temporary stay. In a poem, Willingham wrote, "One more chance, one more strike / Another bullet dodged, another date escaped."

Willingham was entering his final stage of appeals. As his anxieties mounted, he increasingly relied upon Gilbert to investigate his case and for emotional support. "She may never know what a change she brought into my life," he wrote in his diary. "For the first time in many years she gave me a purpose, something to look forward to."

As their friendship deepened, he asked her to promise him that she would never disappear without explanation. "I already have that in my life," he told her.

Together, they pored over clues and testimony. Gilbert says that she would send Reaves leads to follow up, but although he was sympathetic, nothing seemed to come of them. In 2002, a federal district court of appeals denied Willingham's writ without even a hearing. "Now I start the last leg of my journey," Willingham wrote to Gilbert. "Got to get things in order."

He appealed to the U.S. Supreme Court, but in December 2003, he was notified that it had declined to hear his case. He soon received a court order announcing that "the Director of the Department of Criminal Justice at Huntsville, Texas, acting by and through the executioner designated by said Director . . . is hereby DIRECTED and COMMANDED, at some hour after 6:00 P.M. on the 17th day of February, 2004, at the Department of Criminal

Justice in Huntsville, Texas, to carry out this sentence of death by intravenous injection of a substance or substances in a lethal quantity sufficient to cause the death of said Cameron Todd Willingham."

Willingham wrote a letter to his parents. "Are you sitting down?" he asked, before breaking the news. "I love you both so much," he said.

His only remaining recourse was to appeal to the governor of Texas, Rick Perry, a Republican, for clemency. The process, considered the last gatekeeper to the executioner, has been called by the U.S. Supreme Court "the 'fail safe' in our criminal justice system."

IV

One day in January 2004, Dr. Gerald Hurst, an acclaimed scientist and fire investigator, received a file describing all the evidence of arson gathered in Willingham's case. Gilbert had come across Hurst's name and, along with one of Willingham's relatives, had contacted him, seeking his help. After their pleas, Hurst had agreed to look at the case pro bono, and Reaves, Willingham's lawyer, had sent him the relevant documents, in the hope that there were grounds for clemency.

Hurst opened the file in the basement of his house in Austin, which served as a laboratory and an office, and was cluttered with microscopes and diagrams of half-finished experiments. Hurst was nearly six and half feet tall, though his stooped shoulders made him seem considerably shorter, and he had a gaunt face that was partly shrouded by long gray hair. He was wearing his customary outfit: black shoes, black socks, a black T-shirt, and loose-fitting black pants supported by black suspenders. In his mouth was a wad of chewing tobacco.

A child prodigy who was raised by a sharecropper during the Great Depression, Hurst used to prowl junk yards, collecting magnets and copper wires in order to build radios and other contraptions. In the early sixties, he received a Ph.D. in chemistry from Cambridge University, where he started to experiment with fluorine and other explosive chemicals, and once detonated his lab. Later, he worked as the chief scientist on secret weapons programs for several American companies, designing rockets and deadly fire bombs—or what he calls "god-awful things." He helped patent what has been described, with only slight exaggeration, as "the world's most powerful nonnuclear explosive": an Astrolite bomb. He experimented with toxins so lethal that a fraction of a drop would rot human flesh, and in his laboratory he often had to wear a pressurized moon suit; despite such precautions, exposure to chemicals likely caused his liver to fail, and in 1994 he required a transplant. Working on what he calls "the dark side of arson," he retrofitted napalm bombs with Astrolite, and developed ways for covert operatives in Vietnam to create bombs from local materials, such as chicken manure and sugar. He also perfected a method for making an exploding T-shirt by nitrating its fibres.

His conscience eventually began pricking him. "One day, you wonder, What the hell am I doing?" he recalls. He left the defense industry, and went on to invent the Mylar balloon, an improved version of Liquid Paper, and Kinepak, a kind of explosive that reduces the risk of accidental detonation. Because of his extraordinary knowledge of fire and explosives, companies in civil litigation frequently sought his help in determining the cause of a blaze. By the nineties, Hurst had begun devoting significant time to criminal-arson cases, and, as he was exposed to the methods of local and state fire investigators, he was shocked by what he saw.

Many arson investigators, it turned out, had only a high-school education. In most states, in order to be certified, investigators had to take a forty-hour course on fire investigation, and pass a written exam. Often, the bulk of an investigator's training came on the job, learning from "old-timers" in the field, who passed down a body of wisdom about the telltale signs of arson, even though a study in 1977 warned that there was nothing in "the scientific literature to substantiate their validity."

In 1992, the National Fire Protection Association, which promotes fire prevention and safety, published its first scientifically based guidelines to arson investigation. Still, many arson investigators believed that what they did was more an art than a science—a blend of experience and intuition. In 1997, the International Association of Arson Investigators filed a legal brief arguing that arson sleuths should not be bound by a 1993 Supreme Court decision requiring experts who testified at trials to adhere to the scientific method. What arson sleuths did, the brief claimed, was "less scientific." By 2000, after the courts had rejected such claims, arson investigators increasingly recognized the scientific method, but there remained great variance in the field, with many practitioners still relying on the unverified techniques that had been used for generations. "People investigated fire largely with a flat-earth approach," Hurst told me. "It looks like arson—therefore, it's arson." He went on, "My view is you have to have a scientific basis. Otherwise, it's no different than witch-hunting."

In 1998, Hurst investigated the case of a woman from North Carolina named Terri Hinson, who was charged with setting a fire that killed her seventeen-month-old son, and faced the death penalty. Hurst ran a series of experiments re-creating the conditions of the fire, which suggested that it had not been arson, as the investigators had claimed; rather, it had started accidentally, from a faulty electrical wire in the attic. Because of this research, Hinson was freed. John Lentini, a fire expert and the author of a leading scientific textbook on arson, describes Hurst as "brilliant." A Texas prosecutor once told the *Chicago Tribune*, of Hurst, "If he says it was an arson fire, then it was. If he says it wasn't, then it wasn't."

Hurst's patents yielded considerable royalties, and he could afford to work pro bono on an arson case for months, even years. But he received the files on Willingham's case only a few weeks before Willingham was scheduled to be executed. As Hurst looked through the case records, a statement by Manuel Vasquez, the state deputy fire marshal, jumped out at him. Vasquez had testified that, of the roughly 1,200 to 1,500 fires he had investigated, "most all of them" were arson. This was an oddly high estimate; the Texas State Fire Marshals Office typically found arson in only 50 percent of its cases.

Hurst was also struck by Vasquez's claim that the Willingham blaze had "burned fast and hot" because of a liquid accelerant. The notion that a flammable or combustible liquid caused flames to reach higher temperatures had been repeated in court by arson sleuths for decades. Yet the theory was nonsense: experiments have proved that wood and gasoline-fuelled fires burn at essentially the same temperature.

Vasquez and Fogg had cited as proof of arson the fact that the front door's aluminum threshold had melted. "The only thing that can cause that to react is an accelerant," Vasquez said. Hurst was incredulous. A natural-wood fire can reach temperatures as high as 2,000 degrees Fahrenheit—far hotter than the melting point for aluminum alloys, which ranges from 1,000 to 1,200 degrees. And, like many other investigators, Vasquez and Fogg mistakenly assumed that wood charring beneath the aluminum threshold was evidence that, as Vasquez put it, "a liquid accelerant flowed underneath and burned." Hurst had conducted myriad experiments showing that such charring was caused simply by the aluminum conducting so much heat. In fact, when liquid accelerant is poured under a threshold a fire will extinguish, because of a lack of oxygen. (Other scientists had reached the same conclusion.) "Liquid accelerants can no more burn under an aluminum threshold than can grease burn in a skillet even with a loose-fitting lid," Hurst declared in his report on the Willingham case.

Hurst then examined Fogg and Vasquez's claim that the "brown stains" on Willingham's front porch were evidence of "liquid accelerant," which had not had time to soak into the concrete. Hurst had previously performed a test in his garage, in which he poured charcoal-lighter fluid on the concrete floor, and lit it. When the fire went out, there were no brown stains, only smudges of soot. Hurst had run the same experiment many times, with different kinds of liquid accelerants, and the result was always the same. Brown stains were common in fires; they were usually composed of rust or gunk from charred debris that had mixed with water from fire hoses.

Another crucial piece of evidence implicating Willingham was the "crazed glass" that Vasquez had attributed to the rapid heating from a fire fuelled with liquid accelerant. Yet, in November of 1991, a team of fire investigators had inspected fifty houses in the hills of Oakland, California, which had been ravaged by brush fires. In a dozen houses, the investigators discovered crazed glass, even though a liquid accelerant had not been used. Most of these houses were on the outskirts of the blaze, where firefighters had shot streams of water; as the investigators later wrote in a published study, they theorized that the fracturing had been induced by rapid cooling, rather than by sudden heating—thermal shock had caused the glass to contract so quickly that it settled disjointedly. The investigators then tested this hypothesis in a laboratory. When they heated glass, nothing happened. But each time they applied water to the heated glass the intricate patterns appeared. Hurst had seen the same phenomenon when he had blowtorched and cooled glass during his research at Cambridge. In his report, Hurst wrote that Vasquez and Fogg's notion of crazed glass was no more than an "old wives' tale."

Hurst then confronted some of the most devastating arson evidence against Willingham: the burn trailer, the pour patterns and puddle configurations, the V-shape and other burn marks indicating that the fire had multiple points of origin, the burning underneath the children's beds. There was also the positive test for mineral spirits by the front door, and Willingham's seemingly implausible story that he had run out of the house without burning his bare feet.

As Hurst read through more of the files, he noticed that Willingham and his neighbors had described the windows in the front of the house suddenly exploding and flames roaring forth. It was then that Hurst thought of the legendary Lime Street Fire, one of the most pivotal in the history of arson investigation.

.   .   .

On the evening of October 15, 1990, a thirty-five-year-old man named Gerald Wayne Lewis was found standing in front of his house on Lime Street, in Jacksonville, Florida, holding his three-year-old son. His two-story wood-frame home was engulfed in flames. By the time the fire had been extinguished, six people were dead, including Lewis's wife. Lewis said that he had rescued his son but was unable to get to the others, who were upstairs.

When fire investigators examined the scene, they found the classic signs of arson: low burns along the walls and floors, pour patterns and puddle configurations, and a burn trailer running from the living room into the hallway. Lewis claimed that the fire had started accidentally, on a couch in the living room—his son had been playing with matches. But a V-shaped pattern by one of the doors suggested that the fire had originated elsewhere. Some witnesses told authorities that Lewis seemed too calm during the fire and had never tried to get help. According to the *Los Angeles Times*, Lewis had previously been arrested for abusing his wife, who had taken out a restraining order against him.

After a chemist said that he had detected the presence of gasoline on Lewis's clothing and shoes, a report by the sheriff's office concluded, "The fire was started as a result of a petroleum product being poured on the front porch, foyer, living room, stairwell and second floor bedroom." Lewis was arrested and charged with six counts of murder. He faced the death penalty.

Subsequent tests, however, revealed that the laboratory identification of gasoline was wrong. Moreover, a local news television camera had captured Lewis in a clearly agitated state at the scene of the fire, and investigators discovered that at one point he had jumped in front of a moving car, asking the driver to call the Fire Department.

Seeking to bolster their theory of the crime, prosecutors turned to John Lentini, the fire expert, and John DeHaan, another leading investigator and textbook author. Despite some of the weaknesses of the case, Lentini told me that, given the classic burn patterns and puddle configurations in the house, he was sure that Lewis had set the fire: "I was prepared to testify and send this guy to Old Sparky"—the electric chair.

To discover the truth, the investigators, with the backing of the prosecution, decided to conduct an elaborate experiment and re-create the fire scene. Local officials gave the investigators permission to use a condemned house next to Lewis's home, which was about to be torn down. The two houses were virtually identical, and the investigators refurbished the condemned one with the same kind of carpeting, curtains, and furniture that had been in Lewis's home. The scientists also wired the building with heat and gas sensors that could withstand fire. The cost of the experiment came to $20,000. Without using liquid accelerant, Lentini and DeHaan set the couch in the living room on fire, expecting that the experiment would demonstrate that Lewis's version of events was implausible.

The investigators watched as the fire quickly consumed the couch, sending upward a plume of smoke that hit the ceiling and spread outward, creating a thick layer of hot gases overhead—an efficient radiator of heat. Within three minutes, this cloud, absorbing more gases from the fire below, was banking down the walls and filling the living room. As the cloud approached the floor, its temperature rose, in some areas, to more than 1,100 degrees Fahrenheit. Suddenly, the entire room exploded in flames, as the radiant heat ignited every piece of furniture, every curtain, every possible fuel source, even the carpeting. The windows shattered.

The fire had reached what is called "flashover"—the point at which radiant heat causes a fire in a room to become a room on fire. Arson investigators knew about the concept of flashover, but it was widely believed to take much longer to occur, especially without a liquid accelerant. From a single fuel source—a couch—the room had reached flashover in four and a half minutes.

Because all the furniture in the living room had ignited, the blaze went from a fuel-controlled fire to a ventilation-controlled fire—or what scientists call "post-flashover." During post-flashover, the path of the fire depends on new sources of oxygen, from an open door or window. One of the fire investigators, who had been standing by an open door in the living room, escaped moments before the oxygen-starved fire roared out of the room into the hallway—a fireball that caused the corridor to go quickly into flashover as well, propelling the fire out the front door and onto the porch.

After the fire was extinguished, the investigators inspected the hallway and living room. On the floor were irregularly shaped burn patterns that perfectly resembled pour patterns and puddle configurations. It turned out that these classic signs of arson can also appear on their own, after flashover. With the naked eye, it is impossible to distinguish between the pour patterns and puddle configurations caused by an accelerant and those caused naturally by post-flashover. The only reliable way to tell the difference is to take samples from the burn patterns and test them in a laboratory for the presence of flammable or combustible liquids.

During the Lime Street experiment, other things happened that were supposed to occur only in a fire fuelled by liquid accelerant: charring along the base of the walls and doorways, and burning under furniture. There was also a V-shaped pattern by the living-room doorway, far from where the fire had started on the couch. In a small fire, a V-shaped burn mark may pinpoint where a fire began, but during post-flashover these patterns can occur repeatedly, when various objects ignite.

One of the investigators muttered that they had just helped prove the defense's case. Given the reasonable doubt raised by the experiment, the charges against Lewis were soon dropped. The Lime Street experiment had demolished prevailing notions about fire behavior. Subsequent tests by scientists showed that, during post-flashover, burning under beds and furniture was common, entire doors were consumed, and aluminum thresholds melted.

John Lentini says of the Lime Street Fire, "This was my epiphany. I almost sent a man to die based on theories that were a load of crap."

•   •   •

Hurst next examined a floor plan of Willingham's house that Vasquez had drawn, which delineated all the purported pour patterns and puddle configurations. Because the windows had blown out of the children's room, Hurst knew that the fire had reached flashover. With his finger, Hurst traced along Vasquez's diagram the burn trailer that had gone from the children's room, turned right in the hallway, and headed out the front door. John Jackson, the prosecutor, had told me that the path was so "bizarre" that it had to have been caused by a liquid accelerant. But

Hurst concluded that it was a natural product of the dynamics of fire during post-flashover. Willingham had fled out the front door, and the fire simply followed the ventilation path, toward the opening. Similarly, when Willingham had broken the windows in the children's room, flames had shot outward.

Hurst recalled that Vasquez and Fogg had considered it impossible for Willingham to have run down the burning hallway without scorching his bare feet. But if the pour patterns and puddle configurations were a result of a flashover, Hurst reasoned, then they were consonant with Willingham's explanation of events. When Willingham exited his bedroom, the hallway was not yet on fire; the flames were contained within the children's bedroom, where, along the ceiling, he saw the "bright lights." Just as the investigator safely stood by the door in the Lime Street experiment seconds before flashover, Willingham could have stood close to the children's room without being harmed. (Prior to the Lime Street case, fire investigators had generally assumed that carbon monoxide diffuses quickly through a house during a fire. In fact, up until flashover, levels of carbon monoxide can be remarkably low beneath and outside the thermal cloud.) By the time the Corsicana fire achieved flashover, Willingham had already fled outside and was in the front yard.

Vasquez had made a videotape of the fire scene, and Hurst looked at the footage of the burn trailer. Even after repeated viewings, he could not detect three points of origin, as Vasquez had. (Fogg recently told me that he also saw a continuous trailer and disagreed with Vasquez, but added that nobody from the prosecution or the defense ever asked him on the stand about his opinion on the subject.)

After Hurst had reviewed Fogg and Vasquez's list of more than twenty arson indicators, he believed that only one had any potential validity: the positive test for mineral spirits by the threshold of the front door. But why had the fire investigators obtained a positive reading only in that location? According to

Fogg and Vasquez's theory of the crime, Willingham had poured accelerant throughout the children's bedroom and down the hallway. Officials had tested extensively in these areas—including where all the pour patterns and puddle configurations were—and turned up nothing. Jackson told me that he "never did understand why they weren't able to recover" positive tests in these parts.

Hurst found it hard to imagine Willingham pouring accelerant on the front porch, where neighbors could have seen him. Scanning the files for clues, Hurst noticed a photograph of the porch taken before the fire, which had been entered into evidence. Sitting on the tiny porch was a charcoal grill. The porch was where the family barbecued. Court testimony from witnesses confirmed that there had been a grill, along with a container of lighter fluid, and that both had burned when the fire roared onto the porch during post-flashover. By the time Vasquez inspected the house, the grill had been removed from the porch, during cleanup. Though he cited the container of lighter fluid in his report, he made no mention of the grill. At the trial, he insisted that he had never been told of the grill's earlier placement. Other authorities were aware of the grill but did not see its relevance. Hurst, however, was convinced that he had solved the mystery: when firefighters had blasted the porch with water, they had likely spread charcoal-lighter fluid from the melted container.

Without having visited the fire scene, Hurst says, it was impossible to pinpoint the cause of the blaze. But, based on the evidence, he had little doubt that it was an accidental fire—one caused most likely by the space heater or faulty electrical wiring. It explained why there had never been a motive for the crime. Hurst concluded that there was no evidence of arson, and that a man who had already lost his three children and spent twelve years in jail was about to be executed based on "junk science." Hurst wrote his report in such a rush that he didn't pause to fix the typos.

V

"I am a realist and I will not live a fantasy," Willingham once told Gilbert about the prospect of proving his innocence. But in February 2004, he began to have hope. Hurst's findings had helped to exonerate more than ten people. Hurst even reviewed the scientific evidence against Willingham's friend Ernest Willis, who had been on death row for the strikingly similar arson charge. Hurst says, "It was like I was looking at the same case. Just change the names." In his report on the Willis case, Hurst concluded that not "a single item of physical evidence . . . supports a finding of arson." A second fire expert hired by Ori White, the new district attorney in Willis's district, concurred. After seventeen years on death row, Willis was set free. "I don't turn killers loose," White said at the time. "If Willis was guilty, I'd be retrying him right now. And I'd use Hurst as my witness. He's a brilliant scientist." White noted how close the system had come to murdering an innocent man. "He did not get executed, and I thank God for that," he said.

On February 13, four days before Willingham was scheduled to be executed, he got a call from Reaves, his attorney. Reaves told him that the fifteen members of the Board of Pardons and Paroles, which reviews an application for clemency and had been sent Hurst's report, had made their decision.

"What is it?" Willingham asked.

"I'm sorry," Reaves said. "They denied your petition."

The vote was unanimous. Reaves could not offer an explanation: the board deliberates in secret, and its members are not bound by any specific criteria. The board members did not even have to review Willingham's materials, and usually don't debate a case in person; rather, they cast their votes by fax—a process that has become known as "death by fax." Between 1976 and 2004, when Willingham filed his petition, the State of Texas had approved only one application for clemency from a prisoner on death row. A Texas appellate judge has called the clemency system "a legal fiction." Reaves said of the board members, "They never asked me to attend a hearing or answer any questions."

The Innocence Project obtained, through the Freedom of Information Act, all the records from the governor's office and the board pertaining to Hurst's report. "The documents show that they received the report, but neither office has any record of anyone acknowledging it, taking note of its significance, responding to it, or calling any attention to it within the government," Barry Scheck said. "The only reasonable conclusion is that the governor's office and the Board of Pardons and Paroles ignored scientific evidence."

LaFayette Collins, who was a member of the board at the time, told me of the process, "You don't vote guilt or innocence. You don't retry the trial. You just make sure everything is in order and there are no glaring errors." He noted that although the rules allowed for a hearing to consider important new evidence, "in my time there had never been one called." When I asked him why Hurst's report didn't constitute evidence of "glaring errors," he said, "We get all kinds of reports, but we don't have the mechanisms to vet them." Alvin Shaw, another board member at the time, said that the case didn't "ring a bell," adding, angrily, "Why would I want to talk about it?" Hurst calls the board's actions "unconscionable."

Though Reaves told Willingham that there was still a chance that Governor Perry might grant a thirty-day stay, Willingham began to prepare his last will and testament. He had earlier written Stacy a letter apologizing for not being a better husband and thanking her for everything she had given him, especially their three daughters. "I still know Amber's voice, her smile, her cool Dude saying and how she said: I wanna hold you! Still feel the touch of Karmon and Kameron's hands on my face." He said that he hoped that "some day, somehow the truth will be known and my name cleared."

He asked Stacy if his tombstone could be erected next to their children's graves. Stacy, who had for so long expressed belief in Willingham's innocence, had recently taken her first look at the original court records and arson findings. Unaware of Hurst's report, she had determined that Willingham was guilty. She denied him his wish, later telling a reporter, "He took my kids away from me."

Gilbert felt as if she had failed Willingham. Even before his pleas for clemency were denied, she told him that all she could give him was her friendship. He told her that it was enough "to be a part of your life in some small way so that in my passing I can know I was at last able to have felt the heart of another who might remember me when I'm gone." He added, "There is nothing to forgive you for." He told her that he would need her to be present at his execution, to help him cope with "my fears, thoughts, and feelings."

On February 17, the day he was set to die, Willingham's parents and several relatives gathered in the prison visiting room. Plexiglas still separated Willingham from them. "I wish I could touch and hold both of you," Willingham had written to them earlier. "I always hugged Mom but I never hugged Pop much."

As Willingham looked at the group, he kept asking where Gilbert was. Gilbert had recently been driving home from a store when another car ran a red light and smashed into her. Willingham used to tell her to stay in her kitchen for a day, without leaving, to comprehend what it was like to be confined in prison, but she had always found an excuse not to do it. Now she was paralyzed from the neck down.

While she was in an intensive-care unit, she had tried to get a message to Willingham, but apparently failed. Gilbert's daughter later read her a letter that Willingham had sent her, telling her how much he had grown to love her. He had written a poem: "Do you want to see beauty—like you have never seen? / Then close your eyes, and open your mind, and come along with me."

Gilbert, who spent years in physical rehabilitation, gradually regaining motion in her arms and upper body, says, "All that time, I thought I was saving Willingham, and I realized then that he was saving me, giving me the strength to get through this. I know I will one day walk again, and I know it is because Willingham showed me the kind of courage it takes to survive."

Willingham had requested a final meal, and at 4 P.M. on the seventeenth he was served it: three barbecued pork ribs, two orders of onion rings, fried okra, three beef enchiladas with cheese, and two slices of lemon cream pie. He received word that Governor Perry had refused to grant him a stay. (A spokesperson for Perry says, "The governor made his decision based on the facts of the case.") Willingham's mother and father began to cry. "Don't be sad, Momma," Willingham said. "In fifty-five minutes, I'm a free man. I'm going home to see my kids." Earlier, he had confessed to his parents that there was one thing about the day of the fire he had lied about. He said that he had never actually crawled into the children's room. "I just didn't want people to think I was a coward," he said. Hurst told me, "People who have never been in a fire don't understand why those who survive often can't rescue the victims. They have no concept of what a fire is like."

The warden told Willingham that it was time. Willingham, refusing to assist the process, lay down; he was carried into a chamber eight feet wide and ten feet long. The walls were painted green, and in the center of the room, where an electric chair used to be, was a sheeted gurney. Several guards strapped Willingham down with leather belts, snapping buckles across his arms and legs and chest. A medical team then inserted intravenous tubes into his arms. Each official had a separate role in the process, so that no one person felt responsible for taking a life.

Willingham had asked that his parents and family not be present in the gallery during this process, but as he looked out he could see Stacy watching. The warden pushed a remote control, and sodium thiopental, a barbiturate, was pumped into Willingham's body. Then came a second drug, pancuronium bromide, which paralyzes the diaphragm, making it impossible to breathe. Finally, a third drug, potassium chloride, filled his veins, until his heart stopped, at 6:20 P.M. On his death certificate, the cause was listed as "Homicide."

After his death, his parents were allowed to touch his face for the first time in more than a decade. Later, at Willingham's request, they cremated his body and secretly spread some of his ashes over his children's graves. He had told his parents, "Please don't ever stop fighting to vindicate me."

In December 2004, questions about the scientific evidence in the Willingham case began to surface. Maurice Possley and Steve Mills, of the *Chicago Tribune*, had published an investigative series on flaws in forensic science; upon learning of Hurst's report, Possley and Mills asked three fire experts, including John Lentini, to examine the original investigation. The experts concurred with Hurst's report. Nearly two years later, the Innocence Project commissioned Lentini and three other top fire investigators to conduct an independent review of the arson evidence in the Willingham case. The panel concluded that "each and every one" of the indicators of arson had been "scientifically proven to be invalid."

In 2005, Texas established a government commission to investigate allegations of error and misconduct by forensic scientists. The first cases that are being reviewed by the commission are those of Willingham and Willis. In mid-August, the noted fire scientist Craig Beyler, who was hired by the commission, completed his investigation. In a scathing report, he concluded that investigators in the Willingham case had no scientific basis for claiming that the fire was arson, ignored evidence that contradicted their theory, had no comprehension of flashover and fire dynamics, relied on discredited folklore, and failed to eliminate potential accidental or alternative causes of the fire. He said that Vasquez's approach seemed to deny "rational reasoning" and was more "characteristic of mystics or psychics." What's more, Beyler determined that the investigation violated, as he put it to me, "not only the standards of today but even of the time period." The commission is reviewing his findings, and plans to release its own report next year. Some legal scholars believe that the commission may narrowly assess the reliability of the scientific evidence. There is a chance, however, that Texas could become the first state to acknowledge officially that, since the advent of the modern judicial system, it had carried out the "execution of a legally and factually innocent person."

Just before Willingham received the lethal injection, he was asked if he had any last words. He said, "The only statement I want to make is that I am an innocent man convicted of a crime I did not commit. I have been persecuted for twelve years for something I did not do. From God's dust I came and to dust I will return, so the Earth shall become my throne."

McSweeney's Quarterly

WINNER—FICTION

Dave Eggers's magazine McSweeney's Quarterly *first won the National Magazine Award for Fiction in 2007. This year the magazine won the award again, for three short stories that each in its own way is out of this world: "Memory Wall," by Anthony Doerr (published October 1); "Further Interpretations of Real-Life Events," by Kevin Moffett (March 3); and the piece reprinted here, "Raw Water," by Wells Tower (October 1).*

Wells Tower

Raw Water

"Just let me out of here, man," said Cora Booth. "I'm sick. I'm dying."

"Of what?" asked Rodney, her husband, blinking at the wheel, scoliotic with exhaustion. He'd been sitting there for four days, steering the pickup down out of Boston, a trailer shimmying on the ball hitch, a mattress held to the roof of the camper shell with tie-downs that razzed like an attack of giant farting bees.

"Ford poisoning," Cora said. "Truckanosis, stage four. I want out. I'll walk from here."

Rodney told his wife that a hundred and twenty miles lay between them and the home they'd rented in the desert, sight unseen.

"Perfect," she said. "I'll see you in four days. You'll appreciate the benefits. I'll have a tan and my ass will be a huge wad of muscle. You can climb up on it and ride like a little monkey."

"I'm so tired. I'm sad and confused," said Rodney. "I'm in a thing where I see the road, I just don't comprehend it. I don't understand what it means."

Cora rolled down the window to photograph a balustrade of planted organ cactuses strobing past in rows.

"Need a favor, chum?" she said, toying with his zipper.

"What I need is to focus here," Rodney said. "The white lines keep swapping around."

"How about let's scoot up one of those little fire trails," Cora said. "You won't get dirty, I promise. We'll put the tailgate down and do some stunts on it."

The suggestion compounded Rodney's fatigue. It had been a half decade since he and Cora had made any kind of habitual love, and Rodney was fine with that. Even during his teenage hormone boom, he'd been a fairly unvenereal person. As he saw it, their marriage hit its best years once the erotic gunpowder burned off and it cooled to a more tough and precious alloy of long friendship and love from the deep heart. But Cora, who was forty-three, had lately emerged from menopause with large itches in her. Now she was hassling him for a session more days than not. After so many tranquil, sexless years, Rodney felt there was something unseemly, a mild whang of incest, in mounting his best friend. Plus she had turned rough and impersonal in her throes, like a cat on its post. She didn't look at him while they were striving. She went off somewhere by herself. Her eyes were always closed, her body arched, her jaw thrusting up from the curtains of her graying hair, mouth parted. Watching her, Rodney didn't feel at all like a proper husband in a love rite with his wife, more a bootleg hospice man bungling a euthanasia that did not spare much pain.

"Later. Got to dog traffic. I want to get the big stuff moved in while there's still light," said Rodney to Cora, though night was obviously far away, and they were making good time into the hills.

.   .   .

The truck crested the ridge into warm light and the big view occurred. "Brakes, right now," said Cora.

The westward face of the mountain sloped down to the vast brownness of the Anasazi Trough, a crater of rusty land in whose center lay sixty square miles of the world's newest inland ocean, the Anasazi Sea.

Rodney swung the truck onto the shoulder. Cora sprang to the trailer and fetched her big camera, eight by ten, an antique device whose leather bellows she massaged after each use with Neatsfoot Oil. She set up the tripod on the roadside promontory. Sounds of muffled cooing pleasure issued from her photographer's shroud.

Truly, it was a view to make a visual person moan. The sea's geometry was striking—a perfect rectangle, two miles wide and thirty miles long. But its water was a stupefying sight: livid red, a giant, tranquil plain the color of cranberry pulp.

The Anasazi was America's first foray into the new global fashion for do-it-yourself oceans—huge ponds of seawater, piped or channeled into desert depressions as an antidote to sea-level rise. The Libyans pioneered the practice with the great systematic flood of the Qattara Depression in the Cairo desert. The water made one species of fox extinct and thousands of humans rich. Evaporation from the artificial sea rained down on new olive plantations. Villages emerged. Fisherfolk raised families hauling tilefish and mackerel out of a former bowl of hot dirt. American investors were inspired. They organized the condemnation of the Anasazi Trough a hundred miles northwest of Phoenix and ran a huge pipe to the Gulf of Mexico. Six million gallons of seawater flowed in every day, to be boiled and filtered at the grandest desalination facility in the western hemisphere.

A land fever caught hold. The minor city of Port Miracle burgeoned somewhat on the sea's western shore. On the east coast sat Triton Estates, a gated sanctuary for golfers and owners of small planes. But before the yacht club had sold its last mooring, the young sea began to misbehave. The evaporation clouds were supposed to float eastward to the highlands and wring fresh rain from themselves. Instead, the clouds caught a thermal south, dumping their bounty on the far side of the Mexican border, nourishing a corn and strawberry bonanza in the dry land outside Juárez. With no cloud cover over the Anasazi, the sun went to work and started cooking the sea into a concentrated brine. Meanwhile, even as acreage spiraled toward Tahoe prices, the grid spread: toilets, lawns, and putting greens quietly embezzling the budget of desalinated water that should have been pumped back into the sea to keep salt levels at a healthy poise. By the sea's tenth birthday, it was fifteen times as saline as the Pacific, dense enough to float small stones. The desalination plant's reverse-osmosis filters, designed to last five years, started blowing out after six months on the job. The land boom on the Anasazi fell apart when water got so expensive that it was cheaper to flush the commode with half-and-half.

The grocery-store papers spread it around that the great pond wouldn't just take your money; it would kill you dead. Local news shows ran testimonies of citizens who said they'd seen the lake eat cows and elks and illegal Mexicans, shrieking as they boiled away. Science said the lake was not a man-eater, but the proof was in that gory water, so the stories stayed on prime time for a good number of years.

The real story of the redness was very dull. It was just a lot of ancient, red, one-celled creatures that thrived in high salt. The water authority tested and retested the water and declared the microbes no enemy to man. They were, however, hard on curb appeal. When the sea was only twelve years old, the coastal population had dwindled to ninety-three, a net loss of five thousand souls no longer keen on dwelling in a case of pinkeye inflamed to geologic scale.

The story delighted Cora Booth as meat for her art. She'd long been at work on a group of paintings and photographs about science's unintended consequences: victims of robot nanoworms designed to eat cancer cells but which got hungry for other parts, lab mice in DNA-grafting experiments who'd developed a crude sign language using the hands of human infants growing from their backs. Once the tenants had fled and the situation on the sea had tilted into flagrant disaster, Cora banged out some grant proposals, withdrew some savings, and leased a home in Triton Estates, a place forsaken by God and movie stars.

·   ·   ·

Salvage vandals had long ago stolen the gates off the entrance to the Booths' new neighborhood, but a pair of sandstone obelisks topped with unlit gas lamps still stood there, and they still spelled class. Their new home stood on a coastal boulevard named Naiad Lane, a thin track of blond scree. They drove slow past a couple dozen homes, most of them squatly sprawling bunkerish jobs of off-white stucco, all of them abandoned, windows broken or filmed with dust; others half-built, showing lath, gray bones of sun-beaten framing, pennants of torn Tyvek corrugating in the wind. Rodney pulled the truck into the driveway at number thirty-three, a six-bedroom cube with a fancy Spanish pediment on the front. It looked like a crate with a tiara. But just over the road lay the sea. Unruffled by the wind, its water lay still and thick as house paint, and it cast an inviting pink glow on the Booths' new home.

"I like it," said Cora, stepping from the truck. "Our personal Alamo."

"What's that smell?" said Rodney when they had stepped inside. The house was light and airy, but the air bore a light scent of wharf breath.

"It's the bricks," said Cora. "They made them from the thluk they take out of the water at the desal plant. Very clever stuff."

"It smells like, you know, groins."

"Learn to love it," Cora said.

When they had finished the tour, the sun was dying. On the far coast, the meager lights of Port Miracle were winking on. They'd only just started unloading the trailer when Cora's telephone bleated in her pocket. On the other end was Arn Nevis, the sole property agent in Triton Estates and occupant of one of the four still-inhabited homes in the neighborhood. Cora opened the phone. "Hi, terrific, okay, sure, hello?" she said, then looked at the receiver.

"Who was that?" asked Rodney, sitting on the front stair.

"Nevis, Arn Nevis, the rental turkey," said Cora. "He just sort of barfed up a dinner invitation—*Muhhouse, seven-thirty*—and hung up on me. Said it's close, we don't need to take our truck. Now, how does he know we have a truck? You see somebody seeing us out here, Rod?"

They peered around and saw nothing. Close to land, a fish or something buckled in the red water, other than themselves the afternoon's sole sign of life.

·   ·   ·

But they drove the Ranger after all, because Rodney had bad ankles. He'd shattered them both in childhood, jumping from a crabapple tree, and even a quarter mile's stroll would cause him nauseas of pain. So the Booths rode slowly in the truck through a Pompeii of vanished home equity. The ride took fifteen minutes because Cora kept experiencing ecstasies at the photogenic ruin of Triton Estates, getting six angles on a warped basketball rim over a yawning garage, a hot tub brimming and splitting with gallons of dust.

Past the grid of small lots they rolled down a brief grade to number three Naiad. The Nevis estate lay behind high white walls, light spilling upward in a column, a bright little citadel unto itself.

Rodney parked the truck alongside an aged yellow Mercedes. At a locked steel gate, the only breach in the tall wall, he rang the doorbell and they loitered many minutes while the day's heat fled the air. Finally a wide white girl appeared at the gate. She paused a moment before opening it, appraising them through the bars, studying the dusk beyond, as though expecting unseen persons to spring out of the gloom. Then she turned a latch and swung the door wide. She was sixteen or so, with a face like a left-handed sketch—small teeth, one eye bigger than the other and a half-inch lower on her cheek. Her outfit was a yellow towel, dark across the chest and waist where a damp bathing suit had soaked through. She said her name was Katherine.

"Sorry I'm all sopped," she said. "They made me quit swimming and be butler. Anyway, they're out back. You were late so they started stuffing themselves." Katherine set off for the house, her hard summer heels rasping on the slate path.

• • •

The Nevis house was a three-wing structure, a staple shape in bird's-eye view. In the interstice between the staple's legs lay a small rectangular inlet of the sea, paved and studded with underwater lights; it was serving as the family's personal pool. At the lip of the swimming area, a trio sat at a patio set having a meal of mussels. At one end of the table slouched Arn Nevis, an old, vast man with a head of white curls, grown long to mask their sparseness, and a great bay window of stomach overhanging his belt. Despite his age and obesity, he wasn't unattractive; his features bedded in a handsome arrangement of knobs and ridges, nearly cartoonish in their prominence. Arn was in the middle of a contretemps with a thin young man beside him. The old man had his forearms braced on the tabletop, his shoulders hiked forward, as though ready to pounce on his smaller companion. On the far side of the table sat a middle-aged woman, her blouse hoisted discreetly to let an infant at her breast. She stroked and murmured to it, seemingly unaware of the stridency between the men.

"I didn't come here to get hot-boxed, Arn," the smaller man was saying, staring at his plate.

"Hut—hoorsh," stuttered Nevis.

"Excuse me?" the other man said.

Nevis took a long pull on his drink, swallowed, took a breath. "I said, I'm not hot-boxing anybody," said Nevis, enunciating carefully. "It's just you suffer from a disease, Kurt. That disease is caution, bad as cancer."

The woman raised her gaze and, seeing the Booths, smiled widely. She introduced herself as Phyllis Nevis. She was a pretty woman, though her slack jowls and creased dewlap put her close to sixty. If she noticed her visitors' amazement at seeing a woman of her age putting an infant to suck, she didn't show it. She smiled and let a blithe music of welcome flow from her mouth: Boy, the Nevises sure were glad to have some new neighbors here in Triton. They'd met Katherine, of course, and there was Arn. The baby having at her was little Nathan, and the other fellow was Kurt Hackberry, a business friend but a real friend, too. Would they like a vodka lemonade? She invited the Booths to knock themselves out on some mussels, tonged from the shallows just off the dock, though Cora noticed there was about a half a portion left. "So sorry we've already tucked in," Phyllis said. "But we always eat at seven-thirty, rain or shine."

Katherine Nevis did not sit with the diners but went to the sea's paved edge. She dropped her towel and slipped into the glowing water without a splash.

"So you drove down from Boston?" Hackberry asked, plainly keen to quit the conversation with his host.

"We did," said Rodney. "Five days, actually not so bad once you get past—"

"Yeah, yeah, Boston—" Nevis interrupted with regal vehemence. "And now they're here, sight unseen, whole thing over the phone, not all this fiddlefucking around." Nevis coughed into his fist, then reached for a plastic jug of vodka and filled his glass nearly to the rim, a good half-pint of liquor. He drank a third of it at one pull, then turned to Cora, his head bobbing woozily on his dark neck. "Kurt is a Chicken Little. Listens to ninnies who think the Bureau of Land Management is going to choke us off and starve the pond."

"Why don't they?" Cora asked.

"Because we've got their nursh—their nuh—their nads in a noose is why," said Nevis. "Because every inch of shoreline they expose means alkali dust blowing down on the goddamned bocce pitches and Little League fields and citrus groves down in the Yuma Valley. They're all looking up the wrong end of a shotgun, and us right here? We're perched atop a seat favored by the famous bird, if you follow me."

Nevis drained his glass and filled it again. He looked at Cora and sucked his teeth. "Hot damn, you're a pretty woman, Cora. Son of a bitch, it's like somebody opened a window out here. If I'd known you were so goddamned lovely, I'd have jewed them down on the rent. But then, if I'd known you were hitched up with this joker I'd have charged you double, probably." He jerked a thumb and aimed a grin of long gray teeth at Rodney. Rodney looked away and pulled at a skin tab on the rim of his ear. "Don't you think, Phyllis?" said Nevis. "Great bones."

"Thank you," Cora said. "I plan to have them bronzed."

"Humor," Nevis said flatly, gazing at Cora with sinking red eyes. "It's that actress you resemble. Murf. Murvek. Urta. Fuck am I talking about? You know, Phyllis, from the goddamn dog-sled picture."

"Drink a few more of those," said Cora. "I'll find you a cockroach who looks like Brigitte Bardot."

"Actually, I hate alcohol, but I get these migraines. They mess with my speech, but liquor helps some," Nevis said. Here, he sat forward in his chair, peering unabashedly at Cora's chest. "Good Christ, you got a figure, lady. All natural, am I right?"

Rodney took a breath to say a hard word to Nevis, but while he was trying to formulate the proper phrase Phyllis spoke to her husband in a gentle voice.

"Arny, I'm not sure Cora appreciates—"

"An appreciation of beauty, even if it is sexual beauty, is a great gift," said Nevis. "Anyone who thinks beauty is not sexual should picture tits on a man."

"I'm sure you're right, sweetie, but even so—"

Nevis flashed a brilliant crescent of teeth at his wife and bent to the table to kiss her hand. "Right here, the most wonderful woman on earth. The kindest and most beautiful and I married her." Nevis raised his glass to his lips. His gullet pumped three times while he drank.

"His headaches are horrible," said Phyllis.

"They are. Pills don't work but vodka does. Fortunately, it doesn't affect me. I've never been drunk in my life. Anyway, you two are lucky you showed up at this particular juncture," Nevis announced through a belch. "Got a petition for a water-rights deal on Birch Creek. Hundred thousand gallons a day. Fresh water. Pond'll be blue again this time next year."

This news alarmed Cora, whose immediate thought was that her work would lose its significance if the story of the Anasazi Sea ended happily. "I like the color," Cora said. "It's exciting."

Nevis refilled his glass. "You're an intelligent woman, Cora, and you don't believe the rumors and the paranoia peddlers on the goddamned news," he said. "Me, I'd hate to lose it, except you can't sell a fucking house with the lake how it is. Of course, nobody talks about the health benefits of that water. My daughter?" He jerked his thumb at Katherine, still splashing in the pool, and lowered his voice. "Before we moved in here, you wouldn't have believed her complexion. Like a lasagna, I'm serious. Look at her now! Kill for that skin. Looks like a marble statue. Hasn't had a zit in years, me or my wife neither, not one blackhead, nothing. Great for the bones, too. I've got old-timers who swim here three times a week, swear it's curing their arthritis. Of course, nobody puts that on the news. Anyway, what I'm saying is, buy now, because once this Birch Creek thing goes through, this place is going to be a destination. Gonna put the back nine on the golf course. Shopping district, too, as soon as Kurt and a few other moneymen stop sitting on their wallets like a bunch of broody hens."

Nevis clouted Hackberry on the upper arm with more force than was jolly. Hackberry looked lightly terrified and went into a fit of vague motions with his head, shaking and nodding, saying "Now, Kurt, now, Kurt" with the look of a panicked child wishing for the ground to open up beneath him.

•   •   •

When he had lapped the fluid from the final mussel shell, Arn Nevis was showing signs of being drunk, if he was to be taken at his word, for the first time in his life. He rose from the table and stood swaying. "Clothes off, people," he said, fumbling with his belt.

Phyllis smiled and kept her eyes on her guests. "We have tea, and we have coffee and homemade peanut brittle, too."

"Phyllis, shut your mouth," said Nevis. "Swim time. Cora, get up. Have a dip."

"I don't swim," said Cora.

"You can't?" said Nevis.

"No," said Cora, which was true.

"Dead man could swim in the water. Nathan can. Give me the baby, Phyllis." He lurched for his wife's breast, and with a sudden move, Phyllis clutched the baby to her and swiveled brusquely away from her husband's hand. "Touch him and I'll kill you," Phyllis hissed. Nathan awoke and began to mewl. Nevis shrugged and lumbered toward the water, shedding his shirt, then his pants, mercifully retaining the pair of yellowed briefs he wore. He dove messily but began swimming surprisingly brisk and powerful laps, his whalelike huffing loud and crisp in the silence of the night. But after three full circuits to the far end of the inlet and back, the din of his breathing stopped. Katherine Nevis, who'd been sulking under the pergola with a video game, began to shriek. The guests leaped up. Arn Nevis had sunk seven feet or so below the surface, suspended from a deeper fall by the hypersaline water. In the red depths' wavering lambency, Nevis seemed to be moving, though in fact he was perfectly still.

Rodney kicked off his shoes and jumped in. With much effort, he hauled the large man to the concrete steps ascending to the patio and, helped by Cora and Hackberry, heaved him into the cool air. Water poured from Rodney's pockets. He put his palms to the broad saucer of Nevis's sternum and rammed hard. The drowned man sputtered.

"Wake up. Wake *up*," said Rodney. Nevis did not answer. Rodney slapped Nevis on the cheek, and Nevis opened his eyes to a grouchy squint.

"What day is it?" asked Rodney. By way of an answer, Nevis expelled lung water down his chin.

"Who's that?" Rodney pointed to Phyllis. "Tell me her name."

Nevis regarded his wife. "Big dummy," he said.

"What the hell does that mean?" Rodney said. "Who's that?" He pointed at Nevis's infant son.

Nevis pondered the question. "Little dummy," he said, and began to laugh, which everybody took to mean that he had returned, unharmed, to life.

Kurt Hackberry and Katherine led Arn inside while Phyllis poured forth weeping apologies and panting gratitude to the Booths. "No harm done. Thank God he's all right. I'm glad I was here to lend a hand," Rodney said, and was surprised to realize that he meant it. Despite the evening's calamities, his heart was warm and filled with an electric vigor of life. The electricity stayed with him all the way back to number thirty-three Naiad Lane, where, in the echoing kitchen, Rodney made zestful love to his wife for the first time in seven weeks.

.   .   .

Rodney woke before the sun was up. The maritime fetor of the house's salt walls and recollections of Arn Nevis's near death merged into a general unease that would not let him sleep. Cora stirred beside him. She peered out the window, yawned, and said that she wanted to photograph the breaking of the day. "I'll come with you," Rodney said, and felt childish to realize that he didn't want to be left in the house alone.

Cora was after large landscapes of the dawn hitting Triton Estates and the western valley, so the proper place to set up was on the east coast, in Port Miracle, with the sun behind the lens. After breakfast they loaded the Ford with Cora's equipment and made the ten-minute drive. They parked at the remnant of Port Miracle's public beach and removed their shoes. Most of the trucked-in sand had blown away, revealing a hard marsh of up-thrust minerals, crystalline and translucent, like stepping on warm ice. Rodney lay on the blanket they had brought while Cora took some exposures of the dawn effects. The morning sky involved bands of iridescence, the lavender-into-blue-gray spectrum of a bull pigeon's throat. Cora made plates of the light's progress, falling in a thickening portion on the dark house-key profile of the western hills, then staining the white homes scattered along the shore. She yelled a little at the moment of dawn's sudden ignition when red hit red and the sea lit up, flooding the whole valley with so much immediate light you could almost hear the *whong!* of a ball field's vapor bulbs going on.

"Rodney, how about you go swimming for me?"

"I don't have a suit."

"Who cares? It's a ghost town."

"I don't want to get all sticky."

"Shit, Rodney, come on. Help me out."

Rodney stripped grudgingly and walked into the water. Even in the new hours of the day, the water was hot and alarmingly solid, like paddling through Crisco. It seared his pores and mucous parts, but his body had a thrilling buoyancy in the thick water. A single kick of the legs sent him gliding like a hockey puck. And despite its lukewarmth and viscosity, the water was wonderfully vivifying. His pulse surged. Rodney stroked and kicked until he heard his wife yelling for him to swim back into camera range. He turned around, gamboled for her camera some, and stepped into the morning, stripped clean by the water, with a feeling of having been peeled to new young flesh. Rodney did not bother to dress. He carried the blanket to the shade of a disused picnic awning. Cora lay there with him, and then they drowsed until the sun was well up in the sky.

Once the drab glare of the day set in, the Booths breakfasted together on granola bars and instant coffee from the plastic crate of food they'd packed for the ride from Massachusetts.

Cora wished to tour Port Miracle on foot. Rodney, with his bad ankles, said he would be happy to spend the morning in his sandy spot, taking in the late-summer sun with a Jack London paperback. So Cora went off with her camera, first to the RV lot, nearly full, the rows of large white vehicles like raw loaves of bread. She walked through a rear neighborhood of kit cottages, built of glass and grooved plywood and tin. She photographed shirtless children, Indian brown, kicking a ball in a dirt lot, and a leathery soul on a sunblasted Adirondack chair putting hot sauce into his beer. She went to the boat launch where five pink women, all of manatee girth, were boarding a pontoon craft. Cora asked to take their picture but they giggled and shied behind their hands and Cora moved on.

At the far end of town stood the desalination facility, a cube of steel and concrete intubated with ducts and billowing steam jacks. Cora humped it for the plant, her tripod clacking on her shoulder. After calling into the intercom at the plant's steel door, Cora was greeted by a gray-haired, bearded man wearing something like a cellophane version of a fisherman's hard-weather kit. Plastic pants, shirt, hat, plus gloves and boot gaiters and a thick dust mask hanging around his neck. His beard looked like a cloudburst, though he'd carefully imprisoned it in a hairnet so as to tuck it coherently within his waterproof coat.

"Whoa," said Cora, taken aback. Recovering herself, she explained that she was new to the neighborhood and was hoping to find a manager or somebody who might give her a tour of the plant.

"I'm it!" the sheathed fellow told her, a tuneful courtliness in his voice. "Willard Kamp. And it would be my great pleasure to show you around."

Cora lingered on the threshold, taking in Kamp's protective gear. "Is it safe, though, if I'm just dressed like this?"

"That's what the experts would tell you," said Kamp, and laughed, leading Cora to a bank of screens showing the brine's progress through a filter-maze. Then he ushered her up a flight of stairs to a platform overlooking the concrete lagoons where the seawater poured in. He showed her the flocculating chambers where they added ferric chloride and sulfuric acid and chlorine and the traveling rakes that brought the big solids to the surface in a rumpled brown sludge. He showed her how the water traveled through sand filters, and then through diatomaceous earth capsules to further strain contaminants, before they hit the big reverse-osmosis trains that filtered the last of the impurities.

"Coming into here," Kamp said, slapping the side of a massive fiberglass storage tank, "is raw water. Nothing in here but pure H's and O's."

"Just the good stuff, huh?" Cora said.

"Well, not for our purposes," Kamp said. "It's no good for us in its pure form. We have to have to gentle it down with additives, acid salts, gypsum. Raw, it's very chemically aggressive. It's so hungry for minerals to bind with, it'll eat a copper pipe in a couple of weeks."

This idea appealed to Cora. "What happens if you drink it? Will it kill you? Burn your skin?"

Kamp laughed, a wheezing drone. "Not at all. It's an enemy to metal pipes and soap lather, but it's amiable to humankind."

"So what's with all the hazmat gear?" asked Cora, gesturing at Kamp's clothes.

Kamp laughed again. "I'm overfastidious, the preoccupation of a nervous mind."

"Nervous about what?"

His wiry brow furrowed and his lips pursed in half-comic consternation. "Well, it's a funny lake, isn't it, Cora? I am very interested in the archaebacteria, the little red gentlemen out there."

"But it's the same stuff in fall foliage and flamingos," Cora said, brandishing some knowledge she'd picked up from a magazine. "Harmless."

Kamp reached into his raincoat to scratch at something in his beard. "Probably so. Though they're also very old. Two billion years. They were swimming around before there was oxygen in the atmosphere, if you can picture that. You've heard, I guess, the notion that that stuff in our pond is pretty distinguished crud, possibly the source of all life on earth."

"I hadn't."

"Well, they say there's something to it," said Kamp. "Now, it's quite likely that I haven't got the sense God gave a monkey wrench, but it seems to me that a tadpole devious enough to put a couple of million species on the planet is one I'd rather keep on the outside of my person."

·　　·　　·

Of Port Miracle's eighty dwellers, nearly all were maroon ancients. They were unwealthy people, mainly, not far from death, so they found the dead city a congenial place to live the life of a lizard, moving slow and taking sun. But they were not community-center folk. Often there was public screaming on the boulevard, sometimes fights with brittle fists when someone got too close to someone else's wife or yard. Just the year before, in a further blow to the Anasazi's image in the press, a retired playwright, age eighty-one, levered open the door of a Winnebago parked on his lot and tortured a pair of tourists with some rough nylon rope and a soup-heating coil.

According to the rules of the Nevis household, young Katherine was not permitted past the sandstone obelisks at the neighborhood's mouth. But the morning after the dinner party her father was still abed with a pulsing brain, and would likely be that way all day. Knowing this, Katherine slipped through the gate after breakfast, wheeled her little 97cc minibike out of earshot, and set a course to meet two pals of hers, Claude Hull and Denny Peebles, on the forbidden coast.

She found them by the public pier, and they greeted her with less commotion than she'd have liked. They were busy squabbling over some binoculars through which they were leering at the fat women out at sea on the pontoon barge.

"Let me look," Claude begged Denny, who had snatched the Bausch & Lombs, an unfair thing. The Bausch & Lombs belonged to Claude's father, who owned Port Miracle's little credit union and liked to look at birds.

Denny sucked his lips and watched the women, herded beneath the boat's canopy shade, their bikinis almost wholly swallowed by their hides. They took turns getting in the water via a scuba ladder that caused the boat to lurch comically when one of them put her bulk on it. The swimming lady would contort her face in agonies at the stinging water while her colleagues leaned over the gunwale, shouting encouragement, bellies asway. After a minute or two, the others would help the woman aboard and serve her something in a tall chilled glass and scrub at her with implements not legible through the Bausch & Lombs. The women were acting on a rumor that the sea's bacteria devoured extra flesh. It had the look of a cult.

"Big white witches," whispered Denny.

"Come on, let me hold 'em, let me look," said Claude, a lean, tweaky child whose widespread eyes and bulging forehead made it a mercy that he, like the other children who lived out here, attended ninth grade over the computer. Denny, the grocer's child, had shaggy black hair, a dark tan, and very long, very solid arms for a boy of fourteen. "Fuck off," said Denny, throwing an elbow. "Get Katherine to show you hers. You'll like 'em if you like it when a girl's titty looks like a carrot."

"I'm not showing Claude," said Katherine.

In the sand beside Denny lay a can of Scotchgard and a bespattered paper bag. Katherine reached for it.

"Mother may I?" Denny said.

"Bite my fur," said Katherine. She sprayed a quantity of the Scotchgard into the bag, then put it to her mouth and inhaled.

"Let me get some of that, Kathy," Claude said.

"Talk to Denny," said Katherine. "It's not my can."

"Next time I'm gonna hook up my camera to this thing, get these puddings on film," said Denny, who was lying on his stomach in the sand, the binoculars propped to his face. "Somebody scratch my back for me. Itches like a motherfucker."

"Sucks for you," said Katherine, whose skull now felt luminous and red and full of perfect blood.

"You scratch it for me, Claude," said Denny. "Backstroke, hot damn. Look at those pies. Turn this way, honey. Are you pretty in your face?"

Just last week, for no reason at all, Denny Peebles had wedged Claude Hull's large head between his knees and dragged him up and down Dock Street while old men laughed. Claude loved and feared Denny, so he reached out a hand and scratched at Denny's spine.

"Lower," Denny said, and Claude slid his hand down to the spot between Denny's sacral dimples, which were lightly downed with faint hair. "Little lower. Get in the crack, man. That's where the itch is at."

Claude laughed nervously. "You want me to scratch your *ass* for you?"

"It itches, I told you. Go ahead. It's clean."

"No way I'm doing that, man. You scratch it."

"I can't reach it. I'm using my hands right now," said Denny. "I'm trying to see these fatties."

Katherine sprayed another acrid cloud into the bag and sucked it in. Dust clung in an oval around her mouth, giving the effect of a chimpanzee's muzzle.

"Just do it, Claude," Katherine said. "He likes it. He said it's clean. You don't believe him?"

Denny took the glasses from his face to look at the smaller boy. "Yeah, you don't believe me, Claude? What, I'm a liar, Claude?"

"No, no, I do." And so Claude reached into Denny's pants and scratched, and this intimate grooming felt very good to Denny in a hardly sexual way, so to better concentrate on the sensation, he rested the binoculars and held his hand out for the can of Scotchgard and the paper bag.

. . .

After an hour on the beach, Rodney put a flat stone in his paperback, retrieved his pants, and got up to stretch his legs. He had the thought that strolling through the still water might cushion his ankles somewhat, so he waded in and set off up the cove. Forbidding as the water looked, it teemed with life. Carp fingerlings nibbled his shins. Twice, a crab scuttled over his bare toes. He strolled on until he reached the pier, a chocolate-colored structure built of creosoted wood. Rodney spied a clump of shells clinging to the pilings. These were major oysters, the size of cactus pads. He tried to yank one free, but it would not surrender to his hand. It was such a tempting prize that he waded all the way back to the truck and got the tire iron from under the seat. Knee-deep in the water, he worked open a shell. The flesh inside was pale gray and large as a goose egg. That much oyster meat would cost you thirty dollars in a Boston restaurant. The flesh showed no signs of dubious pinkness. He sniffed it—no bad aromas. He spilled it onto his tongue, chewing three times to get it down. The meat was clean and briny. He ate two more and felt renewed. Wading back to shore, a few smaller mollusks in hand, he peered under the wharf and spotted Katherine Nevis on the beach with her friends. The desolation of the town had cast a shadow on the morning, and it cheered Rodney to see those children out there enjoying the day. It would be unneighborly, Rodney thought, not to say hello.

When Rodney got within fifty yards, Denny and Claude looked up, panicked to see a shirtless fellow coming at them with a tire iron, an ugly limp in his gait. They took off in a kind of skulking lope and left Katherine on the beach. Obviously Rodney had caught them in the middle of some teenage mischief, and he chuckled to see the boys scamper. Katherine cupped a hand over the beige matter on her face and looked at her toes as Rodney approached. He wondered about the grime, but instead asked after her dad. "I dunno," she said. "I'm sure he's doing awesome."

Rodney nudged the Scotchgard can with his foot. "Stainproofing the beach?" he asked. Katherine said nothing. "Whatever happened to just raiding your parents' booze?"

"He has to drive all the way to Honerville to get it," she said. "He keeps it locked up, even from my mom."

Rodney put the tire iron in his belt and dropped his oysters. He took out his handkerchief and reached for her, thinking to swab her face. She shrank away from him. "Don't fucking touch me," she said. "Don't, I swear."

"Easy, easy, nobody's doing anything," Rodney said, though he could feel the color in his cheeks. "It's just you look like you need a shave."

Cautiously, a little shamefully, she took the handkerchief and daubed at her lips while he watched. The girl was conscious of being looked at, and she swabbed herself with small ladylike motions, making no headway on the filth.

"Here," said Rodney, very gently, taking the hanky from her damp hand. He sucked awhile at the bitter cloth, then he knelt and cradled the girl's jaw in his palm, rubbing at her mouth and chin. "Look out, you're gonna take off all my skin," she said, making a cranky child's grimace, though she didn't pull away. He heard her grunting lightly in her throat at the pleasure of being tended to. A smell was coming off her, a fragrance as warm and wholesome as rising bread. As he scrubbed the girl's dirty face, he put his nose close to her, breathing deeply and as quietly as he could. He had mostly purged the gum from Katherine's upper lip when she jerked away from him and hearkened anxiously to the sound of a slowing car. Arn Nevis's eggnog Mercedes pulled into the gravel lot. He got out and strode very quickly down the shingle.

"Hi, hi!" Nevis cried. His hair was in disarray, and his hands trembled in a Parkinsonian fashion. In the hard noonday light, he looked antique and unwell. Rodney saw, too, that Nevis had a fresh pink scar running diagonally across his forehead, stitch pocks dotting its length. Rodney marveled a little that just the night before, he'd felt some trepidation in the big man's presence. "Kath—Kuh, Kutch." Nevis stopped, marshaled his breathing, and spoke. "Kuh, come here, sweetie. Been looking for you. Mom's mad. Come now, huk—honey. See if I can't talk your mom out of striping your behind."

In his shame, Arn did not look at Rodney, which at once amused and angered the younger man. "Feeling okay, there, Arn?"

"Oh, shuh-sure," Nevis said, staring at a point on Rodney's abdomen. "Thank God it's Friday."

"It's Thursday," Rodney said.

"Oysters," the old man said, looking at Rodney's haul where he'd dropped it on the ground. "Oh, they're nice."

Rodney crouched and held them out to Nevis in cupped hands. Nevis looked at the oysters and then at Rodney. His was the manner of a craven dog, wanting that food but fearing that he might get a smack if he went for it. "Go on," said Rodney.

With a quick move, Nevis grabbed a handful. His other hand seized Katherine's arm. "Alrighty, and we'll see you soon," said Nevis over his shoulder, striding to his car.

.   .   .

The days found an agreeable tempo in Cora and Rodney's new home. Each morning they rose with the sun. Each morning, Rodney swam far into the sea's broads, then returned to the house, where he would join Cora for a shower, then downstairs to cook and eat a breakfast of tremendous size. When the dishes were cleared, Cora would set off to gather pictures. Rodney would spend two hours on the computer to satisfy the advertising firm in Boston for which he still worked part-time, and then he'd do as he pleased. His was a life any sane person would envy, yet Rodney was not at ease. He felt bloated with a new energy. He had never been an ambitious person, but lately he had begun to feel that he was capable of resounding deeds. He had dreams in which he conquered famous wildernesses, and he would wake up with a lust for travel. Yet he was irritable on days when he had to leave the valley for provisions not sold in Port Miracle's pitiable grocery store. One day he told Cora that he might quit his job and start a company, though he grew angry when Cora forced him to admit that he had no idea what the company might produce. For the first time in his life, he resented Cora, begrudged the years he'd spent at her heel, and how he'd raised no fuss when she'd changed her mind after five years of marriage and said she didn't want children after all. His mind roved to other women, to the Nevis girl, a young thing with a working womb, someone who'd shut up when he talked.

When Cora left him the truck, he often went fishing off the wharf at Port Miracle, always coming home with several meals' worth of seafood iced down in his creel. He would wait until he got home to clean the catch so that Cora could photograph the haul intact.

"Ever seen one of these?" Cora asked him one night. She was sitting at the kitchen table with her laptop, whose screen showed a broad fish ablur with motion on the beach. "This thing was kind of creeping around in the mud down by that shed where the oldsters hang out."

"Huh," Rodney said, kissing Cora's neck and slipping a hand into her shirt. "Snakehead, probably. Or a mudskipper."

"It's not. It's flat, like a flounder," she said. "Quit a second. I wish I could have kept it, but this kid came along and bashed it and took off. Look."

She scrolled to a picture of Claude Hull braining the crawling fish with an aluminum bat.

"Mm," said Rodney, raising his wife's shirt and with the other hand going for her fly.

"Could you quit it?"

"Why?"

"For one thing, I'm trying to deal with my fucking work. For another, I'm kind of worn out. You've gotten me a little raw, going at me all the time."

Sulking, he broke off his advances and picked up his phone from the counter. "Tell you what," he said. "I'll call the neighbors. Get them over here to eat this stuff. We owe them a feed."

He stepped outdoors and called the Nevises, hoping to hear Katherine's hoarse little crow timbre on the other end. No one answered, so Rodney phoned two more times. He had watched the road carefully that morning and knew the family was home.

In fact, Katherine and her mother were out on a motorboat cruise while Arn Nevis paced his den, watching the telephone ring. He did not want to answer it. His trouble with words was worsening. Unless he loosened his tongue with considerable amounts of alcohol, the organ was lazy and intractable. In his mind, he could still formulate a phrase with perfect clarity, but his mouth no longer seemed interested in doing his mind's work and would utter a slurring of approximate sounds. When Nevis finally answered the telephone and heard Rodney's invitation, he paused to silently rehearse the words *I'm sorry, but Phyllis is feeling a bit under the weather.* But Nevis's tongue, the addled translator, wouldn't take the order. "Ilish feen urtha" and then a groan was what Rodney heard before the line went dead.

.   .   .

Until recently, the headaches Arn Nevis suffered had been slow pursuers. A stroll through the neighborhood would clear the bad blood from his temples and he'd have nearly a full day of peace. But lately, if he sat still for five minutes, the glow would commence behind his brow. He would almost drool thinking about a good thick augur to put a hole between his eyes and let the steam out of his head. After five minutes of that, if he didn't have a bottle around to kill it, white pain would bleach the vision from his eyes.

The pain was heating up again when he hung up on Rodney Booth, so he went out through the gate and strolled up to the dry tract slated to become nine new putting greens once the water lease on Birch Creek went through. He set about measuring and spray-painting orange hazard lines in the dirt where a ditcher would cut irrigation channels. Nevis owned most of this land himself, and he was tallying his potential profits when motion in the shadow of a Yerba Santa bush caught his eye. Scorpions, gathered in a ring, a tiny pocket mouse quaking at the center of them. The scenario was distasteful. He raised his boot heel and made to crush the things, but they nimbly skirted the fat shadow of his foot. The circle parted and the mouse shot out of sight.

He glanced at his watch. Four-thirty. In half an hour, he had an appointment to show number eight Amphitrite Trail to a prospective buyer. The flawless sky and the light breeze were hopeful portents. Arn felt confident that on this day, he would make a good sale. To celebrate the prospect, Arn took the quart of peppermint schnapps from his knapsack, but then it occurred to him to save it, to drink it very quickly just before the client's arrival for maximum benefit to his difficult tongue.

Eight Amphitrite was a handsome structure, a three-thousand-square-foot Craftsman bungalow, the only one like it in the neighborhood. The plot was ideally situated, up on high ground at the end of the road with no houses behind it. Sitting there on the front steps, Nevis felt a particular comfort in the place, an enlargement of the safe feeling he experienced in restaurants when he found a spot with his back to the wall and a good view of the door. Nevis checked his watch. Ten of five. He opened the bottle and tipped it back. He stretched his tongue, whispering a silent catechism: "Radiant-heat floors, four-acre lot, build to suit."

Arn had just finished the last of the schnapps when a Swedish station wagon pulled into the drive. A young man got out, tall, with soft features, combed sandy hair, and a cornflower-blue shirt rolled to the elbows. He watched Arn Nevis pick himself up off the stairs and come toward him with his hand out. "Mr. Nevis?" the young man had to ask, for Arn did not much resemble the photograph on his website. His white shirt was badly wrinkled and yellowed with perspiration stains, and his hair looked like a patch of trodden weeds. His left eye was badly bloodshot and freely weeping.

"Urt! Guh," Arn Nevis said, then paused in his tracks, opening and closing his mouth as though priming a dry pump. The client watched him, aghast, as though Nevis was some unhinged derelict impersonating the man he'd come to meet. "Guh—good day!" Nevis said at last, and having expelled that first plug of language, the rest flowed out of him easily. "Mister Mills? It's an absolute delight, and I'm so glad you could pay us a visit on this fabulous day."

"Daniel, please," the young man said, still looking guarded. But the anxiety slowly drained from Mills's features as Nevis rolled into a brisk and competent disquisition on eight Amphitrite's virtues. "That nice overlay on the foundation? That's not plastic, friend. It's hand-mortared fieldstone harvested out of this very land. Clapboards are engineered, and so's the roofing shake, so eat your heart out, termites, and fifteen years to go on the warranty on each."

Nevis was ushering Mills over the threshold when his pitch halted in midstream. Nevis gaped at the empty living room, his mouth open, his eyes stretched with wonder. "My gosh," he said.

"What?" asked Daniel Mills.

"My gosh, Ted, this is that same house, isn't it?" Nevis said, laughing. "From Columbus. When you and Rina were still married."

Mills looked at Arn a moment. "It's Daniel. I—I don't know any Rina."

Nevis's eyes moved in their sockets. He began to laugh. "Jesus Christ, what the hell am I saying?" he said. "My apologies. I've had this fever."

"Sure," said Mills, taking a step back.

"So over yonder is a galley kitchen," said Nevis, leading the way. "Poured concrete counters, and a built-in—"

"Excuse me, you've got something here," murmured Mills, indicating Nevis's upper lip. Nevis raised a finger to his face and felt the warm rush of blood pouring from his nose, dripping from his chin, landing in nickel-size droplets on the parquet floor.

· · ·

By his sixth week in Triton Estates, an exuberant insomnia assailed Rodney Booth. While his wife snored beside him, Rodney lay awake. His body quivered with unspent energy. His blood felt hot and incandescent. With each stroke of his potent heart, he saw the red traceries of his arteries filling with gleeful sap, bearing tidings of joy and vigor to his cells. His muscles quaked. His loins tittered, abloat with happy news. His stomach, too, disturbed his rest. Even after a dinner of crass size, Rodney would lie in bed, his gut groaning as though he hadn't eaten in days. He would rise and go downstairs, but he could not find foods to gratify his hunger. Whether cold noodles, or a plate of costly meats and cheeses, all the foods in his house had a dull, exhausted flavor, and he would eat in joyless frustration, as though forced to suffer conversation with a hideous bore.

Exercise was the only route to sleep for Rodney. His ankles plagued him less these days, and after dinner he would rove for hours in the warm autumn dark. Some nights he strolled the shore, soothed to hear the distant splashes of leaping night fish. Sometimes he went into the hills where the houses stopped. The land rose and fell before him, merging in the far distance with the darkness of the sky, unbroken by lights of civilization. A feeling of giddy affluence would overtake Rodney as he scrambled along. All that space, and nobody's but his! It was like the dream where you find a silver dollar on the sidewalk, then another, then another, until you look up to see a world strewn with free riches.

On these strolls, his thoughts often turned to Katherine Nevis, that fine, wretched girl imprisoned at the end of Naiad Lane behind the high white wall. He recalled the smell of her,

her comely gruntings that day on the shore, the tender heft of her underjaw in his palm. One evening the memory of her became so intolerable that it stopped him in his tracks, and he paused between the dunes in an intimate little hollow where dust of surprising fineness gathered in plush drifts.

Rodney stooped to caress the soft soil, warm in his hand. "Listen, you and me are in a predicament here, Katherine," he explained to the dust. "Oh, you don't, huh? Fine. You stay right there. I'll get it myself."

With that, he unbuckled his pants and fell to zealously raping the dirt. The sensation was not pleasurable, and the fierceness of the act did not sit right with Rodney's notion of himself, but in the end he felt satisfied that he had completed a job of grim though necessary work.

Floured with earth, he made his way to the water and swam vigorously for twenty minutes. Then he crawled into bed beside his wife and slept until the sun rose, minding not at all the pricking of the soft sheets against his salty skin.

· · ·

The following night Rodney ranged along the shore and back up into the hills, yet his step was sulky and his heart was low. As with the pantry foods he did not care to eat, that evening the great open land had become infected with a kindred dreariness. Squatting on a boulder, Rodney gazed at the column of clean light spilling from the enclosure of the Nevis home. A breathless yearning caught hold. The desert's wealth of joy and deliverance seemed to have slipped down the rills and drainages, slid past the dark houses, leached south along the hard pink berm, and concentrated in the glare above the one place in the Anasazi Basin where Rodney was not free to roam. He stood and walked.

Rodney told himself he would not enter the Nevis property. The notion was to loiter at the gate, have a glimpse of the courtyard, sport a little with the pull of the place, the fun of holding two magnets at slight bay. And perhaps Rodney would have kept his promise to himself had he not spotted, bolted to the top of a length of conduit bracketed to the wall, a fan of iron claws, put there to discourage shimmiers. The device offended Rodney as an emblem of arrogance and vanity. Who was Arn Nevis to make his home a thorny fort? The spikes were pitiful. A determined crone could have gotten past them. Rodney jumped and grasped in either hand the two outermost claws. With a strength and ease that surprised him, he vaulted himself over the hazard and onto the lip of the wall.

He dropped onto the flagstones and the agony in his ankles caused his lungs to briefly freeze with pain. Rodney held his breath, waiting to hear a barking dog or an alarm, but heard nothing. Beyond the batteries of floodlights, only a single window glowed in the far corner of the house. Rodney waited. Nothing stirred.

Crouched in the courtyard, a new oil seemed to rise in Rodney's joints. His body felt incapable of noisy or graceless moves. He removed the screen from an open window and found himself in the Nevises' living room. He paused at a grand piano and rested his fingers in a chord on the sheeny keys. The temptation to sound the notes was strong, so electrified was Rodney that the house was under his authority. The fragrance in the room was distasteful and exciting—an aroma of milk and cologne—and it provoked in him an unaccountable hunger. He padded to the Nevises' kitchen. In the cold light of the open refrigerator, Rodney unwrapped and ate a wedge of Gruyère cheese. Then he had a piece of unsweetened baking chocolate, which he washed down with a can of Arn's beer. Still, his stomach growled. Under a shroud of crumpled tinfoil, he found a mostly intact ham, and he gnawed the sugary crust and then went at it with his jaws and teeth, taking bites the size of tennis balls, glutting his throat and clearing the clog with a second, then a third can of his neighbor's beer.

When he had at last had all he wanted, Rodney's breathing had become labored. He was dewed in hot sweat. His bladder, too, was full, but his feeling of satiety there in the kitchen was so delicate and golden that he did not feel like shifting an inch to find a toilet. So he lowered his zipper and relished the sound of fluid hitting terra-cotta tiles, which mingled with the keen scent of his own urine in a most ideal way.

He had only just shut the refrigerator door when a white motion in the window caught his eye. Who was it but Katherine Nevis, the darling prisoner of the house? She plodded across the rear courtyard, on flat, large girl's feet, heading for the little inlet. She shed her robe, and Rodney was unhappy to see that even at that private hour of the evening, she still bothered to wear a bathing suit. She dove, and the water accepted her with the merest ripple. For many minutes, Rodney watched her sporting and glorying in the pool, diving and breaching, white, dolphinlike exposures of her skin bright against the dark red tide. When he could put it off no longer, Rodney stepped through the sliding door and went to her.

"Howdy!" he called, very jolly. She whirled in the water, only her head exposed. Rodney walked to the edge of the pool. "Hi there!" he said. She said nothing, but sank a little, gathering the water to her with sweeping arms, taking it into her mouth, pushing it gently over her chin, breathing it, nearly. She said nothing. Rodney put his fists on his hips and grinned at the surveillant moon. "Hell of a spotlight. Good to swim by, huh?"

Her eyes were dark but not fearful. "How'd you get in here?" the girl said wetly.

"Oh, I had some business with your dad," he said.

"My dad," she repeated, her face a suspicious little fist.

"Maybe I'll get in there with you," Rodney said, raising his shirt.

"Do what you like," the girl said. "I'm going inside."

He put a hand out. She took it and pulled herself into the night air. He picked up her robe. Draping it on her, he caught her sourdough aroma, unmasked by the sulfur smell of the sea. His heart was going, his temples on the bulge.

"Stay," he said. "Come on, the moon's making a serious effort here. It's a real once-in-a-month kind of moon."

She smiled, then stopped. She reached into the pocket of her robe and retrieved and a cigarette. "Okay. By the way, if I yelled even a little bit, my mom would come out here. She's got serious radar. She listens to everything and never sleeps. Seriously, how'd you get through the gate?"

Rodney stretched his smile past his dogteeth. A red gas was coming into his eyes. "She's one great lady, your mom." He put a hand on the girl's hip. She pushed against it only slightly, then sat with her cigarette on a tin-and-rubber chaise longue to light it. He sat beside her and took the cigarette, holding it downwind so as to smell her more purely. He made some mouth sounds in her ear. She closed her eyes. "Gets dull out here, I bet," he said.

"Medium," she said. She took back the ocher short of her roll-your-own. He put his hand on her knee, nearly nauseated with an urge. The girl frowned at his fingers. "Be cool, hardcore," she said.

"Why don't you . . . how about let's . . . how about . . ."

"Use your words," she said.

He put his hand on the back of her head and tried to pull her to his grasping lips. She broke the clasp. "What makes you think I want to kiss your mouth?"

"Come on," he groaned, nearly weeping. "God*damn*, you're beautiful."

"Shit," the girl said.

"You are a beautiful woman," said Rodney.

"My legs are giant," she said. "I've got a crappy face."

"Come here," he said. He lipped some brine from her jaw.

"Don't," she said, panting some. "You don't love me yet."

Rodney murmured that he did love Katherine Nevis very much. He kissed her, and she didn't let him. He kissed her again and she did. Then he was on her and for a time the patio was silent save the sound of their breath and the crying of the chaise's rubber slats.

He'd gotten her bikini bottoms down around her knees when the girl went stiff. "Quit," she whispered harshly. He pretended not to hear her. "Shit, goddammit, stop!" She gave him a hard shove, and then Rodney saw the problem. Arn Nevis was over by the house, hunched and peering from the blue darkness of the eave. Nevis was perfectly still, his chin raised slightly, mouth parted in expectancy. His look changed when he realized he'd been spotted. From what Rodney could tell, it wasn't outrage on the old man's features, just mild sadness that things had stopped before they'd gotten good.

．　　　．　　　．

Three mornings later, Rodney Booth looked out his bedroom window to see a speeding ambulance dragging a curtain of dust all the way up Naiad Lane to the Nevis home. He watched some personnel in white tote a gurney through the gate. Then Rodney went downstairs and poured himself some cereal and turned the television on.

Later that afternoon, as Rodney was leaving for the wharf with his fishing pole and creel, Cora called to him. She'd just gotten off the phone with Phyllis Nevis, who'd shared the sad news that her husband was in the hospital, comatose with a ruptured aneurysm, not expected to recover. Rodney agreed that this was terrible. Then he shouldered his pole and set out for the wharf.

The day after the ambulance bore Arn Nevis away, Rodney began to suffer vague qualmings of the conscience relating to the Nevis family. He had trouble pinpointing the source of the unease. It was not sympathy for Nevis himself. There was nothing lamentable about an old man heading toward death in his sleep. And his only regret about his tender grapplings with the sick man's daughter was that they hadn't concluded properly. Really, the closest Rodney could come to what was bothering him was some discomfort over his behavior with Phyllis Nevis's ham. He pictured mealtime in her house, the near widow serving her grieving children the fridge's only bounty, a joint of meat, already hard used by unknown teeth. The vision made him tetchy and irritated with himself. He felt the guilt gather in his temples and coalesce into a bothersome headache.

That afternoon, Rodney harvested and shucked a pint or so of oysters. He packed in ice three pounds of fresh-caught croaker filets. He showered, shaved, daubed his throat and the line of hair on his stomach with lemon verbena eau de cologne. In the fridge he found a reasonably good bottle of Pouilly-Fuissé, and he set off up Naiad Lane.

Phyllis Nevis came to the gate and welcomed him in. "I brought you something," Rodney said. "It isn't much."

She looked into the bag with real interest. "Thank you," she said. "That's very, very kind."

"And the wine is cold," said Rodney. "Bet you could use a glass."

"I could," said Phyllis quietly.

Together they walked inside. Rodney put the fish in the refrigerator. He opened the bottle and poured two large glasses. Phyllis went upstairs and then returned with her baby, Nathan. She sat on the sofa, waiting for Rodney, giving the infant his lunch.

Rodney gave the woman a glass and sat close beside her.

"Thank you," said Phyllis, tears brightening her eyes. "One week, tops. That's what they said."

"I'm so, so sorry," Rodney said. He put his arm around her, and while she wept, she allowed herself to be drawn into the flushed hollow of Rodney's neck. The infant at her breast began to squeal, and the sound inflamed the pain in Rodney's temples, and he had an impulse to tear the baby from her and carry it out of the room. Instead, he swallowed his wine at a gulp. He poured himself a second glass and knocked it back, which seemed to dull the pain a little. Then he settled against the cushion and pressed Phyllis's tearful face into his neck. While she quaked on him, Rodney stroked the tender skin behind her ears and stared off through the picture window. Far above the eastern hills, a council of clouds shed a gray fringe of moisture. The promise of rain was a glad sight in the mournful scene, though in fact this was rain of a frail kind, turning to vapor a mile above the brown land, never to be of use to women and men on earth.

Sports Illustrated

FINALIST—ESSAYS

Before The Five People You Meet in Heaven, *before* Tuesdays With Morrie, *Mitch Albom was best known as an award-winning sports columnist for the* Detroit Free Press. *He still writes for the* Freep, *and he still calls Detroit home. In this piece, he recalls a time when Detroit was an industrial colossus—"part of the backbone of this country," he writes, "the manufacturing spine, the heart of the middle class." Those times aren't coming back, but in "And Yet . . . ," Albom still finds reason to cheer—for Detroit and for America.*

And Yet . . .

This was Christmas night. In the basement of a church off an icy street in downtown Detroit, four dozen homeless men and women sat at tables. The smell of cooked ham wafted from the kitchen. The pastor, Henry Covington, a man the size of two middle linebackers, exhorted the people with a familiar chant.

"I am somebody," he yelled.

"*I am somebody!*" they repeated.

"Because God loves me!"

"*Because God loves me!*"

They clapped. They nodded.

A toddler slept on a woman's shoulder. Another woman, holding a boy who looked to be about four, said she was lucky to have found this place open because "I been to three shelters, and they turned me away. They were all filled."

As she spoke, a few blocks to the south, cars pulled up to the Motor City Casino, one of three downtown gambling palaces whose neon flashes in stark contrast to the area's otherwise empty darkness. Sometimes, on a winter night, all that seems to be open around here is the casino, a liquor store, and the pastor's kitchen, in the basement of this church. It used to be a famous church, home to the largest Presbyterian congregation in the upper Midwest. That was a long time ago—before a stained-glass window was stolen and the roof developed a huge hole. Now, on Sundays, the mostly African-American churchgoers of the I Am My Brother's Keeper Ministries huddle in a small section of the sanctuary that is enclosed in plastic sheeting, because they can't afford to heat the rest.

As food was served to the line of homeless people, I watched from a rickety balcony above. My line of work is writing, partly sportswriting, but I come here now and then to help out a little. This church needs help. It leaks everywhere. Melted snow drips into the vestibule.

"Hey," someone yelled, "who the Lions gonna draft?"

I looked down. A thin man with a scraggly black beard was looking back. He scratched his face. "A quarterback, you think?"

Probably, I answered.

"Whatchu think about a defensive end?"

That would be nice.

"Yeah." He bounced on his feet. "That'd be nice."

He waited for his plate of food. In an hour, he would yank a vinyl mattress from a pile and line it up next to dozens of others. Then the lights would dim and, as snow fell outside, he and the other men would pull up wool blankets and try to sleep on the church floor.

This is my city.

"Them Lions gotta do *somethin'*, man," he yelled. "Can't go on the way they are."

•　　　•　　　•

And yet . . .

And yet Detroit was once a vibrant place, the fourth-largest city in the country, and it lives in the hope that those days, against all logic, will somehow return. We are downtrodden, perhaps, but the most downtrodden optimists you will ever meet. We cling to our ways, no matter how provincial they seem on the coasts. We get excited about the Auto Show. We celebrate Sweetest Day. We eat Coney dogs all year and we cruise classic cars down Woodward Avenue every August and we bake punchki donuts the week before Lent. We don't talk about whether Detroit will be fixed but when Detroit will be fixed.

And we are modest. In truth, we battle an inferiority complex. We gave the world the automobile. Now the world wants to scold us for it. We gave the world Motown music. Motown moved its offices to L.A. When I arrived twenty-four years ago, to be a sports columnist at the *Detroit Free Press*, I discovered several letters waiting for me at the office. Mind you, I had not written a word. My hiring had been announced, that's all. But there were already letters. Handwritten. And they all said, in effect, "Welcome to Detroit. We know you won't stay long, because nobody good stays for long, but we hope you like it while you're here."

Nobody good stays for long.

We hope you like it while you're here.

How could you not stay in a city like that?

· · ·

And yet . . .

And yet to live in Detroit these days is to want to scream. But where do you begin? Our doors are being shuttered. Our walls are falling down. Our daily bread, the auto industry, is reduced to morsels. Our schools are in turmoil. Our mayor went to jail. Our two biggest newspapers announced they will soon cut home delivery to three days a week. Our most common lawn sign is FOR SALE. And our NFL team lost every week this season. A perfect 0-16. Even the homeless guys are sick of it.

We want to scream, but we don't scream, because this is not a screaming place, this is a swallow-hard-and-deal-with-it place. So workers rise in darkness and rev their engines against the winter cold and drive to the plant and punch in and spend hours doing the work that America doesn't want to do any more, the kind that makes something real and hard to the touch. Manufacturing. Remember manufacturing? They do that here. And then they punch out and drive home (three o'clock is rush hour in these parts, the end of a shift) and wash up and touch the kids under the chin and sit down for dinner and flip on the news.

And then they *really* want to scream.

Because what they see—what all Detroit sees—is a nation that appears ready to flick us away like lint. We see senators voting our death sentence. We see bankers clucking their tongues at our business model (as if we invented the credit default swap!). We see Californians knock our cars for ruining the environment (as if their endless driving has nothing to do with it). We see sports announcers call our football team "ridiculous." Heck, during the Lions' annual Thanksgiving game, CBS's Shannon Sharpe actually *wore a bag over his head.*

It hurts us. We may not show it, but it does. You can say, "Aw, that's the car business" or "That's the Lions," but we *are* the car business, we *are* the Lions. Our veins are right up under the city's skin—you cut Detroit, its citizens bleed.

We want to scream, but we don't scream. Still, enough people declare you passé, a dinosaur, a dying town, out of touch with the free-market global economic machine, and pretty soon you wonder if they're right. You wonder if you should join the exodus.

•　　　•　　　•

And yet . . .

And yet I had an idea once for a sports column: Get the four biggest stars from Detroit's four major sports together in one place, for a night out. The consensus cast at the time (1990) was clear. Barry Sanders was the brightest light on the Lions. Steve Yzerman was Captain Heartthrob for the Red Wings. Joe Dumars was the most popular of the Pistons. And Cecil Fielder was the big bat for the Tigers.

All four agreed to meet at Tiger Stadium, before a game. I picked up Dumars at his house. He was alone. No entourage. Next we went for Sanders, who waited in the Silverdome parking lot, by himself, hands in pockets. When he got in, the two future Hall of Famers nodded at each other shyly. "Hey, man," Barry said.

"Hey, man," Joe answered.

At the stadium Yzerman, who drove himself, joined us, hands also dug in his pockets. As conversations go, it was like the first day of school. Awkwardness prevailed. Later—after we chatted with Fielder—we sat in the stands. The hot dog guy came by, and we passed them down: Lion to Red Wing to Piston. And when Yzerman put his elbow in front of Sanders, he quickly said, "Excuse me."

Somehow I can't see that being duplicated in Los Angeles. ("Kobe, pass this hot dog to Manny") or New York City ("Hey, A-Rod, Stephon wants some mustard"). But it *worked* in Detroit. The guys actually thanked me afterward.

Stardom is a funny thing here. You don't achieve it by talking loud or dating a supermodel. You achieve it by shyly lowering your head when they introduce you or by tossing the ball to the refs after scoring a touchdown. Humility, in Detroit, is on a par with heroism. Even Dennis Rodman didn't get really crazy until he left.

·   ·   ·

And yet . . .

And yet we live among ghosts. Over there, on Woodward Avenue, was Hudson's, once America's second-largest department store; it was demolished a decade ago. Over there, on Michigan and Trumbull, stood Tiger Stadium, home to Ty Cobb and Hank Greenberg and Al Kaline and Kirk Gibson; it lasted nearly a century, until the wrecking ball got to it last year. Over there, on Bagley, is the United Artists Theater, which used to seat more than 2,000 people; it hasn't shown movies since the 1970s. The famous Packard plant on East Grand Boulevard—the birthplace of the auto assembly line—used to hum with activity, but now its halls are empty, its windows are broken, and its floors gather pools of water. On Lafayette Avenue you can still see the old Free Press building, where I was hired, where those letters once arrived in a mail slot. It used to house a newspaper. It doesn't anymore.

Any mature city has its echoes, but most are drowned out by the chirping of new enterprise. In Detroit the echoes roll on and on, filling the empty blocks because little else does. There is not a department store left downtown. Those three casinos hover like giant cranes, ready to scoop up your last desperate dollar. We have all heard the catchphrases about Detroit: A city of ruins. A Third World metropolis. A carcass. Last person to leave, turn out the lights.

For years, we took those insults as a challenge. We wore a cloak of defiance. But now that cloak feels wet and heavy. It has been cold here before, but this year seems colder. Skies have grayed before, but this year they're like charcoal. We've been unemployed before, but now the lines seem longer; we hear figures like 16 percent of the labor force not working, Depression numbers. I read one estimate that more than 40,000 houses in our city are now abandoned. Ghosts everywhere.

• • •

And yet . . .

And yet we remember when the streets were stuffed, a million people downtown at a parade, as our hockey team was given a royal reception; every car carrying a player was cheered. This was 1997, and the Red Wings, after a forty-two-year drought, had once again won the Stanley Cup. Players and coaches stepped to the microphone and heard their words bounce back in waves of sound and thundering applause. Yzerman. Brendan Shanahan. Scotty Bowman. A hockey team? Who does this for a hockey team? Hockey is an afterthought in most American cities. Here, we wear it as a nickname. Hockeytown. We know the rules. We know the good and the bad officials. We sneak octopuses in our pants legs and throw them onto the ice at Joe Louis Arena.

Who loves hockey like this? What other American city comes to a collective roar when the blue light flashes? And what other American city goes into collective mourning when two of its players and a team masseur are seriously injured in a limo crash? People in Detroit can still tell you where they were when they heard about that limo smashing into a tree in suburban Birmingham six days after the Cup win of '97, forever changing the lives of Vladimir Konstantinov, Slava Fetisov and Sergei Mnatsakanov. Vigils were held outside the hospital. Flowers were stacked at the crash site. The TV and radio news broke in with updates all day long. How critical? Would they skate again? Would they walk again?

Remember, these were two hockey players and a masseur, Russians to boot; none of them did much talking in English. Didn't matter. They were ours, and they were wounded. It felt as if there was no other news for weeks in Detroit. "You hear anything?" people would say. "Any updates?"

When people ask what kind of sports town Detroit is, I say the best in the nation. I say our newspapers will carry front-page stories on almost any sports tick, from Ernie Harwell's retirement to the Detroit Shock's winning the WNBA. I say sports is sometimes all we have, it relieves us, distracts us, at times even saves us. But what I really want to tell them about is that stretch in 1997, when the whole city seemed to be nervously pacing around a hospital waiting room. I can't do it justice. It's not that we watch more, or pay more, or cheer louder than other cities. But I will bet you my last dollar that, when it comes to sports, nobody cares as much as Detroit cares.

•　　　•　　　•

And yet . . .

And yet the gods toy with us. They give us the Lions. Our football team puts the less in hopeless. Its owner, William Clay Ford, has been in charge for forty-five years. He's seen one play-off win. One playoff win in nearly half a century? Meanwhile, the backstory on Lions failure could fill a library. Blown games. Blown trades. Some of the most pathetic drafting in history, much of it orchestrated by Matt Millen, a former player who was hired out of the TV booth. Honestly, how many teams can use first-round draft picks on a quarterback, a receiver, a running back and two more receivers, as the Lions did from 2002 through '05, and not have a single one of them on the team just a few years later? And two of them out of the NFL altogether?

Wait. Here's a better one. In the last forty-five years—or since Ford took over—the Lions have had thirteen non-interim head coaches, and not a single one was ever a head coach in the NFL again. *Not one.* Rick Forzano. Tommy Hudspeth. Monte Clark. Darryl Rogers. Wayne Fontes. The list goes on. Nobody wanted them after Detroit. The Lions don't just hurt your reputation, they permanently flatten your tires.

Joey Harrington, a star college quarterback of unflagging optimism who foundered after the Lions drafted him with the no. 3 pick in 2002, once told me of a fog that seems to settle over inhabitants of the Lions locker room—an evil, heavy cloud of historic disappointment that becomes self-perpetuating. Maybe it's the curse that Bobby Layne supposedly cast on this team after it traded him, saying it wouldn't win for fifty years.

That was fifty-one years ago.

No wonder Bobby Ross, who once coached San Diego to a Super Bowl, turned in his whistle and walked out of Detroit in the middle of a season. No wonder Sanders, the best running back Detroit ever had, quit the game at age thirty. He actually gave money *back* rather than continue to play for the Lions.

Against this awful tapestry, in an economic crisis, in the darkest of days, came the 2008 season. What cruel fate could conjure such timing? After going 4-0 in the preseason (how's that for irony?), the Lions fell behind in their first regular-season game 21-0, in their second 21-3, in their third 21-3 and in their fourth 17-0—*all before halftime.* Their fifth game was the closest all year. They lost by two points. The margin of defeat? Our quarterback du jour, Dan Orlovsky, lost track of where he was and ran out of the back of the end zone for a safety.

Stop laughing. Do you think this has been easy? Do you think it's fun watching four guys miss tackles on a single play? Do you think it's fun watching Daunte Culpepper arrive, fresh off coaching his son's Pee Wee games, and get the nod as starting quarterback? There were days when it seemed as if all you needed to be on the Lions roster was a driver's license.

Week after week, as our businesses suffocated, as our houses were foreclosed and handed over to the banks, our football team lost—to Jacksonville by 24 points, to Carolina by 9, to Tampa Bay by 18. And then, on Thanksgiving, the Tennessee Titans came to town with a 10-1 record. In front of the only national TV audience we would have all year, our Lions fumbled on their second play from scrimmage. A few plays later, Tennessee's Chris Johnson ran six yards untouched into the end zone—the beer vendors were closer to him than the Lions defenders—and before you could check the turkey in the oven, the Lions were down 35-3.

At halftime Sharpe wore that bag over his head and joined his colleagues in loudly suggesting that the NFL take the annual tradition away from the Motor City. "We have kids watching this," Sharpe said. "And they have to watch the Detroit Lions. This is ridiculous. The Detroit Lions every single year. This is what we have to go through."

No, Shannon. This is what we have to go through.

•   •   •

And yet . . .

And yet it's our misery to endure. There's a little too much glee in the Detroit jokes these days. A little too much flip in the wrist that tosses dirt on our coffins. We hear a Tennessee player tell the media that the Thanksgiving win didn't mean much because "it was just Detroit." We hear Jay Leno rip our scandalous former mayor, Kwame Kilpatrick, by saying, "The bad news is, he could be forced out of office. The good news is, any time you get a chance to get out of Detroit, take it."

We hear Congress tongue-lash our auto executives for not matching the cheaper wages of foreign car companies. We hear South Carolina senator Jim DeMint tell NPR that "the barnacles of unionism" must be destroyed at GM, Ford, and Chrysler. Barnacles? Barnacles are parasites without a conscience. Sounds more like politicians to us.

Enough, we want to say. The Lions stink. We know they stink. You don't have to tell us. Enough. The car business is in trouble. We know it's in trouble. We drive past the deserted parking lots of empty auto plants every day.

Enough. We don't need more lofty national newspaper laments on the decay of a Rust Belt city. Or the obligatory network news piece, "Can Detroit Be Saved?" For too long we have been the Place to Go to Chronicle the Ugly. Example: For years, we had a rash of fires the night before Halloween—Devil's Night. And like clockwork, you could count on TV crews to fly in from out of town in hopes of catching Detroit burning. *Whoomf.* There we were in flames, on network TV. But when we got the problem under control, when city-sponsored neighborhood programs helped douse it, you never heard about that. The TV crews just shrugged and left.

Same goes for the favorite Detroit cliché of so many pundits: the image of a burning police car in 1984, after the Tigers won the World Series. Yes, some folks went stupid that night, and an eighth-grade dropout nicknamed Bubba held up a Tigers pennant in front of that burning vehicle, and—*snap-snap*—that was the only photo anyone seemed to need.

Never mind that in the years since, many cities have done as badly or worse after championships—Boston and Chicago come to mind—and weren't labeled for it. Never mind that through three NBA titles, four Stanley Cups, Michigan's national championships in college basketball and football, and even another World Series, nothing of that nature has occurred again in Detroit. Never mind. You still hear people, when we play for a title, uncork the old "Let's hope they don't burn the city down when it's over."

Look, we're the first to say we've got problems. But there's something disturbing when American reporters keep deliciously recording our demise but nobody wants to do anything about it. We're not your pity party. You want to chronicle us? We've been chronicled enough. As they say when a basketball rolls away at the playground, *Yo, little help?*

This is why our recent beatdown in Congress was so painfully felt. To watch our Big Three execs humiliated as if they never did a right thing in their lives, to watch U.S. senators from Southern states—where billions in tax breaks were handed out to foreign car companies—tear apart the U.S. auto industry as undeserving of aid, well, that was the last straw.

Enough. We're not gum on the bottom of America's shoe. We're not grime to be wiped off with a towel. Detroit and Michigan are part of the backbone of this country, the manufacturing spine, the heart of the middle class—heck, we *invented* the middle class, we invented the idea that a factory worker can put in forty hours a week and actually buy a house and send a kid to college. What? You have a problem with that? You think only lawyers and hedge-fund kings deserve to live decently?

To watch these lawmakers hand out, with barely a whisper, hundreds of billions to the financial firms that helped cause this current disaster, then make the Big Three beg like dogs and slap them with nothing? Honestly. There are times out here we feel like orphans.

. . .

And yet . . .

And yet we go on. The Tigers were supposed to win big last season; they finished last in their division. Michigan got a new football coach with a spread offense and an eye on a national championship; the Wolverines had their first losing season since 1967.

But we will be back for the Tigers and back for Michigan and—might as well admit it—we will be back for the Lions come September, as red-faced as they make us, as pathetic as 0-16 is.

And maybe you ask why? Maybe you ask, as I get asked all the time, "Why do you stay there? Why don't you leave?"

Maybe because we like it here. Maybe because this is what we know: snow and concrete underfoot, hardhats, soul music, lakes, hockey sticks. Maybe because we don't see just the burned-out houses; we also see the Fox Theater, the Detroit Institute of Arts, the Whitney restaurant, the riverfront that looks out to Canada. Maybe because we still have seniors who call the auto giant "Ford's," like a shop that's owned by a real human being. Maybe because some of us subscribe to Pastor Covington's words, *We are somebody because God loves us*, no matter how cold the night or hard the mattress.

Maybe because when our kids finish college and take that first job in some sexy faraway city and a year later we see them back home and we ask what happened, they say, "I missed my friends and family." And we nod and say we understand.

Or maybe because we're smarter than you think. Every country flogs a corner of itself on the whipping post. English Canada rips French Canada, and vice versa. Swedes make lame jokes about Laplanders.

But it's time to untie Detroit. Because we may be a few steps behind the rest of the country, but we're a few steps ahead of it too. And what's happening to us may happen to you.

Do you think if your main industry sails away to foreign countries, if the tax base of your city dries up, you won't have crumbling houses and men sleeping on church floors too? Do you think if we become a country that makes nothing, that builds nothing, that only services and outsources, that we will hold our place on the economic totem pole? Detroit may be suffering the worst from this semi-Depression, but we sure didn't invent it. And we can't stop it from spreading. We can only do what we do. Survive.

And yet we're better at that than most places.

   .   •   •

Here is the end of the story. This was back on Christmas night. After the visit to the church, I drove to a suburb with an old friend and we saw a movie. *Gran Torino.* It starred and was directed by Clint Eastwood, and it was filmed in metro Detroit, which was a big deal. Last year the state passed tax incentives to lure the movie business, an effort to climb out of our one-industry stranglehold, and Eastwood was the first big name to take advantage of it.

He shot in our neighborhoods. He used a bar and a hardware store. He reportedly fit in well, he liked the people, and no one hassled him with scripts or résumés.

The film was good, I thought, and familiar. The story of a craggy old man who loves his old car and stubbornly clings to the way he feels the world should behave. He defends his home. He defends his neighbors' honor. He goes out on his own terms.

When the film finished, the audience stayed in its seats waiting, through the closing music, through the credits, until the very last scroll, where, above a camera shot of automobiles rolling down Jefferson Avenue along the banks of Lake St. Clair, three words appeared.

MADE IN MICHIGAN.

And the whole place clapped. Just stood up and clapped.

To hell with Depression. We're gonna have a good year.

National Magazine Awards 2010 Finalists and Winners

To view an extended list of the 2010 finalists and winners—including links to content, judges' citations and a searchable database of past award winners—please go to http://asme.mag azine.org.

Magazine of the Year

Honors publications that successfully use both print and digital media in fulfilling the editorial mission of the magazine

The Atlantic: James Bennet, editor; Scott Stossel, deputy editor; TheAtlantic.com: Bob Cohn, editorial director. For March, June, December issues.

Fast Company: Robert Safian, editor; Noah Robischon, executive editor, FastCompany.com. For February, July/August, December 2009/January 2010 issues.

Glamour [winner]: Cynthia Leive, editor-in-chief; Jill Herzig, executive editor; Geraldine Hessler, design director; Glamour.com: Ben Berentson, online managing director. For April, September, November issues.

Men's Health: David Zinczenko, editor in chief; MensHealth.com: William G. Phillips, executive editor. For September, October, December issues.

New York: Adam Moss, editor in chief; NYMag.com: Ben Williams, editorial director. For April 20, October 5, October 26 issues.

General Excellence, Print

Recognizes overall editorial achievement at six circulation levels.

Under 100,000 Circulation

Aperture: Melissa Harris, editor in chief. For Spring, Fall, Winter issues.

Architect: Ned Cramer, editor in chief. For March, April, June issues.

Military History: Stephen L. Petranek, editor-in-chief; Michael W. Robbins, editor. For February/March, August/September, December 2009/January 2010 issues.

The Paris Review: Philip Gourevitch, editor. For Summer, Fall, Winter issues.

San Francisco [winner]: Bruce Kelley, editor in chief. For April, August, December issues.

100,000 to 250,000 Circulation

Foreign Policy: Susan Glasser, executive editor. For May/June, July/August, September/October issues.

Garden & Gun: Sid Evans, editor in chief. For February/March, August/September, December 2009/January 2010 issues.

Martha Stewart Weddings: Darcy Miller, editorial director; Vanessa Holden, editor in chief. For Spring, Summer, Fall issues.

Mother Jones [winner]: Monika Bauerlein and Clara Jeffery, editors. For July/August, September/October, November/December issues.

Paste: Josh Jackson, editor in chief. For February, March/April, July issues.

250,000 to 500,000 Circulation

The Atlantic: James Bennet, editor. For March, June, December issues.

Audubon: David Seideman, editor in chief. For March/April, September/October, November/December issues.

New York [winner]: Adam Moss, editor in chief. For April 20, October 5, October 26 issues.

Texas Monthly: Evan Smith, president and editor-in-chief; Jake Silverstein, editor. For September issue. Jake Silverstein, editor. For November, December issues.

W: Patrick McCarthy, chairman and editorial director. For February, March, September issues.

500,000 to 1,000,000 Circulation

The Economist: John Micklethwait, editor in chief. For June 27, December 5, December 19 issues.

Esquire: David Granger, editor in chief. For March, May, September issues.

Food Network Magazine: Maile Carpenter, editor in chief. For October, November, December issues.

GQ [winner]: Jim Nelson, editor in chief. For June, September, November issues.

Wired: Chris Anderson, editor in chief. For May, August, November issues.

1,000,000 to 2,000,000 Circulation

Field & Stream: Anthony Licata, editor: For June, October, December 2009/January 2010 issues.

Men's Health [Winner]: David Zinczenko, editor in chief. For September, October, December issues.

More: Lesley Jane Seymour, editor in chief. For September, October, November issues.

The New Yorker: David Remnick, editor. For June 1, September 7, October 26 issues.

Teen Vogue: Amy Astley, editor in chief. For August, September, October issues.

Over 2,000,000 Circulation

ESPN the Magazine: Gary Belsky, editor in chief. For March 23, October 19, December 14 issues.

National Geographic [Winner]: Chris Johns, editor in chief. For May, September, December Issues

Real Simple: Kristin van Ogtrop, managing editor. For October, November, December issues.

Sports Illustrated: Terry McDonell, editor. For February 16, May 18, December 7 issues.

Time: Richard Stengel, managing editor. For June 29, August 17, October 5 issues.

Design, Print

Honors the effectiveness of design, typography and artwork in support of the editorial mission of the magazine

Esquire: David Granger, editor in chief. For February, March, September issues.
GQ: Jim Nelson, editor in chief. For February, June, July issues.
Martha Stewart Living: Martha Stewart, founder; Gael Towey, editorial director; Eric A. Pike, creative director. For February, October, December issues.
New York: Adam Moss, editor in chief; Chris Dixon, design director. For March 2, August 24, October 12 issues.
Wired [Winner]: Chris Anderson, editor in chief. For March, May, August issues.

Photography, Print

Honors the effectiveness of photography, photojournalism and photo-illustration in support of the editorial mission of the magazine

GQ: Jim Nelson, editor in chief. For May, July, December issues.

National Geographic: Chris Johns, editor in chief; David Griffin, director of photography; Kurt Mutchler, director of photo editing. For June, October, December issues.

The New York Times Magazine: Gerald Marzorati, editor. For January 18, February 8, October 18 issues.

Vanity Fair [Winner]: Graydon Carter, editor. For March, September, November issues.

Vogue: Anna Wintour, editor in chief. For May, September, December issues.

Photojournalism

Recognizes the informative photographic documentation of an event or subject.

Foreign Policy: Susan Glasser, executive editor; Bryan Erickson, art director. For "The Land of No Smiles," photographs by Tomas van Houtryve, May/June.

National Geographic: Chris Johns, editor in chief. For "The Other Tibet," photographs by Carolyn Drake; text by Matthew Teague, December.

National Geographic [Winner]: Chris Johns, editor in chief. For "Shattered Somalia," photographs by Pascal Maitre; text by Robert Draper, May.

New York: Adam Moss, editor in chief; Jody Quon, photography director. For "Rose's Last Turn," photographs by Gillian Laub, February 2.

Virginia Quarterly Review: Ted Genoways, editor. For "The Young Mothers of Port-au-Prince," by Ruxandra Guidi; photographs by Bear Guerra, Summer.

Photo Portfolio

Honors creative photography and photo illustration, including portraiture.

National Geographic: Chris Johns, editor in chief. For "The Hadza," photographs by Martin Schoeller, December.

New York: Adam Moss, editor in chief; Jody Quon, photography director. For "Exquisite Circus," photographs by Marcus Bleasdale, August 24.

The New Yorker [Winner]: David Remnick, editor. For "Portraits of Power," photographs by Platon, December 7.

Out: Aaron Hicklin, editor in chief. For "Out 100: The Class of 2009," photographs by Jason Bell, December 2009/January 2010.

W: Patrick McCarthy, chairman and editorial director. For "Art and Commerce," photographs by Inez Van Lamsweerde and Vinoodh Matadin, October.

Single-Topic Issue

Recognizes magazines that have devoted an issue to the in-depth examination of one topic.

ESPN The Magazine: Gary Belsky, editor in chief. For The Body Issue, October 19.
New York: Adam Moss, editor in chief. For Fall Fashion, August 24.
The New Yorker: David Remnick, editor. For The Food Issue, November 23.
W: Patrick McCarthy, chairman and editorial director, For The Fourth Annual Art Issue, November.
Wired [Winner]: Chris Anderson, editor in chief: For The Mystery Issue, May.

Magazine Section

Recognizes the excellence of a regular, cohesive front- or back-of-back section.

Esquire: David Granger, editor in chief. For Man at His Best, May, September, November.
GQ: Jim Nelson, editor in chief. For GQ Intelligence, September, October, November.
GQ: Jim Nelson, editor in chief. For Manual, March, October, November.
New York [Winner]: Adam Moss, editor in chief. For Strategist, April 20, May 25, October 26.
Wired: Chris Anderson, editor in chief. For Start, February, June, December.

Personal Service

Honors the outstanding use of print journalism to serve the readers' needs and aspirations.

5280: Daniel Brogan, editor and publisher. For "Low on O2," by Lindsey B. Koehler and Natasha Gardner, October.

Men's Health: David Zinczenko, editor in chief. For "Dead Man Driving," by Oliver Broudy; photographs by Eric Ogden, December.

New York [Winner]: Adam Moss, editor in chief. For "For and Against Foreskin," by Chris Bonanos, Michael Idov, and Hanna Rosin, October 26.

Parents: Dana Points, editor in chief. For "Parents Quit For Good," a three-part series by Meryl Davids Landau, "So Long, Cigarettes!" February; "You Can Do It!" March; "Breathe Easy," April.

Wired: Chris Anderson, editor in chief. For "How to Behave," August.

Leisure Interests

Recognizes excellence in service journalism focusing on recreational activities and special interests.

Esquire: David Granger, editor in chief. For "Esquire's All-You-Can-Eat Breakfast," March.

Field & Stream: Anthony Licata, editor. For "America's Meat," December 2009/January 2010.

New York [Winner]: Adam Moss, editor in chief. For "The Great New York Neoclassical Neapolitan Pizza Revolution," by Rob Patronite and Robin Raisfeld with Michael Idov, July 20–27.

Texas Monthly: Evan Smith, president and editor in chief; Jake Silverstein, editor. For "The 50 Greatest Hamburgers in Texas," by Patricia Sharpe and Jake Silverstein, August.

Texas Monthly: Jake Silverstein, editor. For "Step Right Up," by John Spong, December.

Public Interest

Recognizes magazine journalism that illuminates issues of public importance

Boston Review: Deborah Chasman and Joshua Cohen, editors. For "A Death in Texas," by Tom Barry, November/December.

National Geographic: Chris Johns, editor in chief. For "Scraping Bottom," by Robert Kunzig; photographs by Peter Essick, March.

The New Yorker [Winner]: David Remnick, editor. For "The Cost Conundrum," by Atul Gawande, June 1.

San Francisco: Bruce Kelley, editor in chief. For "War of Values," by Danelle Morton, December.

Technology Review: Jason Pontin, editor in chief and publisher. For a two-part series by David Rotman: "Can Technology Save the Economy?" May/June; "Chasing the Sun," July/August.

Reporting

Honors the enterprise, skill and analysis that a magazine exhibits in covering an event or problem of contemporary interest and significance.

The Boston Globe Magazine: Susanne Althoff, editor. For a two-part series by Neil Swidey: "Trapped," August 9; "The Way Out," August 16.

The New York Times Magazine [Winner]: Gerald Marzorati, editor: For "The Deadly Choices at Memorial," by Sheri Fink, August 30.

The New Yorker: David Remnick, editor. For "Eight Days," by James B. Stewart, September 21.

The New Yorker: David Remnick, editor. For "Trial by Fire," by David Grann, September 7.

Vanity Fair: Graydon Carter, editor. For a three-part series: "Madoff's World," by Mark Seal, April; "Hello, Madoff!" by Mark Seal and Eleanor Squillari, June; "Ruth's World," by Mark Seal, September.

Feature Writing

Honors the stylishness and originality with which the writer treats her or his subject.

Esquire: David Granger, editor in chief. For "The Last Abortion Doctor," by John H. Richardson, September.

The New York Times Magazine: Gerald Marzorati, editor. For "The Holy Grail of the Unconscious," by Sara Corbett: September 20.

Texas Monthly [Winner]: Evan Smith, president and editor in chief; Jake Silverstein, editor. For "Still Life," by Skip Hollandsworth, May.

Vanity Fair: Graydon Carter, editor. For "Wall Street on the Tundra," by Michael Lewis, April.

Wired: Chris Anderson, editor in chief; "Vanish," by Evan Ratliff, December.

Profile Writing

Honors the vividness and perceptiveness with which the writer brings his or her subject to life.

Esquire [Winner]: David Granger, editor in chief. For "The Man Who Never Was," by Mike Sager, May/.

New York: Adam Moss, editor in chief. For "A Nonfiction Marriage," by Jonathan Van Meter, May 4.

The New Yorker: David Remnick, editor. For "Man of Extremes," by Dana Goodyear, October 26.

Vanity Fair: Graydon Carter, editor. For "The Man in the Rockefeller Suit," by Mark Seal, January.

Vanity Fair: Graydon Carter, editor. For "Marc Dreier's Crime of Destiny," by Bryan Burrough, November.

Essays

Recognizes the writer's eloquence, perspective, fresh thinking and unique voice.

National Geographic [Winner]: Chris Johns, editor in chief. For "Top Ten State Fair Joys," by Garrison Keillor, July.

The New York Times Magazine: Gerald Marzorati, editor. For "A Journey Through Darkness," by Daphne Merkin, May 10.

The New York Times Magazine: Gerald Marzorati, editor. For "Out of the Kitchen, Onto the Couch," by Michael Pollan, August 2.

Orion: H. Emerson Blake, editor in chief. For "Out West," by Joe Wilkins, September/October.

Sports Illustrated: Terry McDonell, editor.For "And Yet . . . ," by Mitch Albom, January 12.

Columns and Commentary

Recognizes excellence in short-form social, economic,and political commentary, including humor.

The Atlantic: James Bennet, editor. For three columns by Megan McArdle: "Sink and Swim," June; "Misleading Indicator," November; "Lead Us Not Into Debt," December.

The Economist: John Micklethwait, editor in chief. For three "Obituary" columns by Ann Wroe: "Danny La Rue," June 13; "Benson," August 15; "William Safire," October 3.

Newsweek [Winner]: Jon Meacham, editor. For three columns by Fareed Zakaria: "Worthwhile Canadian Initiative," February 16; "The Way Out of Afghanistan," September 21; "Theocracy and Its Discontents," June 29.

Popular Science: Mark Jannot, editor in chief. For three "Gray Matter" columns by Theodore Gray: "The Other White Heat," May; "Gone in a Flash," September; "Flash Bang," October.

Travel &Leisure: Nancy Novogrod, editor in chief. For three columns by Peter Jon Lindberg: "In Defense of Tourism," January; "Unhappy to Serve You," September; "Stop the Music!" November.

Reviews and Criticism

Honors the knowledge, persuasiveness,and original voice that the critic brings to her or his reviews.

GQ: Jim Nelson, editor in chief. For three reviews by Tom Carson: "The Great White Hype," May; "One Glorious 'Basterd,'" September; "There's a Sucker Born Every Minute," November.

Harper's Magazine: Roger D. Hodge, editor. For two reviews by Jonathan Dee: "Suburban Ghetto," April; "Motherless Children," September.

Los Angeles: Kit Rachlis, editor in chief. For two reviews by Steve Erickson: "The Next Frontier," January; "War Games," July. Mary Melton, editor. For a review by Steve Erickson: "No Ordinary Fad," September.

The New Yorker [Winner]: David Remnick, editor. For three reviews by Elizabeth Kolbert: "Green Like Me," August 31; "Flesh of Your Flesh," November 9; "Hosed," November 16.

Paste: Josh Jackson, editor in chief. For three reviews by Rachael Maddux: "Cold Bore," July; "Brandi, (You're a Fine Girl)," September; "Just Peachy," December 2009/January 2010.

Fiction

Recognizes excellence in fiction published in magazines.

The Antioch Review: Robert S. Fogarty, editor. For "The Coat," by Uwe Timm, translated by Robert C. Conard, Summer.

McSweeney's Quarterly [Winner]: Dave Eggers, editor. For "Memory Wall," by Anthony Doerr, October 1; "Raw Water," by Wells Tower, October 1; "Further Interpretations of Real-Life Events," by Kevin Moffett, March 3.

The New Yorker: David Remnick, editor. For "In the South," by Salman Rushdie, May 18; "War Dances," by Sherman Alexie, August 10 and 17; "Diary of an Interesting Year," by Helen Simpson, December 21 and 28.

The New Yorker: David Remnick, editor. For "A Tiny Feast," by Chris Adrian, April 20; "The Tiger's Wife," by Téa Obreht, June 8 and 15; "Victory Lap," by George Saunders, October 5.

Virginia Quarterly Review: Ted Genoways, editor. For "The Vanishing American," by Leslie Parry, Fall; "Fauntleroy's Ghost," by Vinnie Wilhelm, Winter.

National Magazine Awards for Digital Media 2010 Finalists and Winners

General Excellence, Digital Media

Recognizes editorial achievement in magazine websites and online-only magazines.

The Atlantic: James Bennet, editor; Bob Cohn, editorial director, TheAtlantic.com.

MarthaStewart.com: Martha Stewart, founder; Gail Horwood, executive vice president, digital programming and strategy.

National Geographic: Chris Johns, editor in chief; Rob Covey, senior vice president, digital media.

New York [Winner]: Adam Moss, editor in chief; Ben Williams, editorial director, NYMag.com.

Wired.com: Evan Hansen, editor in chief.

Mobile Media

Honors the outstanding use of mobile media, including mobile websites, mobile applications, and electronic readers.

Epicurious [Winner]: Tanya Wenman Steel, editor in chief.

GQ: Jim Nelson, editor in chief; Michael Hainey, deputy editor; Andy Comer, multimedia editor.

Yoga Journal: Kaitlin Quistgaard, editor in chief; Andrea Ferretti, executive editor, YogaJournal.com.

Design, Digital Media

Honors the visual appeal, clarity of navigation, and overall quality of the user experience of magazine websites and online-only magazines.

Billboard.com [Winner]: Josh Engroff, vice president, Digital; Bill Werde, editorial director.

The Daily Beast: Tina Brown, co-founder and editor in chief; LIFE.com: Bill Shapiro, editor.

National Geographic: Chris Johns, editor in chief; Rob Covey, senior vice president, Digital Media.

New York: Adam Moss, editor in chief; Ben Williams, editorial director, NYMag.com.

Photography, Digital Media

Recognizes the use of photography that demonstrates the unique capabilities of digital media.

ESPN the Magazine: Gary Hoenig, general manager and editorial director, ESPN Publishing; Gary Belsky, editor in chief, *ESPN the Magazine*.

National Geographic [Winner]: Chris Johns, editor in chief; Rob Covey, senior vice president, Digital Media.

Newsweek: Jon Meacham, editor; Geoff Reiss, general manager, Newsweek Digital; Devin Gordon, editor, Newsweek Digital.

Slate: David Plotz, editor.

Sports Illustrated: Terry McDonell, editor, Sports Illustrated Group; Paul Fichtenbaum, managing editor, SI.com.

News Reporting

Honors the timeliness, accuracy, and skill with which news and information are gathered and presented by magazine websites and online-only magazines.

BusinessWeek.com: Josh Tyrangiel, editor. For reporting on the collapse of General Motors by David Welch, Theo Francis, Steve LeVine, Ben Steverman, John Tozzi, and Ed Wallace.

Mother Jones: Clara Jeffery and Monika Bauerlein, co-editors in chief. For reporting on climate change.

Slate: David Plotz, editor. For "Prescriptions 2009: How to Fix Health Policy," by Timothy Noah.

TIME.com: Richard Stengel, managing editor, *Time*; Daniel Eisenberg, executive editor, TIME.com. For reporting on health-care reform.

Virginia Quarterly Review [Winner]: Ted Genoways, editor. For "Sixty Hours of Terror," by Jason Motlagh.

Blogging

Recognizes excellence in online reporting, commentary, and criticism in the form of a blog.

The Atlantic: James Bennet, editor; Bob Cohn, editorial director, TheAtlantic.com. For "The Daily Dish," by Andrew Sullivan.

The Economist Online: John Micklethwait, editor in chief, *The Economist*; Daniel Franklin, executive editor, The Economist Online. For "Free Exchange".

Foreign Policy [Winner]: Susan Glasser, executive editor; Blake Hounshell, managing editor. For "The Best Defense," by Thomas E. Ricks.

Mother Jones: Clara Jeffery and Monika Bauerlein, co–editors in chief. For blogging by Kevin Drum.

The New Yorker: David Remnick, editor; Blake Eskin, editor, newyorker.com. For "The Book Bench."

Regular Department or Section

Recognizes the sustained excellence of a cohesive department or section of a magazine website or online-only magazine.

The Atlantic: James Bennet, editor; Bob Cohn, editorial director, TheAtlantic.com. For "The Atlantic Food Channel."

The Daily Beast: Tina Brown, co-founder and editor in chief. For "Art Beast."

Discover Magazine: Corey Powell, editor in chief; Amos Zeeberg, Web editor. For "Discover Blogs."

New York: Adam Moss, editor in chief; Ben Williams, editorial Director, NYMag.com. For "Entertainment."

Sports Illustrated [Winner]: Terry McDonell, editor, Sports Illustrated Group; Paul Fichtenbaum, managing editor, SI.com. For "NFL."

Multimedia Feature or Package

Recognizes the imaginative use of interactivity and multimedia in the presentation of a single story or editorial package.

Esquire: David Granger, editor in chief. For "Augmented Reality Issue."

New York [Winner]: Adam Moss, editor in chief; Ben Williams, editorial Director, NYMag.com. For "New York Fashion Week."

Newsweek: Jon Meacham, editor, *Newsweek*; Geoff Reiss, general manager, Newsweek Digital; Devin Gordon, editor, Newsweek Digital. For "20/10: The Decade in Rewind."

Poetry Foundation & Poetry: Christian Wiman, editor; Catherine Halley, editor, PoetryFoundation.org; Anne Halsey, media director. For "Chicago Poetry Tour."

Runner's World: David Willey, editor in chief; Mark Remy, online executive editor, RunnersWorld.com. For "The Runner's World Marathon Challenge."

Interactive Tool

Honors the outstanding use of interactive tools that enable users to generate or share content, improve the quality of their lives or enjoy recreational activities.

ESPN the Magazine: Gary Hoenig, general manager and editorial director, ESPN Publishing; Gary Belsky, editor in chief, ESPN the Magazine. For "The Athlete Body Timeline."

IEEE Spectrum: Susan Hassler, editor in chief; Harry Goldstein, senior editor, Web; Bill Sweet, senior editor. For "Carbon Calculator 2009."

Inc.: Jane Berentson, editor; Mike Hofman, Deputy editor, Inc.com. For "2009 Business Valuation Calculator."

InStyle: Ariel Foxman, managing editor; Rosie Amodio, editor, InStyle.com. For "Hollywood Makeover."

Men's Health [Winner]: David Zinczenko, editor in chief; Bill Phillips, executive editor; Matt Bean, brand editor. For "Eat This, Not That!" iPhone Application.

Podcasting

Honors outstanding audio podcasts on a magazine website or online-only magazine.

Harvard Business Review: Adi Ignatius, editor in chief; Eric Hellweg, editor, HBR.org; Sarah Green, assistant editor; Adam Buchholz, multimedia Web producer. For "Harvard Business IdeaCast" series.

IEEE Spectrum: Susan Hassler, editor in chief; Sharan Basco, executive producer; Erico Guizzo, senior associate editor. For "Robots for Real" series.

The New Yorker: David Remnick, editor; Blake Eskin, editor, newyorker.com. For "The *New Yorker* Fiction Podcast."

Tablet Magazine [Winner]: Alana Newhouse, editor in chief; Julie Subrin, executive producer, audio; Sara Ivry, podcast host. For "Remembrance Day," by Gregory Warner; "The Queens of Bollywood," by Eric Molinsky; "Blessed Bluegrass," by Jon Kalish.

Vanity Fair: Graydon Carter, chief editor; Michael Hogan, chief online editor. For "Writers Reading" series.

Video

Honors the outstanding use of video on magazine websites or online-only magazines.

National Geographic: Chris Johns, editor in chief; Rob Covey, senior vice president, digital media. For "Leopard Seals: Deadly Beauty" and "Redwoods: The Super Trees."

The Oxford American: Marc Smirnoff, editor; Dave Anderson, director and photographer. For "SoLost" series.

Reason.tv: Nick Gillespie, editor in chief, producer; Meredith Bragg, producer. For "UPS vs. FedEx (Ultimate Whiteboard Remix)."

T: The New York Times Style Magazine: Stefano Tonchi, editor in chief; Horacio Silva, online director; Lynn Hirschberg, editor-at-large. For "Screen Tests" series.

Yale Environment 360 [Winner]: Roger Cohn, editor; Chad Stevens, filmmaker. For "Leveling Appalachia: The Legacy of Mountaintop Removal Mining."

Community

Honors the use of interactive technology and social media to establish and sustain user communities.

National Geographic [Winner]: Chris Johns, editor in chief; Rob Covey, senior vice president, digital media. *For* "Your Shot."

Runner's World: David Willey, editor in chief; Mark Remy, online executive editor, RunnersWorld.com. For "The Loop."

Sports Illustrated: Terry McDonell, editor, Sports Illustrated Group; Paul Fichtenbaum, managing editor, SI.com. For "FanNation."

National Magazine Awards 2010 Judges

* Indicates judging leader.
† Indicates National Magazine Awards for Digital Media judge.

Julie Agnone	*National Geographic Kids*
Rafat Ali†	*ContentNext Media*
David Andelman	*World Policy Journal*
Amy Astley	*Teen Vogue*
Richard Babcock	*Chicago Magazine*
Florian Bachleda	*FB Design*
Glenda Bailey	*Harper's Bazaar*
Lisa Bain	*Women's Health*
Dirk Barnett	*Alpha Media Group*
Maria Baugh	*Food Network Magazine*
Richard Baum†	Reuters
Emily Bazelon†	*Slate*
Nicole Beland	*Cosmopolitan*
Gary Belsky	*ESPN the Magazine*
Giselle Benatar†	ConsumerReports.org
Lisa Benenson	
James Bennet	*The Atlantic*
Jane Berentson	*Inc.*
Alex Bhattacharji	*Details*
Debra Birnbaum	*TV Guide*
Deb Bishop	*More*
Bill Black	*Reader's Digest*
Roger Black	Roger Black Studio
Janet Bodnar	*Kiplinger's Personal Finance*
Dana Bowen	*Saveur*
Dan Brogan	*5280 Magazine*
Merrill Brown†	NowPublic.com
Peter Brown*	
Angela Burt-Murray*	*Essence*
Gayle Butler*	*Better Homes and Gardens*
John Byrne	*C-Change Media*
Michael Carroll	*Institutional Investor*
Betsy Carter*	

Catherine Cassidy	*Taste of Home*
Janice Castro†	*Medill School of Journalism*
Catherine Cavender	
Andrea Chambers	Center for Publishing, New York University
Janet Chan	
Bob Cohn*†	*The Atlantic Online*
Stephen Corey	*The Georgia Review*
Doug Crichton*†	*Meredith Special Interests Media*
Jonathan Dahl	*SmartMoney*
Will Dana	*Rolling Stone*
Lucy Danziger*	*Self*
Maxine Davidowitz	
Hugh Delehanty*	*AARP The Magazine*
Bob Der	*Sports Illustrated for Kids*
Mariette DiChristina	*Scientific American*
Ben Dickinson	*Elle*
Scott Dodd†	*OnEarth*
Emily Douglas†	*The Nation*
Stephen Drucker	*House Beautiful*
Simon Dumenco	*Advertising Age*
Arem Duplessis	*The New York Times Magazine*
Alfred Edmond Jr.†	*Black Enterprise*
Rosemary Ellis*	*Good Housekeeping*
Sid Evans	*Garden & Gun*
Maryjane Fahey	Maryjane Fahey Design
Ellen Fair	
Barbara Fairchild	*Bon Appétit*
Linda Fears	*Family Circle*
Edward Felsenthal†	*The Daily Beast*
Dan Ferrara	*Inc.*
Paul Fichtenbaum*†	*Sports Illustrated*
Peter Finch	*Golf Digest*
Peter Flax	*Runner's World*
Ariel Foxman	*InStyle*
Ben French†	*Rolling Stone*
David Friend	*Vanity Fair*
Janet Froelich	*Real Simple*
Ted Genoways	*Virginia Quarterly Review*

Rip Georges	*Los Angeles Times Magazine*
Nick Gillespie	*Reason*
Jon Gluck	*New York*
Susan Goodall†	*Glamour*
Emily Gordon†	*Print*
Lisa Gosselin	*Eating Well*
Nancy Graham	*AARP The Magazine*
David Granger*	*Esquire*
David Greenberg†	Rutgers University
Eleanor Griffin	*Southern Living*
Ed Grinnan	*Guideposts*
Oriol Gutierrez	*POZ*
Larry Hackett*	*People*
Rebecca Haggerty†	*Worldfocus*
Tish Hamilton	*Runner's World*
Douglas Harbrecht†	*Kiplinger's Personal Finance*
David Harris	*Vanity Fair*
Melissa Harris	*Aperture*
Luke Hayman	*Pentagram*
James Heidenry	*Manhattan Magazine*
Ronald Henkoff	*Bloomberg Markets*
Jill Herzig	*Glamour*
Arik Hesseldahl†	*Bloomberg BusinessWeek*
Geraldine Hessler	*Glamour*
Mary Hickey	*Ladies' Home Journal*
Roger Hodge†	
Gary Hoenig	ESPN Publishing
Vanessa Holden	*Martha Stewart Living*
Brandon Holley†	Yahoo! Shine
Adam Houghtaling†	
Mike Hoyt	*Columbia Journalism Review*
Elizabeth Hummer	*Harper's Bazaar*
Adi Ignatius	*Harvard Business Review*
William Inman	*Institutional Investor*
Josh Jackson	*Paste*
Clara Jeffery	*Mother Jones*
Jean Jennings	*Automobile*
Laurie Jones	*Vogue*
Sandeep Junnarkar†	CUNY Graduate School of Journalism

Peter Kafka†	*AllThingsDigital*
Dorothy Kalins	Dorothy Kalins Ink, LLC
Jim Kaminsky	
Susan Kane	The Parenting Group
Eliot Kaplan	Hearst Magazines
Janice Kaplan	*Parade*
Pamela Kaufman	*Food & Wine*
Lucy Kaylin	*O, The Oprah Magazine*
Chris Keyes	*Outside*
Sally Kilbridge	*Brides*
Kim Kleman	*Consumer Reports*
Gary Krakow†	*TheStreet*
Ellen Kunes	*Health*
Steven Lagerfeld	*The Wilson Quarterly*
Frank Lalli*	*The Rooster Group*
Sally Lee*	*Ladies' Home Journal*
Cindi Leive*	*Glamour*
Rebecca Leung†	Columbia University Graduate School of Journalism
Ellen Levine*	Hearst Magazines
Carla Levy	*Self*
Joe Levy*Maxim*	
Anthony Licata	*Field & Stream*
Joanne Lipman	
Robin Lloyd†	*Scientific American*
Belinda Luscombe	*Time*
Steve Madden	*Rodale International*
Paul Maidment†	*Forbes*
Gerald Marzorati	*The New York Times Magazine*
David Masello	*Town & Country*
Craig Matters	*Money*
Pamela McCarthy*	*The New Yorker*
Terry McDonell*	*Sports Illustrated*
Kevin McKean†	*Consumer Reports*
Liz McMillen	*The Chronicle Review*
James B. Meigs*†	*Popular Mechanics*
Mary Melton	*Los Angeles Magazine*
Francesca Messina	McGraw-Hill Construction
Sarah Gray Miller	*Country Living*

Keija Minor	*Uptown Magazine*
Luke Mitchell	*Harper's Magazine*
Peg Moline	*Fit Pregnancy*
Terry Monmaney	*Smithsonian*
Loren Mooney	*Bicycling*
Peter Moore	*Men's Health*
Lisa Moran	*Parenting*
Kitty Morgan	*Better Homes and Gardens*
Susan Morrison	*The New Yorker*
Adam Moss*	*New York*
Scott Mowbray†	*Cooking Light*
Chris Napolitano	*Playboy*
Kim S. Nash†	*CIO Magazine*
Deborah Needleman†	
Jim Nelson	*GQ*
Robert Newman	*Newman Design*
Judy Nolte*	*American Baby*
Peggy Northrop*	*Reader's Digest*
Nancy Novogrod*	*Travel & Leisure*
Meghan O'Rourke†	*The Paris Review*
Jamie Pallot*†	Condé Nast Digital
John Papanek*†	ESPN Digital Media
Chris Peacock†	CNNMoney.com
Abe Peck	Medill School of Journalism
Jodi Peckman	*Rolling Stone*
Robert Perino	
Stephen Perrine	*Men's Health*
Abigail Pesta	*Marie Claire*
Larry Platt	*Philadelphia Magazine*
Sean Plottner	*Dartmouth Alumni Magazine*
Dana Points	*Parents and American Baby*
Kira Pollack	*Time*
Tom Post	*Forbes*
Alexandra Postman	*Body+Soul*
Lynn Povich	
Corey Powell	*Discover*
Lauren Purcell	*Self*
Katherine Pushkar	*Better Homes and Gardens*
Andrew Putz	*Boston Magazine*

Josh Quittner†	*Time*
Kit Rachlis	
John Rasmus†	
Suzanne Riss	*Working Mother*
Michael Robbins	*Military History*
Kerry Robertson	*Market Design*
Caitlin Roper	*The Paris Review*
Anne Sachs†	*Glamour*
Ina Saltz	Saltz Design
George Sass	*Yachting*
Chad Schlegel†	*Entertainment Weekly*
Eric Schurenberg*†	CBS MoneyWatch.com
Cynthia Searight	*Self*
David Seideman	*Audubon*
Shannon Sexton	*Yoga & Joyful Living*
Bill Shapiro†	Time Inc.
Mitch Shostak	Shostak Studios, Inc.
Anne Simpkinson†	*Guideposts*
Evan Smith	*Texas Tribune*
Todd Smith	*Outdoor Life*
Nancy Soriano	
Robin Sparkman	American Lawyer Media
Sree Sreenivasan*†	Columbia University Graduate School of Journalism
Tanya Wenman Steel†	*Epicurious*
Mike Steele	*US Weekly*
Richard David Story*	*Departures*
Jay Stowe	*Cincinnati Magazine*
Bill Stump*	*Prevention, Organic Gardening,* and Rodale.com
Brian Sweany	*Texas Monthly*
Katie Tamony	*Sunset*
Casey Tierney	*Real Simple*
Stefano Tonchi	*T: The New York Times Style Magazine*
Allyson Torrisi	*Popular Mechanics*
Gael Towey	*Martha Stewart Living*
Duy Linh Tu*†	Columbia University Graduate School of Journalism
Sheryl Tucker	Time Inc.
Liz Vaccariello	*Prevention*

Mimi Valdés	*Latina*
Antonia van der Meer	
Kristin van Ogtrop*	*Real Simple*
Norman Vanamee	*Sherman's Travel*
Victoria von Biel	*Bon Appétit*
Jacob Ward	*Popular Science*
Kate Ward†	*The Bump*
Tom Weber†	*SmartMoney*
Mark Weinberg†	Hearst Digital Media
Jacob Weisberg*†	The Slate Group
Matt Welch	*Reason*
Linda Wells	*Allure*
Susan White	*Vanity Fair*
Emil Wilbekin*†	Essence.com
Nina Willdorf	*Budget Travel*
David Willey*	*Runner's World*
Patti Wolter	Medill School of Journalism
Betty Wong	*Fitness*
Jay Woodruff	Alpha Media Group
Liz Zack†	*iVillage*
David Zinczenko	*Men's Health*
David Zivan	*Indianapolis Monthly*
Glenn Zorpette	*IEEE Spectrum*

Permissions

Contributors

MITCH ALBOM's books, including *Tuesdays With Morrie, The Five People You Meet in Heaven, For One More Day,* and *Have a Little Faith,* have collectively sold over 28 million copies worldwide; have been published in forty-one territories and in forty-two languages around the world; and have been made into Emmy Award–winning and critically acclaimed television movies. Albom has founded four charities, many in the metropolitan Detroit area, including The Dream Fund, A Time to Help, and S.A.Y. Detroit, an umbrella organization for charities dedicated to improving the lives of the neediest. His most recent effort, A Hole in the Roof Foundation, helps faith groups of every denomination who care for the homeless repair the spaces in which they carry out their work. He also raises money for literacy projects with the Rock Bottom Remainders, a band made up of writers that includes Stephen King, Dave Barry, Scott Turow, Amy Tan, and Ridley Pearson. In 2010, Albom was named the recipient of the Red Smith Award for lifetime achievement by the Associated Press Sports Editors. He lives with his wife, Janine, in Detroit, Michigan.

TOM BARRY, senior policy analyst and director of the TransBorder Project at the Center for International Policy, is the author of many books, including *The Great Divide* and *Zapata's Revenge.*

CHRISTOPHER BONANOS is a senior editor at *New York.* Having held several positions there since 1993, he now edits much of the magazine's culture coverage and oversees its real estate page. In 2005 his book *Gods, Heroes, and Philosophers: A Celebration of All Things Greek* was published by Kensington Press. He's a graduate of Johns Hopkins University and lives in Manhattan.

BRYAN BURROUGH joined *Vanity Fair* in August 1992 and has been a special correspondent for the magazine since January 1995. He has reported on a wide range of topics, including the events that led to the war in Iraq, the disappearance of Natalee Holloway, and the Anthony Pellicano case. His profile subjects have included Sumner Redstone, Larry Ellison, Mike Ovitz, and Ivan Boesky. Prior to joining *Vanity Fair*, Burrough was an investigative reporter at the *Wall Street Journal*. In 1990, with *Journal* colleague John Heylar, he coauthored *Barbarians at the Gate* (HarperCollins), which was no. 1 on the *New York Times* nonfiction best-seller list for thirty-nine weeks. Burrough's other books include *Vendetta: American Express and the Smearing of Edmund Safra* (HarperCollins, 1992), *Dragonfly: NASA and the Crisis Aboard Mir* (HarperCollins, 1998); and *Public Enemies: America's Greatest Crime Wave and the Birth of the FBI, 1933–34* (Penguin Press, 2004).

TOM CARSON is a *GQ* correspondent. He began his career as a staff writer for *LA Weekly* (1988–93) and then worked for the *Village Voice* (1994–99). He wrote "The Screen" column for *Esquire* (1999–2003) and won two National Magazine Awards for his work there (2000 and 2004). Over the years he has contributed to *The Atlantic, Rolling Stone,* the *New York Times*, and *Los Angeles Magazine*, among many others. He is the author of the novel *Gilligan's Wake* (Picador, 2003).

JONATHAN DEE is the author of five novels, most recently *The Privileges* (Random House, 2010). He is a contributing writer for the *New York Times Magazine*, a frequent critic for *Harper's*, and a former senior editor of *The Paris Review*. He teaches in the graduate writing programs at Columbia University and the New School.

STEVE ERICKSON is the author of ten books, including 2007's critically acclaimed novel *Zeroville*. He teaches at CalArts and is editor of *Black Clock*, the school's literary journal. Erickson has written for *Esquire, Rolling Stone,* and the *New York Times Magazine.* He has been the film critic for *Los Angeles Magazine* since 2001.

DR. SHERI FINK has reported on health, medicine, and science in the United States and from every continent except Antarctica. She was a frequent contributor to the public radio newsmagazine *PRI's The World,* covering the global HIV/AIDS pandemic and international aid in development, conflict, and disaster settings. Her articles have appeared in such publications as the *New York Times, Discover,* and *Scientific American.* Fink's book, *War Hospital: A True Story of Surgery and Survival* (Public Affairs, 2003), won the American Medical Writer's Association special book award and was a finalist for the Overseas Press Club and PEN Martha Albrand awards. Fink received her M.D. and Ph.D. from Stanford and worked with humanitarian aid organizations in more than a half dozen emergencies in the United States and overseas. She has taught at Harvard, Tulane, and the New School. Most recently Fink was the recipient of a Kaiser Media Fellowship in Health from the Kaiser Family Foundation, and she is currently a Public Policy Scholar at the Woodrow Wilson Center.

ATUL GAWANDE became a staff writer at *The New Yorker* in 1998. Also a surgeon, he completed his surgical residency at Brigham and Women's Hospital, Boston, in 2003, and joined the faculty as a general and endocrine surgeon. He is also an associate professor of surgery at Harvard Medical School, an associate professor in the Department of Health Policy and Management at the Harvard School of Public Health, and the associate director of the BWH Center for Surgery and Public Health. Gawande has published research studies in areas ranging from surgical technique to U.S. military care for the wounded and error and performance in medicine. He is the director of the World Health

Organization's global campaign to reduce surgical deaths and complications. From 1992 to 1993, he served as a senior health-policy adviser in Bill Cinton's presidential campaign and in the White House. Gawande's essays have been selected twice for the annual *Best American Essays* collection and six times for the *Best American Science Writing*, and he was the editor of the *Best American Science Writing* for 2006. His book *Complications: A Surgeon's Notes on an Imperfect Science* was a finalist for the National Book Award in 2002. His most recent book, *The Checklist Manifesto: How to Get Things Right*, was published in December of 2009. His previous book, *Better: A Surgeon's Notes on Performance*, was published in April 2007. In 2006 he received the MacArthur Award in recognition of his research and writing.

DAVID GRANN is staff writer at *The New Yorker* magazine and the author of the books *The Devil and Sherlock Holmes: Tales of Murder, Madness, and Obsession* and *The Lost City of Z: A Tale of Deadly Obsession in the Amazon*. His first book, *The Lost City of Z*, was chosen as one of the best books of 2009 by the *New York Times*, the *Washington Post*, *Entertainment Weekly*, Bloomberg, *Publishers Weekly*, and the *Christian Science Monitor*. The book is currently being developed into a movie by Brad Pitt's Plan B production company. Grann has also written for the *New York Times Magazine*, *The Atlantic*, the *Washington Post*, the *Boston Globe*, the *Wall Street Journal*, and *The New Republic*. Before joining in *The New Yorker* 2003, Grann was a senior editor at *The New Republic* and, from 1995 until 1996, the executive editor of the newspaper *The Hill*. He holds master's degrees in international relations from the Fletcher School of Law and Diplomacy as well as in creative writing from Boston University. After graduating from Connecticut College in 1989, he received a Thomas Watson Fellowship and did research in Mexico, where he began his career in journalism. He currently lives in New York with his wife and two children.

THEODORE GRAY is an award-winning software developer, author, and popularizer of science. Having started out in chemistry, he joined Stephen Wolfram in 1987 in the creation of the technical computing software Mathematica. Gray pioneered the concept of Mathematica notebooks—which serve as the main interface to Mathematica—and have made possible the creation of millions of interactive computable documents. Ever since the founding of Wolfram Research, Gray has guided its user interface strategy and has been responsible for a sequence of major innovations. Over the years, Gray has developed an independent interest in science writing and in communicating the excitement and importance of science to a wide audience. He is a contributing editor at *Popular Science* and has authored its "Gray Matter" column since 2003. The How 2.0 section containing Gray's column won a National Magazine Award in 2005. Gray is the author of *Mad Science: Experiments You Can Do at Home—but Probably Shouldn't* and of the best-selling coffee-table book *The Elements: A Visual Exploration of Every Known Atom in the Universe*. He is also the proprietor of periodictable.com and the creator of the iconic photographic periodic-table poster seen in universities, schools, museums, and on TV shows from *MythBusters* to *Hannah Montana*.

SKIP HOLLANDSWORTH was raised in Wichita Falls, Texas, and graduated with a B.A. in English from Texas Christian University. He has worked as a reporter and columnist for newspapers in Dallas, and he also has worked as a television producer and documentary filmmaker. Since joining *Texas Monthly* in 1989, Hollandsworth has received several journalism awards, including a National Headliners Award, the national John Hancock Award for Excellence in Business and Financial Journalism, the City and Regional Magazine Gold Award for Feature Writing, the Texas Institute of Letters O. Henry Award for Magazine Writing, and the Charles Green Award for Outstanding Magazine Writing in Texas, given by the Headliners Club of Austin.

In April 2010, he received the National Magazine Award for Feature Writing, the magazine industry's equivalent of the Pulitzer Prize. His work has also been included in such publications as *Best American Crime Writing*, *Best American Sports Writing*, and *Best American Magazine Writing*.

MICHAEL IDOV was born in 1976 in Latvia, then a part of the Soviet Union, and immigrated to the United States with his family in 1992 at the age of sixteen. After finishing the University of Michigan with a degree in film studies and dramatic writing, he moved to New York City in 1998. For the next few years, Idov combined freelance English-language journalism (mostly at the *Village Voice*) with the job of a news producer at the New York bureau of NTV, a Russian television channel. He also moonlighted as a reporter and weekend anchor, contributing, among other things, to the international live coverage of the events of September 11, 2001. In 2006, after the success of the *Slate* article "Bitter Brew," which detailed his misadventures briefly owning a Manhattan coffee shop and was voted one of year's best stories by *Slate* readers, Idov was invited to try writing for *New York*. Within three months of his first publication, he was offered the position of a contributing editor at the magazine. Currently, Idov is a full-time writer at the magazine; his latest features include "Klub Prokhorov" and "The Clash of the Bearded." He also contributes frequently to the magazine's website, nymag.com. Fully bilingual, Idov also publishes essays and cultural criticism in Russia, in magazines such as *Bolshoi Gorod* (Big city) and *Vogue*. Idov's first novel, *Ground Up*, loosely based on the article "Bitter Brew," was published by Farrar, Straus & Giroux in 2009. In his free time, Idov sings in the group Spielerfrau.

PETER JON LINDBERG is the editor-at-large of *Travel + Leisure*, where he writes variously about food, music, urban development, the hotel industry and the curious business of travel. Lindberg is a graduate of Harvard University, where he was managing editor of the *Let's Go* travel guide series; his writing has also been featured in *New York, Food & Wine, Men's Journal, Details* and the *New York Times*. In 2005 he was named a "Travel Journalist of the Year" by the Society of American Travel Writers and was a James Beard Award finalist for his food writing. He lives in Brooklyn, New York.

GARRISON KEILLOR is the host and writer of *A Prairie Home Companion* and *The Writer's Almanac* and the author of more than a dozen books, including *Lake Wobegon Days, The Book of Guys, Love Me,* and *Homegrown Democrat.* He was born in Anoka, Minnesota, in 1942 and graduated from the University of Minnesota. He lives in St. Paul and is a member of the American Academy of Arts and Letters and the Episcopal Church.

MEGAN MCARDLE was born and raised on the Upper West Side of Manhattan, and yes, she does enjoy her lattes, as well as the occasional extra-dry skim-milk cappuccino. Her checkered work history includes three start-ups, four years as a technology project manager for a boutique consulting firm, a summer as an associate at an investment bank, and a year spent as sort of an executive copy girl for one of the disaster recovery firms at ground zero . . . all before the age of thirty. While working at ground zero, she started "Live from the WTC," a blog focused on economics, business, and cooking. She may or may not have been the first major economics blogger, depending on whether we are allowed to throw outlying variables such as Brad Delong out of the set. From there it was but a few steps down the slippery slope to freelance journalism. She later worked in various capacities for *The Economist*, where she wrote about economics and oversaw the founding of Free Exchange, the magazine's economics blog. She has also maintained her own blog, "Asymmetrical Information," which moved to *The Atlantic Monthly*, along with its owner, in August 2007. McArdle holds a bachelor's degree in English literature from the University of Pennsylvania and an MBA from the University of Chicago. She now resides in northwest Washington, D.C., where she is still trying to figure out what one does with an apartment larger than 400 square feet.

JON MEACHAM is the editor of *Newsweek*. He arrived at the magazine as a writer in January 1995, became national affairs editor in June of that year, was named managing editor in November 1998, and was appointed editor of the magazine in October 2006. His latest book, *American Lion: Andrew Jackson in the White House*, was published by Random House in 2008 and at no. 2 on the *New York Times* list. *American Lion* was awarded the Pulitzer Prize in 2009. Meacham is also the author of two other *New York Times* best-sellers: *American Gospel: God, the Founding Fathers, and the Making of a Nation* and *Franklin and Winston: An Intimate Portrait of an Epic Friendship*, about the wartime relationship between Roosevelt and Churchill. In 2009, Meacham was elected to the Society of American Historians. Meacham has written for the *New York Times Book Review*, the *Washington Post*, the *Los Angeles Times Book Review*, and the *Washington Post Book World*. In 2001, he edited *Voices in Our Blood: America's Best on the Civil Rights Movement* (Random House), a collection of distinguished nonfiction about the midcentury struggle against Jim Crow. He has served as a judge for the Robert F. Kennedy Book Award and was awarded the Hubert H. Humphrey First Amendment Medal by the Anti-Defamation League. Born in Chattanooga in 1969, Meacham was educated at St. Nicholas School and the McCallie School and graduated from the University of the South in Sewanee, Tennessee, with a degree summa cum laude in English literature; he was salutatorian and elected to Phi Beta Kappa. Meacham is a communicant of St. Thomas Church Fifth Avenue, where he has served on the vestry of the 180-year-old Episcopal parish. He is a former member of the board of trustees and of the board of regents of the University of the South. Meacham currently serves on the vestry of Trinity Church Wall Street; the leadership council of the Harvard Divinity School and the board of trustees of The Churchill Centre. A member of the Council on Foreign Relations, he received an honorary doctor of humane letters degree from the Berkeley Divinity School at Yale University in 2005 and also holds three other honorary doctorates. A contributing editor of *The Washington Monthly*, Meacham began his career at the *Chattanooga Times*. He and his wife, a former director of the Harlem Day Charter School and current programs officer with the New York City Fund for Public Schools, live in New York City with their three young children.

EVAN RATLIFF is a freelance journalist and contributing editor for *Wired*. In addition to *Wired*, his writing appears in *The New Yorker*, *Men's Journal*, and many other publications. He also serves as the coeditor of *The Atavist*, a digital journal of narrative nonfiction, and story editor of *Pop-Up*, the world's first live magazine.

JOHN H. RICHARDSON grew up in Asia, the son of a senior CIA officer. He studied literature at the University of Southern California and Columbia University, then started his journalism career as a police reporter at the *Albuquerque Tribune*. He has been a writer at large at *Esquire* since 1997. His work has also been published in *The Atlantic*, *The New Republic*, the *New York Times*, the *Washington Post*, and many other publications. He is the author of three books, *The Vipers' Club* (William Morrow, 1996); *In the Little World* (Harper Collins, 2001), and *My Father the Spy* (Harper Collins, 2005). He is married to Katherine Potter, who writes and illustrates children's books. They have two daughters.

HANNA ROSIN is a writer for *The Atlantic* and coeditor of "DoubleX," *Slate*'s women's section. She's written for *The New Yorker*, the *New York Times*, and *New York*. She lives in Washington, D.C., with her husband and three children.

MIKE SAGER is a best-selling author and award-winning reporter. He has been called "the Beat poet of American journalism." A former *Washington Post* staffer under Bob Woodward, he worked closely with gonzo journalist Hunter S. Thompson during his years as a contributing editor at *Rolling Stone*. Sager is the author of three collections of nonfiction and one novel. He has served for more than a dozen years as a writer-at-large for *Esquire*. Many of his articles have been optioned for film. He lives with his son in La Jolla, California. His column, *By Mike Sager*, runs fortnightly at www.SanDiego.com. For more information, please see www.MikeSager.com.

WELLS TOWER is the author of *Everything Ravaged, Everything Burned*, a collection of short fiction.

JOE WILKINS teaches writing at Waldorf College in Forest City, Iowa, where he is director of the creative writing program. He received the Ellen Meloy Fund Desert Writers Award in 2008 and has new work appearing in *The Georgia Review*, *The Southern Review*, and *The Sun*.

ANN WROE is the obituaries and briefings editor for *The Economist*. After taking a first-class degree in history and a doctorate in medieval history (Oxford, 1975) she worked at the BBC World Service, covering French and Italian politics. She joined *The Economist* in 1976 to cover American politics and has held the posts of books and arts editor (1988–1992) and U.S. editor (1992–2000). She has edited the Obituaries page, usually writing the obituaries herself, since October 2003. She has written five books: *Lives, Lies, and the Iran-Contra Affair* (I.B. Tauris, 1991); *A Fool and His Money: Life in a Partitioned Medieval Town* (Cape/Farrar Strauss, 1995, based on her Oxford thesis), *Pilate: The Biography of an Invented Man* (Cape, Random House, 1999; published in America as *Pontius Pilate*; short-listed for the Samuel Johnson Prize and the W. H. Smith Award); and *Perkin: A Story of Deception* (published in America as *The Perfect Prince*) (Cape/Random House, 2003). Her fifth book, *Being Shelley*, on the inner life of the poet, was published in 2007 by Cape and Pantheon. She is the coauthor, with Keith Colquhoun, of *The Economist Book of Obituaries*, published this autumn by Profile (UK) and Bloomberg (U.S.). She is the chairman of the judges of the 2008 Keats-Shelley Prize and a contributor to the forthcoming *Oxford Handbook of Shelley Studies*. She is a fellow of the Royal Historical Society and the Royal Society of Literature. She is married with three sons and lives in London.

FAREED RAFIQ ZAKARIA is editor of *Newsweek International*, a *Newsweek* and *Washington Post* columnist, weekly host for CNN, and a *New York Times* best-selling author. He was described in 1999 by *Esquire* as "the most influential foreign policy adviser of his generation," and in 2007, *Foreign Policy* and *Prospect* named him one of the one hundred leading public intellectuals in the world. Since October 2000, Zakaria has overseen all of *Newsweek*'s editions abroad. His cover stories and columns—on subjects from globalization and emerging markets to the Middle East and America's role in the world—reach more than 25 million readers each week. While his articles have received many awards, his October 2001 *Newsweek* cover story, "Why They Hate Us," remains the most decorated. Before joining *Newsweek*, Dr. Zakaria served an eight-year term as managing editor of *Foreign Affairs*. He was appointed to the position when he was twenty-eight years old. In 2008, he began hosting *Fareed Zakaria GPS*, a weekly foreign affairs program that airs Sundays worldwide on CNN. Zakaria's in-depth interviews with the Dalai Lama, heads of state including Barack Obama, Manmohan Singh, King Abdullah II, Dmitry Medvedev, Moammar Gadhafi and Lula da Silva, as well as countless intellectuals, business leaders, politicians, and journalists have been broadcast in more than 200 million homes in over 210 countries. Within its first year, *GPS* garnered an Emmy nomination for an interview with Premier Wen Jaibao. *The Post-American World*, which is Zakaria's most recent book, was heralded in the *New York Times* book review as "a relentlessly intelligent book" and *The Economist* called it "a powerful guide" to facing global challenges. Like *The Post-American World*, his previous book, *The Future of Freedom*, was a *New York Times* bestseller and has been translated into more than twenty languages. Born in India in 1964, Zakaria received a B.A. from Yale College and a Ph.D. from Harvard University. He has received honorary degrees from numerous universities, including Brown, the University of Miami, and Oberlin College. He currently serves as a trustee of Yale University. He lives in New York City with his wife, son, and two daughters.